Journalism & PR

This book is is part of the Peter Lang Media and Communication list.
Every volume is peer reviewed and meets
the highest quality standards for content and production.

PETER LANG
New York • Bern • Frankfurt • Berlin
Brussels • Vienna • Oxford • Warsaw

Jim Macnamara

Journalism & PR

Unpacking 'Spin',
Stereotypes,
& Media Myths

PETER LANG
New York • Bern • Frankfurt • Berlin
Brussels • Vienna • Oxford • Warsaw

Library of Congress Cataloging-in-Publication Data

Macnamara, Jim.
Journalism and PR: unpacking 'spin', stereotypes,
and media myths / Jim Macnamara.
pages cm
Includes bibliographical references and index.
1. Journalism—Political aspects. 2. Journalism—Objectivity.
3. Public relations and politics. I. Title.
PN4751.M22   659.2'90704—dc23   2014009388
ISBN 978-1-4331-2427-3 (hardcover)
ISBN 978-1-4331-2426-6 (paperback)
ISBN 978-1-4539-1355-0 (e-book)

Bibliographic information published by **Die Deutsche Nationalbibliothek.**
Die Deutsche Nationalbibliothek lists this publication in the "Deutsche
Nationalbibliografie"; detailed bibliographic data are available
on the Internet at http://dnb.d-nb.de/.

The paper in this book meets the guidelines for permanence and durability
of the Committee on Production Guidelines for Book Longevity
of the Council of Library Resources.

Contents

Acknowledgements

I gratefully thank the journalists and public relations, public affairs, and corporate communication practitioners who generously agreed to be interviewed as part of research that informed this book. In addition, I wish to acknowledge and recognize media and PR professionals who offered suggestions and introductions, particularly Barry Leggetter at the International Association for Measurement and Evaluation of Communication (AMEC) and Nick Grant, the CEO of Mediatrack in London, as well as Amanda Millar in Sydney who undertook interviews in the pilot study while working with me as a postgraduate student.

I am also indebted to my publisher, Peter Lang New York, particularly Mary Savigar, who helped bring this book into existence—the second research monograph that we have worked on together—and to the University of Technology, Sydney, which funded and supported my research.

And as always, a special thank you for everything is due to my wife, friend, and intellectual partner, Dr Gail Kenning.

Jim Macnamara, PhD, FPRIA, FAMI, CPM, FAMEC

Foreword

The interrelationship between journalism and public relations (PR), which is also referred to as public affairs, corporate communication, publicity and other similar titles, is one of the most contentious and controversial in the field of media studies, and it is also an issue of concern in discussion of politics and the public sphere. Politicians today are surrounded by teams of press secretaries, media advisors, and PR consultants who are colloquially referred to as 'spin doctors' and their utterances generalized as 'spin'. The term is highly pejorative, alluding to the process of fabrication in the manufacture of thread and textiles. It also carries connotations of twisting and stretching—applied in a contemporary context to truth in the hands of a secret army of media and communication intermediaries whose work and influence is mostly unknown to the public.

Many journalists and commentators now apply the term 'spin' to all information distributed by governments, companies, and organizations, which is increasingly undertaken in contemporary societies by communication professionals in roles referred to in this book as 'PR' for short. Industry studies and employment data show that PR is growing at the same time as journalist positions are declining. Courses in PR are now more popular than those in journalism in many countries—for instance, more than 300 US universities offered degrees in PR in 2010 (Wilcox & Cameron, 2011). Concerned scholars and media professionals ask what this says about contemporary society and what implications it will have for society.

Some editors and journalists deny that PR influences their work (Davies, 2009, p. 52; Turner, 2010, p. 212). But such claims are either naivety or obfuscation. A century of quantitative research involving many dozens of studies has shown that the growing practices of PR have a significant and substantial influence on what we read, hear, and see in our media every day. Research reported in this book shows that PR practitioners frame the agenda, prime the agenda, build the agenda, set the agenda, and sometimes cut the agenda of what is reported and discussed in our media. Their influence extends beyond the news to so-called lifestyle programs and publications, *infotainment*, and entertainment, where the latest techniques of marketing and promotion are referred to as 'embedded' because they involve promotional messages embedded invisibly into the comments of media personalities and even the storylines of drama shows.

Some of these techniques of promotion are described as advertising rather than PR in some professional texts, but they are not transparent in the way that advertising is. While Vance Packard (1957) collectively labelled both advertising and PR as *The Hidden Persuaders*, advertising is explicit and visible because of its characteristic presentation format in print publications and on Web sites and as 'commercials' on radio and TV. Transparency, more than legitimacy, is a major concern raised in relation to PR. In free speech societies, organizations and their advocates and professional communicators explicitly, or at least implicitly[1], have the right to present their views, including promotional messages and partisan views. But media consumers don't know when they are consuming PR. They don't know what interests have influenced what they are told—and what they are not told. PR practitioners have been called "the invisible hand" behind the news (Cadzow, 2001). Author of *Inside Spin: The Dark Underbelly of the PR Industry* Bob Burton stated in an interview: "Some PR activities are genuinely in the public interest…a lot of campaigns are mostly harmless. But it's the invisibility of it all that's the biggest concern" (as cited in Cadzow, 2001, p. 21). In his 2013 book, media critic Robert McChesney warned that the news is "increasingly…unfiltered public relations generated surreptitiously by corporations and governments" (p. 183). McChesney (2013) says that "one of the reasons the amount of PR is less appreciated than, say, advertising, is that PR tends to be much more effective if it is done surreptitiously" (p. 58).

While McChesney could be expected to be critical of PR, being a political economist with a particular interest in journalism and a free press[2], the same point is made by a number of other scholars such as Joseph Turow (2011) who says to students in his widely used textbook:

You are probably much less familiar with public relations (PR) than with advertising. In fact, it wouldn't be surprising if you've never talked with anyone about a public relations campaign. Most people aren't aware that many of the media materials they read, hear, or watch are part of a PR campaign. That's OK with public relations practitioners. They try very hard to avoid getting public recognition for stories that appear in the press, because they believe that, for their work to be most effective, viewers and readers should not know when TV programs and newspaper articles are influenced by the PR industry (p. 560).

In reviewing Nick Davies' popular book, *Flat Earth News*, one senior journalist admitted "the fingerprints of PR are all over the news" (Cosic, 2008, para. 7). But how did they get there? Do they matter? If not, why are the practices of PR surreptitious? Why are they largely invisible and little talked about except in dismissive clichés—even denied? What really happens in journalism and PR behind the stereotypes of *Thank You for Smoking* and *Spin City*? Looking ahead, are social media really 'citizen media' expressing the voice of the people and contributing to democracy? How is the public interest protected and served in contemporary media practice? Is it being protected?

Some scholars and commentators argue that PR and spin have been over-analyzed and that the discussion is now out-dated, given new developments in social media in which everyone potentially becomes a journalist—and a PR person (e.g., Smith, 2008). In a critical review of the book *A Complicated, Antagonistic, Symbiotic Affair: Journalism, Public Relations and Their Struggle for Public Attention* (Merkel, Russ-Mohl, & Zavaritt, 2007), Brian Smith states that "journalism and public relations are converging around new developments in social media" such as blogs, message boards, social networking sites, and online videos that disseminate opinion, commentary, and advocacy mixed with news and researched information (2008, p. 926). Smith suggests that user-generated content and social media should be the focus of analysis. In many respects he is correct—and these significant developments are discussed in this analysis and are addressed elsewhere in considerable detail (e.g., Macnamara, 2014). The evolution of new types of open 'gatekeeperless'[3] media and the development of new content formats such as 'embedded marketing' make it more relevant and important than ever to study the interrelationship between journalism and PR. PR is developing new tactics and techniques at the same time as journalism is struggling to adapt in a digital networked world and these developments and evolving interconnections need to be examined.

However, in traditional as well as emerging forms of media and public communication, the functions, role and influence of PR are poorly understood. Far from being over-analyzed, there is a blind spot in journalism and media studies, sociology, cultural studies, and even in many political economy analyses in relation to PR. Furthermore, the discourse of denial propagated by many journalists and the generalized labelling of PR as 'spin' and 'puffery', which are discussed in Chapter 1, serve only to marginalize and trivialize PR. As New Zealand political scientist Joe Atkinson eloquently says, "media complaints about spin are both disproportionate to the offence and inadequate for its repair" (2005, p. 27). Despite its massive growth and complaints about its increasing pervasiveness, PR is largely unstudied and unexamined outside the specialist disciplinary field of public relations scholarship.

For instance, in mass communication and media studies, Denis McQuail's classic text, *Mass Communication Theory*, even in its sixth edition (McQuail, 2010), does not mention PR, even though it devotes sections to discussing the influence of advertisers and interest groups (pp. 290–292). Pamela Shoemaker and Stephen Reese's widely used text devoted specifically to examining internal and external influences on media content, *Mediating the Message: Theories of Influence on Mass Media Content* (1996), contains just two and a half pages discussing PR. *The Media Book* by Chris Newbold, Oliver Boyd-Barrett, and Hilde Van den Bulck (2002) contains one small section with 37 lines (less than one page) specifically discussing PR, along with two other brief mentions. In his numerous texts, eminent media scholar James Curran identifies that "modern media fell under the sway of public relations" in the 20th century (2002, p. 34), but he discusses PR only in passing in relation to its growth since 1980 (2011, p. 131) and Habermas's concerns about corruption of the public sphere (p. 194), despite his focus on media sources (p. 104) and the effects of commercialization and market liberalism/neoliberalism (pp. 196–204). In *Understanding the Media*, Eoin Devereux (2007a) says, "researchers have examined news media organizations with a view to understanding more about the workings of agenda setting, the use of particular sources in writing news stories, and the increasing importance of other media professionals such as PR experts who attempt to generate a 'spin' on specific stories" (p. 121). But this otherwise informative media text does not analyze or comment on PR beyond this one reference. Devereux's other text on media studies also only mentions PR in passing (Devereux, 2007b). The third edition of *The Media and Communications in Australia*, edited by Stuart Cunningham and Graeme Turner (2010), contains a chapter on PR but, while usefully identifying PR as part of 'promotional culture', it is short (just nine and a half pages) and mainly presents a historical perspective. Furthermore, despite the admonition in this chapter that "it might be wise to acknowledge, rather than merely lament, the structural importance of publicity in order to understand better how the media work today" (Turner, 2010, p. 212), the fourth edition of this media text released in 2014 (Cunningham & Turnbull, 2014) does not have a chapter on PR. Joseph Turow's *Media Today: An*

Introduction to Mass Communication (4th edition) is one of the few media studies texts that addresses PR in any serious way, with a 37-page chapter on the 'The Public Relations Industry' (Turow, 2011, pp. 558–595).

For all the concerns expressed by some journalists and journalism scholars about PR, journalism textbooks also remain surprisingly silent on PR. Some do not mention PR at all. Others make brief references under glib headings such as 'When the Spin-doctors Spin Out' (Lamble, 2011, p. 77). This heading is followed by just 19 lines about PR with statements such as "our state and federal governments in particular, but also many local governments, employ small armies of public relations staff and media advisers: 'minders' whose sole responsibility is to do their utmost to portray their governments to the public." The role of PR is then described as "two-pronged" involving "blowing their own trumpets" and "targeting journalists with a deluge of media releases and deflecting criticism". Ironically, the same section adds: "But on the positive side, media releases can sometimes provide great story leads" (Lamble, 2011, pp. 77–78). *Melvin Mencher's News Reporting and Writing* (e.g., Mencher, 2010), a long-standing journalism text in the US, includes a chapter on writing news releases but does not address PR. *The Professional Journalist*, written by long-time Columbia University journalism professor and administrator of the Pulitzer Prizes for more than 20 years John Hohenberg, is one exception to what is either ostrich-like denial or shameful reticence in relation to PR within journalism. The third edition of this book, which was highly recommended to me by a former editor when I was a very young wide-eyed journalist, has a full chapter devoted to 'The News Media and Public Relations'. This opens with the acknowledgement that "a powerful and ever-growing public relations apparatus filters much of today's news flow before it ever reaches the reporter" (1973, p. 346). However, the last (5th) edition of this book was published in 1983 and it is now listed on Web sites among rare books. Despite much protest and populist rhetoric, journalists are very short on research and rigorous analysis of PR if journalism texts are anything to go by.

Despite Pierre Bourdieu (1984) naming public relations as part of the 'new petite bourgeoisie' involved in "presentations and representation" and "providing symbolic goods and services" in contemporary societies along with advertising, marketing, and other 'cultural intermediaries' (p. 359), sociologists and cultural studies scholars similarly have a blind spot or only peripheral vision in relation to PR. In his examination of promotional culture, Andrew Wernick (1991) focuses on advertising as stated in the title of his seminal book *Promotional Culture: Advertising, Ideology and Symbolic Expression*. Other studies such as that of Mike Featherstone (1991), who broadly critiqued the role of cultural intermediaries in postmodern consumer culture; Keith Negus (1992, 1999), who studied promotion in the music industry in the US and UK; and examinations of the popularizing of art by art institution marketers (e.g., Durrer & Miles, 2009) usefully highlight the role of new types of cultural intermediaries, but mostly ignore PR. Jonathon Gray (2010) notes "the omnipresence of promotion in much media and popular culture" (p. 815), but only Negus refers to PR in saying that "studies have shown that the cultural intermediaries of marketing and public relations can play a critical role in connecting production and consumption" (2002, p. 507). Beyond Bourdieu's passing mention of PR and Negus's inclusion of PR in the "cluster of occupations" involved in cultural mediation, there has been little examination of PR practitioners as cultural or promotional intermediaries in cultural studies.

More recently in discussing the origins of objectivity in 20th century journalism, David Croteau, William Hoynes, and Stefania Milan (2012) say; "At the same time, the field of PR emerged, and professional publicists became early 'spin doctors'" (p. 131). However, no further discussion of PR is offered in their *Media/Society: Industries, Images and Audiences*. Nick Couldry's many highly regarded books and articles on media ignore PR, even though his focus on media practices (2004) provides an ideal lens for examining the journalism–PR interface, and his critique of the effects of neoliberal capitalism on media (2010, 2012) invites political economy analysis of the role of PR.

While Robert McChesney expresses concern about PR in his recent writing (e.g., McChesney, 2013), he does not examine its practices in any detail, and a number of political economy critiques, even those specifically focussed on media and communication, make no mention of PR at all (e.g., Vincent Mosco's *The Political Economy of Communication*, 2009).

It needs to be acknowledged that these texts have other work to do and make valuable contributions to knowledge. But the point is, outside of PR journals and texts, PR receives limited attention, and discussion that does occur is mostly superficial because it is based on clichés, stereotypes, and, in many cases, media mythology, as will be shown.

When editors and journalists do grudgingly acknowledge the influence of PR, claims of victimhood are often advanced. These cite the decline in journalist jobs, which has resulted in reduced time for research and writing, as the reason for the 'PR-ization' of media (Blessing & Marren, 2013; Moloney, 2000, p. 120)[4]. However, research shows that there were high levels of influence and usage of PR material even during the halcyon days of mass media when journalist staff levels were at their highest, as discussed in Chapter 5.

Meanwhile, PR texts often sound like 'PR for PR' rather than scholarly research and critical analysis. Claims that PR is about building mutually beneficial relationships and engaging in dialogue with 'publics'[5] and 'stakeholders'[6] are normative and rarely applied, even in the view of some PR scholars (e.g., Murphy, 1991). The widely advanced image of PR practitioners as 'honest brokers' of information (Hohenberg, 1973) is frequently sullied by episodes such as those described in *Toxic Sludge Is Good for You* (Stauber & Rampton, 1995), the farcical untruths perpetrated by several governments and their 'PR machines' about 'weapons of mass destruction' in Iraq, cover-ups of the damage caused by dangerous products such as asbestos, and many other examples of misinformation and manipulation discussed in this book and others.

These gaps, contradictions, paradoxes, stereotypes, discourses, and myths mask an important interrelationship that warrants close examination—now more than ever. The fingerprints of PR are not being erased and the independence of journalism is not being enhanced in the 21st century. To the contrary, this analysis will show that these issues remain problematic and may be of even greater concern in the era of collapsing media models, widespread concern about a 'crisis in journalism', and open Internet communication in which there are fewer and sometimes no 'gatekeepers', little regulation, and therefore greater potential for misinformation and disinformation.

This book has two important and timely objectives. First, it summarizes and synthesizes existing research and diverse, often conflicting, perspectives on the topic to present an informed overview and balanced insights. Second, it reports new in-depth qualitative research that looks beyond the numerous quantitative surveys and anecdotal claims that have been reported to explore how journalists and PR practitioners interact despite denials and tensions, how and why media–PR interdependency is increasing, how PR is also bypassing journalists to directly create and distribute media content, and the implications of these practices for journalism, media independence, and the public sphere. Findings presented, based on in-depth interviews with senior practitioners in both fields as well as case study analysis and autoethnographic reflections, are relevant and important for researchers, educators, and students in journalism, public relations, and media studies in particular. They also help address the blind spot in sociology, political science, and cultural studies in relation to public relations.

In-depth interviews were conducted with 32 senior journalists and PR practitioners in the US, UK, Australia, and one developing country, mostly during 2013, to gain contemporary information. To gain informed insights, the sampling frame for interviewees was journalists and PR practitioners with 20 years or more of experience in their field (some had experience in both fields). Several had 30–35 years of experience in journalism and/or PR. The sample of interviewees was drawn from general news as well as a range of specialist sectors (i.e., industries or what media refer to as 'rounds' or 'beats'), including business and finance, IT and telecommunications, health and pharmaceuticals, energy/petroleum and gas, food, transport, politics, and non-profits.

Some journalists and PR practitioners were reluctant to speak openly. However, the offer of anonymity, as well as use of some snowball sampling in which interviewees gave introductions to others in their field, paved the way for cooperation, trust, and frankness in the interviews. A number were happy to speak on the record and their seniority and years of experience provided insightful vantage points and authenticity. For example, interviewees included the principal deputy assistant secretary of the Office of Public Affairs in the US Department of Homeland Security. Prior to his senior role with DHS, he was deputy director of external affairs for the US Federal Emergency Management Agency (FEMA) in Washington, DC, where his experiences included setting up government communication field operations and handling media and public communication following the Haiti earthquake and the Deepwater Horizon oil spill in 2010 and during Hurricane Sandy in 2012. Other positions he has held include assistant press secretary for foreign affairs at the National Security Council based at the White House, executive officer and acting spokesman in Baghdad with the State Department, and director of communication operations for the US Department of Defense in Iraq and Afghanistan between 2006 and 2008.

On the corporate and PR agency side, interviewees included the senior vice president, corporate affairs of McDonalds (UK/Europe); the former head of PR for British Airways for a decade, the global head of corporate affairs for one of the largest American food and agriculture companies, and the CEOs of a number of the largest global PR agencies as well as several specialist in-house communication heads and consultants working in fields such as finance, engineering, transport, and not-for-profit.

Experienced journalists interviewed included a former executive editor of Britain's top-rating morning TV program, a multi-award-winning BBC reporter, a former 'Fleet Street' editor, senior reporters from one of the major wire services and one of the leading newspapers in the US, a former editor in chief of one of Australia's leading daily newspapers, as well as a number of senior business, finance, technology, health, transport, and media writers and broadcasters in the US, UK, and Australia.

Their frank comments, combined with analysis of other research studies and first-hand observations reported in this book, provide deep insights into this influential area of media practice that for too long has been obscured by stereotypes, media mythology, contradictions, ambiguity, ambivalence, and institutionalized acrimony that belie the reality of media and public communication today.

Jim Macnamara

Notes

1. This notes that freedom of speech is not guaranteed in the constitution of some countries, as it is in the United States, but it is a convention in most democratic countries.
2. Robert McChesney founded the non-profit group Free Press (http://www.freepress.net/).
3. The term 'gatekeeper' was coined by social psychologist Kurt Lewin (1947) and was used to refer to editors, producers, and journalists who control access to and content of media by David Manning White (1950) and a number of other media scholars since.
4. Eric Louw (2010) also referred to the 'PR-ization of politics' (p. 93) and the 'PR-ization of warfare' (p. 150).
5. While the singular term 'the public' is often used to refer to citizens generally or to groups of people, eminent sociologists such as John Dewey (1927) and Herbert Blumer (1948) have critiqued the notion of a single mass public, pointing to the diversity of interests and groups that comprise societies. Sociologist and political scientist Nina Eliasoph (2004) called for broad-based replacement of the term 'public' with the plural 'publics' to recognize sociological diversity. Based on this thinking, PR theoreticians Jim Grunig and Todd Hunt (1984) and others use the term 'publics' (plural) to refer to various groups of people with whom interaction is desirable or necessary (see further discussion in Chapter 3).
6. 'Stakeholders' is an alternative term for 'publics' used in public relations and by some researchers and political scientists to refer to individuals and groups of people who have an interest in an issue or the activities of an organization, or who are affected by the issue or organization (see further discussion in Chapter 3).

CHAPTER ONE

The Contentious Relationship between Journalism and PR

"The fingerprints of PR are all over the news" (journalist Miriam Cosic, 2008, para. 7).

"It's the invisible hand behind much of the news, the sophisticated spin machine that can rescue reputations or crucify a competitor. And some of its practitioners will stop at nothing" (journalist Jane Cadzow, 2001, p. 20, in a major feature article titled 'The Hidden Persuaders').

"The PR industry…consciously fabricates news" (Nick Davies, 2009, p. 203, in *Flat Earth News*).

"PR fabricates pseudo-evidence…pseudo-events…pseudo-leaks…pseudo-pictures… pseudo-illnesses…pseudo-groups" (Nick Davies, 2009, pp. 172–193).

"Increasingly…[news] is unfiltered public relations generated surreptitiously by corporations and governments" (critical media scholar Robert McChesney, 2013, p. 183).

"The PR industry now plays a powerful and pivotal role in the gathering, packaging, and distribution of news and information" (Andrew Currah, 2009, p. 61, in a report by The Reuters Institute for the Study of Journalism at Oxford University).

"This huge industry of manipulation—targeted at structurally vulnerable media— feeds falsehood and distortion directly into our news channels" (Nick Davies, 2009, p. 167).

"The growth of PR is threatening the integrity of the press" (title of Westminster University debate, as cited in McCrystal, 2008, p. 47).

"Spin has been the most corrosive element to hit journalism in my lifetime…the tentacles of spin reach into every part of news gathering, clouding or corrupting the facts" (journalist Mark Day, 2013).

"In some cases the line between news story and press release has become so blurred that reporters are using direct quotes from press releases in their stories without acknowledging the source" (Christine Russell, 2008, para. 2, writing in *Columbia Journalism Review*).

"Some short-staffed newspapers are only too grateful to be stuffed full of scarcely rewritten news releases" (Tony Harcup, 2009, p. 32, in the journalism textbook *Journalism: Principles and Practices*).

"Journalists tend to take the line of least resistance and select those news items that are easiest to find and edit. The items are those provided by public relations companies, corporate communications departments and political image-makers" (Lynette Sheridan Burns, 2002, p. 27, in *Understanding Journalism*).

"Almost every journalist knows the extent to which public relations has infiltrated the [media] business. But, like so many elements of the respectable and glossy façade erected around journalism…they don't like talking about it" (former newspaper editor and now publisher of online publications including *Crikey.com*, Eric Beecher, 2008, p. 14).

"Spin in intensifying. Its significance is growing…people are complaining about something that they once ignored or took for granted because it now dominates our public culture" (Lindsay Tanner, 2011, former Australian Minister for Finance and Deregulation in his book *Sideshow: Dumbing Down Democracy*, as cited in Knott, 2012a, para. 3).

The Profession that Dares Not Speak its Name

As noted in the foreword, the functions and practices discussed in this book as public relations (PR) go under a number of different names. These include *corporate communication*, *corporate relations*, *corporate affairs*, *public affairs*, *corporate public affairs*, *public information*, and *external relations* (Broom, 2009, p. 23; De Bussy, 2009, p. 225; Macnamara, 2005, pp. 22–23; Sterne, 2008). While there are some differences in focus and specialization within these areas, long-time PR practitioner and author Fraser Seitel (1998) notes that these are largely synonyms for public relations. PR scholar Bruce Berger (2007) observes that "public relations is characterized by historical dissensus in the field about what the practice is, who it serves, and what its roles and responsibilities are" (p. 228). There are several reasons for this diversity in terminology, as well as in the bigger issues of purpose, roles, and responsibilities referred to by Berger that will be discussed in Chapter 3. First, as Krishnamurthy Sriramesh has reported, some languages do not have an equivalent term for public relations (2004, p. 328). Second, some societies see PR as denoting a particularly US-centric model of practice and body of literature and wish to distinguish local practice and ways of thinking. For example, a study conducted in 25 European countries found that the term 'public relations' is not widely used in Europe (van Ruler, Verčič, Büetschi, & Flodin, 2001). The practices and activities referred to as PR in Anglo-American terms certainly are used in Europe (Bentele, 2004), but "rarely under that name" (van Ruler & Verčič, 2004, p. 1), instead being referred to as *communication management* (van Ruler & Verčič, 2005), *strategic communication* (Aarts & Van Woerkum, 2008; Aarts, 2009), and *corporate communication* (Van Riel, 1995; Van Riel & Fombrun, 2007; Zerfass, 2008; Cornelissen, 2011).

Some organizations and practitioners consciously eschew the title public relations and its abbreviation PR in favour of other labels to avoid negative connotations that the term has acquired (Johnston, Zawawi, & Brand, 2009, p. 4; Wilcox & Cameron, 2010, p. 12). In a higher education feature in Australia's national newspaper *The Australian*, PR academics Nigel de Bussy and Katharina Wolf described PR as "a profession that dare not speak its name" (Matchett, 2010, para. 7). The reasons for this are introduced in this chapter and explored throughout this book.

Another complicating factor in relation to nomenclature is that, along with titles such as public relations officer, manager, or director and similar levels in corporate communication, public affairs, and so on, some use terms such as *publicity*, *press relations*, and *media relations* for activities that others include within the rubric of PR. Job titles for roles that are essentially PR also include *press secretary* (particularly in government and political organizations), *media officer*, and *media adviser*. These are more correctly seen as sub-disciplines and specific practices within the field (Macnamara, 2012a)—albeit PR is often narrowly and incorrectly perceived as being focussed only on dealing with mass media, as will be discussed in Chapter 3.

Author of one of the most widely used PR textbooks, Glen Broom, reported that public relations was the most commonly used title in *O'Dwyer's Directory of Corporate Communications*, which listed 7,800 communication departments in public and private sector organizations in the US in 2004 (Cutlip, Center, & Broom, 2006, p. 64). Also, Dennis Wilcox and Glen Cameron (2006, p. 11) note that 64 of 69 national associations and institutes representing public communication professionals other than those in advertising identify themselves as public relations—for example, the Public Relations Society of America (PRSA), the Institute for Public Relations (IPR) in the US, the Chartered Institute of Public Relations (CIPR) in the UK, and the Public Relations Consultants Association (PRCA) in the UK. Even those practitioners and departments using different titles frequently refer to their work as 'PR'. Therefore, for convenience, the term 'public relations', abbreviated to PR for short, is used in this text for the range of professional practices referred to above.

PR also has a number of other names given to it by editors, journalists, and critics. The most widely used pejorative term today is *spin*, with its insidious connotations of fabrication and stretching and twisting the truth, along with the associated terms *spin doctor* and *spinmeister* for its practitioners. The practice of PR is widely described as "the dark side" by journalists and media professionals (Parker, 2011) and as a "dark art" (Burt, 2012). Apart from a wide range of formal titles, PR practitioners are also referred to as *flacks*, fakers, propagandists, and even liars and their work is described as *flackery*, *puff* or *puffery*, *ballyhoo*, *bunco*, *boosterism*, hype, cover-up, and a range of other derogatory terms. Bob Franklin (1997) refers to the rise of *newzak*, a news media equivalent of *muzak*, partly caused by problems in the media, but also largely blamed on PR.

A 2002 study of PR in the UK by Echo Research reported that PR practitioners were described in British media as "scumbags", "manipulative charlatans", "sleazy", and "disingenuous" (as cited in Simpson, 2002, para. 4). A US study reports that journalists also describe PR practitioners as "unethical, manipulative, one-sided and deceptive" (DeLorme & Fedler, 2003, p. 99). A stinging attack on PR by CBS commentator Andrew Cohen in 2009 was not atypical of media rhetoric in relation to PR. Commenting after revelations of lying by a White House press secretary, Cohen said on air:

> Show me a PR person who is 'accurate' and 'truthful' and I'll show you a PR person who is unemployed...the reason companies or governments hire oodles of PR people is because PR people are trained to be slickly untruthful or half-truthful (2009, paras. 6–7).

Over the past two decades, PR has increasingly become a subject of public as well as scholarly attention, including lampooning and criticism in articles and books as well as TV shows and films. Some representations and discussions have been light-hearted and humorous, such as "the air-head opportunists of TV's *Absolutely*

Fabulous" (Matchett, 2010, para. 3), the glamorous character Samantha Jones in the HBO blockbuster *Sex and the City* who owns a PR company (although she never seems to work there), the TV series *Spin City*, starring Michael J. Fox, and Christopher Buckley's novel that was made into 2006 Golden Globe nominated movie *Thank You for Smoking*. However, other criticism has been more serious, such as the provocative book by John Stauber and Sheldon Rampton (1995), *Toxic Sludge Is Good for You: Lies, Damn Lies and the Public Relations Industry*. PR spin has been the subject of more than a dozen books, including the following far from complete list:

- *Spin Control: The White House Office of Communications and the Management of Presidential News* (John Maltese, 1994);
- *PR: A Social History of Spin* (Stuart Ewen, 1996);
- *Spin Man: The Topsy-turvy World of Public Relations: A Tell-all Tale* (Thomas Madden, 1997);
- *The Father of Spin: Edward L. Bernays and the Birth of Public Relations* (Larry Tye, 1998, 2002);
- *Spin: How to Turn the Power of the Press to Your Advantage* (Michael Sitrick, 1998);
- *Spin Cycle: How the White House and the Media Manipulate the News* (Howard Kurtz, 1998);
- *Open Scotland? Journalists, Spin Doctors and Lobbyists* (Philip Schlesinger, David Miller, & William Dinan, 2001);
- *Inside Spin: The Dark Underbelly of the PR Industry* (Bob Burton, 2007);
- *A Century of Spin: How Public Relations Became the Cutting Edge of Corporate Power* (David Miller & William Dinan, 2008);
- *My Spin in PR: A Memoir* (Noel Tennison, 2008);
- *A Persuasive Industry? Spin, Public Relations and the Shaping of the Modern Media* (Trevor Morris & Simon Goldsworthy, 2008);
- *An Insurance Company Insider Speaks Out on How Corporate PR Is Killing Health Care and Deceiving Americans* (Wendell Potter, 2010);
- *Removing the Spin: Towards a New Theory of Public Relations History* (Margot Lamme & Karen Miller, 2010);
- *Stay on Message: The Spin Doctor's Guide to Effective Authentic Communication* (Paul Ritchie, 2010).

Concern about spin prompted the establishment of Spinwatch in the UK in 2005 by the non-profit company Public Interest Investigations to "investigate the way that the public relations (PR) industry and corporate and government propaganda distort public debate and undermine democracy" (2014, para. 3). A similar Web site, PR Watch, dedicated to "exposing corporate spin and government propaganda", has been operated in the US since 1993 by the Center for Media and Democracy, a non-profit investigative reporting group founded by the co-author of *Toxic Sludge Is Good for You*, John Stauber (PR Watch, 2014).

Journalists allege that PR practitioners obstruct reporters in their search for 'the truth' and obfuscate and clutter the channels of communication with *pseudo-events* (Grunig & Hunt, 1984, p. 224; Jeffers, 1977). Author of *Flat Earth News*, Nick Davies, says that along with pseudo-events, PR creates *pseudo-evidence, pseudo-leaks, pseudo-pictures, pseudo-illnesses*, and *pseudo-groups* (2009, pp. 172–193). As well as being the first to identify and criticize pseudo-events in his critique of image-making and "boosterism", Daniel Boorstin (1961) also gave an early warning of the creation of *pseudo-people*—what he called "human pseudo-events" (p. 66)—and pointed to PR as instrumental in their creation.

Criticisms of PR continue unabated, such as Robert McChesney's warning in his 2013 book in which he says that news is "increasingly…unfiltered public relations generated surreptitiously by corporations and governments in a manner that would make Walter Lippmann—whose vision guided the creation of professional journalism in the 1920s—roll in his grave" (2013, p. 183). In the latest edition of his classic media text, Joseph Turow (2011) concludes in an epilogue that a central concern with media today is "people's lack of knowledge about what powers and what agendas lie behind the news, information, and entertainment" and he calls for increased media literacy among citizens and greater transparency by mass media organizations (p. 596). An extensive report produced by the Reuters Institute for the Study of Journalism at Oxford University notes that "in many accounts, PR has been framed as an inherently negative force, a cancer eating away at the heart of modern journalism" (Currah, 2009, p. 62). Specialist areas of media and public communication also complain about PR. For example, Martin Bauer and Massimiano Bucchi say that PR "changes the nature of science communication by displacing the logic of journalistic reportage with the logic of corporate promotion" (2007, p. 2).

On the other hand, PR practitioners say their work is complementary to that of journalists. Many PR scholars and practitioners describe journalist–PR interrelationships as "symbiotic" (Bentele & Nothhaft, 2008, p. 35) or "two sides of the same coin" (Evans, 2010, p. 31). Most editors and journalists rail at such claims and reject them outright, or use them as the basis for a tirade about the woes of journalism in the 21st century, which they see as weakened by economic rationalism and falling into the clutches of predatory PR practitioners. In the least, PR professionals say their work and journalism are mutually dependent and "a two-way street" ("PR: It's not the Dark Side Any More", 2006). PR scholars claim that PR builds relationships and creates dialogue between organizations and their publics (Grunig & Hunt, 1984; L. Grunig, J. Grunig, & Dozier, 2002; Kent & Taylor, 2002). Others go as far as saying that PR is "a resource for nation building" (Curtin & Gaither, 2007, p. 9; Taylor, 2000, p. 180) and that "PR plays a major role in resolving cases of competing interests in society", even referring to PR practitioners as "peacemakers" (Black & Sharpe, 1983, p. vii)—a claim that Benno Signitzer and Carola Wamser describe as "bombastic" (2006, p. 456). A summary of some of the terms, labels, and descriptions of PR commonly found in media reports and in media studies and PR literature is provided in Figure 1.1.

Pejorative views of PR in relation to journalism and the media	Positive descriptions and defences of PR in relation to journalism and the media
"Spin", "spin doctors", "spin doctoring" (Ewen, 1996; Louw, 2005); "spinmeisters" (Potter, 2010, p. 1)	"Honest broker" of information (Hohenberg, 1973, p. 351)
"Fabricators" (Davies, 2009, p. 172)	"Mutually dependent" (Gieber & Johnson, 1961, p. 297)
"Spacegrabbers" (DeLorme & Fedler, 2003, p. 100)	"Interdependent" (Erjavec, 2005, p. 163)
"Flacks" or "flaks"[1] and "flackery" (Salter, 2005; Stegall & Sanders, 1986, p. 341; TIME, 1982; Wilcox & Cameron, 2006, p. 14)	"Two sides of the same coin" (Evans, 2010, p. 31)
"Obstructionists" (Jeffers, 1977; Kopenhaver, Martinson, & Ryan, 1984, p. 860) and "blocks" (Macnamara, 2012b, p. 40)	"A two-way street" ("PR: It's Not the Dark Side Any More", 2006, para. 7)
"Imagemakers" (Hallahan, 1999a, p. 206)	"PR and journalism…are both parts of the same vehicle" (former journalist now in PR quoted in Frith & Meech, 2007, p. 154)
"Minders" and "filters" (Macnamara, 2012b, p. 40)	"Symbiosis" (Bentele & Northhaft, 2008, p. 35) and "symbiotic" (Currah, 2009, p. 66)
"Fakers and phonies" (Blessing & Marren, 2013, para. 6)	"Siamese twins" (Bentele & Northhaft, 2008, p. 35)
"Shysters" (Sallot, 2002, p. 150)	"Tacit coordination" (Schelling, 1960)
"Liars" and "lying" (Cohen, 2009; Wilcox & Cameron, 2006, p. 14)	"Peacemakers" (Black & Sharpe, 1983, p. vii)
"Hype" (Wilcox & Cameron, 2006, p. 14)	"Converging professions?" (Bowen, 2012)
"Puff" and "puffery" (Kinnick, 2005, pp. 721–723)	
"Ballyhoo" (DeLorme & Fedler, 2003, p. 103)	
"Bunco" (Green, 1940; Zolotow, 1949)	

Pejorative views of PR in relation to journalism and the media	Positive descriptions and defences of PR in relation to journalism and the media
"Boosterism" (Boorstin, 1961)	
"Cover up" (Wilcox & Cameron, 2006, p. 14)	
"Propaganda" (Moloney, 2006, p. 41)	
"Dark art" (Burt, 2012)	
"The dark side" (Parker, 2011)	
"A necessary evil" (Sallot & Johnson, 2006, p. 154)	
Greedy Lying Bastards (the title of a 2012 film produced and narrated by Craig Rosebraugh about climate change misinformation distributed by oil companies)	

Figure 1.1. Views expressed in relation to public relations and its relationship with media.

'Churnalism'

On the other side of this contentious relationship, journalism also faces considerable criticism. Leaving aside longstanding condemnations such as British Prime Minister Stanley Baldwin's claim that media seek "power without responsibility —the prerogative of the harlot through the ages"[2], contemporary critiques of media relate to a perceived lack of quality, accuracy, and independence—some of which are linked to the media's reliance on what Oscar Gandy (1982) termed "information subsidies". Low cost and free content are increasingly provided to and used by media, including syndicated stories from wire services such as Associated Press, Reuters, Agence France Presse, and United Press International, as well as news releases, photographs, and videos provided by PR practitioners working for governments, corporations, and organizations.

As a number of scholars and practitioners have noted, journalism relies heavily on sources saying something or providing information in other forms, such as documents (Gans, 1979; Manning, 2001; Reich, 2009, 2013; Sigal, 1973, 1986). Leon Sigal observed that much news is "not what happens, but what someone says has happened or will happen" (1986, p. 25). Therefore, as James Curran says, journalists and journalism are "strongly influenced by their main news sources" (2011, p. 104). Journalism has been criticized for over-reliance on official sources of information, leading to domination of public discourse by elites (McChesney, 2003, 2013; Sigal,

1973). Journalists also encounter misinformation, deceit, and even outright lies from unscrupulous sources. To deal with such distortions and biases, conventions have been developed in journalistic practice to facilitate balance and accuracy, such as seeking alternative sources to verify information and provide confirming or disconfirming comments. However, a growing contemporary criticism of news media is that editors and journalists often fail to verify, corroborate, counter-balance, or even check information and statements that they receive and, instead, publish, broadcast, and post them online with minimal editing or even unchanged.

Nick Davies (2009) coined the term *churnalism* in his book *Flat Earth News* to refer to media reporting that churns out content which is little more than regurgitated wire service reports and PR material. Davies bases his claim on a study conducted by researchers at Cardiff University involving content analysis of Britain's four 'quality' daily newspapers (*The Times, The Guardian, The Independent,* and *The Daily Telegraph*) as well as *The Daily Mail*, the highest circulation popular newspaper in the UK, over a two-week period. The study collected 2,207 media articles and, with the help of staff on *The Guardian* news desk, attempted to capture all of the incoming material that was passed on to reporters during the two weeks. This included wire service stories and press releases. Whenever there was uncertainty about the source of an article, the researchers interviewed the journalists concerned.

As reported in more detail in Chapter 5 along with the findings of other similar studies, the Cardiff University research found almost 60 per cent of printed news stories was comprised wholly or mainly of wire service copy and/or PR material. Davies (2009) reports: "With 8 per cent of the stories, they were unable to be sure about their source. That left only 12 per cent of stories where the researchers could say that all the material was generated by the reporters themselves" (p. 52).

Concern about churnalism led to the Media Standards Trust in the UK establishing an independent non-profit Web site called http://churnalism.com which provides a free 'churn engine' (an online software application) that allows users to compare PR news releases with media articles published on major national news sites including those of *BBC News, Sky News,* and a number of national newspapers. Similarly, Churnalism US (http://churnalism.sunlightfoundation.com) compares media articles with a database of news releases from Fortune 500 companies, congressional offices, major trade organizations, and 'think tanks' collected through clearing houses such as MarketWire and by using Rich Site Summary (RSS) feeds.

A number of studies reported in Chapter 5 show that the Cardiff University research reported by Davies was far from an exception, particularly in relation to PR material. Dozens of studies over the past 100 years have shown that 40–50 per cent of the content of most media is routinely sourced from PR, with some specialist sections of the media comprised of up to 98 per cent PR material (Strahan, 2011).

Studies of influences that shape media agendas and content have examined a range of forces and factors. Based on Pamela Shoemaker and Stephen Reese's hierarchal model of media influences, which they described (from macro- to micro-level) as ideological, extramedia, organizational, media routines, and individual (1996, p. 64), Rita Colistra (2012) developed a model focussed on expounding *extramedia* forces, media organization (*organizational*) forces, and *intramedia* (which she called 'within media') forces. In her Influences on Media Content (IOMC) model, Colistra identified organizational forces as media owners, the predominant focus of early political economy studies of mass media influence and bias, as well as economic pressures and resources issues such as staff size. Intramedia influences include ideological factors, media routines and individual routines, beliefs and practices among media workers, as well as pressures that are exerted downwards from media organization management. Significantly in terms of this study, Colistra identified that extramedia influences include "public relations efforts" as well as advertisers, government, and political and interest groups (2012, p. 88). Colistra's model and research monograph described "public relations pressures" and influence on media as including "press releases, public service announcements (PSAs), broadcast news releases (BNRs), video news releases (VNRs), press conferences" and other PR activities which will be examined in Chapter 3. She reported that some TV stations broadcast VNRs "without revealing that the video segments were produced by outside sponsors, agencies or corporations", which is contrary to the ethical guidelines of the US Radio Television Digital New Association (Colistra, 2012, p. 91). Numerous examples of churnalism and use of PR material by media are reported in Chapter 5.

The Discourse of Denial

Despite the evidence available, a number of researchers and a few media practitioners have noted that editors and journalists often deny using PR material. For example, in a historical analysis reviewing journalists' attitudes towards PR, Denise DeLorme and Fred Fedler (2003) conclude that journalists rarely acknowledge PR practitioners' contributions, a stance also noted by Nick Davies (2009, p. 52) and veteran Australian media researcher Graeme Turner (2010, p. 212). In reporting his findings of high levels of PR material and influence in leading British newspapers, Davies notes that "newspapers do not admit to this" (2009, p. 52). Former newspaper editor and now publisher of a stable of online publications including *Crikey.com* Eric Beecher says that "almost every journalist knows the extent to which public relations has infiltrated the [media] business. But, like so many elements of the respectable and glossy facade erected around journalism…they don't like talking about it" (2008, p. 14).

Some journalists go as far as specifically arguing that they are not influenced at all by PR and do not use information from PR sources. For instance, veteran editor of *The Charlotte Observer* Ed Williams (1999) said of PR practitioners: "It's their job to call you about their client, but you don't have to waste your time listening to them…and often the stuff they send goes directly into the waste basket". The editor of information technology magazine *InformationWeek* Richard Wood (2001a) launched a strident attack on PR and simultaneous denial of PR influence in an editorial headed 'The dark side of communications', in which he wrote: "IT journalists…resent the constant nagging of PR people who, quite simply, get in the way". He went on: "Many PR people think they are actually the drivers of the news". Wood concluded his editorial saying: "We're constantly on guard against that sort of circus act and I'm sure you'll concur that the results in this publication, and on our news site *itnews.com.au*, speak for themselves". In a reply to a series of letters the following week, Wood (2001b) further affirmed an oft-claimed view in the media that PR materials and activity have no impact or influence stating:"The idea that journalists would call a PR person for stories is simply weird… strong stories virtually never come from PR people". Research reported in Chapter 5 shows that media stories certainly do come from PR—and particularly in the information technology sector.

In her research monograph reporting a study of intramedia and extramedia influences on TV news agendas and content, Rita Colistra (2012) identifies PR as one of the major extramedia influences, but she reports that forces outside the media including PR professionals and political/government officials "do not appear to have a significant amount of *direct* influence" (p. 121) [original emphasis]. Her research indicated that outside influences such as PR apply pressures at the media organization level which may be passed on to media workers and eventually influence media content. However, Colistra's study was based on a Web-based survey sent to 2,068 TV reporters which yielded 618 usable responses (p. 106). Journalists surveyed were 'self-reporting' and, based on views and attitudes expressed in other studies, it can be concluded that they were unlikely to admit being influenced by PR. Furthermore, the claim that PR practitioners seek to influence media organizations at management level is contradicted by literature on PR practices reported in Chapter 3 and interviews with senior PR professionals reported in Chapter 6. While major advertisers may occasionally seek to use their financial leverage with media organization management, the currency of PR is information which is targeted at media 'gatekeepers' (i.e., editors and journalists) as well as audiences directly.

A few journalists are more realistic and acknowledge the influence of PR—albeit almost always in pejorative terms. For instance, in a critical review of PR, Australian 'shock jock' and outspoken columnist and commentator Mark Day wrote: "Journalists and publishers could see the dangers of receiving slanted information, but they could also see the attraction of having an army of PR 'helpers' gathering the information for them" (2013, para. 6).

Some journalism texts acknowledge and address PR, such as John Hohenberg's classic *The Professional Journalist* (e.g., 1973, 1983). More recently, Tony Harcup (2009) admits in *Journalism: Principles and Practices* that "some short-staffed newspapers are only too grateful to be stuffed full of scarcely rewritten news releases" (p. 32). In an analysis of journalism education focussed on journalistic independence, David Baines and Ciara Kennedy note that "boundaries between work in journalism, PR and information brokerage are porous" (2010, p. 97). But, as noted in the foreword and discussed further in the following, most discussions of sources in journalism, as well as analyses of media ecology and media sociology either do not acknowledge PR or, when they do, it is usually identified as an unwelcome intruder in the mediascape and a corrupting influence that is resisted.

The Discourse of 'Spin'

The term 'spin doctor' was coined by American novelist Saul Bellow, who spoke in his 1977 Jefferson Lecture about political actors "capturing the presidency itself with the aid of spin doctors", according to Frank Esser (2008, p. 4783). The term 'spin' was first used in the media in relation to promotional material and rhetoric in an article in *The Guardian Weekly* on January 22, 1979, according to Esser's analysis of spin in *The International Encylopedia of Communication* (Donsbach, 2008). The term 'spin doctor' was reportedly first published in a *New York Times* editorial written by Jack Rosenthal titled 'Spin Doctors', published on October 21, 1984, the day of the second Ronald Reagan–Walter Mondale debate, referring to the political advisers working with the presidential candidates (Butterick, 2011; Louw, 2005, p. 297). Some reports allege that Reagan's press secretary, Lyn Nofziger, recalls Reagan's senior political adviser Lee Atwater using the term two weeks earlier after the first presidential debate when he allegedly said: "Now, we're going to want to go out there and spin this afterward" (Butterick, 2011, pp. 182–183; "Spin", 2002). From this we can see that spin entered our lexicon from politics in the late 1970s and early 1980s.

William Safire's *New Political Dictionary* defines spin as "deliberate shading of news perception, attempted control of political reactions" (as cited in Butterick,

2011, p. 182). In criticizing what he calls the "PR-ization" of political processes (p. 150), Eric Louw says that "journalists see spin-doctors as practitioners of the dark arts and demagoguery. Spin-doctors are experts in 'hype'…they craft the 'faces' of politicians and script and stage manage political performances" (2005, p. 297).

While originating in the political arena, the term 'spin' is now increasingly applied to PR generally. In a detailed analysis of spin, Leighton Andrews (2006) identifies four stages in usage of the term. While initially spin was used to describe specific US political campaign tactics used in connection with televised presidential debates, in the second stage the term spread to other countries and broadened in meaning. By the third stage, spin became "an encompassing word for media operations of political institutions", analyzed in books such as John Maltese's *Spin Control* (1994), Howard Kurtz's *Spin Cycle* (1998), and Dick Morris's insider account *Behind the Oval Office* (1997) (as cited in Esser, 2008, p. 4785). However, in the fourth stage, any type of commercial PR activity is equated with spin and spin doctoring (Andrews, 2006). Even though they noted differences between spin and established theories and models of PR, Randall Sumpter and James Tankard (1994) were among the first to discuss spin as a model of PR. In *Understanding the Media*, Eoin Devereux describes 'PR experts' as media professionals "who attempt to generate a 'spin' on specific stories" (2007a, p. 121). Former award-winning journalist turned PR practitioner Keith Butterick observes that spin is now "a shorthand way to describe PR" (2011, p. 182). However, as Frank Esser notes, spin is "a biased term used by journalists to discredit, hype, or mystify the work of political public relations (PR) experts" (2008, p. 4784).

While calling PR spin seems to suggest critical analysis, in reality it achieves the opposite. The term 'spin' is thrown around so broadly that it has become a generalization. Like all generalizations, the term masks diversity, ambiguity, and even contradiction and presents a falsely coherent unified view of PR that is a stereotype. Even within politics, Eric Louw (2005) points out that 'spinning' has never been coherent or homogeneous. He says "spin-doctors work for different employers who are often in competition with each other. Consequently the spin industry does not have a single effect; rather it has multiple (sometimes contradictory) effects" (p. 298). Furthermore, the discourse of spin trivializes and marginalizes PR. As the National Public Radio (NPR) Web site says in its report on the origins of spin: "It's not quite lying. It's not quite the truth. It's spin" ("Spin", 2002, para. 1). Spin is often presented as facile but innocuous, something to be dismissed or ridiculed rather than be taken seriously (Esser, 2008). Drawing on an article by Mark Levy (1981), Joe Atkinson (2005) notes that when media content is shown to be "tainted" with spin, "journalists try to reclaim their professional autonomy by rhetorically distancing themselves from the 'tainted' item". However, paraphrasing Levy, he added that "even though such journalistic responses could be highly critical, scornful or derisive, they were more likely to offer exculpatory explanations or apologies, or to invoke a comic mocking tone to suggest the offence is relatively trivial" (p. 21).

Such rhetorical techniques and discourses lull media consumers into a false sense of security in which they assume that journalists proactively and independently research and write stories and that media 'gatekeepers' scrupulously guard the gates of mass media communication—apart from a few relatively insignificant breaches. Frank Esser says that "demonization of spin is to be understood as a counter-strategy of journalists to prove their independence and legitimacy" (2008, p. 4786). But, as Atkinson argues, "demonized spin is a derogatory form of news discourse where journalists pose as heroic fighters against manipulative politicians and their staffs" when, in reality, research shows "glaring blind spots" in relation to "the media's own contributory role" in spin (p. 17). The role of journalists and other media producers in soliciting and co-creating PR and spin will be explored in Chapters 4–6, which report and analyze research into the interface and interrelationships between journalism and PR.

Intriguingly, at the same time as they trivialize, marginalize, and demonize spin, media fetishize prominent spin doctors and engage in what Atkinson (2005) calls *metaspin*, also referred to as *metacommunication*, about media manipulation by Frank Esser, Carsten Reinemann, and David Fan (2001) in their analysis of spin doctors in the US, Great Britain, and Germany. Focussing on the political sphere, Esser et al. note the "news media's self-referential reflections on the nature of the interplay between political public relations and political journalism" (p. 16). They identify two types of metacommunication in mass media reporting: *self-coverage* in which reporters and media decision makers "treat themselves as the subjects of their own political stories" (i.e., media reporting media) and what Esser et al. call *process stories*, which focus on the "strategies, stage-craft and spin doctors employed" (p. 19). Aeron Davis (2000) went further and argued that mass media "have themselves become obsessed with the activities of the more powerful political spin doctors" (p. 41). An exemplar of this tendency is media reporting on Alastair Campbell who became one of the most high-profile so-called spin doctors of recent times because of his work as director of communications and strategy for UK Prime Minister Tony Blair from 1997 to 2003. Campbell was widely cited in British and international media during the early 2000s as a spin doctor because of his active media promotion of Tony Blair and his policies (MacIntyre, 2003) and he regularly featured in media profiles as a 'personality' and even a celebrity. Ironically, Campbell was a journalist before entering political communication—not a PR practitioner—writing for *The Tavistock Times* before joining *The Sunday Independent*. It is not unusual that those who journalists label spin doctors are often former journalists and not specialist PR practitioners with PR education and training.

It also needs to be said that some generalized uses of the term 'spin' are disingenuous. Labelling any statement that is partisan or which presents a particular perspective as spin is problematic because it devalues legitimate viewpoints. All statements are made from a perspective and framed within particular worldviews with particular ontological, epistemological, and axiological assumptions. Only journalists operating within a high modernism paradigm (Flew, 2014; Hallin, 1994) believe that objectivity is possible and that a single truth exists. This modernist framing of journalism is discussed in detail in the next chapter. While condemning lying, blatant misrepresentation, and manipulative framing and presentation of information, democratic societies must accept the right of individuals and organizations to present information and arguments from their perspective. Providing they do so in good faith, this is legitimate free speech and should not be trivialized or marginalized under labels such as spin. To an extent, the discourse of spin is a self-serving attempt by journalists to exclude information and viewpoints other than their own and those they favour and to try to maintain their central position as 'gatekeepers' of news and information that is veracious and valid. Ironically, many of the same journalists write editorials, opinion columns, and commentary with impunity and frequently inject their views into news reporting as well. An authoritative report titled 'The State of Press Freedom in Australia', while criticizing spin, noted that "journalists are spinning it for themselves", stating that "the 'opinion cycle' which now dominates the news agenda…is often led by the journalists themselves" (Walkley Foundation, 2012, p. 53).

The Discourse of Victimhood

When journalists do acknowledge the influence of PR on media, they often present themselves as victims. PR is represented as relentless, ruthless, and overpowering. For instance, in a five-page cover story titled 'The Hidden Persuaders' published in the *Sydney Morning Herald GoodWeekend* magazine, journalist Jane Cadzow (2001) says of public relations: "It's the invisible hand behind much of the news, the sophisticated spin machine that can rescue reputations or crucify a competitor. And some of its practitioners will stop at nothing" (p. 20)[3]. The discourse of victimhood resonates with Joe Atkinson's metaphor of journalists as "heroic fighters against anti-democratic public relations, information management and marketing activities" (2005, p. 17). Journalists have created a mythology that they stand like the proverbial boy with his finger in the dyke holding back the tide of misinformation and disinformation that threatens to flood society and destroy democracy. They point to PR stereotypes such as highly paid 'flacks' and 'spin doctors' as the enemies of the Fourth Estate held at bay by courageous, independent journalists seeking out and presenting 'the truth', but increasingly being overcome in their struggle.

The discourse of victimhood points to the growth of PR, which ranges between 10 per cent a year in major Western markets where the industry is maturing (Sorrell, 2008) to 23 per cent a year in some fast-developing countries such as Brazil (ICCO, 2011), occurring concurrently with a reduction in journalists' jobs in many media because of declining audiences and advertising revenue. A study by Robert McChesney and John Nichols (2010) based on US Bureau of Labor Statistics data and media reports (e.g., Knott, 2012a, para. 4) estimated that PR practitioners outnumbered journalists by more than 3:1 in the US in 2008 and some, including journalist John Nichols, claim that the ratio is now up to 4:1 (Nichols, as cited in Verel, 2010, para. 4). These trends are forcing many journalists and media organizations to rely on PR-sourced information, some argue. For instance, in a debate hosted by the Media Standards Trust in the UK and the University of Westminster in 2008 titled 'Journalism Versus PR', author of *Flat Earth News,* Nick Davies (2008), acknowledged that many journalists have become "passive processors of material other people provide", but he blamed this on reduced journalistic staff levels resulting in less time for journalists to research stories and check facts. In *Flat Earth News* he describes PR as a "huge industry of manipulation targeted at structurally vulnerable media" (2009, p. 167).

However, while the decline in journalists' positions is a cause for considerable concern, this phenomenon, which has occurred mainly since the second half of the 1980s[4] and escalated through the 1990s and first decade of the 21st century, does not correlate with increases in use of PR material in mass media. US daily newspapers reached their circulation peak in 1984, according to Newspaper Association of America (2012a) data. Television was also reaching maturity, with cable networks joining free-to-air broadcast networks and massive TV audiences being assembled in the US, UK, and other developed countries. Yet, content analyses reported in Chapter 5 show that PR-sourced content was already well demonstrated and reaching close to today's levels during the 1970s and early 1980s— that is, at a time when mass media audiences, revenues, and journalist staff levels were at or close to their highest. While understaffed newsrooms, accelerated news cycles, multimedia convergence, and hyper-competition in the era of social media are exacerbating the problems of journalism, the relationship between journalism and PR has been going on for more than a century.

The discourses of denial, spin, and victimhood propagated by journalists and other media producers fail to take any responsibility for or admit any complicity in the PR-ization of media that is widely identified as problematic. Canadian radio producer and CanWest Fellow Ira Basen said in an interview that, in developing a training program for CBC Radio journalists in 2012, his initial concept was to talk about journalism and PR in terms of "white hats and black hats". However, after delving into the issue more deeply, he reported:

> I realized that the story I needed to tell was not us *versus* them (i.e., journalism vs. PR) but us *and* them…what these journalists needed to know was not how evil public relations was perverting the news, but about all the ways that we, as journalists, were becoming enablers of spin…and how we are part of the problem rather than part of the solution" (Gombita, 2012, paras. 6–8) [original emphasis].

In Australia, Matthew Knott, who has written a series of profiles on influential 'spin doctors' and PR advisers, has similarly noted what many journalists and editors fail to acknowledge. In a report on the 'State of Press Freedom in Australia', he notes:

> Journalists love to bag spin doctors. Bewailing the growth of the PR industry is one of our favourite pastimes…. The incredible proliferation of spin, we tell ourselves, is a threat to journalism and to democracy. We're right—but let's now wallow in self-righteous despair. We in the media are key players in the spin cycle, not passive, powerless observers of it. At our best, we disrupt spin; at our worst, we encourage it (2012b, p. 53).

These various discourses within journalism cloud the issues and obscure media practices that many believe ought to be transparent. They also fly in the face of facts, maintained by defensive rhetoric, media mythology, stereotypes, and *metaspin* (spin about spin). Meanwhile, journalists and PR practitioners interact every minute of the day around the world in a dance that is variously described as a two-step, a tango, and a "Rumba of relationships" (Ross, 2010, p. 272). Given the contradictions and paradoxes, as well as the importance of the engagement, it might well be appropriate to borrow Karen Ross's description of the relationship between journalists and politicians and describe the relationship between journalism and PR as a *danse macabre* (Ross, 2010).

The Discourses of 'Honest Brokers', Dialogue, and Relationships

On the other hand, the PR industry argues that its services are valuable and even essential for organizations to communicate publicly, and points to complicity and hypocrisy among journalists who attack PR at the same time as relying on it for information and even courting favours such as *junkets*[5] and *payola*[6]. PR practitioners say that many organizations from community associations to multinational corporations feel that they often do not receive a fair hearing or are ignored by media and social and political institutions. In one of my early handbooks on PR, I noted: "A company or organization today without an active public relations program soon finds itself ignored by the media, threatened by hysterical minorities, and faced with political and economic neglect" (Macnamara, 1985, p. 16). Models of PR practice will be examined in Chapter 3 but, in overview, contemporary approaches claim to disseminate truthful information—what John Hohenberg (1973) refers to as the "honest broker"—and to facilitate dialogue (Kent & Taylor, 2002) and build and maintain relationships between organizations and their publics (Ledingham, 2006; Ledingham & Bruning, 2000; Hon & Grunig, 1999).

However, all too many reports emerge of PR firms and practitioners engaging in propaganda techniques not dissimilar to those employed during the two World Wars and in the promotion of smoking and the tobacco industry from the time of Edward Bernays (Pollay, 1990)[7]. The PR industry continues to be haunted by associations with propaganda and, in particular, its pejorative and sinister meaning gained during the rise of Nazism and the two World Wars. Even though he referred to propaganda as a "much maligned and often misunderstood word", the Minister for Popular Enlightenment and Propaganda in Adolf Hitler's first government, Joseph Goebbels, did much to ensure that it created what he called a "bitter after-taste" (as cited in Welsh, 2013, p. 2).

Edward Bernays, often referred to as the "father of public relations" (Guth & Marsh, 2007, p. 70) and the "father of spin" (Tye, 1998), set out in the early part of his career to apply wartime mass persuasion and propaganda techniques to private enterprise and peacetime government (Lamme, 2012, p. 37). Even though he (and/or his wife Doris Fleischman)[8] later proposed and advocated the function of *public relations counsel*, which involves advising management to act openly and ethically, it did not help that his second book was titled *Propaganda* (Bernays, 1928). In it Bernays advocated "manipulation of the…opinions of the masses" and said that "those who manipulate this unseen mechanism of society constitute an invisible government which is the true ruling power of our country" (p. 9).

Bernays himself was an ardent self-promoter (Lamme, 2012, p. 38) and his 1955 book *The Engineering of Consent* (Bernays, 1955) further raised concerns about the growing practice of PR. PR scholars and practitioners today agree that PR involves persuasion—for example, Gerald Miller (1989) called PR and persuasion "Two Ps in a pod"—but they argue that persuasion is quite different from propaganda. Garth Jowett and Victoria O'Donnell (2006) say that "the purpose of propaganda is to promote a partisan or competitive cause in the best interest of the propagandist, but not necessarily in the best interest of the recipient" (p. 30). In further comparing propaganda and persuasion, they say in an earlier text:

> Propaganda is a form of communication that is different from persuasion because it attempts to achieve a response that furthers the desired intent of the propagandist. Persuasion is interactive and attempts to satisfy the needs of both persuader and persuadee (Jowett & O'Donnell, 1986, p. 13).

However, PR practitioners today do themselves no favours and some are only too happy to play along with and even boast about their exploits at 'spinning' and manipulation. For example, in an interview with the online media trade journal *mUmBRELLA* in 2009, Sydney publicist Max Markson openly talked about feeding sensational stories to media to create publicity for his celebrity clients, saying: "That's the game, that's what it's about...that's the Machiavellian, behind the scenes, spin-doctoring, you know, controlling the puppetry if you like" (2009). In calling for entries in its annual Gold Quill Awards in 2014, the International Association of Business Communicators[9] e-mailed an information flyer to its members titled "Spin your words into gold" (IABC, 2014).

A report to the Global Alliance for Public Relations and Communication Management on PR education acknowledged that many authors describe PR as propagandist (e.g., Stauber & Rampton, 1995; Chomsky, 2002). It went on to note that "public relations texts do not offer very robust refutations to this charge" (Leeds Metropolitan University, 2008, p. 16). A report prepared jointly by the UK Department of Trade and Industry and the UK Institute of Public Relations titled 'Unlocking the Potential of Public Relations: Developing Good Practice' notes that PR makes a significant contribution to the UK economy, but concludes:

> Equally the report shows that there is also much to be done by public relations professionals themselves, across all the industry sectors, to take forward and strengthen industry initiatives in ethics, training and education, public relations planning and evaluation (DTI/IPR, 2003).

The theories, models, and practices of PR are more fully explained in Chapter 3, including a frank review of 'the good, the bad and the ugly'. This informs an evidence-based analysis of PR today and its interrelationships with journalism and the media.

The 'Doctrine of Selective Depravity' vs. the Moral Majority

Many PR texts skirt around criticisms, choosing instead to engage in what PR scholars William Hatherell and Jennifer Bartlett refer to as "a rhetorical defence of public relations" (2005, p. 9). Some read like recruiting brochures in places, according to an analysis of international PR textbooks (Macnamara, 2012a, p. xvii). Unethical and questionable practices are dismissed as approaches of the past or aberrant actions of a marginal few. Marvin Olasky refers to this rhetorical strategy as "the doctrine of selective depravity, otherwise known as 'don't blame us, it's them—the immoral outsiders who cause the trouble'" (1989, p. 88). This suggests that the field is comprised primarily of a moral majority and, therefore, no intervention or transformative change is required. But even if the majority of PR practitioners are ethical and behave responsibly, there are still practices that warrant critical examination and need to be changed, as will be shown in Chapters 3 and 4.

The continuing harsh criticisms of PR and 'churnalism' and the hollow resonances of the discourses of denial, victimhood, and spin and the rhetorical defences offered by both sides are enough to justify further deeper analysis of this contested terrain. When the changes sweeping journalism and PR in the era of Web 2.0 are also considered, as discussed in the following chapters, further research and critical analysis become essential.

Notes

1. In the 'propaganda model of media' described by Herman and Chomsky (1988), 'flak' is one of five filters that influence media, comprised of negative responses and pressure such as letters to the editor, complaints, threats of regulation, lawsuits, and so forth, while 'flack' is a derogatory term for PR practitioners and publicists. However, the two terms are often conflated to denote PR and publicity.

2. Baldwin used this phrase in relation to Britain's two main press barons of the 1930s, Lord Beaverbrook and Lord Rothermere, reportedly at the suggestion of his cousin Rudyard Kipling.

3. In the interest of transparency, the author notes that the PR consultancy firm which he co-founded and headed as chairman from 1985 to 1997, MACRO Communication, was named in the Jane Cadzow article, in relation to an ethics complaint made against the joint managing director. See further details in Chapter 4 under 'Postscript on a PR Career'.

4. For instance, Rupert Murdoch's union-busting move of his Fleet Street newspapers to a new 'high-tech' facility at Wapping in the London Docklands district, which led to redundancies, occurred in 1986. Robert Maxwell sacked around one-third of his workforce in the UK in the same period (Snoddy, 1992, p. 14).

5. 'Junkets' are a media and PR trade term for non-cash benefits such as free travel and accommodation provided to journalists.

6. 'Payola' refers to payments that are made to journalists, editors, and publishers in some markets. For instance, in 2001 the International Public Relations Association exposed the practice of *Zakazukha* in Russia in which media routinely charge to publish press releases. In Australia, the 'cash for comment' scandal involving Sydney radio announcer John Laws

and others in 1999 is an example. In addition, many media in developed and developing markets publish *advertorial* which refers to promotional content for which media demand payment at advertising rates, but offer to publish in a form that looks like editorial.

7. Bernays organized models to light up Lucky Strike cigarettes in the 1929 Easter Parade in New York City on behalf of American Tobacco and subsequently convinced women's rights marchers during the 1930s to smoke cigarettes as symbolic 'Torches of Freedom', a campaign that is seen as having substantially contributed to the proliferation of smoking among women (Heath, 2005, p. 498; Museum of Public Relations, 2013).

8. Historian Meg Lamme (2012) has reported that Edward Bernays acknowledged that he developed the concept of 'public relations counsel' in collaboration with his wife, Doris Freishman.

9. The International Association of Business Communicators (IABC) is an industry organization operating in 70 countries. In describing its membership it lists "public relations/media relations" first, followed by "corporate communications" and "public affairs" (http://www.iabc.com/about).

CHAPTER TWO

Understanding Journalism

In order to examine the relationship between journalism and public relations, we need an agreed understanding of each field of practice—a starting point from which to proceed. While this is not a textbook on journalism or PR, and does not purport to present a comprehensive analysis of journalism and the role of media, the key concepts and theories of what journalism is and what it does in societies need to be identified so that the interventions and impact of PR can be studied in appropriate and relevant ways. Also, new and emerging forms of journalism are examined in order to look forward in this analysis and not simply review the past. While the basic principles and models of journalism may be well understood by journalism scholars and students, they may find analysis of new forms of journalism useful. For researchers, educators, and students in other disciplines, this chapter provides a foundation for critical analysis of the interrelationship between journalism and PR and its implications and impact.

Models and Theories of Media—What Media and Journalism Do (or Should Do)

The role and functions of media in society are understood and examined within a number of broad theoretical frameworks. These include political economy, which focuses on ownership and financial and political influence on media (Mosco, 2009; McChesney, 2003, 2013); neomarxism, which sees media as part of a 'culture industry' that creates inauthentic culture and coerces citizens as 'consumers' (Adorno, 1991; Adorno & Horkheimer, 1972); and the *potpourri* of cultural studies, which draws on French structuralism and poststructuralism, UK 'Birmingham School' critical thinking of the 1960s and 1970s, and American positivism and mass communication theory (Carey, 2009, pp. 73–75). Some identify American empiricism as a distinct influential tradition of media studies (Sinclair, 2014), while others claim that McLuhan's medium theory remains relevant to understanding media today (Bryant & Miron, 2004), along with more contemporary media studies approaches such as media sociology (Gitlin, 1978) and Nick Couldry's (2004) concept of 'media as practice', which is informed by anthropology. However, the focus here is specifically on news media and journalism in particular.

Journalism has been understood within three or four main theoretical frameworks. *Four Theories of the Press*, published in the mid-1950s by Fred Siebert, Theodore Peterson, and Wilbur Schramm, was the "bible of comparative media studies" for many decades (Curran, 2011, p. 28). It proposed the mass media around the world operated within one of four main models—Authoritarian, Libertarian, Social Responsibility, and Soviet Communist (Siebert, Peterson, & Schramm, 1956). The term 'models' is used here despite Siebert et al.'s title referring to theories, as subsequent analyses such as that by John Nerone (1995) noted that *Four Theories of the Press* is "a bit slippery in its sense of theory" (p. 3). As well as agreeing that the four theories of the press "are not theories in a proper sense", Clifford Christians and colleagues also noted that they are "badly out-dated" (Christians, Glasser, McQuail, Nordenstreng, & White, 2009, pp. vii, x). Nevertheless, they provide some useful insights into how media operate (descriptive) and how they should operate (their normative dimension) in various types of societies.

Siebert and his colleagues summarized that the Authoritarian model of media is designed "to support and advance the policies of the government in power, and to service the state". The Libertarian model is to "inform", "entertain", and "sell" as well as "to help discover truth and check on government". The Social Responsibility model of media, in Siebert et al.'s words, is committed "to inform, entertain, sell—but chiefly to raise conflict to the plane of discussion", while the Soviet Communist model serves "to contribute to the success and continuance of the Soviet socialist system, and especially to the dictatorship of the party" (1956, p. 6).

Some other scholars have suggested Developmental media as a fifth model (e.g., Baran & Davis, 2009, p. 122; Flor, 1992) in which media play a key role in national and social development through communication that addresses basic needs such as health and nutrition information. This model is evident in countries such as Indonesia, the Philippines, the Solomon Islands, and some parts of Africa and Latin America. On the other hand, the Soviet Communist model is no longer relevant following the collapse of the Soviet Union.

While authoritarianism has its roots in the 16th century when rulers claimed Divine Right and it was believed that paternalistic elites should guide the masses, authoritarian media continue to operate in countries such as China, Singapore, Malaysia to a significant extent, Brunei, a number of South American and African countries, and in Russia, which is described as having a neo-authoritarian media system (Becker, 2004).

Media in the USA, Britain, and other Western liberal democratic countries such as Australia and New Zealand have been primarily and often stalwartly Libertarian over the past 200 years. The Libertarian model is largely aligned with what is colloquially referred to as the *watchdog* role of the media and the concept of the Fourth Estate. However, as Nerone (1995) notes, the Libertarian model associates media freedom closely with property rights and, despite its call to "help discover truth", many critics point out that in contemporary neoliberal capitalist societies, Libertarian media primarily represent the interests of economic and political power elites. Also, Libertarian media have been criticized as overly focussed on entertainment and celebrity.

Siebert et al. (1956) conceptualized the Social Responsibility model of media as a response to the 'new Libertarianism' and calls for media reform that followed the 1947 Hutchins Commission on Freedom of the Press inquiry in the US, which found Libertarian media paid too much attention to the trivial and sensational and that media were not meeting their responsibility to provide "a truthful, comprehensive, and intelligent account of the day's events in a context which gives them meaning" (Commission on the Freedom of the Press, 1947). In its final report the Commission stated that media needed to not only provide comprehensive and truthful reporting, but should also "serve as a forum for the exchange of comment and criticism" and provide "a representative picture of constituent groups in society" (as cited in McQuail, 2005, p. 171, and Grossberg, Wartella, Whitney, & Wise, 2006, p. 406). The Social Responsibility model of media is designed to reconcile the ideas of freedom and independence with responsibility towards society. Siebert et al. (1956) list six key functions of what they call the Social Responsibility theory of the press, as follows:

1. Serving the political system by providing information, discussion and debate on public affairs;

2. Enlightening the public so as to make it capable of self-government;

3. Safeguarding the rights of the individual by serving as a watchdog against government;

4. Servicing the economic system, primarily by bringing together the buyers and sellers of goods and services through the medium of advertising;

5. Providing entertainment;

6. Maintaining its own financial self-sufficiency so as to be free from the pressures of special interests (p. 74).

A more recent theoretical framework for understanding the role of media and journalism was provided by Daniel Hallin and Paolo Mancini's *Comparing Media Systems* published in 2004. Rather than presenting normative theories of media, Hallin and Mancini (2004) focus on describing media systems that exist around the world and how they operate. They also pay close attention to the relationship between political systems and media systems, rather than examining media in isolation to the political economy in which they operate—an important contextualization, according to media scholars such as James Curran (2011). From their analysis, Hallin and Mancini identify three "models of media and politics", which they describe as the Liberal model, the Democratic Corporatist model, and the Polarized Pluralist model.

The Liberal model of media, according to Hallin and Mancini, is characterized by limited government intervention, strong market orientation leading to largely commercial media, a strong legal system and legitimate basis of authority, and majority rule democracy. Liberal systems tend to exist in countries with moderate or individualized pluralism (i.e., diverse interests and individualism), but with some sense of the common good and social equity. Such systems exist in the US, Canada, Britain, and Ireland, according to Hallin and Mancini—although they could be accused of ignoring other similar societies such as Australia and New Zealand.

The Democratic Corporatist model of media has much in common with the Liberal model, but differs in having highly organized social groups which are integrated into a corporatist system of governance, operating within a consensual democratic political system. States that adopt this model of media tend to be committed to *societal corporatism* as defined by Phillipe Schmitter (1974, 1979) and Harmon Ziegler (1988), also described as *corporate pluralism* and *neocorporatism* by Alan Cawson (1986), *postpluralism* by A. Paul Pross (1986), and *liberal corporatism* by David Held (1989)[1]. As well as having highly developed corporatism, such systems usually have active, although legally limited, government intervention. A Democratic Corporatist model of media involves substantial media regulation and often public subsidies supporting a strong commitment to public broadcasting. This makes this model different from the Social Responsibility model of media, which seeks voluntary social responsibility from media organizations, with minimal government regulation, a limited commitment to public broadcasting, and usually no subsidization. The Democratic Corporatist model is seen in northern continental Europe, including in the Scandinavian countries of Sweden, Norway, Denmark, Finland, Germany, Austria, Switzerland, and Belgium, according to Hallin and Mancini.

The Polarized Pluralist model is characterized by weak rational-legal authority, sharp political and ideological divisions, tightly controlled economic systems often involving subsidies and direct government investment, strong political parties, and highly organized social groups. Such systems usually feature close alignment between media and political parties and partisan reporting. Hallin and Mancini say this model is to be found in the Mediterranean countries of southern Europe, including France, Italy, Spain, Portugal, and Greece, and is particularly common in new democracies (Curran, 2011, p. 29; Hallin & Mancini, 2004, pp. 10–11).

Hallin and Mancini cautiously point out that media systems are not homogenous and that there is often "complex co-existence" of media systems operating according to different principles (2004, p. 12). Denis McQuail similarly notes that the media "do not constitute any single system…but are composed of many separate, overlapping, often inconsistent elements" (1994, p. 133). However, these models broadly indicate the different types of media that operate in different countries and the varying roles and functions that they play in society. The most common in developed democratic countries are the largely synonymous Liberal/Libertarian model, which is particularly in evidence in the US and UK as well as countries such as Australia, and the Social Responsibility and Democratic Corporatist models, which exist to varying degrees in northern continental and southern Europe.

A more recent and explicitly normative analysis of the media and the role of journalism was presented by Christians et al. (2009) in their book *Normative Theories of the Media: Journalism in Democratic Societies*. They identify four distinct but overlapping roles of media: a monitorial and vigilant informer role of collecting and publishing information of potential interest to the public; a facilitative role that not only reports on but also seeks to support and strengthen civil society; a radical role that challenges authority and voices support for reform, which could be equated to the aphorism "speak truth to power"[2] (AFSC & Rustin, 1955); and a collaborative role that creates partnerships between journalists and centers of power in society including the state as well as citizens to advance mutually acceptable interests.

A number of models of journalism have been identified within these models of media. The most relevant to contemporary democratic countries and this discussion are five models described by Joyce Nip (2010) as *traditional* journalism, *public* journalism (also known as civic or communitarian journalism), *interactive* journalism, *participatory* journalism, and *citizen* journalism. The first two are the most established models of journalism, while the others are emergent models triggered by Web 2.0 and social media. Charlie Beckett and Robin Mansell (2008) advocate *networked journalism*, which they describe as interactive and collaborative with professional journalists and 'amateurs' often working together and "digital and online technologies…at the heart of the process of newsgathering, processing and dissemination" (p. 94)[3]. While different from citizen journalism, which may be entirely produced by non-professionals, this concept is closely related to what others call interactive or participatory journalism. There are also other models of journalism practiced in *community* and *alternative* media and *developmental* media, as discussed by Angela Romano (2010) and others. Furthermore, there are developments such as *peace journalism*, which is based on the argument that traditional reporting of conflicts and wars focusses on confrontation and violence and relies on official sources, thereby deepening divisions and failing to examine underlying and often complex structural origins of conflicts (see Keeble, Tulloch, & Zollman, 2010; Robie, 2011). Based on his observations, renowned war correspondent John Pilger reports: "So-called mainstream journalism was committed almost exclusively in the interests of power, not people" (2010, p. ix). Alternative models of journalism such as public and civic journalism, as well as evolving forms such as interactive, participatory, networked, and citizen journalism, are designed to broaden the range of voices that receive a megaphone through media and broaden the range of viewpoints and interests represented in media. Some of these will be discussed further later in this chapter.

The Fourth Estate and Watchdog Journalism

A simplified but enduring model of what media and journalists do and should do in democratic countries is the concept of the Fourth Estate. Irish philosopher and statesman Edmund Burke coined the term in a parliamentary debate in 1787 on the opening of the House of Commons of Great Britain to press reporting, according to historian Thomas Carlyle—although Eric Louw (2005, p. 288) claims that it was first proposed by John Locke. Carlyle reported that "Burke said there were three Estates in Parliament; but, in the reporters' gallery yonder, there sat a Fourth Estate more important far than they all" (1840, 1993, p. 349). For a detailed analysis of the origins and rationale of the Fourth Estate, see the monograph 'Emergence of the Fourth Estate: 1640–1789' by Carl Burrowes (2011). The role of the press operating as a Fourth Estate or watchdog of society, and its self-proclaimed ability to identify truth, was expounded by editor of *The Times* John Delane in a widely quoted 1852 editorial in which he said:

> The first duty of the press is to obtain the earliest and most correct intelligence of the events of the time and instantly by disclosing them to make them the common property of the nation. The press lives by disclosures…bound to tell the *truth* as we find

it without fear of consequences...the duty of the journalist is the same as that of the historian—to seek out *truth*, above all things, and to present to his readers not such things as statecraft would wish them to know, but the *truth* as near as he can attain it (Delane as cited in Schultz, 1998, p. 25; Louw, 2005, p. 61) [emphasis added].

This statement, like many others about the role of the media, reflects modernist and somewhat paternalistic notions of truth, which will be critically examined later in this chapter. However, notwithstanding contested understandings of truth, media have come to be seen and accepted as an important part of the infrastructure of democratic societies. Even more specifically, 'free' media that are unencumbered by government control or other sources of power or influence are regarded as essential to protect the interests of citizens. In an essay titled 'The Watchdog Role of the Press', W. Lance Bennett and William Serrin (2011) list three roles for what they term "watchdog journalism". At a day-to-day level, they say watchdog journalism involves "documenting the activities of government, business and other public institutions in ways that expose little-publicized or hidden activities to public scrutiny" (p. 396). Second, they state that journalism serves as a watchdog by going further and "clarifying the significance of documented activities by asking probing questions of public officials and authorities". At the third level, they argue that the watchdog role involves "enterprise or investigative reporting aimed at finding hidden evidence of social ills, official deception, and institutional corruption" (p. 396).

Journalism in its day-to-day reporting mode, in its questioning on behalf of citizens, and in its most aggressive form of investigative reporting is seen by many as the heart of democracy[4]. Writing about US politics and civic life, Bennett and Serrin say: "Without journalists acting as watchdogs, American democracy—at least in anything close to the form we know it today—would not exist" (2011, p. 397).

Some argue that media acting as a Fourth Estate was important and necessary in liberal, republican/representative, and deliberative forms of democracy that applied, or were aspired to, in Western democratic countries throughout the 19th and 20th centuries, but that this is less the case in new emerging forms of democracy. For instance, in what John Keane (2009) calls *monitory democracy*, there are thousands of non-government organizations (NGOs) that now engage in a watchdog role as well as advocacy and activism on behalf of citizens on a range of issues—a phenomenon that did not exist to any extent before 1945 and which has escalated since the 1970s and particularly since the 1990s, according to Keane. For example, the United Nations Department of Economic and Social Affairs reports that there are now more than 37,000 NGOs in the world, one-fifth of which were formed in the 1990s (Bimber, Flanagin, & Stohl, 2012, p. 8). Organizations such as Greenpeace, consumer activist groups, quasi-government standards bodies, industry regulators, and even local citizens' action groups now play a Fourth Estate role. The changing role of media in monitory and radical democratic contexts in which citizens are represented by a growing range of often highly effective pressure groups and take direct participatory action, warrants close attention in journalism and media studies. Simply invoking old clichés will not save journalism in the 21st century. Whether they accept it or not, journalists are now not the only, or even the principal, representatives of the public interest. The role of "keeping the bastards honest", in the words of former Australian Democrats Senator Don Chipp (Bean, 2012), is shared by a number of organizations, advocacy groups, minority political parties, and "monitorial citizens" who Michael Schudson (1998) says are a postmodern evolution of the informed citizen with an active interest in public affairs, albeit acting outside traditional political and media institutions. The role of social media as a potential *Fifth Estate* (Cooper, 2006; Dutton, 2007) is also changing the role and relevance of the Fourth Estate as it has been understood—a development that will be examined in Chapter 7.

Bennett and Serrin (2011) also warn that mass media have an uneven track record as watchdogs, that this role has become "overly stylized" and "ritualized", and that media are often a "sleeping watchdog" (pp. 400–402). They also say that many journalists "have sold their souls for access to public officials" (p. 402)—a criticism also made in a number of studies showing heavy reliance on official sources of news and information (e.g., McChesney, 2003, 2013; Sigal, 1973, 1986).

Nevertheless, a robust Fourth Estate continues to have a place in democracy in the view of most. Questions remain over how many citizens are prepared to be monitorial citizens, minority political parties come and go, and representative organizations and institutions become colonized by power elites or rendered incompetent by bureaucracy. What remains, and must remain, in the view of many scholars and practitioners, are media—ideally, strong independent media free of government control and other subverting influences. In their important essay on 'The Watchdog Role of the Press', Bennett and Serrin (2011) say watchdog journalism may need these institutional partners and they welcome "more probing voices", but they conclude that there continues to be a need for alert and effective media (p. 399).

Key Political Actors in the Public Sphere

The Social Responsibility model of media, in particular, is linked to the concept of the *public sphere* which Jürgen Habermas (1989, 2006) envisaged as a space for "rational-critical debate" through which citizens can become informed, contribute to political discourse, and reach consensus expressed in the form of public opinion. While Habermas took his idea of the public sphere from the coffee houses, salons, and literary societies of 18th-century France and England, in contemporary societies the public sphere is primarily understood as a mediated space rather than a physical site involving face-to-face communication (Castells, 2009; Corner, 2007; Dahlgren, 2009; Keane, 2009). Journalists, along with politicians, lobbyists, intellectuals, and various other social leaders and advocates, are key political 'actors' in this public sphere, according to Habermas (2006, p. 416).

The public sphere provides a more critical framework in which to examine the role and performance of media than the romanticized notions of the Fourth Estate and journalists as watchdogs. Even in his classic text that introduced the concept, *The Structural Transformation of the Public Sphere*, Habermas (1989) identified public relations as problematic—even more so than advertising. Habermas saw advertising addressed to private citizens as "consumers", whereas "the addressee of public relations is 'public opinion'". While advertising is explicit, Habermas comments of PR: "The sender of the message hides his business intentions in the role of someone interested in the public welfare". He lamented that "the accepted functions of the public sphere are integrated into the competition of organized private interests" through the practices of PR (Habermas, 1991, p. 193).

More recently, in their book on collective action, Bruce Bimber, Andrew Flanagin, and Cynthia Stohl note that the US public sphere in particular is characterized by "its vibrant and extensive population of interest groups" (2012, p. 33) and, increasingly, these groups ranging from the 'gun lobby' to environmental organizations are represented and spearheaded by PR practitioners. As Peter Dahlgren (2009) notes, a number of media and political science scholars are concerned that "spin doctors, public relations experts, media advisors, and political consultants using the techniques of advertising, market research, public relations, and opinion analysis have entered the fray to help political actors and economic elites shape their communication strategies" (p. 49).

Governments themselves are also major users of PR. David Deacon and Peter Golding (1994) in their widely cited study of taxation and representation in the US point out the extensive use of media advisers and communication professionals by governments to promote policies and out-manoeuvre their opponents and warn: "We cannot ignore the massive expansion of the *public relations state*" (pp. 5–6) [emphasis added]. Nevertheless, the institutionalization of PR as part of government has been largely ignored, with the focus of most political communication studies being election campaigns and specific, often spectacular, cases of political spin, as noted by Ian Ward (2003, 2007) in his analysis of "an Australian PR state". Furthermore, the *PR state* has expanded massively since Deacon and Golding's study and even since Ward's updated 2007 analysis, comprised of politicians' 'media minders' (e.g., media advisers), media units staffed by journalists or PR practitioners who write speeches and media releases for politicians, public affairs units in government departments and agencies, and whole-of-government coordination and promotion agencies (Ward, 2007, pp. 6–17).

In his recent writing, Habermas also critiques contemporary mass media for what he sees as their part in failing to provide a viable public sphere to serve public interests. He said the mass media's focus on spectacle, entertainment, celebrity, and consumerism "goes against the grain of the normative requirements of deliberative politics" (2006, p. 420). Nevertheless, he maintains that a deliberative public sphere is "part of the bedrock of liberal democracies" (p. 412).

While Habermas's concept of the public sphere has been criticized for its "idealization of public reason" (Curran, 2002, p. 45), for imposing "homogeneity" on diverse groups of citizens through consensus seeking and recognition of singular 'public opinion' (Fraser, 1990), and for being based on the bourgeois public sphere, which excludes or marginalizes many people, more general understandings of the public sphere offer a context for understanding what Kenneth Burke (1969) called the "wrangle of the marketplace" of ideas. It may not exist as Habermas envisaged, but democratic societies need a public sphere in which citizens can become informed and engage in discussion and debate. In an age of mobility and declining traditional political institutions such as political parties, media operate as key sites for such activities. In those sites, journalists perform important roles, not only as 'gatekeepers' but also as producers of allegedly independent reporting and analysis. If journalists are merely 'churning' press releases and reporting political, corporate, and organizational rhetoric distributed by PR practitioners in their various guises, they are not performing their role as key political actors.

Whether democracy is worked out in a single cohesive public sphere as envisaged by Habermas, or in multiple public spheres (Dahlgren, 2009) or *public sphericles* as discussed by Nancy Fraser (1992) and others (e.g., Gitlin, 1998; Goode, 2005; Warner, 2002), the creation and participation of informed citizens is critical. The "uninformed citizen" is problematic for democracy, as noted by scholars such as Peter Dahlgren (2009) and Michael Delli Carpini and Scott Keeter (1996). Equally one could argue that the misinformed citizen is problematic. Hence, maintenance of a viable public sphere in which citizens can access independently produced non-partisan information remains crucial.

Cornerstone of Democracy

From a number of perspectives, the role of media—and journalism in particular—is seen in many countries as a cornerstone of democracy (e.g., see Walkley

Foundation, 2012). This is nowhere more apparent than in developing countries in which free independent media are the difference between despotic regimes and free elections; between propaganda and free speech and freedom of information. Yet, according to the latest Freedom House reports, the sobering reality is that more than one-third of all people globally live under highly state-controlled media and information environments classified as 'not free' (Moss & Koenig, 2013, p. 2). While not the main focus of this book, interviews with journalists in developing countries were included in research reported in Chapter 6 and the findings in relation to PR will surprise some.

Investigative journalism, in particular, is seen by many as the heart of democracy in both developed and developing nations, particularly in corrupt states (Bennett & Serrin, 2011). In their widely used text, *The Elements of Journalism: What Newspeople Should Know and the Public Should Expect*, Bill Kovach and Tom Rosenstiel (2007) argue that investigative journalism serves as an independent "monitor of power" and offers "a voice to the voiceless" (chap. 6). To serve this role, they argue that journalists must maintain independence from all factions and forms of influence (chap. 5).

The Propaganda Model of Media

Conversely, it needs to be borne in mind that some critical scholars see the Liberal/Libertarian, Social Responsibility, and Democratic Corporatist models of media, the role of journalists as key political actors in the public sphere, and concepts such as the Fourth Estate as failed or flawed. Edward Herman and Noam Chomsky (1988) argue that most countries including the US and UK are served by a *propaganda model* of media. In *Manufacturing Consent: The Political Economy of Mass Media*, they contend that mass media "serve to mobilize support for the special interests that dominate the state"—that is, political and economic elites (p. xi). In the case of Western capitalist countries, they argue that commercial media operate primarily to sell products and services for other businesses, particularly advertisers, rather than provide quality news and information to citizens. Herman and Chomsky propose that five 'filters' serve to influence and corrupt commercial media: (1) ownership by profit-seeking corporations as well as politically and ideologically motivated proprietors; (2) advertising which provides the predominant source of media revenue; (3) reliance on sources, particularly official and elite sources, which becomes a symbiotic and mutually supporting relationship; (4) 'flak' such as letters, petitions, complaints, proposed regulation or legislation, or other threats such as withdrawal of advertising; and (5) anti-Communism. While the fifth filter related mainly to the period of the Cold War, analyses such as that by J. Michael Sproule (1997) show that media have been used widely for propaganda in democratic as well as centrally controlled states. It is useful to reflect on the continuing relevance of many of these factors today, particularly advertising, sources dependency, and evolving forms of 'flak' including organized campaigns as discussed in the next chapter on PR.

Cultural Intermediaries

Pierre Bourdieu identifies "the producers of cultural programs on TV and radio… the 'critics' of quality newspapers and magazines and all the writer-journalists and journalist-writers" as *cultural intermediaries* (1984, p. 325). It a world that John Keane (2009) calls "media-saturated", or which is even "supersaturated" by media according to Todd Gitlin (2001) and Nick Couldry (2012, p. 5), cultural intermediaries occupy a central role in not only producing symbolic goods and services but also in mediating meaning in society.

While the concept of cultural intermediaries provides another useful theoretical framework to understand journalism and the role of journalists in society, use of the term 'cultural intermediaries' has strayed far from Bourdieu's original description (Curtin & Gaither, 2007), and tracing its evolution is necessary. Others now share the stage and one of the 'new cultural intermediaries' that has emerged is PR (Macnamara & Crawford, 2013). As David Hesmondhalgh notes, Bourdieu's reference to cultural intermediaries in *Distinction* referred to "a particular type of new petite bourgeoisie profession associated with cultural commentary in the mass media" (2007, p. 66). Bourdieu identifies cultural intermediaries as most typically journalists and media program producers (1984, p. 325). However, in contemporary societies it can be argued that the distinction seen by Bourdieu—that cultural intermediaries such as journalists, critics, and commentators alone mediate meaning between producers and consumers, while the new petite bourgeoisie occupations such as advertising and PR simply produce "symbolic goods and services"—is increasingly blurred or non-existent. Keith Negus (2002) sees the term 'cultural intermediaries' as problematic as a descriptive label and as an analytic concept because it privileges "a particular cluster of occupations" (p. 504), and he argues that a wider range of workers including corporate managers, accountants, and even factory workers can constitute cultural intermediaries (pp. 505–507). While this may be stretching the term too far, the long separation between studies of the production and consumption of media and culture has increasingly closed and a broader range of actors and agents involved in cultural production and processes of meaning-making has been identified. Drawing on Sean Nixon and Paul du Gay (2002), Caroline Hodges (2006) says "cultural intermediaries are by definition advertising practitioners, management consultants and public relations practitioners and other occupations" involved in information and knowledge intensive forms of work, and she described these as increasingly central to economic and cultural life (p. 84).

The Decline of Journalism

The last decade of the 20th century and the first decade of the 21st century have seen what a number of media scholars warn is a crisis in journalism (Gitlin, 2009; Curran, 2010; Jones, 2011), the "twilight of journalism" (Dahlgren, 2009, p. 41), or even the "end of journalism" (Jones & Salter, 2012, p. 1)—although, as John Seely Brown and Paul Duguid (2000) state, *endism* is a much over-claimed concept. Tom Laster predicted in *The Boston Globe* in 1993 that the introduction of CD-ROM would mean "the end of books" (as cited in Curran, 2010, p. 464). Philip Meyer (2004) notes widespread speculation on the "end of newspapers". George Gilder confidently predicted "the end of television" (1994, p. 49). And Jon Lewis (2001) wrote about the end of cinema. Despite significant technological, industrial, economic, and social change, none of these predictions have come to pass. Nevertheless, grave fears are held for journalism because of the domino effect of falling newspaper circulation and broadcast audiences, which has led to falling advertising revenue (as advertising prices are based on audience size), which in turn has led to loss of journalists' jobs through cutbacks caused by falling media incomes and even the collapse of many media companies.

Newspapers have lost readers at an escalating rate over the past 25 to 30 years in the US and most other developed countries. From a high of 63.34 million copies a day in 1984, US daily newspapers have plummeted to sales of 44.42 million copies a day in 2011 (Newspaper Association of America, 2012a)—a fall of close to 30 per cent, or almost 20 million readers. Ten million of these readers were lost in the decade 2001–2011. The decline has been relentless, as shown in Figure 2.1, and makes one wonder why it took so long for newspaper proprietors to recognize that major structural change was occurring.

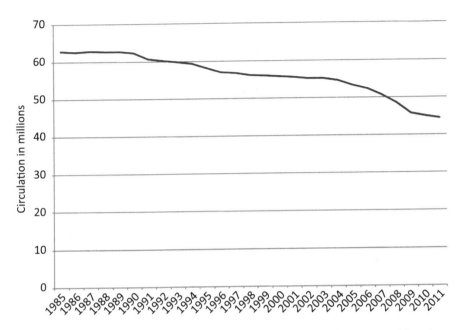

Figure 2.1. US daily newspaper circulation, 1984–2011 (Newspaper Association of America, 2012a).

In the UK, Professor of Journalism at City University, London, and media writer for *The Guardian* Roy Greenslade has noted that Britain's 10 national daily newspapers sold just over eight million copies a day in November 2012, compared with 11 million copies a day in November 2007—a fall of more than 25 per cent in the five years. The turn away from Sunday newspapers in the UK has been even more dramatic, declining from more than 11 million copies a week to just 7.75 million—a fall of more than 30 per cent (Greenslade, 2012).

The Guardian has been more successful than most newspapers in transitioning to the digital age and the Internet but, while increasing traffic to its online news pages by 22 per cent in 2010, it lost 16 per cent of its print readers. This is significant because, as Janet Jones and Lee Salter (2012) note, "online eyeballs were worth a fraction of their print counterparts" (p. 37). They report a media economist's calculations that an online reader was worth just 1.2 Euro a year in terms of advertising earned, whereas a print edition reader was worth 18 a year at that time. This is partly because almost 80 per cent of online users say that they never or hardly ever click on display advertisements, according to the Pew Research Center (2010). Pew also has reported that the average online reader spends only three minutes and four seconds per session visiting a news site (as cited in O'Donnell, McKnight, & Este, 2012, p. 18).

Australian newspapers have fared better than their US and UK counterparts, according to Sydney media analyst Steve Allen, but nevertheless total annual newspaper sales in Australia fell from 888.7 million in 2006 to 789.8 million in 2011—a drop of 11 per cent (Dyer, 2012a). After a temporary respite in 2010 following the circulation bloodbath of 2008–2009, a number of leading Australian newspapers again suffered increasing falls in readership in 2011 compared with previous years. For instance, *The Sydney Morning Herald* suffered a weekday circulation decline of 13.6 per cent in the 12 months to March 2011 and its Saturday edition lost 13.8 per cent in circulation. Similarly, circulation of *The Age* in Melbourne fell 13.5 per cent on weekdays and 12.4 per cent on Saturdays (Dyer, 2012b).

TV has been holding on to its audiences better than newspapers (Pew Research Center, 2012). However, the Pew Research Center's 'State of the News Media' report for 2013 presented data from Nielsen Media Research, comScore, Arbitron, and other sources showing local TV audiences in the US were down 6.5 per cent in one year from 2011 to 2012 and network TV was down almost 2 per cent in 2012 compared with 2011 (Pew Research Center, 2013). Also, alarmingly, TV is losing key demographics, particularly young people. These same key demographics are also abandoning radio. John Pavlik (2008) reports that listenership of radio among teenagers has fallen 20 per cent in the US since 1996 (p. 62) and only 23 per cent of 18–29-year-olds say they rely on major network television as their primary source of news (p. 89). A 2010 US analysis shows that time spent listening to radio per day had almost halved in a decade, and radio, which has traditionally been a favourite medium for youth, has slipped from number one to number three medium among 12–24-year-olds behind TV and the Internet (Stern, 2010).

Because the attractiveness of media to advertisers is directly related to the size of their audience, both overall and in particular demographic segments targeted by advertisers, declining audiences have resulted in declining advertising revenue. The flow-on effect of the declining circulation of US newspapers is graphically illustrated in Figure 2.2, which tabulates advertising revenues from 2000 to 2011. This shows that, even though advertising in online editions of newspapers has brought in a new revenue stream starting from 2003, this has not offset losses in print media advertising. Overall, advertising revenue in leading US newspapers has been in decline since 2007, suffering a substantial 16.6 per cent fall in 2008 and a massive 27.2 per cent drop in 2009. Jones and Salter (2012) report that US newspapers "exited a harrowing 2008 and entered 2009 in something perilously close to free fall" (p. 38). Robert McChesney (2013) similarly notes that a "newspaper meltdown unfolded early in 2009" (p. 199). Even though this plummeting trend has eased somewhat, advertising revenue continued to fall by 6–7 per cent a year in 2010 and 2011 (see Figure 2.2).

US National Newspapers	Print		Online		Total				Change
Year	$ millions	% change	$ millions	% change	$ millions	% change	$ millions		% change
2000	$7,653	5.1%	$48,670	5.1%					
2001	$7,004	-15.2%	$44,305	-9.0%					
2002	$7,210	-4.3%	$44,102	-0.5%					
2003	$7,797	-0.6%	$44,939	1.9%	$1,216		$46,156		
2004	$8,083	5.1%	$46,703	3.9%	$1,541	26.7%	$48,244		4.5%
2005	$7,910	4.2%	$47,408	1.5%	$2,027	31.5%	$49,435		2.5%
2006	$7,505	-1.9%	$46,611	-1.7%	$2,664	31.4%	$49,275		0.3%
2007	$7,005	-16.5%	$42,209	-9.4%	$3,166	18.8%	$45,375		-7.9%
2008	$5,996	-29.7%	$34,740	-17.7%	$3,109	-1.8%	$37,848		-16.6%
2009	$4,424	-38.1%	$24,821	-28.6%	$2,743	-11.8%	$27,564		-27.2%
2010	$4,221	-8.6%	$22,795	-8.2%	$3,042	10.9%	$25,838		-6.3%
2011	$3,777	-11.0%	$20,692	-9.2%	$3,249	6.8%	$23,941		-7.3%

Figure 2.2. Advertising revenue of US national newspapers 2000–2011 (Newspaper Association of America, 2012b).

The 2012 'State of the News Media' report by the Pew Research Center Project for Excellence in Journalism noted that an indexed comparison of circulation and advertising revenue combined showed that the US newspaper industry had shrunk 43 per cent since 2000 (Pew Research Center, 2012). In 2000, US daily newspapers received around US$20 billion a year from classified advertising alone. By 2011, the figure was US$5 billion. In the same period, display advertising revenue fell from US$30 billion to half that amount (McChesney, 2013, p. 172). Not surprisingly, an increasing number of US newspapers are closing their doors. The number of daily newspapers in the US has declined from more than 1,800 in the 1940s to 1,611 by 1990 and was down to 1,382 in 2011 (Newspaper Association of America, 2012a).

While faring better than newspapers in advertising revenue, US network TV also suffered a 3.7 per cent fall in advertising revenue in 2011, local US TV stations suffered a 6.7 per cent fall, and advertising revenue of US magazines declined by 5.6 per cent (Pew Research Center, 2012, p. 9). The Pew Research Center warns that, in the changing news landscape, "even television is vulnerable" (Kohut, Doherty, Dimock, & Keeter, 2012) and the further loss of audiences of local and network TV reported in the 2013 'State of the News Media' report (Pew Research Center, 2013) is likely to cause further revenue losses.

The picture is equally gloomy in the UK and other developed countries such as Australia. In Britain, print media advertising revenue is reported to have fallen by more than 30 per cent in 2009 and, despite a small recovery in 2010, declined 12.8 per cent in 2011 (O'Donnell et al., 2012, p. 10). In Australia, total newspaper advertising revenue declined by 8 per cent in 2011 and was down 18 per cent on 2008. The Newspaper Works, an advocacy group for the Australian newspaper industry, has remained upbeat, commenting in its 2011 annual report that "Australian newspapers are well-placed to take full advantage of the future and are poised to benefit from the burgeoning consumer take-up of digital platforms" (para. 1). However, statistics do not support such optimism and suggest it is a case of what James Curran identifies as "ostrich-like denial" (2011, p. 114). An IBISWorld report forecast that Australian newspaper revenues would fall by a further 4 per cent in 2013 ("Newspaper revenue forecast", 2013). Broadcasting is performing better than print in terms of advertising revenue, but TV and radio advertising is also in a continuing decline. Australian TV advertising revenue for free-to-air networks fell 4.5 per cent in 2011 compared with the previous year ("TV revenues down across the board", 2012), and metropolitan radio advertising revenue declined in all Australian capital cities in 2012 ("Radio ad revenue softer", 2013). These figures may be a lull before a further storm, as Deloitte data published by Commercial Radio Australia showed a 3 per cent fall in the month of January 2013 alone, compared to the same month the year before (Sinclair, 2013).

The sustained and substantial fall in advertising revenue being experienced by most commercial newspapers, magazines, and broadcasting networks in major developed markets has led to large and sometimes massive reductions in the number of journalists employed by these media because news and current affairs, along with other programming, is primarily funded by advertising revenue. Staff reductions started in the late 1980s and early 1990s, particularly in newspapers, such as during Rupert Murdoch's union-busting move of his Fleet Street newspapers to a new 'high-tech' facility at Wapping in the London Docklands district in 1986. Robert Maxwell sacked around one-third of his workforce in the same period (Snoddy, 1992, p. 14).

A fresh round of media staff reductions began in the early 2000s following the economic downturn triggered by the dot.com crash and, even though economies have recovered from this and mostly weathered the Global Financial Crisis of 2007–2008, The Guardian News and Media group announced that it would axe up to 100 of its 650 editorial staff in late 2012 because of losses of more than £44 million a year (Rushton, 2012). In 2013 the publicly funded BBC announced a five-year program to cut 2,000 jobs (Reuters, 2013). In the US, journalists' jobs are being lost through complete collapse of traditional media organizations, as well as through layoffs. According to *Paper Cuts* (2012), a Web site which monitors US media, 15,554 journalists' jobs were lost in the US in 2008 and 14,828 in 2009—a period of massive restructuring in US media. The loss of US journalists' jobs has slowed but not stopped, with a further 2,920 going in 2010, 4,190 in 2011, and 1,859 in 2012. The 'crisis in journalism' is also affecting related jobs such as news photography. In May 2013, *The Chicago Sun-Times* fired all 28 of its photographers with the intent of relying on 'crowdsourcing' and citizen content (Pavlik, 2013, p. 212). The Pew Research Center's 'State of the News Media' report for 2013 notes that US newsroom staff were down 30 per cent since 2,000 and below 40,000 full-time professional employees for the first time since 1978 (Pew Research Center, 2013). After slashing 550 jobs from the staff of its publications in Australia and New Zealand, including 120 journalists, one of the leading Australasian media organizations, Fairfax Media, announced in 2012 that 1,900 more jobs would go, including almost 400 journalists' positions. More than 1,000 journalists' jobs were lost between 2009 and 2012 in Australia, according to Penny O'Donnell and her co-researchers (2012, p. 9).

Journalists worldwide are reacting to reductions in editorial staff and the decline in traditional media with understandable alarm. They argue that an inevitable and concerning result of this loss of journalists' jobs is a lack of time for remaining journalists to do research and fact check, which leads to a loss of quality. Studies have found that quality in journalism is correlated with the size of news staff (e.g., Lacy, Fico, & Simon, 1989). Furthermore, many journalists and editors say that the reductions in editorial staff that have occurred in almost all developed countries have forced them to rely on PR material to fill pages and programs, as there are simply not enough journalists to independently research and report all the content required each day. A study among educators in the US found that both journalism and PR educators believe that journalists depend on PR material due to "inadequate staffing levels in most newspapers" (Shaw & White, 2004, p. 499). More recently, a 'Challenges' study by the Reuters Institute for the Study of Journalism at Oxford University titled 'What's Happening to Our News' reports:

> The sophisticated and fast-growing public relations industry (financed by wealthy individuals and corporate clients) appears to benefit from this trend. The client-driven, self-promoting incentives of PR align with the cost-cutting incentives of publishers to encourage the rapid absorption of pre-packaged PR material into the twenty-first news factories (Currah, 2009, p. 6).

In *Flat Earth News*, Nick Davies says: "The media…have become structurally weakened to the point where they routinely betray their own function by passing on unchecked PR to their readers and viewers" (2009, p. 194). He further explains:

Journalists who no longer have the time to go out and find their own stories and to check the material which they are handling, are consistently vulnerable to ingesting and reproducing the packages of information which are provided for them by this PR industry (p. 203).

However, there are two important qualifications that need to be made in relation to claims that external factors are the root of the media's weakened position, particularly its infiltration by PR. Newspaper circulation in the US reached its peak in 1984 and cutbacks in journalists' jobs did not begin to any significant extent until the late 1980s. As reported in Chapter 5, use of PR material was already well established in the 1920s and was clearly documented through the 1960s, 1970s, and 1980s. In fact, 100 years of content analyses summarized in Chapter 5 reveal high use of PR material dating back to the very early 1900s. So there is no correlation between the trend lines of increasing use of PR material and loss of journalists' jobs—these two trends have occurred independently of each other, although the decline in journalists' jobs is likely to exacerbate the situation.

The second qualification that needs to be noted is that journalism has contributed to its own problems and, to a significant extent, lives in a glasshouse when it comes to partisanship, spin, and even fabrication. One of the reasons for declining readers, listeners, and viewers of mass media is declining public confidence in them. While pointing the finger at PR as a corrupter of media values and quality, news media have had their own share of questionable practices. In the 19th century and even into the early 20th century, journalists did not separate fact and comment and regularly took sides in political debates (Machin & Van Leeuwen, 2007, p. 7). The popular press has at various times in the not too distant past been involved in "muck-raking" (Mayer, 1968, p. 89) and "yellow journalism" characterized by "gimmicky features, fakery, and hysterical headlines" (McChesney & Scott, 2003, p. xvii). Even worse, longtime professor of journalism and mass communications Tom Goldstein notes that "fabrication was a fixture of journalism for much of the 19th and 20th centuries" (2007, p. 17).

More recently, Goldstein cites Janet Cooke's 1981 Pulitzer Prize-winning account of an eight-year-old heroin addict published in *The Washington Post* in a story called 'Jimmy's world' as a lamentable example of problematic journalistic practices. It was later revealed that there was no 'Jimmy'; the journalist created a fictional composite character based on anecdotal information, but this was not revealed in the article (Goldstein, 2007, p. 17). Any study of the media does not have to go back even to the 1980s to identify an absence of objectivity and a very loose conception of truth. More recent scandals include the Stephen Glass case that was dramatized in the 2003 film *Shattered Glass*. It was discovered in 1998 that 27 of 41 articles written by Glass for *The New Republic* in the previous three years contained fabricated material

(Kurtz, 1998). In 2003, Jayson Blair resigned from *The New York Times* after it was discovered that he had plagiarized and fabricated numerous articles. Blair gained an internship with *The Times* despite falsely claiming he had completed a degree and was rapidly promoted to its Metro section and then the national desk. Often touted as a bastion of media credibility, *The New York Times* was forced to admit:

> He [Jayson Blair] fabricated comments. He concocted scenes. He lifted material from other newspapers and wire services. He selected details from photographs to create the impression he had been somewhere or seen someone, when he had not ("Times Reporter Who Resigned", 2003).

The credibility of major media and contemporary journalism has been severely dented by even more recent sordid behaviour, such as the phone tapping and hacking activities of *News of the World* journalists in the UK, which resulted in a judicial inquiry in 2011 after it was revealed that reporters had hacked into the voicemail of murdered teenager Milly Dowler. Dozens of victims of media phone tapping came forward to testify to the inquiry, including parents of other murdered and missing children who reported being "hounded and harassed" by reporters, as well as celebrities such as Hugh Grant, Sienna Miller, and J. K. Rowling (Basen, 2012, paras. 3–5). In the introduction of *Ethics of Media*, Nick Couldry, Mirca Madianou, and Amit Pinchevski (2013) say that incidents such as the *News of the World* 'phone hacking' have "finally installed the ethics of media at the heart of public debate" (p. 3) and they add that, along with the declining credibility of media, the changing nature of media is a "huge stimulus" for examining the ethics of media (p. 5).

The Pew Research Center's 2009 'State of the News Media' report provides sobering reading in relation to media credibility. It reports that only 25 per cent of citizens said that they believe all or most of what they read in *The Wall Street Journal*. In 1998, that figure stood at 41 per cent and in 2002 it was 33 per cent, showing a continuing decline in the credibility of major media. Similarly, the Pew study found that only 21 per cent of people believe all or most of what they read in *TIME* magazine and only 18 per cent rate *The New York Times* as highly credible. *Newsweek* and *USA Today* were rated even less credible, with only 16 per cent of respondents saying they believe all or most of what they publish. Contrary to some claims, local newspapers also are facing falling credibility. In 1998, 29 per cent of readers said they believed all or most of what they read in their local newspaper—not a great endorsement. But this has fallen further to just 22 per cent in 2008, according to the Pew Research Center (2009). More recently, the annual Gallup survey of confidence in US institutions found that trust in newspapers in 2012 was well down from its peak of 51 per cent in 1979, with just 25 per cent of Americans, on average, having 'a great deal' or 'quite a lot' of confidence in their press (Morales, 2012).

Broadcast media are only marginally more trusted and believed, according to the Pew Research Center (2009). Only 30 per cent of viewers believe all or most of what is reported on *CNN*, only 29 per cent rate *60 Minutes* highly believable, and the ratings for 'believe all or most' fall to 24 per cent for *NBC* News, *ABC News*, and *MSNBC News*, followed by *Fox News* at 23 per cent and *CBS News* at 22 per cent. Interestingly, the Pew Internet Research 'State of the News Media' reports for 2011 and 2012 did not include believability figures. However, a Pew study of the press by Andrew Kohut and colleagues in 2012 found that 77 per cent of Americans feel newspapers lack fairness, 72 per cent believe press are unwilling to admit mistakes, 66 per cent believe they report inaccurately, and 63 per cent perceive political bias (Kohut et al., 2012, p. 6). From its annual survey of confidence in US institutions in 2012, Gallup reported that, overall, only 21 per cent of Americans had 'a great deal' or 'quite a lot' of confidence in television news—less than half the number who trusted TV when Gallup started tracking confidence in television news in 1993.

The decline in media credibility is occurring in many countries. A 2007 Roy Morgan Research poll found 85 per cent of Australians believe newspaper journalists are often biased, 74 per cent believe TV reporters are often biased, and almost 70 per cent believe that talk-back radio announcers are often biased (Roy Morgan Research, 2007). During the March 2008 Malaysian election, the long-reigning coalition, *Barisan Nasional* (National Front), which owns the major newspapers and broadcast networks in Malaysia, found itself facing a political crisis as citizens turned away from these media, claiming that they "were no longer credible" and looked to blogs for independent information. BN suffered a major loss of support in the polls, narrowly holding on to government, and was forced to make major changes in its policies and use of media (Ramli, 2008; "Study Shows Why BN Lost Media War", 2008). Recently, the Edelman Trust Barometer, the largest annual study of trust in the world with almost 32,000 respondents in 2013, reported that in each year from 2010 to 2013 peers ('a person like you') and colleagues ('a regular employee') are trusted more than CEOs, government officials, and even NGOs (Edelman, 2013a, p. 8). Interestingly, the Edelman Trust Barometer has found trust in media still relatively high and even increasing in some countries, including China, Singapore, India, Hong Kong, the United Arab Emirates (UAE), and parts of South America, but it confirmed low trust in media in major developed Western countries.

In a classic example of the discourse of victimhood, some shoot the blame for the media's falling credibility on to PR. Writing in the Sage *Index on Censorship*, Michael Foley (2004) says:

> The increasing power of public relations and the consequent decline in journalism has contributed to a collapse in public trust. The confusion of public and private makes it difficult for the public to judge the information it is given (p. 77).

While the infiltration of PR material into media may be one factor in declining public trust, such claims are disingenuous. In the discourse of victimhood, editors and journalists take little or no responsibility for the troubles in journalism—the crisis in journalism is somebody else's fault! They fail to acknowledge that many, if not most, journalists willingly seek PR material and assistance on a daily basis—even if they deny it to their editors and their audience. Many still fail to give respect and credit to readers, listeners, and viewers, assuming that they are passive and gullible. Research suggests that readers, listeners, and viewers are much smarter than traditional media thought. Those who New York journalism professor Jay Rosen calls "the people formerly known as the audience" (2006, para. 1) have voted with their eyes and ears and their keyboard clicking fingers. They are consuming more media content than ever before in history, but it is increasingly not content produced by journalists.

In response to complaints of inaccuracy in the media and declining credibility, a number of fact-checking initiatives have been launched. These include:

- FactCheck (http://www.factcheck.org), a non-partisan, non-profit organization established by the Annenberg Public Policy Center of the University of Pennsylvania;
- PolitiFact (http://www.politifact.com), a Pulitzer prize-winning site established by *The Tampa Bay Times* and partners in the US;
- Fullfact (http://fullfact.org), a non-partisan, non-profit group in the UK;
- PolitiFact Australia (http://www.politifact.com.au) established by former editor in chief of *The Sydney Morning Herald* Peter Fray; and
- Several individual media fact-checking sites such as *The FactCheck Blog* launched in 2010 by the UK public service broadcaster Channel 4 (http://blogs.channel4.com/factcheck).

However, all of these initiatives are focussed predominantly on political statements, speeches, and policies and do not research media content more generally. Furthermore, it is reasonable to ask why separate organizations are needed to check facts in information provided to the media—surely this is what journalists are meant to do? While a popular aphorism is that journalism is "the first rough draft of history"[5] and a Columbia Journalism School report eloquently describes journalists as "the emergency room doctors of epistemology" (Folkerts, Hamilton, & Lehmann, 2013, p. 62) because they have to work quickly with little time for reflection and revision, Bill Kovach and Tom Rosenstiel state in *The Elements of Journalism* that "verification is what separates journalism from entertainment, propaganda, fiction, or art" (2001, p. 79).

Media writer Tim Dunlop is one who is critical of fact checking becoming a "side-dish rather than an integral part of the normal meal of journalism" (2013a, para. 3). Dunlop says in his 2013 book *The New Front Page: New Media and the Rise of the Audience (2013a) and his blog*:

> If you relied on the mainstream media for your information on incredibly important issues such as the Iraq War, the events leading up to the global financial crisis, climate change and even media reform…you would be badly informed. On all of these issues, the mainstream [media] failed in its most basic duty as a provider of information that allows citizens to inform themselves. It found itself captured by various special interests (2013b, para. 14).

New Forms of Journalism

A cogent and cryptic overview of the main claims and narratives about journalism in the first and second decades of the 21st century has been provided by James Curran (2010, 2011). He has identified four discourses which he describes as: (1) "continuity", characterized by media proprietor survivalism and "ostrich-like denial"; (2) a "crisis of journalism", based on journalists' anxiety and pessimism; (3) "a cleansing purgative" in the eyes of "gleeful millenarians" who see a collapse of traditional media models as an opportunity for change; and (4) "renaissance", based on transformist views of liberal journalism and media academics who optimistically anticipate a new media world of citizen journalism and network journalism (Curran, 2010, pp. 464–470; Curran, 2011, pp. 111–118). Originally presented as a plenary paper to a Future of Journalism conference in Cardiff, Wales in September 2009, before being advanced in his books *Media and Democracy* (Curran, 2011) and *Misunderstanding the Internet* (Curran, Fenton, & Freedman, 2012), Curran's four positions were neatly summarized in a conference report by the Canadian Journalism Project. This described the four scenarios as "boisterous survivalism among industry leaders, gleeful apocalypticism among those disenchanted with the atrophy of the Fourth Estate, a panglossian optimism among academics, and an anxious overwhelmed sense among journalists who fear they might be witnessing their profession's extinction" (2009, para. 2).

While conceptualizing and creating the future of journalism remains a work in progress, there is a continuing role for journalism in the view of most scholars in media studies, politics, and sociology. They say journalism remains of enduring importance in democratic societies. Journalism as it has been practiced and some of the sites where it has been practiced may not have a future, but there are opportunities for journalism to reinvent and relocate itself to become more relevant and competitive in the 21st-century mediascape—to enjoy the 'renaissance' that Curran cites. Some emerging forms of journalism and suggestions for the future of journalism are briefly noted to inform a contemporary analysis of the interrelationship with PR.

Specialist journalism

While some genres of journalism such as general news reporting and some industry sectors such as 'newspaper journalism' are in major decline, it needs to be borne in mind that some specialist fields of journalism are maintaining and even increasing audiences. For example, it is often overlooked that business journalism continues to be in demand, albeit it has largely shifted from business newspapers and magazines to specialist online and subscription services such as Bloomberg (e.g., *BusinessWeek* was acquired by Bloomberg in 2009). Al Jazeera has expanded substantially over the past decade in many countries—for example, Al Jazeera America was hiring journalists when many US media were reducing their editorial staff. Also, fields such as environmental journalism, sports journalism, and entertainment journalism continue to attract audiences—albeit they also are increasingly shifting to online sites. While journalism and media scholars justifiably express concern about genres such as investigative journalism being under threat, educators and practitioners need to recognize the breadth of public information needs and interests served by journalism and think laterally, not only in traditional and elite terms. Furthermore, beyond continuing and evolving specialist and niche markets for journalism, the following more fundamental shifts are noteworthy.

Analysis and sense-making

In an age of ubiquitous mobile/cell phones, social media, and social networks, it is becoming difficult if not impossible for mass media organizations to be first with news, other than that provided to them by official sources, which Richard Perloff described as the "lifeblood of news" (1998, p. 223). Increasingly, news is reported by eye-witnesses via social media and social networks. What is missing and much-needed in information-overloaded contemporary societies is not more news, but analysis to make sense of issues in the news, identify trends, and explain developments. This argument is supported by research findings in relation to paywalls and paid content, which indicate that most people will not pay for news, but many will pay for in-depth analysis (e.g., PriceWaterhouseCoopers, 2009).

Hyperlocal journalism

Pablo Boczkowski (2005), Bob Franklin (2006), and others have identified growing interest in local and micro-local conversations, which offers another opportunity for journalism. While the Internet facilitates globalization of information and culture, particularly when used by large commercial media organizations, it also opens up opportunities for hyperlocal journalism. Online newspapers, newsletters, blogs, forums, and communities can be economically established and operated by and for even very small communities both in terms of geography and interests. The demise of small local newspapers and radio stations that has occurred in many country towns and suburbs over the past few decades can be reversed with the Internet, bringing valuable local news, information, analysis, and commentary back to communities.

Computational and data journalism

The widespread use of computing, and particularly the growth of databases and associated techniques such as database search and data mining, offer new research and investigation opportunities for journalists referred to as 'computational journalism' or 'data journalism'. Terry Flew and colleagues say that computational journalism "involves the application of software and technologies to the activities of journalism" (Flew, Spurgeon, Daniel, & Swift, 2012, p. 157). More specifically, computational or data journalism involves the use of sophisticated tools and methods to drill into, collect, and analyze the vast amounts of information that are now available in digital form. Everything from the minutes of local government meetings and the expense accounts of members of Parliament and Congress to transcripts of inquiries and reports of major development projects are available in digital form and many can be accessed by those with knowledge of databases, database query tools, and sophisticated software programs for data and text analysis. Computational journalism is the news media's strategy in relation to what is referred to as 'big data'—the vast and growing amount of data in the world that IDC estimates has reached 1.8 zettabytes (1.8 trillion gigabytes) in 500 quadrillion files by the end of 2010 (Gantz & Reinsel, 2010). Computational journalism is much the same as what others call *data journalism* (Gray, Bounegru, & Chambers, 2012).

A 2012 report produced by the Tow Center for Digital Journalism at Columbia University, New York, argues that, in addition to having 'soft skills' such as maintaining networks and relationships with sources, understanding audiences and adapting to change, journalists in the 21st century need 'hard skills' including data literacy, an ability to write computer code, and the skills to tell stories using various technologies (Anderson, Bell, & Shirky, 2012, pp. 36–39). The purpose of computational or data journalism is not simply accessing and reporting data, but "sense-making" (Flew, 2014, p. 115), through being able to combine, compare, and analyze large amounts of data to gain insights and identify patterns and trends.

In addition to gaining advanced computing skills, Philip Meyer (2002) and others explain that computational or data journalism utilizes social science research methods including quantitative data collection through polling, surveying, archival records analysis, statistical analysis, and text analysis to collect and make sense of information. This heavy use of data and social science research methods, particularly quantitative research, has led to some calling this approach *precision journalism*.

While the use of computers has been central to journalism for several decades and some journalists have a basic understanding of databases, few feel comfortable with database queries, data mining, statistical analysis, and advanced text analysis. As Terry Flew and colleagues note, journalists have relied on humanistic approaches to sense-making, relying often on intuition as well as understanding of rhetorical communication and information processing. A number of studies have reported that, notwithstanding some notable exceptions, news media have been slow to adopt new technologies (e.g., Himelboim & McCreery, 2012; O'Sullivan & Heinonen, 2008; Reich, 2013). While some blame for this no doubt lies at the feet of media proprietors, this also suggests that major changes are required in the education and training of journalists.

Digital journalism

With digitization of press, radio, and TV content, convergence as discussed by Henry Jenkins (2006) and others is affecting the practices as well as the technologies of traditional news gathering, leading to what Bill Gentile (2013) calls 'backpack journalists' and Stephen Quinn (2012) refers to as the 'MOJO evolution'—mobile multimedia journalists who record video, photos, and sound, as well as write text reports and upload these to media Web sites from the field via Internet-connected digital devices. In *Principles of Convergent Journalism*, US journalism scholars Jeffrey Wilkinson, August Grant, and Douglas Fisher (2012) discuss how the contemporary journalist increasingly needs to work with multiple forms of media across multiple digital platforms. However, digital journalism refers not only to traditional forms of reporting in digital form and online, which is now commonplace, but also to a range of online media types and forms of writing. Peter Dahlgren (2013) says digital journalism includes:

> Mainstream online media, alternative journalism sites, the blogosphere, social media, individual and group productions, including efforts by social movements and other activists and groups of every imaginable persuasion—political, religious, and lifestyle advocates, hobbyists and much more. All manner of 'amateur'—as well as 'para'—or 'quasi journalism' are juxtaposing and blending with each other. Facts and opinions, debates, gossip, nonsense, misinformation, the insightful, the deceptive, the poetic, are all mixed together, scrambling the traditional boundaries between journalism and non-journalism (p. 160).

Dahlgren's definition is broad but useful for its inclusiveness and its suggestion that journalism of the future will be a blending of professionals and amateurs interacting in both complementary and competitive ways and that it will be located at multiple sites, not simply within a small oligopoly of large media organizations. A study by Farida Vis (2013) of the use of Twitter during the 2011 London riots serves as an illustration of this new hybrid model of journalism. Senior journalists Paul Lewis from *The Guardian* and Ravi Somaiya from *The New York Times* exchanged information with citizens, asked questions, checked facts, and kept track of developments by following the Twitter stream through key hashtags such as #ukriots, #tottenham, and #tottenhamriots. They gained valuable information by engaging citizens in the news gathering and production process. Vis further noted that the traditional analogue media approach of sending a TV crew with a large professional camera, and often lights, to a scene can incite crowds to do more than they otherwise might do, whereas a 'MOJO' or 'backpack' journalist with a small mobile/cell phone or handheld digital camera, and active use of Twitter, Facebook, and YouTube can gain a far more authentic and complete account of events.

At the beginning of the 21st century, John Pavlik (2001) predicted digital journalism could be "potentially a better form of journalism", saying it could "re-engage an increasingly distrusting and alienated audience" (p. xi). A 2010 Pew Research Center Project for Excellence in Journalism study in the US found that 37 per cent of Internet users have contributed to the creation of news, commented on news, or disseminated news via postings on social media sites such as Facebook or Twitter (Purcell, Rainie, Mitchell, Rosenstiel, & Olmstead, 2010, p. 2). This demonstrates participation by citizens in news production, news distribution networks, and also growing 'consumption networks' as discussed by Lijun Tang (2013), but often overlooked in the focus on production and distribution and because of the "traditional production-consumption boundary" (Dickinson, Matthews, & Saltzis, 2013, p. 11).

In 2012, Lewis Dvorkin, the chief product officer at Forbes Media, published *The Forbes Model for Journalism in the Digital Age*, which describes journalism as "listening and engaging with news consumers", as well as giving reporters and contributors tools to enable them to easily publish text, photos, and video.

Public, civic, interactive, participatory, and networked journalism—journalism as conversation

Digital journalism in this sense is similar to and facilitates a movement towards 'journalism as conversation' (Kunelius, 2001; Marchionni, 2013). This approach to journalism has its roots in the criticisms of mid-20th-century journalism made by eminent scholars such as James Carey (1992, 2009), James Fallows (1996), and Jay Rosen (1999). Carey says that the primary method by which humans make sense of and establish coherence in the world is communication carried out interactively through conversation (2009, p. 65). He argues that the media "by seeing its role as that of informing the public, abandons its role as an agency for carrying on the conversation of our culture" (pp. 62–63). He says that mass media acts as 'monopolies of knowledge' and in granting freedom of the press, societies sacrificed "the right of people to speak to one another and to inform themselves" and "substituted the more abstract right to be spoken to and to be informed by others" (2009, p. 125). Furthermore, by focussing on elites and experts as sources of information, the media became "one-way top-down lecture to citizens" (Marchionni, 2013, p. 132).

As Tanjev Schultz (1999) observes in an analysis of interactive online journalism: "There is a long tradition of dissatisfaction regarding the limited one-way communication of mass media"—the traditional model of journalism (para. 1). In a widely quoted speech to the American Society of Newspaper Editors in 2005, Rupert Murdoch acknowledged as much, saying that citizens today "don't want to rely on a god-like figure from above to tell them what's important. And to carry the religion analogy a bit further, they certainly don't want news presented as gospel" (2005, para. 16). The co-founder of Hotmail, Sabeer Bhatia, echoed Murdoch's religious analogy in an interview with *The Economist* discussing blogs and other forms of interactive media, predicting that "journalism won't be a sermon any more, it will be a conversation" ("It's the links stupid", 2006). In his book *Digitizing the News*, Pablo Boczkowski says: "News in the online environment is… [changing] from being mostly journalist-centred, communicated as monologue, and primarily local, to also being increasingly audience-centred, part of multiple conversations and micro-local" (2005, p. 21).

Former journalist now journalism academic Sue Robinson (2011) has proposed a framework for viewing *journalism as process*, rather than as a product resulting from news 'production', particularly in the case of online participatory news. She argues this to draw attention to the fact that "a news story now represents a fluid productive process as opposed to a discrete newspaper article" (p. 141). In a research monograph reporting on a study of US Midwestern newspapers transitioning from print to online and from traditional news gathering to emerging participatory models, Robinson describes traditional journalism as a product of industrialization, industrial labour relations, institutional practices, and a particular "production geography". She found that in shifting to online news, many traditional media organizations "appeared to be transferring key aspects of the industrialized work situation into the digital world" (p. 202), rather than fully reviewing and reimagining the spatial and temporal dimensions of news. She proposes that perceiving journalism as process facilitates a fundamental rethinking of the direction of information flow between workers and audiences, the roles and relationships of various participants, and the nature of news and journalism.

The movement towards greater citizen involvement is not new. A shift to engagement of citizens and incorporation of some level of user-generated content has been advocated in *public journalism*, as discussed by Jay Rosen (1999), Michael Schudson (1999), and Jack Rosenberry and Burton St John III (2010), and as part of *civic journalism* (Nip, 2008), *interactive journalism* (Schultz, 1999), *participatory journalism* (Nip, 2006), *networked journalism* (Beckett & Mansell, 2008; Van Der Haak, Parks, & Castells, 2012), and *citizen journalism* (Rosen, 2008). While a number of these terms are largely synonymous, there are some subtle and important differences. Jay Rosen says that "when the people formerly known as the audience employ the press tools they have in their possession to inform one another, that's citizen journalism" (2008, para. 1). However, Joyce Nip (2006) argues that interactive and participatory journalism involve publication or broadcast of user-generated content "within a frame designed by professionals" (p. 217), whereas citizen journalism involves no professionals. In this sense, citizen journalism is more closely related to what others call *street journalism* (Witschge, 2009) and *guerrilla journalism* (Case, 2007).

In a recent analysis, Doreen Marchionni (2013) notes that journalism as conversation "lacks coherent conceptual and operational definitions" and says researchers need to "establish a clear theoretical framework" for this approach (p. 143). She offers a definition of journalism as conversation as "the manner and/ or degree to which interpersonal, reciprocal exchanges between journalists and everyday citizens, whether mediated or unmediated, enhance news work on matters of public import for the common good" (p. 136). Open participatory networked approaches to journalism move practice from creation and production to *aggregation* and *curation*, which were demonstrated in the London riots reporting discussed in the previous section (Vis, 2013) and which are identified as future trends in journalism (Macquarie University, 2013). However, even beyond specific theories and practices of journalism, developing a more coherent and workable approach to interactive participatory journalism requires rethinking of the broad philosophical and paradigmatic framework in which journalism operates.

Postmodern journalism

Despite assertions since the early 1990s that the "high modern" paradigm of journalism that emerged in the early 20th century is waning (e.g., Altheide & Snow, 1991; Hallin, 1992), much discussion of journalism today continues within a worldview of modernism and even high modernism. Since the early days of American journalism when the American Society of Newspaper Editors developed what it called 'Canons of Journalism' and the Society of Professional Journalists developed its code of ethics, it has been argued that "the duty of journalists is to serve *the truth*" (Goldstein, 2007, p. 39) [emphasis added]. For example, in their influential text, *The Elements of Journalism*, Bill Kovach and Tom Rosenstiel assert that "journalism's first obligation is to the truth"—although they do go on to note that identifying truth is complex and can cause "utter confusion" (2001, p. 37). While some contemporary journalism courses teach a more relativist approach to research and writing, much journalism remains anchored in modernism with its metanarratives and ontological, epistemological, and axiological assumptions of a singular truth out there able to be discovered by humans, who allegedly can objectively research, interpret, and report without bias or subjectivity. Many journalists regard themselves and their work as resistant or even immune to the social constructedness of knowledge, the influence of discourses, and the subjectivities that plague other humans.

Journalism needs to more broadly embrace a postmodern/poststructuralist approach to remain relevant in developed societies. As Hunter S. Thompson puts it: "There is no such thing as objective journalism. The phrase itself is a pompous contradiction in terms" (as cited in O'Shaughnessy & Stadler, 2008, p. 76). More recently, Nick Davies (2009) states in *Flat Earth News*:

> The great blockbuster myth of modern journalism is objectivity, the idea that a good newspaper or broadcaster simply collects and reproduces the objective truth. It is a classic Flat Earth tale, widely believed and devoid of reality. It has never happened and never will happen because it cannot happen (p. 111).

Professor of journalism and mass communications at New York University Mitchell Stephens says that for a long time journalists "were content to ignore postmodernism" (as cited in Goldstein, 2007, p. 83). He advocates a 'journalism of openness', acknowledging the complexities of interpreting data and gaining accurate information, even from eyewitnesses who often have multiple different accounts (Goldstein, 2007, pp. 84–90). Chris Anderson (2006) comments in *The Long Tail*: "This is the end of spoon-fed orthodoxy and infallible institutions" (p. 190).

Modernist approaches in journalism, with their gatekeeping role and their focus on experts and elite sources, have in many ways played into the hands of PR. Governments and large corporations have trained, groomed, and air-brushed the image of political leaders, CEOs and a bevy of experts as media spokespersons willing and ready at a moment's notice to deliver a '10-second grab' to the media. The rich and powerful have the resources to make this investment in polished experts available 24/7 and, partly as a result of this, media reporting is dominated by a relatively small group of elite sources, while less accomplished, less erudite, and less available voices miss out. David Miller (1994) and Paul Manning (2001) report that selection of PR sources for media information is correlated with the economic resources of PR and that journalists mostly chose PR sources from groups with what Pierre Bourdieu called 'cultural capital'. Aeron Davis points out that this means that "well-resourced organizations can inundate the media and set the agenda, while the attempts of resource-poor organizations become quickly marginalized" (2000, p. 48). Postmodern thinking would prompt editors and journalists to recognize diversity and multiplicity in sources and content, rather than maintain 'gated' communities of media.

Post-industrial journalism

Postmodern understandings of journalism are similar to what Columbia University's Tow Center for Digital Journalism calls *post-industrial journalism*. In a 2012 report, authors C. W. Anderson, Emily Bell, and Clay Shirky (2012) argue that the survival of journalism requires:

> rethinking every organizational aspect of news production—increased openness to partnerships; increased reliance on publicly available data; increased use of individuals, crowds and machines to produce raw material; even increased reliance on machines to produce some of the output (p. 13).

In advocating *crowdsourcing* of content (pp. 6, 24), using an "artisanal" approach (p. 26), as well as other strategies including non-profit journalism such as that provided by ProPublica in the US, the Tow Center report proposes:

> The journalist has not been replaced but displaced, moved higher up the editorial chain from the production of initial observations to a role that emphasizes verification and interpretation, bringing sense to the streams of text, audio, photos and video produced by the public (p. 22).

Media theorist John Hartley warned before the turn of the millennium that the modernist ideology of journalism and the professional practices associated with it "simply cannot survive unscathed" (1999, p. 27). On the other hand, John Pavlik believes that the "evolution from a one-way [monologue] to a two-way dialogue can strengthen the role of journalism as sense maker in society" (2008, p. 73). Mark Deuze (2005) says interactive and participatory approaches "herald new roles for journalists as bottom-up facilitators and moderators of community-level conversations among citizens rather than functioning as top-down storytellers for an increasingly disinterested public" (para. 4). This view is supported by Jeff Jarvis who says in an essay written for the World Association of Newspapers: "By 2020 I imagine that a wide network of people will report, and the value we add is to organize and enable them: we promote their content and sell ads on it, we educate them (and they us), we moderate discussion" (Jarvis, 2008, p. 20). Axel Bruns (2005) refers to this more open moderating role as *gatewatching* rather than gatekeeping.

Not all agree with these concepts and trends. In his final editorial for *Journalism & Mass Communication Educator* in 2012, Dane Claussen wrote: "I think the term *citizen journalism*, while perhaps a noble ideal and something that a few will strive for and achieve, is almost entirely an oxymoron". He also said, "this goes for the other silly concepts—stand-alone journalism, participatory journalism, open-source journalism, crowd-sourced journalism, and representative journalism" (2012, pp. 329–330). A discourse of denial towards changes taking place as well as PR exists among some media academics as well as practitioners.

Post-journalism

A number of writers refer to *post-journalism* and many use the prefix 'post', not in the sense of transforming or transcending, but to denote a negative and retrograde development. For example, military historian, academic, and columnist Victor Hanson, in lamenting partisan reporting on the 2008 Obama presidential campaign in which some journalists actively supported Obama, wrote:

> We live now in the age of post-journalism. All that was before is now over, as this generation of journalists voluntarily destroyed the hallowed notion of objectivity and they will have no idea quite how to put Humpty-Dumpty back together again (2008, para. 5).

In a widely quoted article in *The Atlantic* in October 2009 discussing a campaign against President Obama's nomination of US Circuit Court Judge Sonia Sotomayor to the Supreme Court in which compromising videos were fed to the mass media by opponents, along with social media attacks, Mark Bowden wrote:

> I would describe their approach as post-journalistic. It sees democracy, by definition, as perpetual political battle. The blogger's role is to help his side. Distortions and inaccuracies, lapses of judgment, the absence of context, all of these things matter only a little, because they are committed by both sides, and tend to come out a wash.... The truth is something that emerges from the cauldron of debate. No, not the truth: *victory*, because winning is way more important than being right.... There is nothing new about this. But we never used to mistake it for journalism. Today it is rapidly replacing journalism, leading us toward a world where all information is spun, and where all "news" is unapologetically propaganda (para. 39).

Others argue that such views reflect nostalgia and romanticization of a mythical golden age of journalism, at best, and defensiveness and a power play to maintain control of information flows in society at worst. Author of *Understanding New Media*[6] Eugenia Siapera wrote in an online post in *The Guardian* 'Media Network' blog in 2013 that the future of journalism did not need a new business model to sustain traditional journalistic practices, but a radicalized "move towards imagining not only post-industrial, but post-journalism" (2013, para. 7). She says that journalism as it has existed for the past century or so is "an institution of modernity" and argues that contemporary societies "cannot sustain a model of journalism that remains wedded to old and currently largely irrelevant norms conceived for a kind of society that no longer exists" (para. 5). While leaving the specifics open for debate, Siapera says post-journalism refers to "the kind of journalism that applies itself to the kind of society we live in", suggesting that "journalists are no longer only reporters, but data miners, media artists, writers, analysts, witnesses and so on" (para. 1) and that journalism needs to be more open, collaborative, accountable, and accepting of a redefining, reordering, and reshuffling of the field as the value of various practices is established, including "data journalism, news aggregation, citizen witnessing, opinion blogs, affective news, and so on" (paras. 5–7).

Scientific journalism and WikiLeaks

A controversial form of reporting that encompasses elements of all of the previous approaches—data mining and digital technologies, participatory and networked ways of working including crowdsourcing, and which has a distinctly post-industrial and postmodern philosophy—is referred to by WikiLeaks founder Julian Assange as *scientific journalism* (Smith, 2011). Assange founded WikiLeaks in 2006 as a non-profit online media organization[7], with the motto "to publish fact-based stories without fear or favour" (Goc, 2012). Phrases such as "without fear of favour" echo the principles of traditional journalism, but the term "scientific journalism" refers to the practice of using full primary sources and content, rather than relying on interviews which is a common basis of most journalism (Smith, 2011).

WikiLeaks and Assange have become globally famous and infamous, as the activities of WikiLeaks have divided media scholars and practitioners as well as social scientists. For example, in 2009, Assange was awarded the Amnesty International Media Award, and in 2011 he was awarded the Martha Gellhorn Prize for journalism named after the renowned American war correspondent Martha Gellhorn. In announcing the award, the judges said:

> WikiLeaks has given the public more scoops than most journalists can imagine: a truth-telling that has empowered people all over the world. As publisher and editor, Julian Assange represents that which journalists once prided themselves in—he's brave, determined, independent: a true agent of people not of power (Deans, 2011, para. 4).

However, fellow countryman, journalist, and journalism text book author David Conley wrote in his national newspaper, *The Australian*:

> Assange isn't a journalist, either by practice, education or training. He is, in fact, a convicted hacker whose WikiLeaks site has operated as a photocopier in publishing everything from soldiers' social security numbers to the names of Afghan informants for United Nations forces. That's not journalism (2010, para. 2).

A number of academics, including a group from the Columbia University Graduate School of Journalism argue that WikiLeaks' activities should be protected under the US First Amendment. However, media support has been "somewhat muted" in other quarters, with the American Society of Professional Journalists and the Newspaper Association of America saying that their efforts to gain a federal reporters' shield law in the US have been "imperiled by WikiLeaks" (Goc, 2012, p. 65). In a recent analysis, Nicola Goc (2012) says WikiLeaks "has divided journalists and academics worldwide" (p. 65). But Assange, who studied physics and mathematics at university and worked with computers from his teens, illustrates the capability of new forms of investigation and reporting and the new skills that are required to access information in an age of 'big data' and 'big brother'.

While media scholars as well as social and political scientists debate developments such as WikiLeaks, and Eugenia Siapera sees the Tow Center report on post-industrial journalism not going far enough in exploring new paradigms, it and other studies such as those of the Pew Research Center make it clear that things can neither remain as they are, nor can they return to an imaginary golden age of journalism. In its 2004 'State of the News Media' report, Pew concludes that "journalism is in the midst of an epochal transformation, as momentous probably as the invention of the telegraph or television" (Pew Research Center, 2004, p. 4). In *Media in the Digital Age*, John Pavlik states the "sea change" occurring will have "far reaching implications for the nature and function of journalism in modern society" (2008, p. 77). And, as Mark Deuze, Axel Bruns, and Christoph Neuberger (2007) point out: "Whether the practitioners in…news publishing are enthusiast participants in the process or not, the process of increasing hybridization and convergence between the bottom-up and top-down models of newswork is already in full swing around the world" (p. 20).

What some refer to as *algorithm journalism* because it involves computer algorithms that search the Internet and collate information on various topics are not discussed in this chapter, as this fully automated form of information reporting is news aggregation aided by artificial intelligence. This is not to dismiss the power of the systems being developed by companies such as Narrative Science in Chicago (http://narrativescience.com), but it does not, at this stage, offer a realistic career for journalists or a site for journalism as it is currently conceptualized. Nevertheless, Figure 2.3 presents a 'tag cloud' overviewing this and many other terms and perceptions of the future of journalism drawn from extensive research literature and discussion.

Figure 2.3. Tag cloud of concepts and models of journalism proposed in contemporary debate.

Brand/corporate journalism and content creation

A final controversial development in journalism and media content production that needs to be noted, as it is highly relevant to this analysis, is arising from the substantial growth in demand for content by the burgeoning number of Web sites and social media sites created and controlled by non-media corporations, organizations, and government agencies (i.e., *owned media*, vis-à-vis advertising, which is *paid media*, and editorial publicity, which is described as *earned media*). To attract and maintain readers, viewers, and followers, the hosts of owned media need to provide quality content that is interesting and informative. Marketing blurbs, advertising, PR media releases, speeches, and bios of organization executives, while expected on traditional organization Web sites, do not attract substantial audiences to blogs, online newsletters and magazines, videos, and rich media sites. Organizations are increasingly turning to journalists to produce content for their owned media because of their ability to research and create content that is concise, interesting, and written in a way that broad audiences can understand, rather than in technical or bureaucratic language.

Journalists are being engaged to produce what is referred to as *brand journalism* or *corporate journalism* as freelancers, or as employees of organizations, or through media partnerships in which media organizations contract to produce owned media for corporations, institutions, or government agencies. For example, GE has entered into an agreement with Atlantic Media, publisher of *The Atlantic*, to produce *Ideas Lab* (http://www.ideaslaboratory.com), described as "an interactive platform around the most critical issues impacting America's economic future" (Atlantic Media, 2014). Cash-strapped media organizations desperately looking for new revenue streams and business models are enthusiastically embracing such commercial arrangements. Such developments also create work and jobs for journalists—a not insignificant consideration for journalists faced with precarity (Deuze, 2007) or unemployment. However, while providing new job opportunities and well-paid work, employment of journalists on a freelance, staff, or contract basis to write sponsored content sits outside traditional and contemporary theories and models of media and journalism and their role in society. This trend, and a number of other developments referred to as sponsored content, 'native advertising', and embedded marketing communication are further blurring the boundaries between journalism and PR and are critically examined in Chapter 7.

Notes

1. Corporatism as discussed here is a system of representation and intermediation of interests in which the state creates or recognizes a number of constituent units or interests groups as having a representational monopoly within their respective categories in exchange for observing certain controls on their selection of leaders and articulation of demands and supports (Schmitter, 1979). While early 20th century corporatism was associated with Fascism because the state controlled each constituent unit, in the 'new corporatism' that emerged from the 1970s, referred to as *societal corporatism*, *neocorporatism*, and *corporate pluralism*, a range of interests, including labour and business as well as various institutions, are recognized and engaged in both decision making and governance in partnership with the state.
2. The phrase 'speak truth to power' originates from the title of a pamphlet produced by the American Friends Service Committee (Quakers) in 1955, written by a number of authors, including Bayard Rustin who was excluded from recognition but later reinstated as an author (see AFSC & Rustin, 1955).

3. See the J-Lab networked journalism project for more information (http://www.j-lab.org/projects/networked-journalism).

4. The phrase 'journalism is the heart of democracy' was reportedly used by author and radio personality Garrison Keillor, according to Bennett & Serrin (2011, p. 397) who endorse the notion.

5. The saying "journalism is the first rough draft of history" is widely attributed to publisher of *The Washington Post* Phillip Graham, reportedly used in a speech to *Newsweek*'s overseas correspondents in London in 1963 and possibly earlier in a letter to readers in *The Washington Post* in 1948. However, other reports attribute the phrase to a 1943 book review in *The New Republic* by Allan Barth (Shafer, 2010).

6. Siapera, E. (2012). *Understanding new media*. London, UK: Sage.

7. WikiLeaks was founded as part of The Sunshine Press (Goc, 2012, p. 62).

CHAPTER THREE

Understanding Public Relations

As in Chapter 2, the purpose of this chapter is not to explain public relations in detail but to ensure our analysis proceeds with an informed understanding of this diverse and often misunderstood field of practice. This chapter briefly summarizes the main models and theories of PR, the evolution and growth of PR over the past century, and the key functions and activities of PR. Outside of PR monographs, textbooks, journals, and practical manuals, these are little understood. As noted in the foreword, a blind spot exists in sociology, political science, cultural studies, and even to a large extent in media studies in relation to PR. It is not that PR is unknown or undiscussed. It is often mentioned, but it is typically trivialized and marginalized, which prevents serious analysis, generalized with stereotypes, and often demonized with extreme claims that do not productively contribute to discussion. Equally, this chapter is not a defence of PR, as it presents a none-too-pretty picture in many respects. But it is important to look past the rhetoric of both sides of the debate to gain some concrete sense of reality, to recognize diversity in practices and evolution and progress, as well as anomalies and questions about equity and ethics.

This chapter provides a useful recap of contemporary theories and models for PR scholars and students and particularly serves as an overview for researchers, educators, and students in journalism, media studies, and disciplinary fields such as sociology, political science, and cultural studies to inform and ground their critical analysis.

Press Agents and 'Flacks'—The Murky World of 19th-Century PR

Unbeknown to most people who watched movies and television and read comics during the 20th century, many of the heroes of the American West, including Daniel Boone, Davy Crockett, and Buffalo Bill, were the creations of publicists, and the reality was often quite different from the publicity. Daniel Boone, for example, was largely the creation of a press agent working for landowners wanting to promote settlement in Kentucky (Grunig & Hunt, 1984, p. 27). When President Andrew Jackson became popular among 'common folk' in the American West, the opposition political party created the legend of Davy Crockett to combat Jackson's frontier popularity. In reality, a number of America's frontier heroes were out-of-work actors and drunkards who had rarely if ever set foot in the 'Wild West'.

Techniques referred to as 'press agentry' achieved widespread public notoriety in the 1830s through practitioners such as the noted American showman Phineas Taylor Barnum, founder of a circus that bore his name and later became the Ringling Bros and Barnum and Bailey Circus. He became infamous for his stunts and hoaxes, which included exhibition of purported mermaids and popular characters such as the dwarf 'General Tom Thumb', who he passed off as 11 years of age when he was only four. Through his press agent, Richard 'Tody' Hamilton, P. T. Barnum also promoted Joice Heth, purportedly a black slave who nursed George Washington 100 years previously. When she died allegedly at 161 years of age, an autopsy revealed that she was actually around 80 years old and the story, like many of Barnum's publicity stunts, was a fraud. However, Barnum reportedly earned up to US$1,500 a week from people eager to see the old woman (Boorstin, 1961, p. 207). He unashamedly coined the phrase "there's a sucker born every minute" (Grunig & Hunt, 1984, p. 28). Like a number of publicists, P. T. Barnum seemingly stopped at nothing to generate publicity for his show which he called 'The Greatest Show on Earth' (Kunhardt, Kunhardt, & Kunhardt, 1995). Daniel Boorstin (1961) called Barnum "the first modern master of pseudoevents" (p. 210) and his style of promotion was referred to as 'ballyhoo' (DeLorme & Fedler, 2003, p. 103).

One of the movie industry's first PR practitioners, Harry L. Reichenbach, similarly promoted movies and their 'stars' by staging stunts and even hoaxes (DeLorme & Fedler, 2003, p. 106). Another publicist, James S. Moran, who once dyed a cow purple to gain publicity, became known as "the last great bunco[1] artist in the profession of publicity" (Green, 1940; Zolotow, 1949). Somewhat ironically in terms of this discussion, both P. T. Barnum and Moran were former journalists.

The oft-quoted but misleading aphorism 'there's no such thing as bad publicity' originated in the era of press agentry and gained currency during a time described in Eric Goldman's history of public relations as the era of "the public be fooled" (1948, p. 1). Whereas the early 19th century period of industrialization and growth of 'big business' in America was described as the era of "the public be damned"—a phrase allegedly used by railroads magnate William Vanderbilt (Marchand, 1998, p. 9)—focus shifted in the late 19th century from not telling publics anything to hoodwinking and manipulating them. However, the mantra 'any publicity is good publicity' no longer holds currency today, as increasing education and the rise of consumerism and activist groups mean that people are not so easily fooled. Publicity can be extremely damaging, as many companies and organizations have found.

In the 1800s and into the early 1900s, press agents operated in major cities such as New York, acting as intermediaries between organizations and the media. Many early press agents arranged advertising (referred to in the trade as 'paid media') as well as editorial publicity (referred to as 'earned media') for their clients, although they increasingly focussed on 'free publicity' as the advertising industry grew and specialized quite separately to the PR industry. In his history of American journalism, Willard Bleyer (1973) reported that a census of accredited press agents conducted by New York newspapers in the first decade of the 20th century found 1,200 press agents working to influence public opinion through mass media in New York alone (p. 421).

"That the rise of the press agent would pose a problem for the press was obvious", according to George Bird and Frederic Merwin (1955) in their historically significant book of articles by some of the 20th century's most eminent media scholars, *The Press and Society*[2]. However, they concluded that "the newspaper faced a choice between accepting the releases of press agents, or failing to report many facts needed for the record" (p. 521). Bird and Merwin added that censorship and the inaccessibility of much news combined to strengthen the press agent's position. The complex duality of press agentry, and its contemporary cousin PR, is well summarized in this quote from *The Press and Society*.

> The influence of the press agent on the press has been far-reaching. Biographies, investigations, and research studies all attest to his success. From his personal standpoint, the press agent has performed a vital function. He has helped to make clear many events that might otherwise have gone unnoticed, and he has proved an invaluable aid in cutting away the barriers that so often separate the reporter from the hidden facts. From the point of view of the newspaper, the publicity man is far from being an unmixed blessing. Most editors concede that his assistance is perhaps necessary in making the record complete, but, at the same time, they realize that he will never do more than present the picture which he, or his employer, wishes the public to see. Thus editors see that they have replaced negative censorship with

positive censorship while saddling themselves with a propaganda burden (Bird & Merwin, 1955, p. 521).

PR as Counsel

Bird and Merwin's claim that the press agent would "never do more than present the picture which he, or his employer, wishes the public to see" was challenged by a role of PR practitioner as counsellor to management. The role of counsel was introduced into the lexicon of public relations by Edward Bernays (1923), described by some as "the father of modern public relations" (Guth & Marsh, 2007, p. 70)—although historian Meg Lamme (2012) notes that he developed the concept in collaboration with his wife, Doris Fleischman, a respected PR practitioner in her own right and a feminist activist. In this role, senior PR practitioners often reflect the views of publics and stakeholders to management and urge organizational change, or at least compromise. This is a side of PR work that is never seen outside an organization. Indeed, it requires negotiation skills and considerable delicacy at times, as senior management rarely likes to have its policies and decisions challenged. But a PR practitioner who can see an organization heading for trouble does have a vested interest in taking a preventative approach, and many senior PR professionals report spending a good deal of their time as advisors and counsellors (see research findings reported in Chapter 6).

This dual role of representing the organization and also representing public interests to the organization is often referred to in PR literature as *boundary spanning*. This function is described as the *boundary spanner* role because it involves crossing or breaking down the boundaries between an organization and its environment and seeking to integrate the interests of both (Grunig, 1992; Grunig & Hunt, 1984; Grunig, Grunig, & Dozier, 2002). In their seminal text, PR scholars Jim Grunig and Todd Hunt (1984) argue that practitioners should "have one foot in the organization and one outside" (p. 9).

The Four Models—PR Becomes Theorized and Legitimized?

In 1984, now retired Emeritus Professor of Public Relations Jim Grunig co-authored with Todd Hunt a landmark book that outlined four models of PR. These models were useful and widely referenced because they illustrated the historical evolution of the field, common existing practices, as well as what Grunig and Hunt posit as ideal practice. The four models therefore presented both a *positive* theory in social science terms (a description and explanation of actual practice) and a *normative* theory (a description and explanation of what ideally ought to be)—although later iterations of Grunig's theory became criticized as normative and not practical as we will see. The four models identified were:

- Press agentry/publicity;
- Public information;
- Two-way asymmetrical PR;
- Two-way symmetrical PR (Grunig & Hunt, 1984).

Press agentry/publicity

While media publicity is still a focus of many PR campaigns today and can be gained through honest and responsible means, the press agentry/publicity model of PR refers to the type of exaggeration, hyperbole, and stunts that were common practice in the promotion of Wild West figures and P. T. Barnum. Grunig and Hunt note that the American railroads used publicity stunts from the 1870s to the turn of the century to promote settlement across the American West (1984, p. 30). The romanticization of the American West was largely a press agentry/publicity campaign designed to encourage inland settlement and generate traffic for the railroads. Press agents also were extensively used by the Hollywood movie industry and introduced their techniques to other countries such as Australia during the 1920s and 1930s, as noted by Clara Zawawi (2009) in her history of PR in Australia. Most PR scholars and practitioners today regard the press agentry/publicity model as a somewhat embarrassing relic of the past. However, in some sectors, such as the entertainment industry, celebrity publicists still use these techniques.

Public information model of PR

A shift occurred in PR, according to Grunig and Hunt, with the arrival in New York in 1899 of a young Princeton graduate by the name of Ivy Leadbetter Lee who worked as a journalist for *The New York Times* and *New York World*, before opening America's third PR firm, Parker & Lee[3]. While still focussed on media publicity, Lee developed a policy of 'the public be informed', which he spelled out in a *Declaration of Principles* that he distributed to his clients and media. These set out a new approach to PR focussed on distributing truthful, accurate information and assisting media in obtaining news (Hiebert, 1966, pp. 47–48).

Lee's approach marked the beginning of the public information model of PR, according to Grunig and Hunt (1984, pp. 22, 30–36). This model was demonstrated when Lee's advice was sought after Pennsylvania Railroad had a major accident. The railroad's management initially wanted to suppress all news of the accident. However, Lee convinced them to invite reporters to the scene and help them cover the story. The result was improved relations with media and relatively favourable publicity. Ivy Lee was also the pioneer of the press release—the handouts of information to media that continue today as media releases or news releases. Lee famously worked for the Rockefeller family from 1914 when he assisted John D. Rockefeller Jr. combat negative publicity over a strike by 9,000 miners in Colorado during which several miners, two women, and 11 children were killed after an accidental shot sparked a battle between protesting miners and the Rockefeller-owned mining company. Lee convinced Rockefeller to visit the mining camps to observe conditions first-hand, which PR historian Ray Hiebert described as "a landmark in public relations" (as cited in Grunig & Hunt, 1984, p. 34). Lee also promoted the Rockefellers' major charity donations and helped rehabilitate the name and legacy of John D. Rockefeller, who prior to this time was branded a 'robber baron' by American media.

The central proposition of the public information model of PR is that citizens in a democracy need information about a wide range of matters from a range of perspectives in order to make informed decisions. This model draws on the 'marketplace of ideas' discussed by Kenneth Burke (1969) and proposes that organizations—government, corporate, institutional, and non-profit—make available and actively distribute information on their policies, products, services, and on public issues. Importantly, this model advocates that information distributed is accurate, truthful, and as complete as possible. The public information approach represented the first step towards responsible and ethical PR.

The public information model of PR is described by many as the 'journalist-in-residence' approach because of its primary focus on distributing information to and through media and the recruitment of journalists into many PR positions during the 20th century (Broom, 1982; Dozier & Broom, 2006, p. 140; Grunig & Hunt, 1984, p. 35; Hagan, 2007, p. 421). Their ability to recognize news, write in media style, and their media contacts meant that journalists were adept in helping organizations gain publicity. PR practitioners working within this model often maintained a journalistic ethic and this mode of practice fostered the view that journalism and PR are 'symbiotic' and 'two sides of the same coin'. Walter Lippmann was referring to this model of PR when he wrote that "the publicity man… saves the reporter much trouble by presenting him a clear picture of a situation out of which he might otherwise make neither head nor tail" (Lippmann, 1922, p. 218). Some government PR positions are still advertised with titles such as press secretary, media officer, or media adviser, reflecting a long-standing PR focus on media publicity—although the role of PR has broadened in more recent times.

Despite his Declaration of Principles, Ivy Lee "lapsed from his declared policy to the extent of whitewashing his clients", according to fellow PR pioneer Edward Bernays (1952, p. 70). Lee died in disgrace in 1934 at the age of 54 after advising a German company, subsequently taken over by the Nazis, on how to improve German-American relations. Lee was investigated by the House Special Committee on Un-American Activities and labelled a "Hitler press agent" (Grunig & Hunt, 1984, p. 35). Lee maintained that he gave the German company the same advice that he gave to the Rockefellers and other clients—be open and honest and, if organization policies are unacceptable to people, change the policies—although PR is often accused of trying to change people through persuasion and propaganda. To be fair, Lee's German client was not connected with the rising Nazi movement when he advised them. But his and Edward Bernays' backgrounds illustrate the troubled history of contemporary PR.

Two-way asymmetrical model of PR

In the 'four models' and other writing, Jim Grunig proposed two types of two-way transactional models of PR practice—one imbalanced which he called *asymmetrical* and the other balanced which he called *symmetrical*. Grunig drew on Eric Goldman's (1948) notion of communication as a 'two-way street' and Theodore Newcomb's (1953) theories of symmetry, orientation, and co-orientation in developing the two-way asymmetrical and symmetrical models of PR.

Two-way asymmetrical PR is grounded in behaviourist psychology with its objective of "scientific persuasion", which was a prominent scholarly tradition in early 20th-century America (Grunig & Hunt, 1984, p. 22; Hagan, 2007, p. 422). In this model, organizations use communication to try to persuade their publics to the views and behaviour desired by the organization. Whereas Ivy Lee pioneered the public information model of PR, Grunig cites Edward Bernays as a key influence in the two-way asymmetrical model. Bernays, who was a nephew of Sigmund Freud, helped Freud publish English translations of his books, which stimulated Bernays' interest in behavioural psychology and social science in general (Grunig & Hunt, 1984, p. 38). While focussing on orientation of publics to the organization through persuasion, this model of PR is described as two-way because it utilizes research to understand the views, interests, and needs of publics, and takes these into consideration. However, research is mostly deployed in the two-way asymmetrical model of PR to gain insights in order to most effectively persuade publics to align their views and/or behaviour with those of the organization. Grunig and Hunt (1984) say: "As did Ivy Lee, Bernays stressed the importance of communicating the public's point of view to management. In practice, however, both did much more to explain management's view to the public" (p. 39).

Bernays' first book, *Crystallising Public Opinion*, published in 1923, articulates his concept of public relations counsel that involved presenting the views and interests of publics to the organization and giving advice to management, as well as presenting the organization's messages to publics (Bernays, 1923). However, his second book, titled *Propaganda*, attests to Bernays' focus on persuasive communication to mould public opinion to that desired by the users of PR. The opening paragraph of *Propaganda* makes clear Bernays' belief in the power of persuasion and an *asymmetric* view of PR, as he states:

> The conscious and intelligent manipulation of the organized habits and opinions of the masses is an important element in democratic society. Those who manipulate this unseen mechanism of society constitute an invisible government which is the true ruling power of our country (1928, p. 9).

On reading such a paragraph, and noting that Bernays is cited in a number of PR texts as "the father of modern public relations" (e.g., Guth & Marsh, 2007, p. 70), it is not surprising that PR has critics. In the two-way asymmetrical model of PR, organizations engage in some interaction with their publics or stakeholders, but the interests of the organization remain paramount and there is more outbound information flow than inbound information flow. Hunt and Grunig (1994) acknowledged that the two-way asymmetrical model of PR is "a selfish model... because the organization that uses it believes it is right (and the public wrong) and that any change needed to resolve a conflict must come from the public and not the organization" (p. 8).

Grunig and White (1992) go as far as saying that the "asymmetrical worldview steers public relations toward actions that are unethical and ineffective" (p. 40). This view has been criticized by other PR scholars as too generalized and naïve. For instance, most people would agree that a public health campaign designed to combat AIDS is justified in employing persuasion and seeking behavioural change among its target publics. Nevertheless, Grunig and his co-researchers strongly advocate the fourth of the four models.

Two-way symmetrical model of PR

The two-way symmetrical model of PR aims to create understanding, harmony, and agreement, or at least mutual acceptance, between organizations and their publics through 50/50 *co-orientation*. That is, the organization should adapt to the interests, demands, and expectations of its publics, as much as it expects them to adapt to it.

Some scoff at this notion of PR, seeing it as 'pie in the sky' and question whether many or even any organizations would be so altruistic. Why would organizations voluntarily accommodate external interests, sometimes to the extent of making considerable compromises? Jim Grunig and other symmetrical PR proponents say that two-way symmetrical public relations can occur through "enlightened self-interest" (Grunig et al., 2002, p. 472). Long-term success requires organizations to maintain the support of key stakeholders such as their customers, suppliers, business partners, governments, and local communities. Even small activist groups such as environmentalists or human rights campaigners can disrupt the operations of organizations—e.g., campaigns against Nike in the 1990s and early 2000s because of its use of 'sweat shops' to manufacture its products in Southeast Asia, which resulted in boycotts of Nike products in the US and some other major markets. Jim Grunig and his various co-authors, including his wife and fellow scholar Larissa Grunig, have argued for several decades that two-way symmetrical public relations is the only truly ethical method of practicing PR, as well as the most effective method.

However, critics and many practitioners say that the two-way symmetrical model is normative (i.e., it describes what ought to be, rather than what is) and that it is unrealistic and unachievable in the 'real' world (Kersten, 1994; L'Etang, 1995; Murphy, 1991; Pieczka, 1996). Grunig admits to a gap between theory and practice, observing in 1984 that only around 15 per cent of PR practice employed a two-way symmetrical approach (Grunig & Hunt, 1984, p. 22). PR scholar Priscilla Murphy (1991) argues that two-way symmetrical PR is "exceedingly rare in actual practice" (p. 120) and that there are severe limits to its achievement. This led to a number of further developments in PR theories and models.

The four models of public relations as originally outlined by Grunig and Hunt (1984) and their key characteristics are summarized in Figure 3.1.

Characteristics	Press agentry/ publicity	Public information	Two-way asymmetrical	Two-way symmetrical
Purpose	Propaganda	Dissemination of information	Scientific persuasion	Mutual understanding
Nature of communication	One-way; complete truth not essential	One-way; truth important	Two-way; imbalanced effects	Two-way; balanced effects
Communication model	Source to receiver	Source to receiver	Source to receiver plus feedback	Source to group; group to source
Nature of research	Little (e.g., counting clips)	Little (e.g., readability; readership)	Formative; evaluative of attitudes	Formative; evaluative of understanding

Character-istics	Press agentry/publicity	Public information	Two-way asymmetrical	Two-way symmetrical
Leading historical figures	P. T. Barnum	Ivy Lee	Edward Bernays	Bernays; educators, professional leaders
Where practiced today	Sports, the-atre, product promotion	Government, non-profit organizations, business	Competitive business; agencies	Regulated business; agencies
Estimated % of orga-nizations practicing today*	15 per cent	50 per cent	20 per cent	15 per cent

Figure 3.1. The four models of public relations and their characteristics (Grunig & Hunt, 1984, p. 22). (*Estimated as at 1984.)

Publics and stakeholders

While the singular term 'public' is used in the title public relations and in the public information model of PR, it will have become evident in the preceding discussion that the plural terms 'publics' and also 'stakeholders' are used when referring to those addressed through PR. This stems from criticisms of the notion of a single mass public by sociologists, including eminent 'Chicago School' scholars John Dewey (1927) and Herbert Blumer (1948) who noted that society is comprised of diverse groups of people with diverse interests. Lawrence Grossberg et al. say "there is no such thing as 'the public'" (2006, p. 379). Sociologist and political scientist Nina Eliasoph (2004) calls for broad-based replacement of the term 'public' with the plural 'publics' to recognize sociological diversity, and this term is now used widely in PR literature. Variations and alternative terms include 'target publics' and 'target audiences'.

Some PR and social science scholars prefer the term 'stakeholders.' For instance, in writing about research, Yvonna Lincoln argues that "stakeholders is a more appropriate term" for those with whom researchers, authors, journalists, and other communication practitioners seek to engage (1997, p. 46). Stakeholder thinking in contemporary PR was influenced by R. Edward Freeman's seminal book, *Strategic Management: A Stakeholder Approach*, which defined stakeholders as "any group or individual who can affect or is affected by the achievement of the firm's objectives" (1984, p. 25). Putting aside Freeman's commercial contextualiza-tion in terms of 'firms', an important aspect of this definition is that it identifies stakeholders as both those who are able to affect an organization, as well as those who are affected by an organization. This two-way interrelationship is an important part of stakeholder theory today and aligns, at least in theory, with the two-way asymmetrical and symmetrical models of PR.

Excellence Theory of PR—Normative Notions and Professionalization

Following the critique of two-way symmetrical PR by Priscilla Murphy (1991) in which she proposed what she called a *mixed-motive model* of PR involving a combination of two-way asymmetrical and two-way symmetrical communication, Grunig and his colleagues modified their models by combining the former two-way symmetrical and two-way asymmetrical models into a *two-way contingency model* of PR (Grunig et al., 2002, p. 472)—also referred to by the same authors as the "the new model of symmetry" (Dozier, J. Grunig, & L. Grunig, 1995, p. 48) and the "new contingency model" (Grunig et al., pp. 355, 358). In the contingency model, the target of persuasion—publics, the organization, or both—is contingent on the circumstances. In a public health communication campaign, as cited previously, it may be legitimate and ethical to seek to change public attitudes and behaviour (e.g., to reduce smoking), whereas in other situations it may be more appropriate or necessary for the organization to change. Thus, in this model, advocacy with the intention of persuasion is accepted as a legitimate and ethical practice. However, Grunig et al. (2002) state that "these contingent decisions must be made...with the interest of both the organization and the public in mind" (p. 472). Furthermore, they argue that the aim of symmetrical PR is to achieve a "win-win" for organizations and their publics (p. 358).

A major initiative in developing contemporary theory and models of PR was the Excellence Study, which was conducted in three stages over more than 15 years between 1985 and 2002, involving a global survey of PR practitioners, organization managers, and employees in more than 300 organizations and interviews with CEOs to identify how different types of communication correlate with organizational excellence[4] (Grunig et al., 2002, pp. 4–5). The Excellence Study identified 14 communication attributes linked to organizational excellence. Prominent among these attributes (not in original order) are:

1. A participative rather than authoritarian organizational culture;
2. The senior public relations executive has influence within the *dominant coalition*—the senior management group of the organization;
3. A *two-way symmetrical* model of public relations is practiced;

4. The senior public relations practitioner has *knowledge and professionalism*, including relevant academic qualifications and training in ethics;

5. Public relations is managed *strategically* in that it is focussed on achieving goals and objectives, which are ideally measured and evaluated (Grunig et al., 2002, pp. 12–17).

These attributes, along with elements of a number of other theories and models that were developed between the 1970s and early 2000s, form the basis of Excellence theory of PR, which has become the dominant paradigm of PR globally (Pieczka, 1996, pp. 143–144; 2006, pp. 349–350; Spicer, 2007). Other noteworthy PR theories and models that influenced Excellence theory and directly define and explain contemporary PR practice include:

- *Co-orientation* theory proposed by Glen Broom (1977) and Broom and Dozier (1990), which advocates mutual orientation and adaptation between organizations and their publics;
- *Rhetorical* theory of public relations advocated by Robert Heath and others (e.g., Heath, Toth, & Waymer, 2009), which describes PR in terms of persuasion, argumentation, and storytelling, but maintaining honesty and truthfulness (*logos* and *ethos* as well as *pathos*);
- *Dialogic* theory (Kent & Taylor, 2002), which emphasizes two-way dialogue between organizations and their publics; and
- *Relationship* theory (Ledingham, 2006; Ledingham & Bruning, 2000), which identifies building and maintaining relationships between organizations and their key publics as the central focus of PR.

Contemporary Critical Thinking in and about PR

Despite claims of dialogue, relationships, co-orientation, and symmetry as central to PR, critical scholars point out that the dominant theories and models of PR practice emanating from North America are grounded in behaviourism and functionalism—that is, designed to influence the behaviour of publics to serve the interests of the organization—as well as being shaped to serve neoliberal capitalism. European models of *strategic communication* and *communication management* are similarly seen as organization-centric. A number of PR scholars and practitioners continue to argue that Excellence theory with its focus on symmetrical communication and relationships—even in Grunig et al.'s modified contingent view—is normative and rare in practice (L'Etang & Pieczka, 2006; Macnamara, 2012a). In reality, most PR practitioners go about their business with the majority of them still practicing the public information model of PR at best and a few still practicing press agentry.

Along with criticisms of the two-way symmetrical model of PR in Grunig and Hunt's four models and Excellence theory of PR by scholars such as Priscilla Murphy (1991), the beginnings of what Jacquie L'Etang (2009) calls "radical PR" thinking began to emerge from the late 1990s in books such as L'Etang and Pieczka's (1996) *Critical Perspectives in Public Relations*. This and other critical analyses examined issues such as power differentials between organizations and their publics, access to media, ethics, and societal interests. Rethinking of PR and non-US perspectives started to enter the mainstream of PR literature in texts such as *Handbook of Public Relations*, edited by Robert Heath (2001), and a decade later critical PR scholar Lee Edwards noted that "much of the research presented in the 2010 *Sage Handbook of Public Relations* (Heath, 2010) contests functional PR theory" (Edwards, 2012, p. 11).

The launch of *Public Relations Inquiry* in 2012 as a journal devoted to critical PR scholarship extended this rethinking and in 2014 Routledge published *The Routledge Handbook of Critical Public Relations* devoted to alternative perspectives (L'Etang, McKie, Snow, & Xifra, 2014). Along with Edwards, L'Etang, Leitch, McKie, Murphy, Pieczka, and Xifra, other leading critical PR scholars who call for a reconceptualization of PR include Derina Holtzhausen in Europe; Caroline Hodges in the UK; Robert Heath, Bruce Berger, and Kevin Moloney in the US; Judy Motion, Johanna Fawkes, and Kristen Demetrious, as well as this author, in Australia; and Debashish Munshi and Kay Weaver in New Zealand, to name but some. Journalism academics and practitioners who resist calls for journalism students to receive at least some lectures on PR fail to recognize the resource of thinkers who have informed critical perspectives to contribute in place of the clichés, stereotypes, and myths that journalism courses often trot out in relation to PR. Consider the following quotation.

> 'Spin' is one of the most lamented aspects of modern society: the exaggeration, the puffery, the blinding obfuscation and the trickery of words. Sometimes it's like a mouth full of fairy floss, sweet and sickly, other times it can be brutal, ugly and searing. Journalists hate it, the public is bewildered and angry about it—but no one really can say…how to arrest the debasement of public debate (Demetrious, 2013a, para. 1).

Many journalists and media scholars will be surprised to know that this statement comes, not from a journalist or social activist, but from a PR scholar—Associate Professor Kristen Demetrious, author of *Public Relations, Activism and Social Change* (Demetrious, 2013b). Many PR scholars and those in neighbouring fields such as public communication, political communication, and organizational communication are calling for change in PR, offering opportunities for productive dialogue with journalism, media studies, and social science researchers and educators, as proposed in the concluding chapter examining future directions.

The 'Sociocultural Turn' in PR

In the past decade, critical PR scholars have cited and advocated a 'sociocultural turn' in PR. UK PR scholars Lee Edwards and Caroline Hodges (2011) argue that increasing focus on sociological and cultural theories "constitutes a 'turn' in PR theory that shifts the ontological and epistemological focus of the field" (p. 3). In simple terms, what they are discussing—and advocating because the 'turn' is nascent by even the most optimistic accounts—is that the very nature of PR (its ontology) should be taken out of strategic organization management and relocated in a sociological and cultural context. This would shift its centre of gravity away from the service of power elites towards the interests of society—or at least to a position where balance could be achieved. Furthermore, the 'sociocultural turn' refers to a transition from a functionalist behaviourist approach based on systems theory, which informs and shapes the dominant paradigm of PR, to a recognition of the social construction of reality, the importance of social interaction, culture, and more humanistic understandings of the world based on social theory. The sociocultural turn is also associated with postmodernism, cultural studies, feminism, and participatory approaches in research and politics. As noted in Chapter 2, along with journalists, PR practitioners are now recognized as 'cultural intermediaries' involved in not only the production of symbolic goods and services but also in mediating meaning in society (Hodges, 2006; Macnamara & Crawford, 2013). Sociocultural approaches to PR argue that this role should be enacted ethically and with social responsibility, not simply to serve the interests of employers and clients.

This is not to say that critical thinking within PR and emergent 'turns' have materialized in new modes of practice, a fact that the critics of the critics in PR point out. However, this chapter seeks to show that PR is more than a motley collection of ex-journalists and Machiavellian spin doctors with PR or psych degrees blithely manipulating the media and trying to shape public opinion at the behest of self-interested, corrupt, incompetent, or simply dull and uninteresting corporations, governments, and organizations. PR has a substantial body of knowledge based on scholarly research. The introduction of undergraduate and postgraduate university degrees in public relations and public communication has facilitated some level of critical thinking and ethics training among current and future generations of PR practitioners.

The industry also has sought to professionalize. For example, in the UK the former Institute for Public Relations is now the Chartered Institute for Public

Relations, with the power to accredit members and censure them for conduct that breaches the organization's Code of Ethics. The UK also has a Public Relations Consultants Association (PRCA) representing PR consultancy firms. In the US, the Public Relations Society of America (PRSA) provides a major ongoing program of professional development for its members as well as codes of ethics, and the US-based Institute for Public Relations (IPR) is a specialist non-profit research institute dedicated to fostering research into PR. In Europe, the European Association of Communication Directors (EACD) is a pan-European body operating to promote professionalism, along with country PR and communication associations throughout Europe. Similar country and regional institutes and associations operate in other parts of the world also, such as Australia, New Zealand, Asia, South America, and the Middle East. There are also several international organizations that promote standards, such as the Global Alliance for Public Relations and Communication Management (2010), which has developed a global code of ethics; the International Communications Consultancy Association (ICCO); the International Public Relations Association (IPRA); and the Association for Measurement and Evaluation of Communication (AMEC).

The Growth of PR

While scholars and thinking practitioners debate the nature, purpose, and most appropriate approach of PR, the field continues to grow. Worldwide, PR was estimated to be a US$8 billion a year industry in the first decade of the 21st century (Wilcox & Cameron, 2010) and growing by 10 per cent a year according to Martin Sorrell (2008), CEO of the global advertising, marketing, and PR group WPP[5]. A 2011 study by the International Communications Consultancy Organisation (ICCO), which collated data from 24 countries, reported that US PR consultancies grew by 11 per cent in 2010 and UK consultancies increased their turnover by 13 per cent. Some developing countries experienced considerably higher rates of growth in PR, such as Brazil with a 23 per cent increase in PR spending between 2009 and 2010, Russia with a 17 per cent increase, and parts of Eastern Europe such as Slovenia up 12 per cent (ICCO, 2011).

The 2011 PR Census study conducted by the Public Relations Consultants Association (PRCA) in the UK estimated that the PR industry in Britain is worth £7.5 billion a year (around US$12.7 billion), making it the second largest in the world (PRCA, 2012; Spinwatch, 2014). This figure, and the reported growth rates in the US and elsewhere, suggest that spending on PR worldwide is now well over US$20 billion a year. In late 2013, the CEO of global PR agency Ketchum, Rob Flaherty, stated that the US 'PR business' was worth US$10–12 billion a year (Flaherty, 2013). However, this is almost certainly conservative, as *Fox News* reported in 2009 that an Associated Press (AP) investigation found US Department of Defense spending on PR had risen by 63 per cent in the preceding five years to US$4.7 billion (*Fox News*, 2009).

Because of definitional imprecision and varying nomenclature, it is difficult to identify total budgets and the number of PR practitioners, but the Global Alliance for Public Relations and Communication Management, an international confederation of PR institutes and associations, estimated that there are more than 3 million PR practitioners worldwide in 2005 (Valin, 2005; Wilcox & Cameron, 2010, p. 3). An industry-sizing study conducted by Toni Falconi (2006) estimates that there were between 2.3 and 4.5 million PR practitioners globally in 2006. Even conservative census and official membership figures from PR associations indicate that today there are around a quarter of a million professional PR practitioners in the US and more than 60,000 in the UK (Morris & Goldsworthy, 2012, p. 19; PRCA, 2012, p. 7).

In his book *Public Relations Democracy: Politics, Public Relations and the Mass Media in Britain*, Aeron Davis (2002) reports that 28 per cent of the top 50 companies in *The Times* 1,000 list used PR agencies in 1979, while 90 per cent of them were doing so just five years later (as cited in Davies, 2009, p. 85). Almost all of the Fortune 500 companies invest heavily in PR, either with in-house staff, consultancies, or both. Government departments and agencies are also spending more and more each year on PR. For instance, in *Packaging Politics*, Bob Franklin (1994) reported that 90 per cent of metropolitan authorities in the UK had set up PR departments. Fifteen years later, Nick Davies (2009) reported that Britain had 47,800 PR practitioners, compared with 45,000 journalists.

Former crime reporter Nigel Green claimed on the Spinwatch site that the police forces of England and Wales were spending around £30 million pounds a year on "corporate communications departments" in 2010, with budgets rising 40 per cent in the previous five years. He asked whether this expenditure on PR had "shifted the balance of power between the police and the media and whether regional newspapers are now being force fed propaganda" (Green, 2010, paras. 1–2). The phrase "being force-fed propaganda" is interesting for two reasons. It contains a generalized assumption that all information distributed by police PR is propaganda when, in reality, much media communication by police occurs in relation to public appeals for information about crimes and missing persons. Second, the notion of 'force-fed' implies that editors and journalists have no choice in the matter—they are, it is suggested, forced to accept and consume propaganda like victims of water torture or the hapless geese force-fed through a feeding tube for *foie gras* production[6].

Nevertheless, critics and concerned citizens increasingly question the use and growth of PR. A BBC investigation in London in 2013 found that Britain's troubled and often controversial National Health Service (NHS) spent almost £13 million on PR in the previous three years, comprised of £9.7 million for media officers' salaries and a further £3 million on PR consultancy services. Critics called for "medical doctors not spin doctors" (Davey, 2013, paras. 1–3).

Nick Davies (2009) describes PR as a "huge industry of manipulation" that is "targeted at structurally vulnerable media" and "which feeds falsehood and distortion directly into our news channels" (p. 167). Similarly, Damien McCrystal claims that "the growth of PR is threatening the integrity of the press" (2008, p. 47). If taken at face value, these claims are concerning because, as the statistics show, PR is growing rapidly at the same time as the editorial departments of most media are shrinking. However, as will be argued throughout this book, it is necessary to look beyond the rhetoric and popular discourses propagated about PR. Putting aside the pejorative qualitative elements of these statements for the time being, a key question is whether it is true even at a basic quantitative level that this multi-billion dollar industry is lined up against a dwindling force of brave resistant journalists?

The answer is quite simply no. Why? Because, even though media publicity is an important and highly visible part of PR, a substantial part of the PR industry is not concerned with mass media. The structure and operations of the PR industry remain poorly understood by journalists and some media scholars, despite a key part of their role being to do research and check facts. PR involves a range of activities. These are briefly summarized so that we can proceed to review research findings and analyze the effects of PR on journalism and the public sphere with a well-based understanding of what we are talking about when we discuss PR.

The Activities of PR

It is true that some activities undertaken by PR practitioners are focussed on communicating information through what are called 'mainstream' media and we will begin with these, so as not to be disingenuous.

Press/news/media releases

The most well-known and ubiquitous outputs produced by PR practitioners are news releases, also known as media releases and often still referred to as *press releases* even though this term is largely out-of-date because these releases are usually distributed to press, radio, TV, and online media. Since it was introduced by Ivy Lee more than 100 years ago, the news or media release has been used extensively by PR practitioners seeking media publicity—to the extent that many journalists talk about newsroom rubbish bins overflowing with them and, more recently, e-mail accounts regularly reaching their limit. *Financial Times* journalist Tom Foremski launched an attack on press releases as an out-dated mode of communication with media in a widely cited blog post titled 'Die! Press release! Die! Die! Die!' (Foremski, 2006). However, the format of releases of information to media is changing and evolving. BusinessWire introduced the "smart news release" in 1997 which incorporates audio, video, and images as well as text. PRNewswire introduced its more advanced MultiVu multimedia release in 2001 (Solis, 2009, paras. 8–9). The most recent development is the *social media release* (SMR) allegedly first developed by blogger Todd Defren (2008) in response to Foremski's call for change. The social media release is an online version (Web page) that offers quick and easy access to a range of organizational information, photographs, video clips, MP3 sound files such as podcasts of speeches, graphics, blogs and links for RSS feeds, Technorati tags, blog trackbacks, Twitter following, and so on. Increasingly organizations are offering online social media releases as well as *social media newsrooms* where journalists can access material. It has to be recognized that such sites are helpful to journalists in many cases, such as allowing downloading of photographs of organization executives and access to documents such as annual reports during or after hours. Social media releases and social media newsrooms are replacing traditional 'media kits' which comprise media news releases as well as other printed materials such as photos and background documents.

Video news releases (VNRs)

A controversial type of subsidized content produced and distributed by the PR industry is the video news release (VNR). This practice, which gained popularity in the 1990s and early 2000s, involves the production and distribution of video clips emulating the format of news or current affairs reporting—except they are not produced by independent reporters but by production companies commissioned by organizations as PR. Nick Davies (2009) cites examples that became controversial in the US, including pre-packaged VNRs distributed by federal government branches advocating the administration's case for invading Afghanistan, which aired on numerous TV networks as if they were "mainstream journalism". In the UK, despite denials from major media groups that they use VNRs, the BBC was found to have used an unlabelled VNR funded by an insurance company when presenting an interview with an Olympic athlete, who had the insurance company's logo emblazoned on her shirt and also on a board behind her (Davies, 2009, p. 177).

A related form of "information subsidy" is 'pool video', which is shot and distributed by media networks themselves sometimes (e.g., taking turns to save costs) and also by government agencies and institutions. For example, organizers of Congressional hearings, commissions of inquiry, court cases, and major briefings or speeches often arrange for a camera to record the event and then distribute the footage to media free of charge. Mary Bock (2009), who has analyzed political use of pool video, says the premise of the pool system is that "news video is a fungible, objective representation of the day's events; that it does not matter who shot the video", but she notes that media and visual communication scholars challenge this assumption (p. 258).

As well as distributing fully pre-packaged video reports, another stock in trade of PR is what the TV and film industries call 'B roll footage'. This is unedited video footage that can be used as background for media reports presented by a program anchor, or edited into media reports as 'cutaways' (general scenes used to bridge between 'talking head' shots and provide visual variety). PR practitioners routinely provide free footage showing their employers' and clients' products and facilities as a way of gaining free promotion. For instance, a story about food prices needs relevant vision and what better than some free footage from a Dairy Farmers of America milk promotion or even pictures of kids drinking Muscle Milk or TruMoo, complete with logo centre screen. A report on the busy holiday season is a chance for airlines to have images of their new aircraft and livery shown on television. Provision of B roll footage can backfire, of course. No food company or airline wants its products and logo broadcast on television when there is a report of a food poisoning or airline crash. But the risks are usually worth it for the free publicity that is regularly gained.

Advertorial

Another controversial practice in PR and media publishing is the purchase of media space or time at advertising rates and placement of information designed to look like editorial. Hence the content is referred to as *advertorial*. While some media prohibit advertorial being typeset and laid out in the same fonts and style as editorial, many examples closely resemble editorial. In some cases, advertorial content is labelled to signal it is not independent editorial. However, this is rarely done explicitly by labelling such content as advertising. Most often advertorial content is thinly disguised under labels such as 'special feature' or 'special supplement'. Also, such labels are also often printed in very small fonts in page headers or footers where they are easily missed by many readers. The result is that some media consumers cannot distinguish paid promotional content from independent editorial.

A study of reader response to print media advertorial found that more than two thirds of readers who were exposed to labelled advertorial failed to recall the presence of the label and the study concluded that the advertorial format "fools readers into greater involvement with the advertising message and that the presence of advertorial labels may not be particularly effective in alerting consumers to the true nature of the message" (Kim, Pasadeos, & Barban, 2001, p. 265). An analysis published in the *Journal of Information Ethics* by John Ellerbach described advertorial as a form of "information pollution" (2004, p. 61).

Journalists understandably are opposed to advertorial content, as it misrepresents information and confuses readers, as shown in the research. However, advertorial is not solely the fault of PR practitioners. In many cases, the advertising departments or supplements sections of media organizations dangle the promise of advertorial presentation, sometimes even with discounts on regular advertising rates, to make their revenue targets. This author's own experience with advertorial is discussed in Chapter 4.

Media relations

As well as preparing and sending information to editors and journalists, a major part of the work of many PR practitioners is liaising with journalists by telephone, e-mail, and face-to-face. This occurs both proactively and reactively. The PR department is the starting point for many journalists' inquiries to organizations. Effective PR practitioners can be helpful to journalists by answering questions, providing background information, advising them of the best person to speak to about an issue, or even arranging an interview for a journalist. Senior PR practitioners with the ear of their CEO can facilitate access for media when switchboards, secretaries, and personal assistants shield them and filter calls. Similarly, a receptive press/media secretary or media officer can be a conduit to busy Members of Congress, Senators, Members of Parliament, and heads of major organizations. On the other hand, journalists often complain that PR practitioners obstruct access other than for reporters who write positively about their organizations. Proponents of this view quip that PRO stands for 'professional reporter obstacle' or 'prevent reporters operating'.

Some journalists recognize the help that PR practitioners can provide. For instance, in an analysis of 'spinners' and PR advisers Matthew Knott (2012a) wrote in the online journal *Crikey*: "While journalists love to bewail the growth of the PR industry, spinners play an important role in bringing newsworthy stories to light, answering reporters' questions and defending those whose reputation has come under attack" (para. 19). However, note the pejorative language of "spinners" as a general term for PR. And journalists claim to write objectively and accuse others of putting a spin on a story!

PR practitioners also proactively contact editors and journalists to alert them to future events such as launches and announcements and to 'pitch' stories. The latter is the cause of frustration to many journalists. Some PR practitioners with media experience, particularly those who are former journalists, understand news and only try to 'sell' stories that have some newsworthiness or relevance to the audience of the media. However, many inexperienced PRs, eager to please their bosses and clients, over-zealously pitch what journalists call puff or puffery—that is, information that is not news and often thinly disguised promotion or propaganda. Probably no aspect of PR causes as much irritation among media as pitching stories that are not stories from a media perspective.

Media relations also includes occasional 'wining and dining'. Many journalists are reluctant to accept overly gratuitous offers of entertainment and some media have policies prohibiting journalists from accepting what can appear to be bribes. However, it is accepted practice in many countries to invite journalists to lunch occasionally, to seasonal celebrations such as Christmas parties, Chinese New Year celebrations, or Ramadan feasts, and sometimes to sporting matches or other types of events and entertainment. Sometimes this is done simply to say thank you, although PR practitioners also seek to strategically build relationships with key journalists relevant to their industry or sector.

Media training and 'media management'

Another key media-related activity undertaken by PR practitioners, or arranged with specialist trainers, is media training for organization spokespersons. Today, few organizations allow their spokespersons to talk to journalists without special training. PR practitioners justify this on the basis of the common media practice of taking an adversarial approach in interviews. This approach is epitomized in statements such as "news is what somebody somewhere wants to suppress; all the rest is advertising", reportedly said by the late 19th- and early 20th-century British publisher Lord Northcliffe (Ingram, 2012), as well as the motto "the journalist's first line of approach should always be 'why is this bastard lying to me?'", a phrase attributed to the noted foreign correspondent Louis Philip Heren (1919–1995) (MediaWise, 2003). Faced with adversarial and sometimes aggressive journalists, spokespersons and their organizations fear being caught off guard, tricked into saying what they don't mean, or finding themselves tongue-tied.

To some extent, media training of spokespersons can help media. Spokespersons who cannot make their point clearly and briefly are unpopular with reporters and radio and TV audiences. They are not considered good *talent*. Part of media training is teaching spokespersons to answer questions briefly, as media demand much tighter discussion formats than typical management meetings or political speeches. However, most media training has a highly strategic intent, designed to shift the balance of power in an interview from the journalist to the spokesperson and even control the interview. An analysis of 12 media spokesperson training programs and manuals widely used internationally found that all recommended preparing "key messages" and staying "on message", with several stipulating that this practice should be followed irrespective of questions asked (Macnamara, 2009, p. 6). Most significantly, 10 of the 12 programs and guides prominently claimed to help interviewees and PR practitioners control and/or manage media interviews. Eight of the 12 programs and guides explicitly claimed to teach participants to *control* media interviews and messages that they disseminate. Two others used the term 'manage' in relation to media and messages. While ostensibly a more flexible term, the course description of one of the programs told potential participants: "learn to manage the media on YOUR terms" (PRIA, 2009) [original emphasis]. Only two of the media training programs focussed on development of media communication skills without making claims to control or manage media and content. No terms were found in the materials analyzed referring to public benefits or the public interest. All course objectives and statements of outcomes analyzed referred to empowerment of interviewees and achievement of strategic organizational objectives.

In an analysis of media interviews, Philip Bell and Theo van Leeuwen (1994) note that interviewers have four distinct advantages over interviewees, including being able to choose the topic, being able to "direct the answerer towards certain kinds of answers", and "they can compel the answerer to answer (at least in all but a very few situations)" (p. 7). However, analysis of contemporary media interview training programs and guides indicates that this is increasingly not the case. For instance, in his book *Managing the Interview*, which is provided as part of one of the media training programs studied, media trainer Graham Kelly poses the question "who controls the interview" and advises interviewees: "You do, despite what the journalist may think" (1995, p. 36). He proceeds to instruct interviewees on how to "subtly ensure your own agenda is met".

Microsoft provides media training tips to its executives and business partners online under the heading "Six tips for taking control in media interviews". Advice offered includes "stay on track with your message" and "bridge…to deflect any attempts to derail your message" (Krotz, 2009, paras. 16, 17).

Media Training Worldwide (2009), which claims to offer media training to leading corporations and organizations globally, states in an online description of its program:

Whether you are preparing for interviews with *The Wall Street Journal*, CNBC or *Business Week*, we can make you shine. Our goal is simple: to make you confident, comfortable and relaxed in any interview situation AND give you the ability to *control* not only your message but also your exact quotes used by the media (para. 3) [original emphasis].

It is quite clear from analysis of media interview training programs that training is provided to organization spokespersons not only to help them communicate clearly and coherently but also to manage the media and try to control media content.

Speech writing

Few corporation or organization leaders or politicians today write their own speeches. While many politicians employ specialist speech writers—a highly paid niche market in its own right—speeches and presentations by CEOs, organization heads, and government officials are usually produced by or with significant involvement of PR practitioners. Abraham Lincoln and Martin Luther King may have spent time crafting their own oratory, but speeches today are largely the handicraft of PR, created and polished to rhetorical perfection in many cases.

Keeping news out of the media

Another side of PR even less discussed than its role in gaining publicity for organizations is its role in keeping information out of the media, which some media scholars refer to as *agenda cutting* (Colistra, 2012; Wober & Gunter, 1988), as opposed to agenda setting, agenda building, or agenda melding, which will be examined later (McCombs & Shaw, 1972; McCombs, 2004; Shaw & Weaver, 2014). Aeron Davis notes in *Public Relations Democracy* that "for every story fed to the media, there is one being carefully kept out. For many organizations, half or more of the work of PR practitioners involves restricting reporter access and information and/or attempting to quash negative stories" (as cited in Davies, 2009, p. 87). Some corporations want to stay completely out of the news and 'keep a low profile' (Ericson, Baranek, & Chan, 1989). This is undertaken in various ways ranging from defensive strategies such as simply not returning calls and declining interviews to more aggressive strategies such as threatening to deny access to future information. Such threats are often not made explicitly. Seasoned PR practitioners say it is more a case of editors and journalists understanding that 'if they scratch our backs we'll scratch theirs' and, conversely, 'if they don't scratch our backs, we won't scratch theirs'. Media which publish or broadcast negative stories about an organization often find themselves left off the invitation list for important briefings or events when their competitors are invited. No editor wants to miss an important announcement or find their competitors given access to exclusive interviews or information. An example of the sometimes controversial practice of keeping news out of the media is reflected on in Chapter 4 and the practice was discussed with senior practitioners in the research reported in Chapter 6.

Much PR is nothing to do with mass media

Apart from these media-related PR activities, an important contextualization is that PR is not all about dealing with journalists and mass media. Journalists have a tendency to think that the entire industry of PR exists to target them. This ego-centrism-cum-paranoia is evident in many comments made by journalists about PR and in the discourse of victimhood. However, this perception is quite removed from reality. The practice of PR, which is documented in detail in a raft of text-books and handbooks, incorporates a range of communication activities beyond seeking publicity in mass media (e.g., Broom, 2009; Cornelissen, 2011; Mac-namara, 2012a; Tench & Yeomans, 2009; Toth, 2007; Wilcox & Cameron, 2010). PR programs and campaigns today typically include:

- 'House' *publications* such as newsletters, annual reports, brochures, information flyers, and leaflets produced and distributed in hard copy or electronically by organizations—often referred to as corporate publishing and as 'owned media';
- *Events* ranging from media news conferences and briefings to launches, open days, conferences, seminars, and exhibitions;
- *Web sites* including public Web pages, intranets (e.g., for staff), and extranets (sometimes produced for business partners, investors, and other key stakeholders);
- *Social media* such as corporate or organization blogs, microblogging accounts (e.g., on Twitter or internally using applications such as Yammer, Jive, Social Text, and Socialcast), Facebook community pages, YouTube channels, wikis, and so on. Social media are becoming a important channels for corporate and organizational communication and are discussed specifically in Chapter 7;
- *Public affairs/lobbying*, also called *government relations*, which is a highly specialized area of practice designed to influence government decision makers in relation to policy. A range of activities are undertaken in this field, including writing submissions to government inquiries and hearings; writing and distributing briefing papers, fact sheets, and White Papers; undertaking research and producing research reports; and arranging and

attending meetings with government advisers, departmental staff and Congress members, Ministers and Senators;

- *Investor/shareholder relations* (also referred to as financial PR), which includes production of annual reports, analyst briefings, and various other forms of communication such as financial newsletters;
- *Community relations*, which may include local sponsorships, community meetings and consultation, local community newsletters, and local events;
- *Internal/employee communication*, also called *employee relations*, which includes activities such as staff newsletters and intranets, as well as events for staff; and
- *Strategic management advice*—an often overlooked and unrecognized role of PR practitioners, particularly senior corporate relations and public affairs executives and consultants, as discussed under 'PR as counsellor' earlier in this chapter.

Other growing areas of PR include the closely related practices of *issue management* and *crisis communication*. These are specialized applications of PR rather than particular activities. Usually they involve a combination of or all of the preceding activities, deployed in response to an issue with implications for an organization, such as an impending government decision or change of policy, or a crisis that affects its operations. While crises are usually highly visible, issue management is a noteworthy example of PR that is largely unseen or completely invisible—and it is significant because it is reported to be one of the fastest growing areas of PR practice (ICCO, 2011, p. 7). There are many definitions, but one of the earliest by Howard Chase (1982) briefly explains this practice:

> Issue management is the capacity to understand, mobilize, coordinate, and direct all strategic and policy planning functions, and all public affairs/public relations skills, toward achievement of one objective: meaningful participation in creation of public policy that affects personal and institutional destiny (p. 1).

'Managing' issues is one of the activities of PR that draws much criticism both publicly and in scholarly literature because it involves *framing* and reframing of issues, with PR practitioners acting as what a number of researchers call "frame sponsors" (Anderson, 1997; Carragee & Roefs, 2004; Edy & Meirick, 2011), as well as *priming, agenda building*, and *agenda setting* (Kitzinger, 2007; McCombs & Ghanem, 2001; McCombs & Reynolds, 2002). Issue management most often deploys *strategic* communication, as defined by Habermas (1984, 1987)—that is, it is undertaken to achieve the goals of the organization rather than what PR Excellence theorists call symmetrical communication or co-orientation. The concepts and theories of framing, priming, agenda building, agenda setting, and strategic communication, as well as *agenda melding*, will be discussed further in Chapter 5 as frameworks for analyzing research findings presented. For now, having explained the normative and positive theories of PR and its range of professional practices, it is necessary to also note that PR has a chequered history and 'skeletons in the closet' which are regularly found and exposed in the media.

PR's Skeletons—Toxic Sludge, the Gulf War, Asbestos, and Other 'PR Disasters'

One of the most damning and high profile contemporary critiques of PR was the book written by John Stauber and Sheldon Rampton (1995) titled *Toxic Sludge Is Good for You: Lies, Damn Lies and the Public Relations Industry*. The first part of the book's title was originally drawn from a 'Tom Tomorrow' cartoon, but took on special meaning following an investigation by the authors of a campaign by the US Water Environment Federation (formerly known as the Federation of Sewage Works Associations) to rebrand sewage sludge as 'biosolids' and pro-mote it as harmless, even beneficial fertiliser for farms. The authors report: "Our investigation into the PR campaign for 'beneficial use' of sewage sludge revealed a murky tangle of corporate and government bureaucracies, conflicts of interest, and a cover-up of massive hazards to the environment and human health" (p. 101). Their investigation led to a whistle blower in the hazardous site control division of the Environmental Protection Agency, who described the untreated sludge as "the mother lode of toxic waste" (Stauber & Rampton, 1995, p. 101). The publish-er's introduction claims that the book "blows the lid off of today's multi-billion-dollar propaganda-for-hire PR industry; naming names this book reveals how public relations wizards concoct and spin the news, organize phony 'grassroots' front groups, spy on citizens and conspire with lobbyists and politicians to thwart democracy" (Common Courage Press, 2001).

As well as the attempt to whitewash toxic sludge, Stauber and Rampton exposed insidious elements of the PR campaign to convince Americans to go to war in Iraq (allegedly to free Kuwait in the first Persian Gulf invasion). During the first Gulf War, one of the world's largest PR firms, Hill & Knowlton, was engaged in a US$10.8 million campaign to mobilize American support for an invasion of Iraq. While Hill & Knowlton has denied most of the accusations made against it[7], Stauber and Rampton (1995), Corporate Watch (2002), and a number of other sources allege that 'Citizens for a Free Kuwait' was a front organization created by the PR firm, a practice referred to as *astroturfing*[8]. Astroturfing is defined by digital communication specialist and blogger Paull Young (2006) as "the practice of creating fake entities that appear to be real grassroots organizations, when in fact they are the work of people or groups with hidden motives and identities" (para. 1). In addition to creating Citizens for a Free Kuwait as a largely citizen-less organization[9], a key element of the campaign to mobilize American public opinion in support of war against Iraq was testimony by 'Nurse Nayirah' to the Congressional Human Rights Caucus in October 1990 that she had witnessed Iraqi soldiers killing hundreds of premature babies at the Al-Addan Hospital in Kuwait City. The public was told that the identity of Nurse Nayirah was concealed to protect her family. However, it was later disclosed that 'Nurse Nayirah' was Nayirah al-Sabah, daughter of the Kuwaiti Ambassador to the US, and her story was revealed to be untrue. Why would she make up such stories? It has been reported subsequently that she was recruited and coached by Hill & Knowlton as part of its campaign for Citizens for a Free Kuwait (Corporate Watch, 2002; "Deception on Capitol Hill", 1992; Stauber & Rampton, 1995). It is difficult to know if all the allegations made about the campaign are true—and it does need to be recognized that many of the activities undertaken by Hill & Knowlton in the campaign were legitimate practices, such as arranging interviews for visiting Kuwaiti government officials. But it is well established that PR was used to manipulate American public opinion in favour of the war in Iraq and that part of this was misinformation. The case caused considerable controversy in the US PR industry (e.g., see Elliott, 1992) and its reputational implications linger today.

One of the worst examples of spin and pseudo-science of all time may well be the claim which justified the second Iraq war—that Iraq possessed 'weapons of mass destruction' and constituted a threat to its neighbouring countries and regional security. This so-called evidence was used to gain congressional, parliamentary, and public support for the 2003 military invasion of Iraq by US and allied forces. BBC radio reporter Andrew Gilligan reported controversially in May 2003 that Downing Street had demanded that the September 2002 dossier on Iraqi weapons be "sexed up" (as cited in Davies, 2009, p. 199). On the same day that Gilligan's report was aired, the director of communications and strategy for UK Prime Minister Tony Blair, Alistair Campbell, issued a firm denial, saying: "Not one word of the dossier was not entirely the work of intelligence agencies". Subsequent official inquiries revealed that this claim was simply not true. As Nick Davies states, intelligence agencies reported that Iraq was likely to use chemical and biological weapons only if it was attacked and that Iraq "may be able" to deploy such weapons within 45 minutes of an order to do so. 'May be able' was changed by Downing Street to "are able" and, by the time the information was reported in *The Evening Standard* and *The Sun*, it was headlined as '45 minutes from attack' and 'Brits 45 minutes from doom' (Davies, 2009, p. 200).

This infamous and extreme example of spin needs to be understood in the context of politics rather than as a generalized example of PR. While Alastair Campbell was a PR practitioner working for British PM Tony Blair—and a former journalist who worked for *The Sunday Independent, The Mirror,* and *Today* (a fact that media critics of PR conveniently ignore)—his role at the epicentre of spin has to be seen as influenced by and reflecting the practices of politics in contemporary Western democracies. Equally, the PR activities of the George H. W. Bush and George W. Bush administrations in the US to justify the Gulf wars were characteristic of neoliberal politics. This is not to attempt some covert re-categorization of political PR and spin and employ what Marvin Olasky calls "the doctrine of selective depravity" (1989, p. 88) that lets the rest off the hook. It is important, however, to recognize the diversity of practices grouped under the labels of spin and PR.

The corporate world is far from unblemished in terms of PR malpractice. In Australia, Gwyneth Howell (2009a, 2009b) has written extensively about building products company James Hardie Industries, which was found by a commission of inquiry to have "knowingly under-funded a compensation trust…to limit the assets available to compensate victims of asbestos products" and publicly lied about it to the stock exchange, the media, and the public (2009a, p. 281). James Hardie Industries was also found by the commission of inquiry to have selectively released information through financial media which treated news of reduced liability for shareholders as a positive story, and to have restricted the access of other media to information about the inadequacy of compensation funds for victims of asbestos-related diseases (Howell, 2009b, p. 194). While such tactics are not illegal, they comprise media management designed to deflect attention and cover up an inconvenient truth. Furthermore, and even more seriously, a media release issued in February 2001 which stated that the Medical Research and Compensation Foundation established by James Hardie Industries was "fully funded" to meet its compensation liabilities was found to be intentionally misleading—a "lie" designed to absolve the company of its obligations to dying workers who had inhaled asbestos (Eltham, 2009, paras. 13–15). A Special Commission of Inquiry report stated that "the media release seems a pure public relations construct, bereft of substantial truth" (New South Wales Government, 2004, p. 358). Also James Hardie was reported to have engaged in spin to disguise its motives in restructuring the company and moving its head office from Australia to Holland where it came under Dutch jurisdiction, leaving behind its legal responsibilities for asbestos victims in Australia (Howell, 2009b, pp. 194–195).

It should be noted that the company has since accepted responsibility and complied with legal requirements and public expectations in relation to asbestos victims. However, not before seven directors and three senior executives of the company, including the former CEO and chief financial officer, were found by the High Court of Australia to have breached their statutory obligations under the Corporations Act by knowingly approving the 2001 media release that contained misleading and inaccurate information about compensation for asbestos victims[10]. The Special Commission of Inquiry, known as The Jackson Inquiry, found that the compensation fund was under-funded by approximately AUD$1.5 billion—a not trivial shortfall. *The Sydney Morning Herald* reported the outcome of the case under the headline 'When spin spun out of control' (Sexton, 2007, p. 39).

A book by Matt Peacock (2011) reviewing the case, *Killer Company: James Hardie Exposed*, documents how PR was used for decades by James Hardie Industries and other asbestos-producing companies worldwide, as well as industry organizations such as the Asbestos Information Council (AIC) in Britain, to downplay emerging fears and evidence that the product is linked to a number of diseases including asbestosis (scarring of the lungs) and the cancer mesothelioma. Australia and the UK have the highest rates of asbestos-related deaths in the world because of the amount of asbestos used in these countries. It was estimated in 2013 that there had already been at least 4,700 deaths from mesothelioma in Australia since records began in the early 1980s and it was predicted that more than 25,000 Australians will die from it over the next 40 years, as the effects take some years to manifest (National Health and Medical Research Council, 2013).

Some PR abuses are less serious, but still mislead and deceive the public, such as the activities of the allegedly independent organization Working Families for Walmart, which rallied purportedly spontaneous support for the retail giant in its campaign to counter union, media, and public criticism in relation to its treatment of workers and management practices. In 2006, the organization supported a blog titled *Walmarting Across America* written by an allegedly independent retired couple 'Jim and Laura' reporting on their driving adventures across America during which they visited Wal-Mart stores and reported many happy experiences. It did not take long for Internet users to discover that the organization was created by Walmart's PR agency Edelman (another example of astroturfing) and that 'Jim and Laura' were sponsored to write about the company, a form of blogging referred to as *flogging* (Gogoi, 2006; "Walmart, Edelman flogged for blog", 2006).

In discussing the "hidden hand of PR" in creating pseudo-events, pseudo-evidence, pseudo-science, pseudo-leaks, pseudo-pictures, pseudo-illnesses, and even whole organizations that he calls pseudo-groups, Nick Davies (2009) gave a number of examples including the following.

- Echoing the infamous 'torches of freedom' march organized by PR pioneer Edward Bernays to promote smoking to women, events and 'photo ops' (photo opportunities) are routinely created by PR practitioners, such as George W. Bush announcing the end of combat operations in Iraq and "mission accomplished" in May 2003 atop an aircraft carrier in full airman's combat gear. This event was staged by his PR advisers and was both premature and fake. Bush had never been an airman, the aircraft carrier was anchored off the coast of California, and conflict in Iraq raged on for another decade (p. 167).
- A PR firm representing a company that offered a service for finding lost mobile/cell phones claimed that 63,000 mobile/cell phones had been left in London taxis during the previous six months. Davies reported that, according to the Public Carriage Office, the real figure was 779. The PR firm gained its startling statistic by interviewing 131 of the 24,000 cabbies in London—well below a statistically reliable sample. This is what Davies calls pseudo-evidence (p. 173).
- A more serious example of pseudo-evidence and pseudo-science being disseminated to the public cited by Davies was international media reporting in 2005 on the success of genetically modified (GM) crops successfully combatting hunger in Africa, based on quotes from an organization called Africa Harvest headed by Dr Florence Wambugu. The British PR monitoring group Spinwatch later revealed that Africa Harvest was funded by GM companies and Dr Wambugu was an adviser to DuPont, one of the leaders of the GM industry (p. 170).
- Impending resignations of political leaders are often leaked to the media, but Davies comments that many of them are pseudo-leaks, crafted by media and PR advisers to avoid scandal and criticism. He cites the examples of resignation letters of UK MPs Geoffrey Robinson, Peter Mandelson, and Ron Davies, which were later revealed to be written by the Downing Street press office. Alastair Campbell's former deputy Lance Price reported in *Spin Doctor's Diary* that he routinely wrote letters for Members of Parliament (p. 174).
- An alleged new health problem called social anxiety disorder was promoted by PR agency Cohn & Wolfe on behalf of a pharmaceutical client, which resulted in reports of the alleged disorder increasing from 50 in 1997 to more than a billion in 1999 and sales of a drug designed to combat the disorder increasing by 18 per cent. Davies argued that the so-called disorder was nothing more than shyness. This is an example of what Davies calls a pseudo-illness created by PR (p. 175).

- In the infamous cause of tobacco promotion, global PR firm Hill & Knowlton created the Council for Tobacco Research and the Tobacco Institute as apparently independent organizations when, in fact, they were pseudo-groups representing the interests of the tobacco industry—yet another example of astroturfing. Similarly, global PR giant Burson-Marsteller created the National Smokers Alliance (p. 169). The important debate on global climate change has been distorted not only by genuine differences of opinion among scientists and inconsistencies in data, but also by pseudo-groups such as the European Science and Environment Forum which was established with the help of two PR agencies—APCO Worldwide and Burson-Marsteller—to challenge claims of anthropogenic climate change (p. 193). Davies cites a 2007 research study by the Union of Concerned Scientists which reported that ExxonMobil alone spent US$15.8 million creating or supporting 43 different front groups between 1985 and 2005, including the Global Climate Change Coalition (p. 188) and the Global Climate Science Team (p. 187).

There are many other case studies of PR being involved or implicated in scandals, cover-ups, and attempts at manipulation of public opinion, policy, and even government regulation and legislation. A Web search of the words 'PR disasters' in 2013 yielded more than 6 million references. These included a Web site devoted to highlighting PR disasters (http://prdisasters.com); 'The five biggest PR disasters of the past year' published in *Salon* (Gupta, 2013); links to what were rated the biggest PR disasters in the US, UK, Australia, Canada, and a number of other countries; as well as annual almanacs of PR disasters each year since 2009. Many of the reports listed are in fact not related to the activities of PR practitioners, but rather imbroglios created by corporate executives and political leaders. Such is the generalized discourse about PR.

Counter PR

Notwithstanding the unsavoury uses or abuses of PR that occur, a further important contextualization is that, while some of the PR activities listed previously are specifically related to business (e.g., investor relations), most can be and are undertaken by environmental organizations, charities, hospitals, emergency services such as fire brigades, the police, trade unions, local action groups, clubs, and even churches, as well as corporations and governments. Small activist groups, which rarely have budgets for media advertising or the resources for professional lobbying of governments, use PR tactics to draw attention to issues and causes. At a global level, Greenpeace has proved itself a master of PR, gaining publicity around the world to draw attention to illegal whaling activities and other environmental issues.

While expressing concern about the influence of PR deployed by economic elites in political communication, particularly organizations with substantial resources, Peter Dahlgren (2009) notes that the same techniques and practices "can also be used by the less powerful, opening the doors for progressive movements to get their messages onto the media agenda" (p. 49). In contrast with the traditional radical view of the public sphere which sees PR as a means by which "well-resourced organizations can inundate the media and set the agenda while the attempts of resource-poor organizations become quickly marginalized" (Davis, 2000, p. 48), counter PR, which enables non-institutional and resource-poor groups to gain influence, aligns with a radical pluralism perspective (Davis, 2000, p. 40). Pamela Shoemaker (1989), Jay Blumler (1990), and Margaret Scammell (1995) have suggested that PR actually offers greater potential for non-official sources to gain access to voice than many studies have acknowledged, pointing out that PR is less capital-dependent than other forms of public communication such as advertising and can employ strategies that require little institutional legitimacy.

The edited collection *News, Public Relations and Power* by Simon Cottle (2003) provides a number of examples of PR being used for public causes such as environmental and green campaigns in the UK, as well as the 'usual suspects' of big business and government. In 2012, a group of PR scholars at Bournemouth University in the UK, working in collaboration with veteran US PR scholar Kevin Moloney, published a report titled 'Dissent and Protest Public Relations' which specifically identified and explored ways in which PR techniques are increasingly being deployed in campaigns of dissent and protest (Moloney, McQueen, Surowiec, & Yaxley, 2012). In a foreword, Kevin Moloney defines dissent PR as "the dissemination of ideas, commentaries, and policies through PR techniques in order to change current, dominant thinking and behaviour in discrete economic, political and cultural areas of public life" (p. 3). In calling for more pluralist understanding or PR, the authors discussed campaigns by Greenpeace, contemporary feminist protest activities such as 'slut walks' which have gained widespread media attention, and even the 1980s trade union *Solidarity* campaign in Poland as examples of counter-business and counter-government PR.

PR is also used by the Red Cross to collect blood, which is essential to save lives (the organization does not have funds for major advertising campaigns and relies on PR and direct appeals). Health campaigns to combat disease, promote good nutrition, reduce smoking, and promote fitness use PR. So do road safety campaigns. Schools engage in PR when they invite parents and community members to visit and attend school events, and many philanthropic organizations use PR to raise much-needed funds.

In their classic text *Mediating the Message*, Pamela Shoemaker and Stephen Reese (1996) point out that "a government agency might create a public relations message intended to warn the public about an environmental hazard, or it might plan a public information program designed both to teach people about the health risks of cocaine use and to ultimately reduce cocaine's consumption" (p. 179). In an analysis of publicity as one aspect of PR and the one that attracts most criticism, Kirk Hallahan (2010) also notes:

> Publicity is integrally involved in preserving and encouraging public interest in the fine arts and other forms of serious creative expression—painting, sculpture, dance, symphonic and chamber music, theatre, serious fiction, and so on. Publicity is also crucial to the commercial viability of popular culture by creating popular demand for books, plays, movies, music recordings, TV shows, electronic games, and other entertainment (2010, p. 533).

It is important to not generalize about PR based on ignorance, misinformation, stereotypes, or myths. And it is important to not assume that PR is only used by the rich and powerful for selfish or nefarious ends. In a critical review of PR, Kevin Moloney (2006) makes an important observation about PR, saying:

> There is no 'PR' in capital letters that is reprobate, and a 'pr' in lower case that is virtuous. PR cannot be separated into the perverse category of 'propaganda and manipulation' and the laudatory one of 'information and campaigning'. PR techniques do not have integral to them moral values. They are communicative modes. They are used by principals who have moralities, ethics and benign interests in a democracy and in markets—or not (p. 176).

In short, Moloney is pointing out the truism that PR is neither innately good nor bad; neither destructive nor constructive; neither ethical nor unethical. It is what people do with PR that determines its effects in society.

Notes

1. Originally a parlour game in 18th century England, the term 'bunco' became synonymous with any "swindling game or scheme" in the US (Merriam-Webster Online Dictionary, 2013).
2. *The Press and Society*, edited by George Bird and Frederic Merwin, contains articles by Walter Lippmann, Harold Lasswell, Paul Lazarsfeld, Bernard Berelson, Willard Bleyer,

George Gallup, Silas Bent, Kenneth Olson, and many other distinguished media writers. It is available for free download (see Bird & Merwin, 1955).

3. The first US PR agency, established in Boston in 1900, was called The Publicity Bureau, which indicates the early focus on *press agentry/publicity*.

4. In the Excellence Study of PR, the criteria for identifying excellent organizations were based in part on Tom Peters and Robert Waterman's (1982) book *In Search of Excellence*. This is one of the criticisms made of Excellence theory of PR, as many of the organizations identified as excellent in the Peters and Waterman study subsequently declined or went out of business. Nevertheless, the Excellence Study of PR claimed to draw on a wide range of literature that identified the attributes that made organizations excellent and characteristics of public relations that theoretically contributed to organizational excellence (Grunig et al., 2006, p. 26).

5. WPP owns several of the world's largest PR consultancy firms including Hill & Knowlton, Burson-Marsteller, Ogilvy PR, Carl Byoir & Associates, and Cohn & Wolfe, as well as a number of advertising agencies, direct marketing firms, digital communication agencies, and consumer research companies.

6. The force-feeding of geese for *foie gras* production using a feeding tube called a *gavage* is controversial and is not condoned or supported by its reference here.

7. PR firm Hill & Knowlton previously published details and its version of the 'Citizens to Free Kuwait' campaign on its Web site at http://www.hillandknowlton.com/citizensfora-freekuwait, but all references to Citizens to Free Kuwait have been removed from the Hill & Knowlton site.

8. The term 'astroturfing' is derived from the artificial turf developed by the Monsanto Company and famously used at the Astrodome in Houston, Texas, in the late 1960s.

9. PR Watch (2005) reported that, apart from US$11.9 million contributed to Citizens for a Free Kuwait by the Kuwaiti government, US$10.8 million of which went to the PR firm Hill & Knowlton in fees, the only other funding of the organization totalled $17,861 from 78 individuals.

10. It should be noted that the head of PR for James Hardie Industries at the time was not charged or found guilty of any offences in the ensuing 11 years of legal proceedings in relation to the Medical Research and Compensation Foundation for asbestos victims. Even though he drafted the media release that was found to have made false statements and his name appeared on the bottom, the State Supreme and High Court found directors and senior managers of the company had approved the statement and were ultimately responsible for its distribution.

CHAPTER FOUR

What 20 Years of Practice and Case Studies Reveal

While Chapter 3 provides a summary of descriptive and normative theories and models of PR, as well as a brief insight into the specific practices of PR and some widely reported case studies, literature in research monographs, journals, and textbooks gives only a broad brush picture of what PR practitioners actually do. This chapter is designed to put some 'flesh on the bones' of the industry and field of practice outlined in Chapter 3. If we are going to critically analyze what PR practitioners do on a regular basis, and the implications of what they do, we need a close-up view of practices, rather than rely solely on what academics or journalists say they do. A view exclusively from the academy or the external position of an independent researcher can miss the nuances, unwritten rules, and conventions that are learned in daily work and fail to fully appreciate the rich texture of these fast-moving, dynamic fields at the applied level.

This chapter summarizes a number of additional case studies of PR practice based on autoethnography, a derivative of ethnography that uses observations undertaken during personal experience subjected to reflective and reflexive analysis. Autoethnography has its methodological limitations including subjectivity, as will be discussed in this chapter, but it also has its benefits—in particular, its capacity to ground research in deep understanding of a field and provide what is termed 'thick description'.

Clifford Geertz (1973) describes ethnography as a qualitative research method conducted to learn and understand cultural phenomena which reflect the knowledge and system of meanings guiding the life of a cultural group. Thus, ethnography is a useful method for exploring PR and its interface with media. In particular, Geertz described ethnography as "thick description", meaning such analysis is based on detailed observation and interpretation during an extended period of field work. Distinguished anthropologist Barbara Tedlock notes that ethnographers *live in* a society for an extended period of time which she cites as "two years ideally" (2008, p. 151) [emphasis added]. This immersion in a group is important. Thick description cannot be achieved by short-term observations from outside a group, through surveys, or even through structured or semi-structured interviews. Geertz (1973) identifies the primary research methods used in ethnography as participant observation and sometimes participation by the researcher.

John Creswell draws attention to further key characteristics, benefits, and methods of this approach in his definition of ethnography as "a strategy of inquiry in which the researcher studies an intact cultural group in a *natural setting* over a prolonged period of time by collecting, primarily, observational and interview data" (2009, p. 13) [emphasis added]. Unlike the claimed independent, objective, outside-the-studied-group standpoint of the scientific method of research, ethnography involves intensive study using personal observation and sometimes participation inside the world of those studied, as well as interviews. Interviews are necessarily in-depth, or may take the form of open-ended conversations over a period, with data collected in notes, audio or video recordings, diaries, and other records such as documents (e.g., minutes of meetings, transcripts of speeches, and statements, etc.).

While experiences and observations are only summarized here, the analysis fits the definition of thick description as it is based on detailed observation and active participation in the cultural group over an extended period. Observations are drawn from more than 20 years working in PR for American, British, Australian, and Asian companies and several government agencies. This was preceded by nine years working as a journalist, which collectively affords understanding of both 'sides of the fence'. Most importantly, this experience provides an 'inside' vantage point (*emic* perspective) from which to observe and report on practices. The author's later experience working as a full-time media and communication academic (since 2007) affords an *etic* perspective from which to reflect on these observations and experiences. While some ethnographic studies take either an emic or etic approach, Klaus Jensen states that cultural expressions including communication "can and should be studied from both internal and external perspectives" (2012, p. 267). He draws on Kenneth Pike's seminal 1967 work in urging researchers "to relate the two aspects of understanding and interpretation" (Pike, as cited in Jensen, 2012, p. 267). Further elaborating on Geertz's classic definition, researcher W. Lawrence Neuman (2006) emphasizes that ethnography is "very detailed description of a…culture from the viewpoint of an *insider* in the culture to facilitate understanding of it" (p. 381) [emphasis added]. Within these theoretical frameworks, the author has a useful vantage point as both participant and observer, and both practitioner and scholar, over a long period, which offers insights that add another layer to understanding the interface between PR and journalism.

A limitation or weakness of personal observation and reflection (ethnography) as a research method is that it introduces even more subjectivity than applies in other research methods. Autoethnography, in particular, which involves reflection on one's own experiences and actions, can lean towards anecdotes, autobiography, or personal memoirs. However, Tedlock (2008) rejects the binary separation of so-called *objective* observation associated with 'scientific ethnography' and subjective autobiographical accounts. Ethnography and autoethnography, when undertaken carefully and sensitively, incorporate steps to manage and minimize subjectivity and ensure validity of findings.

What separates ethnographic and autoethnographic research from auto-biographical stories and anecdotes, according to Garance Maréchal (2010), is *reflexivity* and the connection of observations to wider cultural, political, and social meanings and understandings—that is, comparing the autoethnographer's observations with other sources or data and reflectively analyzing them within the framework of theoretical knowledge in the field. Ethnography and autoethnography typically rely on field notes (i.e., recorded observations made at the time), but also can draw on journals, diaries, reports, minutes of meetings, scrapbooks, newspaper and trade magazine articles and columns, newsletters, and other relevant documents. In addition, observations in these methods of research can be compared with records in books, journal articles, published memoirs, and other research studies.

The validity and reliability of autoethnographic observations and analysis reported here are addressed in several ways. First, reflexivity is recognized in both senses in which it is understood in the social sciences and used as a tool to acknowledge (1) the role of the researcher in the research and (2) the situated nature of the research (Finlay & Gough, 2003). In a personal sense, the researcher has attempted to be conscious of his relationship to the field of study and how power relations, self-justification, or 'Photoshopping' of history might influence what is reported. This is addressed through applying self-critique as part of the analysis and reflecting with the benefit of time, which affords some distance on the matters discussed. In a broader sense, reflexivity denotes the ways that cultural practices involve self-references and commentary on themselves and how examination can 'bend back on' and affect the entity undertaking the investigation—in short, the ways in which a researcher can become socialized into the culture that she or he is investigating. This is addressed through the second approach for ensuring validity: as far as possible reflections on observed practices are compared with other research and historical literature to confirm and contextualize observations. Reflections that are aberrant with other recorded observations and findings can be questioned, although not necessarily dismissed. Reflexivity is further aided by the researcher having been socialized into both the worlds of journalism and PR.

Home Boy/Girl Stories—Everyday PR

Between 1974 and 1976 I worked in Army Public Relations based at Second Military District headquarters in Sydney and then in Defence Public Relations based at the Department of Defence, Russell Hill in Canberra, Australia's national capital. In addition to doing the press clippings each morning, which in those days involved physically clipping relevant articles from newspapers with a pair of scissors, one of my first assignments in Army Public Relations was called 'home boy' stories. Later, with awareness of gendered language and increasing numbers of women serving in the military, they became 'home girl' stories as well.

Some background on how I came to be writing home boy/girl stories for the Army as a young man in my early twenties is relevant, as it reflects the relationship and frequent crossover between journalism and PR. For as long as I can remember, I wanted to be a journalist and writer. At school I was involved in producing a students' newsletter during Year 10 (junior high). I churned out freelance contributions for small publications on my first Remington manual typewriter from the age of 16, starting with a church magazine. By the time I left school I was writing regular articles for country newspapers in my home state. These were inauspicious and inconspicuous beginnings, I have to say. It was perhaps fortunate that my fledgling journalism career was interrupted by Army service in 1972.

After less than one year of military service in 'rookie' training and then in a Royal Australian Engineers regiment (to which I was posted despite knowing even less about engineering than I did about journalism), the newly elected Labor government ended Australia's engagement in Vietnam and so too the structure of many military units, which were largely comprised of National Service conscripts. With questionable prospects in rural Queensland, my home state, due to a decline in agricultural fortunes, I decided to stay in the Army and was offered a job in Army Public Relations because of my journalism experience, meagre though it was. Thus began my PR career—and my crossing over to the 'dark side' in the eyes of my journalist colleagues.

I learned early on that the journalism–PR nexus is not as simple as two opposing sides in the world of media and public information. It is a narrow strait that I crossed back and forth a number of times. During my time in Army and then Defence Public Relations, the military allowed me to undertake professional development training with media organizations—my early journalism training having been cut short. So it was that I ended up for a time on the main editorial floor of John Fairfax & Sons' Jones Street headquarters in Sydney—a building to which I would fatefully and somewhat ironically return 32 years later when it had become part of the University of Technology, Sydney. With Fairfax, I gained experience writing for *The Sydney Morning Herald* and, occasionally, *The Sun* and *The Sun-Herald*—although tabloids were my first disappointment in journalism. I also spent some time with Radio 2UE and a brief attachment with ATN Channel 7 news (now Seven Network). Despite its glamorous image, television never appealed to me because it seemed to compromise journalism with entertainment values and turned complex issues into what were then 30-second 'grabs' (now more like 5-second grabs). In fact, television reporting fanned the flames of a passion for long-form writing which provides in-depth analysis. I believed then and still believe that journalism done well is a most satisfying form of work and a substantial and essential contribution to society.

There is a thrill, and a considerable ego boost, in seeing one's name in print on the top of an article in a major newspaper or magazine. Less so for me to be on television, although others find the celebrity of TV reporting even more of a 'buzz'. Beyond the 'ego trip', there is also a deep sense of satisfaction when one finds a flaw in policy, a product fault, a wrong-doing, or an injustice that has gone unreported and which the public should know about. There is also a pride that comes from tracking down an inspiring human interest story, revealing insights into an issue or place that others have not discovered, and explaining things that help people in their daily lives—whether that is how to save money, invest wisely, live healthily, or learn about their local community.

In my early years of crossing back and forth between journalism and PR, I started to see that the walls that allegedly separated them were far more permeable than my journalistic colleagues claimed and that there were important public information and communication functions on the so-called 'dark side'. This experience was based in Australia where I grew up and did military service, but interviews with PR practitioners in the US and UK reported in Chapter 6 show that my experiences were not atypical. In doing PR for the Australian armed forces I was involved in media relations (liaising with journalists), distributing media releases and photography produced by Defence PR personnel to media nationally, and producing documentary films. But let's come back to my more humble everyday example of PR.

Doing home boy/girl stories involved going into the field with military units, such as on training exercises, to take photos of and interview soldiers. The photos were a mix of action shots and poses, such as a trooper sitting on top of a tank or decked out in full camouflage kit ready to do simulated battle. The photos and short articles telling of soldiers' exploits were sent to their hometown newspapers in country towns, provincial cities, and suburbs across the country. These activities took me and my military PR colleagues to the Outback on desert training exercises, to the cold damp forests of Gippsland in southern Australia, and to the tropical beaches and rain forests of North Queensland. Sometimes we trained with US and New Zealand troops in combined ANZUS (Australia, New Zealand, and US) exercises. Thousands of young soldiers participated in these exercises—deploying in Armoured Personnel Carriers (APCs) or beach landing craft, parachuting from C-130 Hercules transport aircraft or helicopters, simulating combat in remote bushland or damp jungle, and leaping on and off Iroquois and Chinook military helicopters.

A photo of Johnny Smith or Jenny Smith in combat gear handling military equipment ranging from radios to six-wheel-drive trucks and tanks may not make it into *The Sydney Morning Herald*, but such photos were welcomed by *The Pastoral Times*, *The Western Advocate*, *The Downs Star*, and local suburban papers in the cities such as *The Liverpool Leader* and *The North Shore Times*. Sometimes they even made the front page. The short articles and captions accompanying the photos told of local young people who had gone off to serve their country. They were 'good PR' for the military, but they were also welcome news for families and friends back home. The soldiers, who often received press clippings sent from home, felt proud and enjoyed the recognition. Their story was being told—not by journalists, but by hard-working military PR personnel. The home boy/girl stories were good for morale. And for editors of small newspapers with a staff of one or two, they were a welcome change from photos of the winning cake at a local fair and a farmer's prize-winning cow.

The photos were usually more important than the story—a sobering lesson that I took on board for later in my career. But these 'home boy' and 'home girl' stories required sharp interview skills and an ability to write quickly. Often the interviews were done on the run (literally) during simulated combat exercises, and copy to accompany film back to head office for processing and distribution was written on a typewriter on the tailgate of an Army truck or Land Rover (yes, film and typewriters were used back then). I and my colleagues in Army and Defence

PR were the 'dark side' of public communication in the eyes of many journalists, but we wrote and photographed thousands of stories that were welcomed around Australia and even internationally.

Some years later, I met the mother of a soldier who had been killed. Upon offering my condolences and identifying myself as a former soldier and military PR person, she told me that she treasured a copy of her local newspaper from many years before with a photo of her son taken during training on the front page. "It was the best photo I ever had of him," she said.

Saving an Outback Town in Prime Time

As happens every 7–10 years in Australia, heavy rains caused inland rivers to burst their banks and flood the flat plains of Outback New South Wales in 1976. Towns all along the Darling River that joins the river systems of Queensland's Channel Country to the 'mighty Murray' River in Victoria and South Australia were isolated. The small town of Brewarrina, in particular, was in dire straits—cut off by road, its airport also partly flooded, and the river threatening to break the levy banks that protected the town. The town's hospital was near the river, with many patients too ill or frail to be moved. Besides, where could they go? Roads in all directions were cut by floodwaters and washouts.

The call went out to the Army and Air Force and, within a few hours, emergency flights were taking off from Richmond Air Base west of Sydney ferrying in soldiers and equipment to help reinforce levy banks. Army helicopters were also despatched to help in rescues. There was high media interest in the plight of inland towns such as Brewarrina, but most media networks did not have long-range helicopters at the time. As a military PR officer based in Sydney, I had authority to escort media on military flights and operations during emergencies. Within a day, I had arranged for a number of journalists and photographers, including a crew from the national current affairs TV program *This Day Tonight*, to be accommodated along with cargo and troops on a flight to Brewarrina. We flew into the tiny Outback town in a C-130 Hercules[1], a legendary 'tramp steamer' of the skies, which was able to land on a short dry section of the runway and were then transported into town in an Army engineers flat-bottom boat.

The TV crew and photographers captured the dramatic efforts of soldiers working frantically alongside townsfolk filling sandbags, while others operated machinery such as ditch diggers and front-end loaders. Fortunately, the reinforced levy banks held and the town was saved. Photographers travelled in helicopters to rescue families from remote homesteads that were isolated by floodwaters and gained photo spreads that captured the human drama and the tragedy for some families and local livestock.

It occurred to me on the flight home sitting in orange netting seats in the screaming fuselage of the 'Herc' that this was more than good PR for the Army and the Air Force. These images would never have been seen by the public without the work of military PR. Neither *This Day Tonight* nor any other journalists or camera crews would have been able to get to Brewarrina. State and federal governments may not have understood the need for assistance to the area and may not have been motivated to act were it not for the prime time news and current affairs reporting. The community may have felt ignored, isolated, and forgotten. This was not an isolated instance. Dozens of towns down river were also assisted by the Army and Air Force. Just two years before, the military played a major role in providing emergency services in the northern Australian city of Darwin when it was all but destroyed by Cyclone Tracy on Christmas Day 1974. With all telecommunications cut and travel in and out of the city open only to military aircraft for many days, it was Army and Air Force PR officers who helped journalists gain access and cover the myriad stories of destruction, heartbreak, finding hope, and then rebuilding. During my years doing military PR, I and my colleagues regularly lobbied generals and military headquarters to get seats on aircraft for journalists and media camera crews; we directed the military's own photographers and film crews and openly and freely made the footage available to media; we corralled senior military officers and urged them to communicate with the public via the media, even when their operational responsibilities were onerous; and we provided a steady stream of facts and statistical data to literally hundreds of journalists on a daily basis.

On the flight returning from Brewarrina, like many others, I felt a sense of pride in a good day's work and went home and slept soundly.

The Journalism–PR Two-Step

After completing almost five years in the Army, including three years in Army and Defence PR, I returned to journalism as an A-Grade reporter with Rural Press, publishers of the leading Australian rural newspapers *The Land* and *Country Life*. The job suited me because of my background growing up on a farm and gave me the chance to write feature articles as well as news reports. I even got the opportunity to start a motoring column, which was a great lurk because it involved a regular supply of new cars to drive and review. Therein came my first experience of the incentives that are offered to journalists and the grey zone that exists between the allegedly black-and-white worlds of journalism and PR. The cars rarely if ever came with insistence of a positive review. Only the most inexperienced PR practitioner or crass commercial operator made such requests or demands. But I found myself cautious about criticizing the 'free rides' that I enjoyed, knowing that another one was unlikely to come my way if I 'bit the hand that fed me'. Driving a new model Mercedes Benz for a weekend at the wineries or to pick up a friend provided a mild narcotic that dulled my otherwise sharply critical sensibilities and produced a more tepid form of critical review. I was not bought off and never sold out in any explicit sense. But I discovered the naivety of journalists' claims of objectivity, the subtle art of nuance, and the seduction of ego. PR practitioners are human—and so are journalists.

Hungry for by-lines and success as well as experience, I also wrote freelance for a range of non-competing magazines and journals, a practice that I continued even after I left full-time journalism for the last time and took up a commercial PR position. Over the next seven or eight years, I was a regular freelancer for magazines including *People, Overlander, Wheels, Australian Boating*, and specialist magazines such as *Pacific Defence Reporter*. As I slowly earned a name, I gained commissions from *Australian Playboy* (yes, for the articles), *Cleo*, and feature articles for the 'Op-Ed' page of *The Sydney Morning Herald* and *The Canberra Times*. As can be seen from the list of titles, my writing was not all or even much about world-changing events, but it was diverse and exposed me to a range of media experiences.

I continued my back-and-forth shuffle between journalism and PR over many years, as I wrote freelance during several PR jobs. For instance, while I was director of public relations for the National Farmers Federation in Canberra (1980–1984), I wrote regularly for several magazines. It was there also that I wrote my first book. This was inspired by both journalism and PR. It was a small manual called *Public Relations Handbook for Clubs and Associations* (Macnamara, 1983), the genesis of which was my observation during my years in journalism and PR that many groups in society are effectively disenfranchised because they do not know how to present their information to the media—and media do not have sufficient staff to search out and report every story that deserves and/or has a right to be told. This concern has been recognized in some studies of journalism such as a Reuters Institute for the Study of Journalism conducted by the University of Oxford in 2009, which reported that "entering the unpredictable waters of the media without the guidance of a PR specialist is…as ill-advised as going to court without a lawyer" (Currah, 2009, p. 61). My PR handbook for clubs and associations and subsequent editions written for managers and executives (Macnamara, 1985, 1992, 1996a, 2000) helped journalists as well as businesses and organizations, including many small associations, local community groups, and clubs with scant resources and little or no specialist knowledge of media practices. The PR handbooks advocated being open and honest with media, presenting truthful information, and they explained the format and style of media writing, including brevity and straightforwardness.

MACRO and Microsoft

These qualities and principles were tested during my PR career in the late 1980s and early 1990s when the consultancy firm I co-founded, MACRO Communication[2], was appointed by Microsoft to promote its corporate image and products. One of the major projects that my colleagues and I undertook for Microsoft was the launch and ongoing promotion of Windows 3.0, a major upgrade to Microsoft's graphical user interface (GUI) Windows operating system that replaced MS-DOS. Despite promising significant interface enhancements and technical improvements compared with its predecessor Windows 2.1, Windows 3.0 had major 'bugs' in IT terms. As a *New York Times* technology review reported shortly after the launch, "the adventurous souls who leaped aboard the Windows 3.0 bandwagon had a bumpy ride" (Lewis, 1992, para. 10). The Intel microprocessors in PCs of the day frequently detected a protection violation between Windows 3.0 and software applications, which caused computers to stop executing code and send a general protection fault (GPF) notice to the user. This displayed a screen message saying "Unrecoverable Application Error", upon which the machine crashed and all documents not saved were lost. Faults in computers are hardly new. But this one was quite serious and Microsoft was reportedly aware of the problem before the launch and decided to proceed anyway. The company was locked in combat in the market with Apple Computer, as well as with several major PC software competitors including Lotus, WordPerfect, and Adobe.

From a PR standpoint, this case study illustrates the perilous ethical dilemmas that can arise. I and my agency's staff were aware of the problems in the product and Microsoft's scramble to bring an upgrade with 'bug fixes' to market as quickly as possible, but we were prohibited from acknowledging this publicly. Seasoned IT journalists were soon on to the story and the best we could do was nod and say "sorry, we're working on it". As it turned out, Microsoft released an upgraded version in December 1990—a little more than six months after the high-profile initial launch of the third generation of its Windows operating system. But that was a long time to deflect criticism and maintain a positive PR line. High principled and high-minded critics might say that we should have resigned from the account. But there was almost a million dollars a year of fees at stake and I and my business partners had mortgages and children in school. Walking away or becoming a whistle blower is easier said than done. We prided ourselves that we never lied. But we knew we were skating on thin ice above a dark bottomless lake in terms of our reputations when we hosted media launches and briefings for Windows 3.0 and tried to whip up excitement in the market.

Less problematic but still illustrative of the moral dilemmas encountered in PR was the launch of Microsoft Office. 'Office' software packages, as most now know, are suites of several software applications bundled together and sold as a single product. Microsoft pioneered this practice in 1990 as a strategy to wrest desktop application leadership away from its competitors. At the time, the acknowledged leader in spreadsheets was Lotus 123. The word processing program widely rated as the best was WordPerfect. And Adobe Systems had launched Persuasion, which was arguably the most advanced presentation software program, along with Lotus Freelance. Microsoft did not have the leading PC application in any of the top three categories. However, by bundling together Microsoft Word, Microsoft Excel, and the fledgling Microsoft PowerPoint, it produced and marketed The Microsoft Office, substantially undercutting the total price of competitors' programs sold separately. Even though Microsoft Word was under-developed at the time and PowerPoint was an awkward teenager even in Version 2.0 form, sales success followed, built more on pricing strategy and marketing than technological prowess. The role of the PR agency was to 'sell' a narrative that Office suites were the way to go because they offered integration of functions between applications. The 'apps' allegedly worked together seamlessly with common functions, compared with standalone programs. In reality, there was little integration in the early versions. They were cobbled together as a marketing strategy and PR sold the story. It was not altogether untrue, but it was exaggerated. On reflection, it was spin.

To be fair and to its credit, Microsoft developed Excel to be a highly sophisticated application used widely by accountants and even statisticians, and Microsoft PowerPoint underwent several versions of development until it became the market leader and a generic term for PC presentation tools. Integration between applications did eventuate and offer benefits. Microsoft has softened its image from the days of anti-trust actions in which the company was accused of becoming a monopoly in the Windows computing and Web browser markets and engaging in abusive trade practices (e.g., US Department of Justice action launched in 1998 and settled in 2001). The Bill and Melinda Gates Foundation stands as a global benchmark in philanthropy. Microsoft public relations improved as the company listened to its stakeholders through feedback and research and engaged in dialogue and co-orientation to align itself with customer and public expectations.

MACRO Communication played a small part in one country, but worked for Microsoft for five years, which included coordinating the first visit to Australia by Bill Gates in 1994. While he was addressing a crowd at the Sydney Opera House, a minor crisis broke when *The Daily Telegraph* reported that Bill Gates had declined a meeting requested by the then Australian Prime Minister Paul Keating because he was too busy. The story was based on a phone call by a journalist asking if Mr Gates was meeting with the PM. The person answering the phone said that there was no meeting scheduled and Mr Gates' itinerary was full. That was true, but when the beat-up story broke, the PR team immediately alerted Microsoft management that an apparent snub of the Prime Minister was not a good strategy and was ordered to smooth the troubled waters. As head of the PR consultancy, it was my job to phone the Prime Minister's staff to apologize for the implication in *The Telegraph* report and ascertain if it was true that Mr Keating wanted to meet with Bill Gates. The PM's staff advised that Mr Keating was indeed keen to meet Bill Gates because he had a deep interest in the 'information superhighway' and its potential to benefit society as well as business. So of course I said yes and a meeting was on, with just two days' notice. A team of Microsoft and MACRO Communication staff went to work to reorganize the schedule, find airline seats or a charter flight to Canberra, arrange cars for local transport, organize a photographer to record the occasion, and alert the media. Furthermore, if Bill Gates was going to the national capital to meet the PM, why not try to arrange an address to the National Press Club, which is located there. After a few more phone calls, a special address to the National Press Club by Bill Gates was booked for lunch time immediately following his meeting with the Prime Minister on February 4, 1994.

I flew to Canberra with the entourage that morning, coordinated the photo shoot at Parliament House following the meeting with the PM, and then went to the National Press Club luncheon to assist and manage the swarm of media which had gathered. Bookings were so high that the event had to be moved to the National Convention Centre in Canberra where Bill Gates addressed 1,200 people, breaking the Press Club record previously held by Indira Ghandi and setting a record that has still not been surpassed (Doherty, 2013, para. 6). A 'media scrum' of more than 100 journalists clamoured for interviews and statements, which required considerable management and coordination to balance their needs and the public interest with the practical requirements of Bill Gate's schedule. Many journalists fail to understand that, even though publicity is sought and valued as a form of promotion by companies, VIP visits such as Bill Gate's are not simply arranged for them. The primary purpose of his visit was high-level business meetings in relation to the Australian and Asia Pacific operations of the company. During much of his visit, he was locked away in budget discussions and what Microsoft called its 'sub-review' with the local subsidiary. It was largely the efforts of the PR agency that carved out time for the media.

It is almost impossible for journalists other than the most senior reporters and those representing large national networks to get access to the likes of Bill Gates without facilitation by a media-sympathetic and media-savvy PR person acting as intermediary. It is also very difficult for many journalists to get answers to questions without attentive PR practitioners either inside the organization or in a retained PR consultancy. This is not necessarily because corporation and organization staff are unwilling or deliberately obdurate, as journalists often claim. CEOs and other senior executives are very busy with many competing demands for their attention. Talking to journalists is simply not on their priority list in many cases. PR practitioners represent a dedicated resource and central contact point for journalists seeking information or interviews. While some PR practitioners—particularly those in organizations with something to hide—engage in obfuscation or at least clever footwork to avoid open communication, many genuinely try to help media and distribute information to the public in good faith.

That first visit to Australia by Bill Gates was considered a big success from many perspectives. While it involved many hard-working people, PR staff were front and centre of most arrangements and played a major part in not only Microsoft's success but also in helping many journalists gain access for interviews—and even in helping set up a meeting with the Prime Minister. As I was researching and writing this book, Bill Gates returned to Australia and to the National Press Club to deliver an address in May 2013 and was welcomed as one of the leaders of the 21st century.

Reflection and reflexivity demand admission by this author of some slightly sordid examples of spin in my career. But, on the whole, I only ever felt my principles and journalistic values compromised on a few occasions while working in PR roles. On other occasions, such as in the next case study reported, I found myself even more intimately involved with journalists and engaged in an interdependency that is rarely acknowledged or understood.

The Voice of Vodafone

While working for Microsoft I received a phone call one day in early 1993 from Liz Lette, the sister of bestselling author Kathy Lette. Liz had been headhunted from Apple Computer, along with Tony Fraser, to launch and manage marketing for the Australian subsidiary of British mobile communications giant Vodafone, working with CEO John Rohan. It was a big challenge, as Australia already had two major mobile/cell phone companies, Telstra and Optus (now owned by Singapore Telecom), and the nation was poised on the verge of a changeover from ageing analogue technology to the digital Global System for Mobile (GSM). After an obligatory 'pitch' and several discussions, Liz invited MACRO Communication to work for Vodafone as their PR agency and a key part of their marketing department, which in start-up mode numbered just two (Tony and Liz). I accepted and the next four years of my life were substantially changed.

A third competitor traditionally faces a tough battle in most market sectors, whether it is automotive, computers, telecommunications, or supermarket chains. Marketing researchers and theorists, based on studies of more than 200 industries, have identified that a 'top two' typically dominates most market sectors and that third and later competitors struggle for market share and mindshare unless they are specialists or niche market providers (Sheth & Sisodia, 2002). So Vodafone needed to employ clever marketing and have good public communication.

Furthermore, Vodafone faced an additional communication and marketing challenge because both of the two established competitors, Telstra and Optus, had existing analogue mobile/cell phone networks and the government had announced that there would be a gradual phase-out of analogue so as not to disadvantage users. At the time of Vodafone's entry to the Australian market there were 635,000 analogue mobile/cell phones in use. However, because of the gradual phase-out planned, Telstra continued promotion of analogue services and by March 1994 the number of analogue mobile/cell phone users passed 1 million (Australian Mobile Telecommunications, n.d.). Because it was a new entrant, it was not cost effective for Vodafone to build an analogue network. As well as not having access to this continuing analogue market, Vodafone also faced confusion in the market caused by its decision to focus on GSM digital while the major competitors continued to promote the analogue Advanced Mobile Phone System (AMPS).

A 'PR war' ensued over the next few years, with Vodafone rapidly rolling out its digital GSM network and trying to convince mobile/cell phone buyers that they should switch to digital rather than continue to buy analogue products. The detailed ins and outs of the PR campaign are not the focus here, except insofar as they were based on a genuine belief that the message we were communicating was truthful and in the public interest. Digital mobile communication was coming and it offered superior services on mobile/cell phone networks. To a significant extent, the incumbent market leaders were obfuscating to protect their existing analogue investments and get as much revenue out of them as possible before they had to close them down. As a third competitor, Vodafone was also bringing much-needed competition to the market that had been monopolized for decades by Telstra (formerly Telecom Australia) as a single carrier before Optus entered the market just the year before Vodafone in 1992. Australians were frustrated with decades of monopoly control of the telephone market and my PR colleagues and

I approached our task with enthusiasm and near missionary zeal. It is seldom recognized that PR practitioners often genuinely believe in what they are communicating and promoting and often have good reasons to do so.

The first six months of planning were hectic and Vodafone's GSM mobile/cell phone network was launched in October 1993, just a few months after Telstra and Optus launched their digital networks. We creatively made our point about the superiority of digital technology at the launch when more than 50 journalists and TV crew members sat in a client-less room at the Observatory Hotel while noted jazz musician James Morrison played a trumpet. Puzzled media faces watched as, after playing a traditional instrument for several minutes, Morrison stood up, walked over and picked up a small trumpet connected by a cable to a sound mixer and speakers and then shook the room with the thunderous but crystal clear sound of a digital trumpet. The CEO of Vodafone Australia walked into the room, stood at the lectern, and said quietly: "Before was analogue. That was digital sound." That launch event may sound stage-managed, and it was, but PR practitioners are employed as storytellers and it was our job to tell this story as well as we could. It was a story that we believed and one that we felt was important for the public to hear.

However, the most significant aspect of this case study in the context of this book was the extent and type of interrelationship with media that I experienced over the next four years. The CEO John Rohan was an engineer and was extremely competent and confident talking to technical journalists, and as CEO he was required to handle interviews with major financial and business media. But he had much to do leading the construction of a whole new company and a whole new network. He had neither the time nor the confidence in his public communication skills to handle the numerous media interviews and comments requested on a daily basis from state, city, provincial, trade, and even small-town newspapers, TV networks, and radio stations, as well as magazines of all genres. Because of this, and also because of Vodafone Australia's skeletal staff during the start-up years, he decided that I should be Vodafone's media spokesperson for all general media inquiries.

It is unusual for a PR person to become the authorized spokesperson for a major corporation or organization, particularly for a consultant to have this role. Most often PR practitioners, even in-house PR executives, are communication facilitators working in the background. I wondered and was concerned initially about how media would take to this arrangement. Most journalists knew that I was a PR practitioner from my and my firm's high-profile work with Microsoft. Journalists' criticisms of PR 'gatekeepers' and spin doctors resonated in my mind as this arrangement was put in place.

I need not have worried. Far from being concerned or resenting the arrangement, most journalists welcomed it, as I made myself readily available and knew what media wanted. Also, my consultancy implemented systems to help media, including a 24/7 media contact service. At the time, most companies' PR departments and agencies took calls during working hours only and Web sites were still in early stages of development with only basic information for media. MACRO Communication printed a small card with the mobile/cell phone numbers for all members of the PR team and advised journalists that one of us would be rostered to accept media inquiries at any hour of the day or night seven days a week. Internally, we had a list of after-hours numbers for Vodafone's key technicians to provide information to us when required.

This accessibility and media response capability was tested on Christmas Day 1995 when a journalist called my mobile/cell phone during Christmas lunch with my family to advise that a small child had fallen into a swimming pool in Brisbane and when the mother called the 000 emergency number (equivalent to 911 in the US) on her Vodafone mobile/cell phone, the call failed. The Vodafone network was being blamed. I immediately called an engineer on duty and requested information. Within minutes, he had sourced the problem, which was a crash by the 000 emergency services server in Brisbane. He could produce data to show the Vodafone call reached the server, but it failed to accept the call. With this data I was able to field numerous media interviews and give them convincing information that saved the reputation of the company from potentially serious damage. Fortunately also, the child survived after a further phone call reached the emergency service server that rebooted within minutes. My Christmas lunch went cold and my family were somewhat testy about my job, but again I went home feeling like I had done something important and worthwhile.

Over the next four years, I gave more than 1,000 interviews and comments to journalists on behalf of Vodafone. No journalist ever expressed concern or a problem with having to deal with a PR person—either to me, to the company, or in print or in a broadcast report. To the contrary, without meaning to sound immodest, journalists sought me out. They knew that I would always take their call. They knew that, if I didn't know what they wanted, I would find out—and quickly. They knew that if I didn't know and couldn't find out, I would say 'we don't know'. They knew that I would present my client in the best possible light, but I would not lie or obfuscate. They knew that I would do my best to help them. They knew that I would be fair and even-handed and not give precedence to their competitors except in the case of pre-arranged exclusive stories. Usually, exclusives were only given when a journalist initiated a story; all client information was otherwise distributed openly and equally. An intriguing footnote to this is that I continued to receive media inquiries about Vodafone up to five years after I ceased working for the company and even after I sold my PR firm and moved into full-time media research.

The purpose of recounting these observations and reflections is not to claim high moral ground for myself. They were also the practices of many other PR professionals I knew. I cannot say *all* PR practitioners operated on the same basis. Some following case studies show the other side of the coin. But generalized claims that PR negatively impacts and undermines journalism need to be questioned and subjected to test against empirical evidence. There is no *prima facie* evidence or logic to show that PR practitioners per se are less ethical or more manipulative or sinister than other professionals working in media practices. Many PR practitioners have training and backgrounds in journalism, giving them a grounding in the values, standards, and culture that journalists have or aspire to. Many PR practitioners are more educated than journalists (Sallot, Steinfatt, & Salwen, 1998) with postgraduate education increasingly common in the PR field, which fosters critical thinking and broader societal perspectives than the disciplinary and practice focus of many undergraduate majors in journalism and mass communication. Many PR practitioners take seriously the counsellor role discussed in Chapter 3, often urging and sometimes even arguing with management on behalf of public interests. I have done this many times in my career—not always successfully—but I always tried and often succeeded in negotiating outcomes that were mutually acceptable to the organization as well as its publics. At a day-to-day level, many media comments and interviews are gained by PR practitioners acting as intermediaries and recommending and sometimes lobbying senior management. Also, unlike many journalists, PR practitioners are exposed to regular feedback and evaluation from their employers and, most importantly, from their publics. If their activities irritate or alienate publics—including groups such as local communities, organization employees, and activists—they are held accountable.

Many of the journalists I worked with closely during those years were independent critical thinkers who went about their research diligently and wrote frankly and without fear or favour based on analysis they undertook. That analysis frequently included the perspective of my employers and clients, but often they also sought out other information and opinions. I respected and admired them for that. But, in terms of balance, I also observed many journalists who fell into two other categories. One category succumbed to routinized practices. They cleared their in-boxes and wrote stories based largely on news releases. Sure, they threw out the blatant promotion and the trivial. But they followed a well-established convention and scoured the 'press boxes' at Parliament House or Congress and, more recently, the online newsrooms of major organizations. They trudged along to news media conferences and media briefings and they regularly phoned around an established group of sources relevant to their 'beat' or 'round'. They followed a much-routinized tradition of believing there are 'two sides to a story', so when they received a statement or comment, they sought one oppositional view and believed they had reported fairly and fully. Another category of journalists were simply lazy. They were happy to be spoon fed information. Free products to test and free trips were welcome. When they were looking for a story, they simply called up PR practitioners they knew and asked 'have you got something?' An untold story is the number of times that journalists canvass leads and even whole stories from PR practitioners. When they thought they could get away with it, they slightly revised news releases and put their name on the top. Once, a news release I had written appeared not once but twice in the same newspaper under two different by-lines. A journalist in the press gallery in Canberra filed it as a national political story at the same time as a Sydney journalist 'wrote' it as a business story. Embarrassingly it appeared in two sections of the same newspaper on the same day with two different authors—neither of whom had much to do with researching or writing the story.

The point here is not to apportion blame back to journalists or exaggerate the failings of journalists, although extensive experience supports Joe Atkinson's findings about PR and spin in the media that confirm "glaring blind spots" in relation to "the media's own contributory role" (2005, p. 18). In his analysis of the relations among the media, politicians, and their PR staff in New Zealand, Atkinson concluded that "journalists have been co-opted into a symbiotic relationship with the politicians and spin doctors upon whom they depend as sources and whose efforts are calculated to supply precisely those stories the commercialized media are willing to cover" (p. 19). A key point that emerges from practical experience and research is that the relationship between journalism and PR is not one-way or one-sided. Two decades of personal experience support Canadian Jean Charron's description of the journalism–PR nexus as "relations of exchange" and negotiation and his research conclusion that "influence is not a unidirectional phenomenon by which the public relations practitioner 'manipulates' the journalist". He says "in negotiation influence flow[s] in both directions between public relations practitioners and journalists", although he adds that "such a view does not imply that the game of influence is necessarily balanced" (Charron, 1989, p. 52).

These case studies and reflections indicate that generalizations are misrepresentative on both sides. The reality is much more complex and multi-dimensional than popular discourses suggest. However, the purpose here is not to 'gild the lily'. As this chapter is about 'inside PR', let's complete these observations and reflections about PR practice by examining some more problematic case studies and incidents, before moving on to examine contemporary research and the insights that it provides.

Humas and Brown Envelopes for Journalists in Jakarta

In the late 1980s, just before settling back into life in Australia working for Microsoft and then Vodafone as major clients, I spent two years working in Southeast Asia, particularly in Indonesia. This flashback is useful and informative, as there I witnessed another side of PR, known in the local Malay-based language Bahasa Indonesia as *hubungan masyarakat*, or *humas* for short. I also saw another side of media.

In early 1988, my PR firm MACRO Communication won a major international contract to help promote the relaunch of Indonesia's national airline, Garuda Indonesia, working collaboratively with the advertising agency Foote Cone & Belding (FCB). Shortly after, we also won a contract to promote 'Visit Indonesia Year' coordinated by the Directorate-General Tourism (DGT). Even though much of the work was to generate publicity and distribute promotional materials such as colourful brochures, booklets, and videos internationally, the contracts required my firm to establish an office in Jakarta, the national capital of Indonesia. Initially I left the running of the Jakarta office to local staff under the leadership of a manager recruited from Singapore. However, within a short time, the complexities of doing business in Indonesia, the relative infancy of PR practice there, and the model of media operating in Indonesia forced me to become directly involved or risk financial or reputation losses, or both.

Several revelations were experienced working in Indonesia. The model of media in Indonesia at the time was somewhere between the Developmental model as discussed by Baran and Davis (2009) and the Authoritarian model described by Siebert et al. (1956). There was little sign of the Liberal, Democratic Corporatist, or Polarized Pluralist models identified by Hallin and Mancini (2004). The media were seen as having a key role in *polopor pembangunan*—developing the nation. The Director-General of Tourism at the time, Joop Ave, described it to me in frank terms. He pointed out that many parts of the archipelago of Indonesia—with somewhere between 13,000 and 17,000 islands depending on one's reference—lacked clean drinking water and basic hygiene standards. The country of 300 million citizens was still struggling to combat diseases. Many women did not know of or have access to birth control. "In these circumstances, do we want our media broadcasting American or British soap operas or celebrity news?" Joop Ave asked, pointing to the largely trivial content that dominates Western commercial media. I saw his point. Radio in particular played an instrumental role in communicating health messages and educating citizens in relation to basic services because every village and most families owned or had access to a radio, whereas TV was less accessible and some people could not read. I found the same vital role of radio many years later doing research on developmental journalism in the Solomon Islands, which is reported in Chapter 6.

On the other hand, Indonesia was still under the control of President Suharto in 1988 (he was to rule as Indonesia's second president for another decade) and media freedom was severely restricted. When the leading magazine *Tempo* fell afoul of Indonesia's censorship laws, it was closed down. Journalists knew what they could write and what they could not write—and there was a lot they could not write. Journalists were also poorly paid—as were civil servants, including the police, which resulted in widespread bribery, which many locals viewed as a kind of tipping. I soon found that if I expected journalists to attend a news conference or briefing, we had to pay 'transportation allowances'. Ostensibly the payments were to cover the cost of taxis, as most media organizations allegedly did not pay travel costs for their reporters. But often journalists double-dipped, recovering expenses from both their employers and publicity seekers. Furthermore, bigger and better media coverage could be obtained by paying larger transportation allowances. These were usually discretely handed to journalists in brown envelopes when they arrived for interviews or media briefings.

Such practices have become engrained in Indonesia and in many other countries. And the amounts involved are not always small. For instance, in 2011, the Malaysian news agency *Bernama* reported that an Indonesian journalist admitted demanding bribes over a number of years "of up to hundreds of millions of Rupiah to play up issues in the media, presenting deliberately-biased or inaccurate news reports to benefit those paying him" ("Journalist Reveals Bribery", 2011, para. 1). The amounts paid for stories, which the journalist admitted was a routine practice of a number of Indonesian journalists, were reported to range from Rp7.5 million (US$830) to hundreds of millions of Rupiah, depending on the urgency of the issue (para. 4).

Local PR practitioners rarely questioned such practices. During my years in Indonesia, a few practitioners were former journalists and one or two had international professional experience, but most were locals with 'contacts' and social skills, but little training in journalism or PR. Sometimes their contacts were relatives working in government or other influential places. Some others practiced an Asian version of 'Ad Fab'[3] PR, focussed more on entertainment than public communication. In fact, one of the local contacts introduced to me as a potential employee or even business partner soon after I started working in Jakarta was the head of a model agency who specialized in organizing high society functions with lavish entertainment and believed that her team of young models could do PR work. Paying for publicity did not seem to be a problem to under-trained or untrained PR practitioners or journalists.

Payment of transportation allowances to journalists also has been common over the past decade or two in China where they are called *jiaotongfei* (De Mente, 2012, p. 116). International PR professionals increasingly refuse to pay transportation allowances and other forms of payments for media coverage. For example, East-West Public Relations, which has operated in Singapore for many years and in Beijing since 2006, openly tells its clients and journalists that it will not make these payments. The firm's Web site says:

> Whenever we meet with clients in China who are about to make a major announcement with a press briefing, we must explain to them why we do not have a policy of paying attending journalists. This question comes from the common practice of paying journalists a 'transportation allowance' or *jiaotongfei*, which is a small stipend paid to cover transportation to the briefing or interview. Usually these allowances are much higher than the cost of transportation (Dougoud, 2009, para. 1).

Russia has a long-documented history of bribery and corruption when it comes to media coverage. The practice of *zakazukha*—cash for editorial—was exposed and brought to international attention in 2001 when a PR agency in Moscow, as a research project, issued a fictitious news release on the opening of a new store. No less than 16 media publications subsequently initiated negotiations to run the story, without any checking of the facts, in exchange for payment. Invoices were issued by 13 media which then published articles reporting on the opening of the non-existent shop called Svetophor. This occurred despite Russian law which requires paid advertising to be clearly identified and separated from editorial. The International Public Relations Association (IPRA) called for an end to *zakazukha* in Russia (IPRA, 2001). An international survey of 90 countries conducted on behalf of the International Public Relations Association (IPRA) in 2002, which received 242 responses from 54 countries, reported that "'cash for editorial' and other unethical practices are rife in the print and broadcast media of many countries around the world" ("Unethical Media Practices Revealed", 2002, para. 1).

It would be a mistake to think that these practices only occur in what are sometimes called Third World countries, better described as developing nations. In 2005 in the US, the Bush administration acknowledged that it had paid at least three journalists as commentators to support conservative policies, and several departments announced that they were conducting internal inquiries to see if other journalists were employed under government contracts. New Jersey Democrat Senator Frank Lautenberg demanded several investigations into the so-called payola practices (Kornblut, 2005, para. 12).

In *Flat Earth News*, Nick Davies notes that journalists are often complicit in the use of PR tips, information, and angles in media reporting (i.e., framing, and agenda priming, building, and setting in media theory terms). He gave a number of examples, such as US-syndicated columnist Armstrong Williams, a strong George Bush supporter, being found in 2005 to have received US$240,000 in federal government funds through a contract organized by PR firm Ketchum. Shortly after, two other US columnists, Michael McManus and Maggie Gallagher, admitted taking government money while writing pro-government stories (Davies, 2009, p. 196). In the UK, conservative columnist Roger Scruton was found to have received a retainer of £4,500 a month from a Japanese tobacco company while writing in favour of smoking in *The Financial Times*, *The Daily Telegraph*, *The Independent*, *The Times*, and for *The Wall Street Journal* (Davies, 2009, p. 197). The 'cash for comment' scandal in Australia in 1999 exposed that two of the nation's top-rating radio presenters had taken cash in return for making favourable on-air comments about various banks, airlines, and casino companies (Turner, 2001).

During my time working for Microsoft and Vodafone, several major media organizations only too happily agreed to run what are termed advertorials and special supplements. In several cases, the media organizations, including one leading business magazine, approached us—not the other way round. The business magazine even offered to have its technology writer assist in preparing copy, but made it clear that our client could have final say over the content. As discussed in Chapter 3, advertorial is a shadowy practice in which promotional content is presented in editorial format, but it is effectively advertising as the client pays for the space or time and has control over the content. Advertorial is offered by many media worldwide and the practice is growing rather than declining as media face financial pressures and look for new ways to generate revenue, as will be further discussed in Chapter 7.

Such practices place both journalists and PR practitioners in conflicted positions and pose ethical dilemmas, the resolutions of which are not as simple as some suggest. International PR practitioners are advised not to make payments to journalists. But if they follow this advice, they are likely to find their employers and clients disadvantaged and their own effectiveness questioned in some cases. They can even lose clients or their jobs. On the other hand, some are only too happy to go along with the practice as a short-cut to good publicity. How did my PR firm handle these problems, I am sure you are wondering? I and my colleagues made the decision to not directly make any payments of any kind to any party in Indonesia, other than payment of fair prices for goods and legitimate services. To get around the problem of intractable demands for 'kickbacks' and commissions, we followed a long-standing practice of having a local partner, often referred to as a 'Mr Ten Per Cent', because he or she received 10 per cent of all revenues of the firm and, in return, took care of various licences that were required to operate in the country, expected hospitality for local officials, and also payments that needed to be made to do business.

On reflection, and being self-critical, this was more a case of turning a blind eye and believing that 'what we don't see won't hurt us' than it was ethical and transparent practice. It was at best a work-around. At worst, it was a cop-out and a compromise of our principles. It was rationalized, by both journalists and PR practitioners, as 'the way things are done around here'. Reflectivity and reflexivity also require me to admit that many of the techniques used by spokespersons in media interviews, such as staying 'on message', repeating key messages, and not necessarily answering journalists' questions were taught to clients in media training workshops at MACRO Communication. I conducted such courses for more than a decade and also published a management handbook called *How to Handle the Media* (Macnamara, 1996b). While urging truthfulness and helping journalists to some extent by giving advice to spokespersons, such as "be accessible", "be brief", and "keep it simple", the handbook also explained techniques for "managing the interview" and pursuing the organization's communication objectives irrespective of journalists' questions. Why write such a book and give such advice? Because many organization spokespersons did not have a clue how to get their point across in the pressure-cooker environment of media interviews and also most were extremely vulnerable when confronted with 'attack dog' and ambush interviews—aggressive techniques that media sometimes use that can cause spokespersons to say things they don't mean. Such issues further illustrate the complex interrelationships that exist between journalism and PR, the shared responsibility for many practices, and the over-simplification of blaming one or the other for problems that exist in relation to our media.

Another PR practice referred to in Chapter 3 also has caused me a degree of personal discomfort. On at least two occasions in my career as a PR consultant I advised organizations on how to keep bad news out of the media and implemented the strategy on their behalf. In the first, I was confidentially briefed by international management of a large multinational company that the country CEO was to be fired following a number of 'incidents' and complaints. The most serious was that he had been reported for inappropriate conduct with a young female member of his staff, and there were rumours of other inappropriate advances. However, none of the young women wanted to take the matter further or be identified. While they were offered counselling and support, I was left with the dilemma of how to announce the sacking of the CEO without revealing confidences and without causing speculation that could identify and harm the women and the company. A much less serious but vexing issue in the company at the time was that the CEO had not long before signed up to a multi-million-dollar sport sponsorship that many felt was a waste of money, as it involved an elite sport that was not aligned to the company's market segments. The former 'news hound' in me knew that media would demand a reason for the CEO's sudden departure—I had to 'throw the media a bone', and this was it. I crafted a statement saying that the country CEO was being dismissed for poor financial management and poor judgement in relation to the sponsorship that had cost the company several million dollars and alienated some of its key stakeholders. The media lapped up the story and never looked further. I justified the cover-up on the basis that the young women's privacy was protected (which they requested), the CEO left knowing the real reasons for his dismissal and severely chastened, and the company's reputation was protected, as cancellation of the elite sponsorship was seen as a positive step by shareholders, customers, and staff. It seemed to be a win all round, or at least a best available solution. But was it ethical PR? And what does it say about journalism?

The second case is even more troubling. Its execution was simple. No lies were told. No information was withheld. Timing can be everything in handling bad news, as British Transport Ministry PR head Jo Moore infamously demonstrated after 9/11 (see Chapter 5 under 'Agenda Cutting'). During my years in PR, my consultancy firm was contacted to provide crisis communication after an airliner crashed in Southeast Asia, killing all passengers (I am compelled to be vague on the time and location due to ongoing confidentiality and legal issues). The investigation reported that terrorism was unlikely, given the location and nationalities of passengers, and raised serious questions about safety procedures and the pilot—both of which were likely to seriously damage the airline's reputation and potentially its business if they made the headlines. The crisis communication strategy involved delaying release of the investigation report for several months to allow the airline time to implement changes and then releasing it between Christmas and New Year—a time when Western media are in holiday mode and largely 'asleep' to all but the biggest news stories. Chinese New Year was also looming and the report passed into aviation history with little media coverage. To be fair, it must be said that the airline met all its legal responsibilities, including payment of compensation to victims, and implemented all the recommendations of the investigation. So was this avoidance of ruinous media coverage simply clever PR, or spin at its worst? Or was it a failure of journalism because of its tendency to ignore or quickly forget issues that are no longer new and/or far from home and its focus on entertainment and 'light' stories to match seasons and popular taste. Or was it both?

While PR practitioners are blamed for many questionable and unethical practices, sometimes with good reason, this chapter has sought to illustrate three important points. First, PR is deployed in many day-to-day honest information dissemination functions that are, in the least, useful and which can even be beneficial for society. It bears repeating that generalizing about PR is usually misleading. Second, in recognizing and examining an insidious side of PR and its impact on media and public communication, it needs to be recognized that PR is a service industry engaged by organizations—government departments and agencies, corporations, NGOs, and non-profits. While PR practitioners need to take personal responsibility for their actions, individual practitioners and PR firms are subject to employer and client lines of reporting and power relations, which means that employer organizations should be held most accountable when practices are misleading, manipulative, fraudulent, or cover-ups. Many of the problematic case studies and examples cited in this chapter, and in Chapter 3, involve bad corporate or government behaviour that is often genericized as 'PR' and sheeted home to one group of professionals and one disciplinary practice. The James Hardie Industries case is significant in that it is one in which company directors were held responsible for misleading media releases, rather than assigning blame and punishment to PR as a 'whipping boy'. Third, and perhaps most important of all in terms of the focus of this book, case studies show that PR and journalism are often in lockstep. To some that might sound like PR spin doctors trying to pass the buck. But journalism and the PR industry need to recognize the interconnection and interdependence of their practices and share responsibility for implementing standards and maintaining integrity, while at the same time performing their respective roles in a complex pluralist world.

Postscript to a PR Career

Despite working in various forms of PR, including corporate communication and marketing communication, for almost 20 years spanning government, industry, and consultancy, I maintained a passion for journalism and a deep interest in the role of media. In 1997 I sold the last of my shares in the PR consultancy I co-founded, MACRO Communication, and went into full-time media and communication research. In this role I was involved in media content analysis to track issues and trends and evaluate the effectiveness of communication campaigns, ranging from public health education and promotion to corporate reputation analysis. After crossing from journalism to PR, I crossed to yet another side—that of independent researcher looking back at journalism and PR and systematically and critically analyzing the activities of both.

In 2001, the five-page *Sydney Morning Herald* feature article titled 'The Hidden Persuaders', which was referred to in Chapter 1 (Cadzow, 2001), named MACRO Communication in the second paragraph in relation to an ethics complaint against its joint managing director at the time. As Jane Cadzow reported, the Public Relations Institute of Australia (PRIA) "censured" the PR firm's managing director. She noted, however, that "the reprimand was not reported", not even in the PR Institute's newsletter (p. 20). Even though I had sold my shares in the consultancy and ceased all involvement four years previously, this case was uncomfortably close to home for me, not only because it was my former business but also because I was the national president of the PRIA at the time. In fact, I had the unpleasant task of delivering the censure to the managing director, a former colleague. That the matter was not reported was also an uncomfortable reality. What many critics fail to recognize is that industry and professional associations such as the PRIA, like the PRSA in the US, have no statutory power or legal authority to act against members who breach their codes of ethics or principles. These bodies attempting self-regulation rely on voluntary compliance achieved predominantly through education and promotion of professional standards. Legal advisers informed the PRIA and me that any public statement we made that was damaging to a member would make the institute and me personally liable for defamation and potentially a damages claim. Thus, when breaches of ethics do occur, the only power available to industry and professional associations and institutes, other than those that are 'chartered' (such as the Institute of Chartered Accountants and the Chartered Institute of Public Relations in the UK), is the power to impose the professional shame of censure within their field or, in extreme cases, expel members. This ethics case and several others that I presided over during my time as president of the PRIA and a member of the International Public Relations Association (IPRA) brought me close to the matters that others talk about from a distance. I have seen the good and the bad of PR from the inside, as well as from the vantage point of an outside observer.

On a happier note, in 2005 my wife and I took a few months off work to undertake a driving adventure from our home in Sydney across the centre of Australia to its remote and rugged northwest coast and back—a total distance of more almost 12,000 kilometres (almost 7,500 miles). Along with obligatory emergency supplies and a GPS system, two-way radio, and satellite phone in our four-wheel drive, we took along two cameras and two notebook computers to record images and stories of people and places we encountered. The stories we discovered resulted in several articles that I wrote for travel and lifestyle magazines. Journalism gets into your blood and it never leaves.

More than a decade spent working in a media research company (1995–2006) and doing a PhD in media research led to a full-time academic position in 2007, which I have held since and enjoy greatly. It is important to note that at the time of researching this book I did not work in PR or journalism, but have studied both closely as a media researcher and scholar for almost 20 years. This affords an independent perspective and distance to look back reflectively. Previous experience working in journalism and PR ensures a practice-grounded approach. In addition, this analysis looks laterally in a contemporary context through new primary research reported in Chapter 6, and forward in analysis presented in Chapter 7 and Chapter 8.

Notes

1. The Lockheed Martin C-130 Hercules is a short take-off and landing (STOL) aircraft, which allows it to take off and land in very short distances and without the need for prepared runways. It is widely used around the world and in 2007 became one of the few aircraft to have been in continuous production for 50 years.
2. MACRO Communication was a PR and communication consultancy firm operating in Australia, Singapore, and Indonesia from 1985 to the early 2000s that took its name from the surnames of the two founders, Jim Macnamara and Andrew Royal, as well as the common computing term 'macro', which refers to a sequence of macro-instructions that execute computer functions. After changing its name to MACRO Consulting and then to Upstream Australia in 2003 (Bloomberg, 2014), the consultancy was fully acquired by Upstream Marketing and Communications Inc. in 2007 (LSE, 2007).
3. Abbreviation of the British comedy TV series *Absolutely Fabulous*.

CHAPTER FIVE

What 100 Years of Media Research Reveals

The discourse of denial within journalism and the blind spot in media studies, sociology, and cultural studies about the practices and influence of PR flies in the face of extensive empirical evidence gained from numerous studies conducted over the past 100 years. A review by Lynne Sallot and Elizabeth Johnson in 2006 estimated that "more than 150 studies have examined some aspect of relations between public relations practitioners as news sources and journalists as media gatekeepers since the 1960s" (2006, p. 151). With many other studies dating back to the very early 20th century, and a number conducted since Sallot and Johnson's review, it is likely that 200 or more research studies have examined the interrelationship between journalism and PR.

On the face of it, this might seem to indicate thorough attention, or even over-analysis, as Brian Smith (2008) warns. However, in addition to summarizing the findings of some of these studies which conclusively show substantial influence of PR on mass media news and other forms of content, this chapter also identifies the scant amount of qualitative research undertaken and illustrates the importance of this type of analysis in exploring why and how the ambiguous and contradictory relationship between journalists and PR practitioners is maintained and its implications for society.

The Influence of Press Agents in the Early 20th Century

In a history of American journalism, Willard Bleyer (1973) reported that even before World War I the "system of supplying newspapers with publicity and propaganda in the guise of news became so popular that a census of accredited press agents" was conducted by New York newspapers (p. 421). This identified around 1,200 press agents working to influence public opinion through mass media. As discussed in Chapter 3, the terms 'press agent' and 'publicity counsellor' were forerunners of PR pioneered by Ivy Lee in New York in 1904 (Grunig & Hunt, 1984), before the term 'public relations' was coined and popularized by Edward Bernays (1923).

Editors and journalists increasingly found themselves faced with a growing band of intermediaries standing between the media and sources of news and information. As Bird and Merwin (1955) noted in their historical review: "The newspaper faced a choice between accepting the releases of press agents, or failing to report many facts needed for the record" (p. 521).

The Growing Influence of PR, 1920–2000

In 1926, Silas Bent (1927) reported that a systematic study of *The New York Times* found 147 of the 256 news stories in the newspaper on December 29 of that year had been suggested, created, or supplied by PR practitioners. Only 83 stories were identified as independently generated by journalists and the origin of 26 was uncertain. However, Bent did not analyze sport, society, or real estate stories, and DeLorme and Fedler observe that all of the 50 real estate stories in *The Times* "seemed to have originated with publicists" (2003, p. 111).

Paul Bixler (1930) concluded from a study that women's pages in newspapers were almost totally dependent on publicists and that many stories in business sections were also heavily influenced by these early PR practitioners. He reported that only stories about crime were unaffected by PR at the time. In 1934, Stanley Walker identified 42 of 64 local stories in one newspaper "were written or pasted up from press agent material: a little more than 60 per cent" (1999, p. 147).

In 1963, a series of studies of news media in Milwaukee found that around 45 per cent of news reports in newspapers and around 15 per cent of news on radio and television originated to some extent from PR sources (Grunig & Hunt, 1984, p. 225).

In 1973, Leon Sigal classified the sources of 1,146 stories in *The Washington Post* and *The New York Times* and found that around 75 per cent resulted from what he called "information processing" as opposed to proactively researched information. He concluded that 50 per cent of stories came from routine sources such as official proceedings as well as press releases and press conferences, another 16 per cent came from unofficial sources such as leaks, and only 26 per cent of news resulted from enterprise reporting, interviews, or journalists' own analysis (Grunig & Hunt, 1984, p. 229). Overall, Sigal concluded that around two-thirds of media stories originated from news releases, handouts, and other documents handed to reporters by news sources (Grossberg et al., 2006, p. 352).

Similarly, in a widely reported content analysis of US national TV news and news magazines in 1979, sociologist Herbert Gans reported that 75 per cent of all news came from government and commercial sources. Gans was also one of the first to examine specific sectors of media reporting, referred to by journalists as 'beats' or 'rounds', such as business and finance, crime, transport, entertainment, travel, sport, and so on. He noted: "Beat reporters are drawn into a symbiotic relationship of mutual obligation with their sources, which both facilitates and complicates their work" (1979, p. 133).

Studies of reporting within specific 'beats' have found consistently heavy reliance on PR. For instance, David Sachsman (1976) analyzed environmental coverage in San Francisco newspapers and found that 53 per cent of 200 articles on environmental issues were directly derived from PR sources and half were lightly rewritten press releases. Sharon Dunwoody (1978) wrote a PhD dissertation reporting her study of science reporting during and following an American Association for the Advancement of Science convention, which showed PR efforts were instrumental in gaining national media coverage of science. A content analysis of major US newspapers in 1979–1980 by Jane Brown, Carl Bybee, Stanley Wearden, and Dulcie Straughan (1987) found that 80 per cent of wire service stories on health issues relied on official proceedings (e.g., of conferences and seminars), press releases, and press conferences. Writing in Canada, Jean Charron (1989) observed that journalists in different fields have distinctly different objectives and requirements, noting for example that "in the area of sports, journalists and public relations practitioners do not behave in the same way as in the sphere of politics" (p. 47). This further emphasizes the need to drill down into specific fields of practice rather than treat PR, or journalism, as generic and seek universalized truths.

Lawrence Grossberg et al. (2006, p. 351) cite a number of other 1980s studies in the US (e.g., Whitney, Fritzler, Jones, Mazzarella, & Rakow, 1989), which suggest that up to three-quarters of editorial media content is drawn from PR or government sources. Judy VanSlyke Turk (1986) found that newspapers used 51 per cent of all news releases distributed by six state government agencies, resulting in 183 news stories which accounted for 48 per cent of all stories published about the agencies. A late 1980s study of small television stations found that 59 per cent of their content was linked to PR (Abbott & Brassfield, 1989).

Research in Europe has gained similar findings. Studies by Barbara Baerns in the 1970s and 1980s found that journalists are heavily influenced by PR in terms of both topics and timing, which led her to develop an influence model that she called the *determination model* (Baerns, as cited in Bentele & Nothhaft, 2008, p. 34). Günter Bentele, Tobias Liebert, and Stefan Seeling (1997) developed their *intereffication model* to explain the relationship between journalism and PR, which they argue is more complex and profound than simple commonly used metaphors such as 'symbiosis' which carries positive connotations or 'Siamese twins' which "suggests a negative, somewhat pathological state of affairs" (Bentele & Nothhaft, 2008, p. 35). The term *effication* is not in most English dictionaries, but is used in science to refer to efficacy—the power to cause an effect. Thus, intereffication is a neologism referring to mutual or reciprocal effects.

These studies from the 1920s through the 1980s show that media use of PR information is not a new phenomenon and, therefore, cannot be attributed to comparatively recent reductions in journalist staff levels as often claimed. Newspaper circulation and journalist staff levels were growing during this period, with US weekday newspaper circulation reaching its peak in 1984 (Newspaper Association of America, 2012a). Television, introduced in the 1940s and 1950s, enjoyed rapid growth through the 1960s, 1970s, and 1980s.

Research studies in Australia during the 1990s have similarly found PR influence on media varying from the 30–40 per cent range to the 70–80 per cent range. These include an analysis of the impact of political PR on *The Courier Mail* in Brisbane conducted by Ian Ward in 1992, analysis of the relationship between police and reporters by Paul Grabowski and Paul Wilson in 1996, and studies by Rodney Tiffin that estimated (although did not substantiate) that up to 80 per cent of the content of metropolitan newspapers is provided by PR (as cited in Zawawi, 1994, 2001).

Based on my experiences and observations working both as a journalist and as a PR practitioner, as discussed in Chapter 4, in 1992 I decided to undertake a Master of Arts by research to examine this relationship. This study (Macnamara, 1993) triangulated data from a survey of journalists designed to identify the type and level of their contact with PR, a content analysis of stories published by the same journalists and their publications, and an analysis of news releases and statements issued by PR practitioners during the same period. A survey of 417 journalists and editors in Sydney, Melbourne, Brisbane, and Canberra, which received 143 responses (a 34 per cent response rate), found that 86 per cent reported very frequent contact from PR practitioners, with more than 74 per cent receiving 20 or more PR communications such as news releases, phone calls, or faxes per week. In the same period, 150 news releases from 27 different companies and organizations were obtained and content analysis was undertaken of the media in which the surveyed journalists were employed over a six-month period. Articles were sourced using a national press clipping service which retrieved 2,500 articles from the selected media on the topics discussed in the tracked news releases. The study found that 768 stories (31 per cent) were wholly or substantially based on news releases, including verbatim extracts of statements and facts and figures without alternative attribution. While 360 (47 per cent) of these were published in trade or specialist media, 245 (32 per cent) of PR-based stories were published in national, state, or capital city media. Up to 70 per cent of the content of some small trade, specialist, and suburban media was PR-sourced and only nine news releases out of 150 tracked (1.2 per cent) were not used at all in the media. One news release about a new wine released by Lindeman Wines was published in 69 newspapers, many with a photograph provided by the PR firm.

A subsequent analysis of Australian media use of PR material carried out by Clara Zawawi (1994, 2001) analyzed 1,163 articles published by three leading Australian metropolitan newspapers, *The Courier-Mail* (Brisbane), *The Sydney Morning Herald*, and *The Age* (Melbourne) to identify the origin of media stories. Her research was able to confirm the origin of 683 of the articles, of which 251 (37 per cent) were directly the result of PR activity. Furthermore, Zawawi argued that surveys, papers, and submissions sent to journalists with the intent of gaining media coverage could also be regarded as PR and these accounted for another 88 articles. In total, she concluded that 47 per cent of articles in these three major capital city newspapers emanated from PR.

PR-ization of Media in the 21st Century

Studies of the sources of media content continued in the early 21st century. For example, a national study of health reporting by local TV stations across the US by Andrea Tanner (2004) found that reporters received most of their story ideas from personal contacts with PR practitioners, and news releases were the second most frequently used source of health information. This was acknowledged by reporters themselves, as the study was based on a nationwide survey of journalists who reported on health. Similarly, Lynne Sallot and Elizabeth Johnson (2006) analyzed 413 reports of interviews with US journalists conducted between 1991 and 2004 and found that, on average, journalists estimated that 44 per cent of the content of US news media was the result of PR contact. Journalists' estimates could be expected to be conservative, given negative attitudes towards PR widely expressed among them.

An extensive 2008 study conducted by Cardiff University found that 60 per cent of Britain's leading newspapers and 34 per cent of broadcast stories was comprised wholly of wire service copy or PR material (Lewis, Williams, Franklin, Thomas, & Mosdell, 2008, p. 3). Verifying PR information is difficult because of the secrecy that surrounds PR–journalist interaction and the sheer scale of media releases and PR statements to be tracked—not to mention undocumented contacts such as phone calls, e-mails, text messages, and private conversations. The Cardiff University study commented:

> Since our analysis of the influence of PR is based only on those *verifiable* instances where we could find PR source material, it is almost certainly an underestimate. Nevertheless, our findings suggest that public relations often does much more than merely set the agenda: we found that 19 per cent of newspaper stories and 17 per cent of broadcast stories were verifiably derived *mainly or wholly* from PR material, while less than half the stories we looked at appeared to be entirely independent of traceable PR (Lewis et al., 2008, p. 3).

The study reported that "a further 13 per cent of press articles and 6 per cent of broadcast news items were categorized under the heading 'looks like PR but not found/ongoing'" (Lewis et al., 2008, p. 20). In other words, the Cardiff University study suggested that more than half of the content of leading British newspapers and broadcast networks was influenced by PR in some way. It commented that "many stories apparently written by one of the newspaper's own reporters seem to have been cut and pasted from elsewhere" (Lewis et al., 2008, p. 15) and only 12 per cent of British press articles could be established to be entirely independent (p. 25). The study was based on a substantial sample, involving 2,207 newspaper articles and 402 radio and TV reports. Coverage spanned crime, politics, business, health, and entertainment (Lewis et al., 2008, p. 13–14).

In the US, a 2008 survey of more than 12,000 editors and journalists with 745 responses conducted by research company Cision in conjunction with George Washington University reported that 94 per cent said that they use information from PR practitioners, and 87 per cent said they regularly refer to press/media kits (Bates & Arno, 2009, pp. 8–9).

A 2009 Pew Research Center Project for Excellence in Journalism study of the reporting of 60 media outlets in Baltimore, Maryland, over the course of a week (July 25–29) found that "63 per cent of stories were initiated by government officials", particularly the police, and a further 23 per cent of stories were initiated by interest groups. Thus, up to 86 per cent of media coverage could be attributed to PR. Only 14 per cent of media stories could be identified as proactive research and reporting by journalists (Pew Research Center, 2009, p. 3). The Pew report concluded: "Much of the 'news' people receive contains no original reporting. Fully 8 out of 10 stories studied simply repeated or repackaged previously published information" (p. 1).

Nick Davies reported that a *Columbia University Review* study of a single edition of *The Wall Street Journal* found that more than half of the news stories "were based solely on press releases". Davies further commented that "these were reprinted almost verbatim or in paraphrase, with little additional reporting, but with the classic and dishonest byline 'By a *Wall Street Journal* reporter'" (as cited in Davies, 2009, p. 97).

A 2010 study by the Australian Centre for Independent Journalism at the University of Technology, Sydney, headed by veteran journalism educator Wendy Bacon, similarly found that, on average, almost 55 per cent of the stories in 10 leading Australian newspapers were the result of some form of PR activity. PR influence on content ranged from 42 per cent in *The Sydney Morning Herald* over a five-day working week to 70 per cent in *The Daily Telegraph* ("Over half your news is spin", 2010).

In 2011, Helen Sissons spent more than 70 hours in two newsrooms in New Zealand observing news production and also collected 35 media releases to match against news stories published. Sissons (2012) reported that 23 of the 35 media releases were reproduced word-for-word, or almost word-for-word, in the media. In only eight stories based on the 35 media releases was new material added by the journalists, such as additional quotes or statistics (p. 279). She concluded that "journalists are in many instances not carrying out the traditional practice of checking information. Instead, journalists appear to be replicating the material given to them by public relations professionals" (p. 274). She noted that many studies suggest that journalists usually make significant changes to media releases, but she reported: "My research shows that this is happening less and less. From the data, it appears news outlets are increasingly publishing public relations material almost or completely unchanged" (p. 275).

In some specialist sections of the media, the percentage of PR material used is even higher than these broad studies show. For example, Linda Strahan (2011) conducted a content analysis of the arts pages of two leading Melbourne newspapers and found 97 per cent of articles about the arts in *The Age* and 98 per cent of articles about the arts in *The Herald-Sun* contained high levels of PR content.

The use of PR material is not only a Western media phenomenon. In 2003, Karmen Erjavec from the University of Ljubljana in Slovenia conducted an ethnographic study observing news gathering and production operations inside four daily newspapers in Slovenia over a period of 12 weeks, supported by in-depth interviews. Erjavec (2005) reported that "PR sources are a main source of information". Observed journalists routinely obtained information from news conferences, media releases via e-mail, fax, and Internet access, and via telephone calls and face-to-face conversations with PR practitioners. The study reported "an oversaturation of PR information" with up to 18 different pieces of PR information received per journalist per day in the newsrooms (p. 160).

A 2013 digital journalism study based on a survey of more than 500 journalists in 14 countries including Australia, Brazil, Canada, China, France, Germany, India, Italy, New Zealand, Russia, Spain, Sweden, the UK, and the USA by the Oriella PR Network found that, after 'industry insiders', journalists' main sources of news and verification of news are wire services, corporate spokespeople, and PR agencies, followed by increasing reliance on social media such as microblogs and blogs (see Figure 5.1). While this was a PR industry study, which could be seen to be self-serving in some respects, it echoes the findings of a substantial body of independent scholarly research.

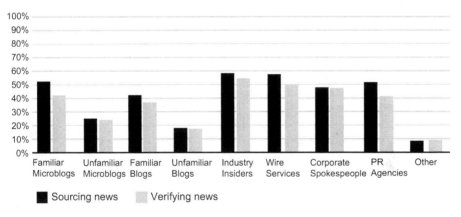

Figure 5.1. Sources of news and verification of news by journalists (Oriella, 2013).

Extensive data from quantitative studies conducted over the past 100 years show that somewhere between 30 and 80 per cent of media content is sourced from or significantly influenced by PR, with estimates of 50–80 per cent common. This wide range is not an indicator of 'rubbery' figures but, rather, reflects varying levels of independence among journalists and differences between types of media (e.g., national, trade, local) and between 'rounds' or 'beats' such as business, sport, property, IT, shipping, crime, and so on. General news sections of large quality newspapers do not seem to be as influenced by PR as some sections—although many media rely on wire services for general news with 47 per cent of UK national newspapers "wholly or mainly wire copy" according to the Cardiff University study (Lewis et al., 2008, p. 4). Police PR departments provide much crime information.

Similarly, finance sections of media rely heavily on financial results released by public companies to stock exchanges and in company annual reports and statements by CEOs. Sectors such as IT and motoring inevitably have an interest in new product launches and product reviews, which in almost all cases requires contact with PR practitioners. Trade media, in particular, have different roles than daily news media and closer affiliation with industrial and commercial interests by the former is to be expected.

In the journalism textbook *Journalism Principles and Practices*, Tony Harcup (2009) says frankly in a discussion of sources of information:

> Journalists and PR people love to hate—or at least poke gentle fun at—each other. But the fruits of the PR industry's labours are there for all to see in the media every day, so the reality is that PR is a major source for many journalists (p. 72).

Reporting on the launch of Editorial Intelligence headed by Julia Hobsbawm in London, John Plunkett wrote in *The Guardian*:

> The normal journalistic approach to PRs—i.e., dogs and lamp posts—is grossly self-serving from the point of view of journalists. It glosses over, ignores or even denies the fact that much of current journalism, both broadcast and press, is public relations in the sense that stories, ideas, features and interviews are either suggested, or in the extreme actually written by public relations people. Until that becomes open and debated between PR people and journalists, we will continue to have this artificially wide gulf where journalists pose as fearless seekers of truth and PRs are slimy creatures trying to put one over on us. It is not remotely like that (Plunkett, 2006, paras. 9–10).

Former journalist Jim Parker[1] who crossed over to the 'dark side' of PR says:

> The 'dark corporate PR forces' are no longer camped *outside*. They broke through the editorial walls long ago. The copy written by publicity agents, corporate communication flaks, advertisers and political minders now makes up the bulk of what is sold to the public as 'journalism' (2011, para. 5) [original emphasis].

While blaming the decline in the number of journalists employed to research, write, and check stories as the main cause of media "passing on unchecked PR to their readers and viewers" (2009, p. 194), Nick Davies challenges the discourse of victimhood by acknowledging that many journalists voluntarily feed from the hand of PR. For instance, he says: "Political reporters—like most of their colleagues—are wholly complicit in assisting PR operatives like Alastair Campbell to have their way with them" (2009, p 196). He adds: "Political correspondents, just like most other reporters, turn to press officers, particularly those who speak for official sources, where they are handed stories on a plate with a sprig of parsley on top" (p. 196).

The 'Culture War' in Media Production

Notwithstanding their reliance on PR-supplied leads and materials and even though many have changed careers to work in PR, a trend that started as early as the 1890s according to Paul Lancaster (1992), many journalists continue to express negative perceptions of and attitudes towards PR (DeLorme & Fedler, 2003; Jeffers, 1977; Kopenhaver, 1985; Kopenhaver, Martinson, & Ryan, 1984; Ryan & Martinson, 1988; Stegall & Sanders, 1986; White & Shaw, 2005; Wilson & Supa, 2013). From their historical review of journalist–PR relations, Denise DeLorme and Fred Fedler (2003, p. 101) conclude that the source–reporter relationship is "tense and complex", existing in a state of what Eric Louw (2005) calls "symbiotic tension" (pp. 149–150). In their study in New Zealand, Elspeth Tilley and James Hollings (2008) describe journalist–PR interaction as an "enduring and impassioned duality" of a "love–hate relationship". Delorme and Fedler go further and state that "journalists seem to treat public relations and its practitioners with contempt" (2003, p. 99). That hate and contempt are not exaggerations is clear in the opening sentence of an article about PR in the online media, politics, and business journal *Crikey* which states: "We all know how much *Crikey* hates the manipulative PR industry." The article referred to PR as "fatuous" and "a sinful industry" ("Spin doctors and manipulators exposed", 2000).

Based on a survey of education reporters and university PR directors, Sandra Stegall and Keith Sanders (1986) report that journalists see PR as "mercenary", "having less honourable intentions", and "unaware of the valuable role reporters play in…a democratic society" (p. 347). Negative attitudes of journalists towards PR identified by Jeffers (1977), DeLorme and Fedler (2003), and others have continued in the 21st century, according to research by Thomas Littlewood (2002) and a 2012 study by Drew Wilson and Dustin Supa (2013), as well as anecdotal evidence provided in media articles and popular texts discussed in Chapter 1.

If the perceptions that journalists have of PR practitioners are accurate—that is, they are "less honourable" or dishonourable (Stegall & Sanders, 1986); "sleazy", "disingenuous" "manipulative charlatans", and "scumbags" (Simpson, 2002, para. 4); "slickly untruthful or half-truthful" (Cohen, 2009, para. 6); involved in fabrication of "pseudo-evidence", "pseudo-events", "pseudo-leaks", "pseudo-pictures", "pseudo-illnesses", and "pseudo-groups" (Davies, 2009, pp. 172–193); "lies" (Stauber & Rampton, 1995); and "manipulation" (Davies, 2009, p. 167), as has been discussed—then the conclusive findings about their substantial influence on media content and public communication reported in this chapter should be a matter of urgent concern. Such a situation would surely warrant a Commission of Inquiry or a Royal Commission?

However, what is more likely the case is that the "myth of the spin doctor", as Frank Esser calls it, and "the demonization of spin" (2008, p. 4786), along with the generalized condemnation of PR that frequents media debate, are a mixture of genuine valid concerns and media rhetoric based on fear, defensiveness, ideological positions, arrogance at times, and a lack of knowledge in many cases. Even though PR practitioners as well as journalists are now recognized as cultural intermediaries involved, for better or worse, in the production of symbolic goods and services in contemporary societies (Hodges, 2006; Negus, 2002; Nixon & du Gay, 2002), journalists are resentful of this encroachment into what many regard as their exclusive domain. To some extent, the animosity expressed, the denials, and the posturing are part of a culture war among the key players involved in media content production. It is important to question these claims and probe behind the rhetoric. As Esser says, the branding of all PR as spin and the wholesale demonizing of spin "conceals the fact that...PR experts provide essential information, without which the media could not possibly carry out their task of informing the public" (p. 4786). While Esser made this comment referring to politics, the same is even truer of many other areas ranging from information on emergency and social services to reporting on war zones. On the other hand, as this analysis has attempted to even-handedly show, the rhetoric about PR ('PR for PR') also needs to be unpacked and critically examined.

A review of social science literature by Glen Cameron, Lynne Sallot, and Patricia Curtin concludes that "assumptions of outright animosity may be exaggerated and generalized" (1997, pp. 111). A number of studies have concluded that journalists and PR practitioners share similar news values (e.g., Kopenhaver, Martinson, & Ryan, 1984; Sallot, Steinfatt, & Salwen, 1998), although research by Sandra Stegall and Keith Sanders (1986) found that they do not perceive each other as having shared values. Michael Ryan and David Martinson (1994) found that journalists and PR practitioners also have similar views on what constitutes lying, although they note that journalists "expect [PR] practitioners to be evasive and withhold information", so the finding may not be entirely positive (p. 210). Nevertheless, Lynne Sallot and Elizabeth Johnson (2006) note that the two fields of practice work together on a regular basis and that "practitioners benefit journalists by offering information journalists would never otherwise have known" (p. 156). Sallot and Johnson (2006) also confirm what they termed the *Jeffers' Syndrome*—the finding by Dennis Jeffers (1977) that, while journalists generally denigrate PR practitioners collectively, they view individual PR practitioners with whom they work closely more favourably and sometimes even quite favourably.

Other research shows a high degree of ambivalence among journalists about PR, possibly based on confusion, or a mixture of confusion, guilt, and ignorance.

For example, a survey of graduates working in journalism conducted by media researchers Simon Frith and Peter Meech in the UK found that, in response to a question asking whether journalism and PR are part of the same occupational field, 22 said they were not, but 8 thought they were. Asked if they were different occupations, 31 per cent said yes, but 7 said no. When asked if journalism and PR were opposed occupations, 15 said yes, 3 were partially of that view, 13 said no, and 19 did not answer (Frith & Meech, 2007, p. 154). Such findings suggest that journalists have very mixed views of PR and many are not sure how to understand the position and role of PR in media practice.

A recent analysis by Göran Eriksson and Johan Östman (2013) presents three perspectives on journalist–politician relations and the same model could be used as a framework to examine the interactions between journalism and PR. They identified a *dependence* model, a more reciprocal *exchange* model, and an *adversary* model (pp. 305–306). In their study they found that none of the three models applied consistently. Rather, they conclude that the relationship between political actors varies at different stages in news gathering and production. For instance, while journalists often rely on news releases and access to officials at the first stage of news gathering (dependence), they often switch to an adversary mode during interviews (referred to as the 'attack dog' interview at its extreme).

However, a significant limitation of the literature available is that most of the studies exploring the relationships between journalists and PR practitioners have used quantitative research methods only, particularly surveys which rely on self-reporting, and do not provide in-depth qualitative information or insights (e.g., Aronoff, 1975; Cho, 2006; Habermann, Kopenhaver, & Martinson, 1988; Kopenhaver, Martinson, & Ryan, 1984; Ryan & Martinson, 1984, 1994; Sallot, Steinfatt, & Salwen, 1998; Shin & Cameron, 2005). Many others have used quantitative content analysis (e.g., Bent, 1927; Eriksson & Östman, 2013); Gans, 1979; Lewis et al., 2008; Macnamara, 1993; Sigal, 1973; Strahan, 2011; Walker, 1999; Zawawi, 1994, 2001. Some others such as Lynne Sallot (2002) have used experiments, administered using questionnaires. While a widely cited study by Candace White and Thomasena Shaw (2005) used qualitative textual analysis, it focussed on how PR is portrayed in the most commonly used textbooks in introductory mass communication courses, rather than first-hand accounts or observations of actual practices. These studies all provide useful information, but only a relatively few studies have used qualitative research methods such as in-depth interviews or ethnography to look beyond the ratings, scores, and tick-a-box evaluations that participants give themselves and each other in surveys and the coding of texts undertaken from a temporal, spatial, and cultural distance.

As noted, Dennis Jeffers (1977) suggests that journalists are more favourably disposed towards PR practitioners whom they know personally and work with closely than those whom they do not know. This potentially significant finding, which indicates that the *personal influence* model of communication may play a part, is supported by the findings of Michael Ryan and David Martinson (1988) and Jae-Hwa Shin and Glen Cameron (2003), but they too rely primarily on quantitative survey methodologies. Of qualitative studies using in-depth interviews that have been undertaken to explore the complex journalism–PR nexus, most have been small and limited to one country or even one city or region. For example, based on interviews, Australian PR scholars Katrina Oakham and Bronwyn Kirby (2006) reported that the personal relationship between PR practitioners and journalists is important in gaining media coverage. Also, a qualitative study of PR and media interaction in regional Australia conducted by Kristy Hess and Lisa Waller (2008) reported that all media officers working with local councils claimed to have excellent and close relationships with local journalists. While adopting a qualitative approach, a weakness of both of these studies is that they interviewed PR practitioners only, which means the results are based on one perspective only. Furthermore, their findings were based on small samples—seven PR practitioners in the research by Oakham and Kirby and six in the study by Hess and Waller. The ethnographic study of newsrooms by Karmen Erjavec (2005) was conducted in Slovenia only and a similar study by Helen Sissons (2012) was undertaken in just one city in New Zealand.

For these reasons, and because of rapid changes in the mediascape influenced by emerging technologies and new media platforms including social media and social networks, further in-depth qualitative research is essential in this important area, informed by the empirical research data and findings gained to date and also by the substantial body of research-based theory relevant to journalism, media, and PR. The cluster of framing and agenda-related theories that are widely applied in media studies are used as a framework for the in-depth qualitative study of the interrelationships between journalism and PR reported in the next chapter, along with a key communication theory that informs analysis of the ethics and societal effects of public communication.

Architects of Framing, Priming, and Agenda Building, Setting, and Cutting

From the past century or more of media research, a number of key theories have been developed which provide frameworks for analyzing media practices in terms of who does what to whom with what effect (to paraphrase Harold Lasswell, 1948, p. 12). *Framing, priming, agenda building*, and *agenda setting* are widely applied in media studies and also in PR theory and research. In addition, in his analysis of spin Frank Esser specifically observes that the theoretical concepts most closely related to spin are priming and framing (2008, p. 4783). Framing theory dates back to the 1950s and scholars observe that "framing is inescapable" in communication (Graber, 2011, p. 316). Also, scholars note that agenda building and priming occur before and contribute to agenda setting (Len-Ríos, Hinnant, Park, Cameron, et al., 2009, p. 316). Chronology and precedence provide a logical order for discussion. However, because agenda setting is "the quintessential political communication concept" according to Richard Perloff (2013 p. 320), and because the term is used broadly and often overlaps with framing, priming, agenda building, and the recently introduced concept of agenda melding, it is simpler and less repetitive to discuss this large body of work and its applicability to this analysis first.

Agenda setting

Agenda setting is one of the most widely known and discussed media theories, originating from a landmark study by Max McCombs and Donald Shaw of undecided voters in Chapel Hill, North Carolina, during the 1968 presidential election contested by Richard Nixon and Hubert Humphrey (McCombs & Shaw, 1972). McCombs and Shaw found a strong correlation between the volume of coverage of various issues reported and discussed in the media and "the salience of those issues among voters" (McCombs & Reynolds, 2002, p. 2). Thus, they concluded that mass media set the agenda of issues, although their initial findings have been criticized and have evolved considerably.

To some extent, McCombs and Shaw's finding was not new. Interest in and concern about the role of media in setting the agenda of public thought and discussion began with Walter Lippmann (1922) and Harold Lasswell (1927), although they did not use the term 'agenda setting'. Reflecting media effects thinking at the time, Bernard Cohen (1963) famously stated that the media "may not be successful much of the time in telling people what to think, but it is stunningly successful in telling its readers what to think *about*" (p. 13). However, McCombs and Shaw went further and did a follow-up study of a representative sample of voters in Charlotte, North Carolina, during the 1972 presidential election campaign further examining issues reported in media compared with public perceptions and opinion (McCombs & Reynolds, 2002, p. 3; Shaw & McCombs, 1977). In this and other studies (e.g., McCombs & Bell, 1996; McCombs & Evatt, 1995; and McCombs & Ghanem, 2001), McCombs and colleagues point to what they term *second-level* as well as *first-level* media effects. Whereas awareness and perceived importance of issues (*salience*) is described as a first-level effect, they argue that the perceived characteristics, properties, and features of various topics discussed in media (*attributes*) are also communicated to audiences. In this step, agenda setting theory challenges and extends Cohen's view by arguing that media not only tell people *what* to think about, but they can also tell people *how* to think about some things (McCombs & Reynolds, 2002, p. 10).

Since the Chapel Hill study, there have been more than 400 studies of the agenda setting influence of news media (Griffin, 2009, p. 367). McCombs provides a useful review of 50 years of agenda setting theory in his 2004 text *Setting the Agenda: The Mass Media and Public Opinion* in which he notes in the introduction that "the theory of agenda setting is a complex intellectual map still in the process of evolving" (2004, p. xiii). McCombs and Jason Yu (2005) subsequently added what they call a *third level* of agenda setting which refers to the tonal qualities of media articles—that is, whether they convey positive or negative tones about topics and issues. Recent debate on agenda setting has included an intellectual joust between Annie Lang (2013) and Richard Perloff (2013) in articles on media effects research, which provide an interesting update and critique, and in 2014 McCombs published a second edition of *Setting the Agenda: The Mass Media and Public Opinion* (McCombs, 2014).

Framing

McCombs and colleagues claim that second-level and third-level agenda setting are similar to what others call 'framing'. As Jenny Kitzinger (2007) points out, framing involves much more than the traditional notion of agenda setting. She says framing goes beyond drawing attention to certain issues and topics "focussing instead on the nature of that attention and the aspects that are highlighted as salient" (p. 137). Framing, therefore, influences "how we think about" issues (Scheufele & Tewksbury, 2007, p. 14).

Developed by anthropologist Gregory Bateson (1955) and sociologist Erving Goffman (1974), framing theory is widely applied in study of language and in the social sciences including psychology, sociology, and political science and is also increasingly used for understanding media practices and functions. There are two types of frames at work in media communication: *media frames* and *audience frames*. Audience frames are the "mentally stored clusters of ideas that guide an individual's processing of information" (Entman, 1993, p. 53). Media frames, which are the main focus here, are the "persistent patterns of cognition, interpretation and presentation, of selection, emphasis and exclusion by which symbol handlers routinely organize discourse" (Gitlin, 1980, p. 7). They are also described as "interpretative packages" that give meaning to an issue, at the core of which is "a central organizing idea, or *frame*, for making sense of relevant events, suggesting what is at issue" (Gamson & Modigliani, 1989, p. 3). A frame acts as "a window or portrait frame drawn around information that delimits the subject matter and, thus, focuses attention on key elements within" (Hallahan, 1999a, p. 207).

Frames and framing do not occur by accident in most cases. Rather, they are intentional constructions designed to serve some interest or objective. Robert Entman (1993) defines the verb 'frame' as "to select some aspects of a perceived reality and make them more salient in a communication text, in such a way as to promote a particular problem definition, causal interpretation, moral evaluation or treatment recommendation for the item described" (p. 52). Entman (1993) also identifies four key elements of framing. He says frames (1) define problems; (2) diagnose causes; (3) make moral judgements; and (4) suggest remedies (p. 55). Importantly, as also noted by Gitlin (1980) and Hallahan (1999a), the defining of problems and moral judgements include processes of inclusion and exclusion. What is left out of the frame, what is not told, or what is withheld or obscured is just as important as what is presented in a frame and this concept is useful for analyzing journalism and PR.

Jenny Kitzinger (2007) says that "journalists are consummate 'framers' of reality" (p. 137). McCombs and Reynolds identify two types of frames deployed by media: (1) *central themes* and (2) *aspects* (2002, p. 12). In the first, they see media determining the main issues that will receive attention in public debate. The second type of frame draws the spotlight of public attention to key attributes of those issues through the use of specific words, phrases, names, and labels—as well as through what is omitted from a story.

A contemporary example of media framing can be seen in reporting of the September 11, 2001 terrorist attacks in the US. Even though the attacks were framed both as criminal acts calling for a criminal response and military acts justifying a military response (Bennett, 1990), Jill Edy and Patrick Meirick point out that media overwhelmingly positioned the attacks in a militaristic frame, drawing attention to militaristic aspects through use of the word 'war' and likening the attacks to Pearl Harbor, and called for a military response rather than a criminal investigation and criminal charges against the offenders (Edy & Meirick, 2011). Shanto Iyengar (1991) studied how television frames political issues and campaigns, often by focussing on personality, gaffes, or 'horse race' analysis comparing polls and popularity, rather than policies.

Beyond the fundamental agenda setting question of 'who sets the agenda' of public debate and findings that media do, at least to some extent, an important follow-up question that a number of researchers have asked is 'who sets the media agenda' (Blood, 1989, p. 12; McCombs & Reynolds, 2002, p. 12; Severin & Tankard, 2001, p. 231; Weaver & Elliot, 1985)? Three types of agenda setting identified by Everett Rogers and James Dearing (1988) aid understanding of the multiple levels of influence that exist and show the overlap between the concepts of agenda setting and framing. They identify *public agenda setting* (the traditional hypothesis and role which McCombs and colleagues attributed to media), *media agenda setting* (who sets the media agenda), and *policy agenda setting*, in which elite policy makers' agendas are influenced. These are useful, as we are concerned here with the agenda setting, framing, priming, and agenda building roles of both journalism and PR, not only the alleged agenda setting role of media.

Along with the question 'who sets the media agenda', a further key question to explore is 'who sets the media's frames?' Are they determined by editors and journalists based on research and independent critical analysis of issues and the attributes that could be highlighted, as some agenda setting thinking supposes? Or are there other influences involved in our pluralist political and media environment?

Frame sponsors, advocates, and strategists

In examining agenda setting at all three levels identified by Rogers and Dearing (1988), a number of scholars have begun to explore the activities of what are increasingly referred to as *frame sponsors* (e.g., Anderson, 1997; Carragee & Roefs, 2004; Edy & Meirick, 2011), also referred to as *frame advocates* (Tewksbury, Jones, Peske, Raymond et al., 2000) and *frame strategists* (Hallahan, 1999a). Following the 9/11 attacks in the US, the Bush administration was clearly involved in promoting its particular view of what had happened and what the appropriate response should be (Edy & Meirick, 2011, p. 142). Similarly, the US and UK governments sponsored particular frames to justify their plans to launch the second Gulf War through the release of intelligence reports and the discourse of the 'war on terror'.

Frames are advanced and promoted by official sponsors, such as governments, political leaders, institutions, and representative organisations. In addition, frames are advanced by a range of unofficial sponsors ranging from 'think tanks' and activist groups to private business interests and individuals. Furthermore, as well as describing journalists as "consummate 'framers' of reality", Jenny Kitzinger adds: "As are professional PR workers who help control and shape the supply of information to the media" (2007, p. 137). PR scholar Kirk Hallahan (1999a) has identified seven ways that PR is engaged in framing of issues—or, more correctly, acting as frame sponsors. He says PR practitioners frame situations, attributes, choices, actions, issues, responsibility, and news itself by providing information to media such as in ready-made news releases and interviews, as well as producing and releasing reports and lobbying policy makers and decision makers. Hallahan uses the term "frame strategist" in describing the framing role of PR practitioners, which can be seen as largely synonymous with the concepts of frame advocates and frame sponsors (p. 224), although it could be argued that PR practitioners' employers and clients are the frame sponsors.

While some areas of PR such as public affairs, also referred to as lobbying or government relations, may be directly involved in framing as well as policy agenda setting, the largely behind-the-scenes role of PR, as well as its heavy focus on communicating through media, indicates that PR practitioners can be more precisely understood and examined in the context of frame advocates or strategists working on behalf of frame sponsors, as well as media agenda setters acting on behalf of agenda sponsors.

Priming

Priming is another long-established concept in social science that was applied to media studies in the 1980s (Iyengar, Peters, & Kinder, 1982; Iyengar & Kinder, 1987; Krosnick & Kinder, 1990). As defined in the political communication literature, priming refers to "changes in the standards that people use to make political evaluations" (Iyengar & Kinder, 1987, p. 63). Priming occurs when news content suggests to news audiences that they ought to use specific issues or attributes as benchmarks for evaluating the performance of leaders or organizations or forming an opinion about an issue. In this sense, it can be seen that priming precedes agenda setting. It is a related and complementary theory to framing in that, whereas framing identifies what is to be considered—and what isn't by being left out of the frame—priming suggests the criteria and standards by which issues should be judged.

For example, leadership of a political candidate or CEO may be an issue that is placed front and centre of the frame for public discussion. This may be done to draw attention away from his or her chaotic personal life—an example of how frames include and exclude. Within that frame, priming can be used to establish how leadership will be assessed—for example, will it be evaluated in terms of successful financial performance, international representation, and diplomacy, or human and social welfare? Thus, priming is an important and integral element of overall agenda setting and framing strategies.

Max McCombs, known as the 'father of agenda setting theory', includes agenda priming as part of agenda setting theory (see McCombs & Reynolds, 2002, pp. 11–15), although others see it as a separate theory and important for understanding the complex range of interactions and effects involved in media communication.

Agenda building

Drawing on the work of Gladys and Kurt Lang (1981), Rogers and Dearing (1988) describe the difference between agenda setting and agenda building in terms of the first representing a media focus, while the second involves a broader macro-level focus on the public sphere and the interaction of various political actors. In short, agenda setting refers to the transfer of a media agenda to the public agenda, while agenda building includes "some degree of reciprocity" between the mass media and society where both media and public agendas influence public policy.

Lang and Lang (1981, 1983), and before them Roger Cobb and Charles Elder (1972), discuss the way that agendas are collectively built in an interactive process involving media, government, organizations, and opinion leaders. Agenda building denotes a more complex process than the original agenda setting theory by recognizing inputs to agendas from multiple sources—not only media. Lang and Lang suggest that the process of putting an issue on the public agenda takes time and goes through a number of stages. They propose six stages from the time media draw attention to an issue, event, or activity, through its framing by media and by others such as politicians, lobby groups, PR practitioners, and individuals who champion or evangelize a viewpoint—what Edy and Meirick (2011) and some others call sponsors—to its ultimate resolution through action or demise. A useful summary of agenda building is available in Joseph Severin and James Tankard's *Communication Theories: Origins, Methods, and Uses in the Mass Media* (2001, pp. 230–231).

Some other researchers use the term *frame building* to describe these multi-actor, multi-stage processes of influencing media and, in turn, influencing public debate and policy (e.g., Scheufele, 1999), although some challenge that frame building is more concerned with the news production process than the broader role and effects of agenda building. For example, Russell Neuman, Marion Just, and Ann Crigler (1992) say frames and frame building relate to how the media "spin" a story, taking into account their "organizational and modality constraints, professional judgements, and certain judgements about audience" (p. 120).

Oscar Gandy (1982) and others such as Dan Berkowitz and Douglas Adams (1990) have highlighted the role of "information subsidies" provided by PR as an agenda building mechanism, and research since by Bruce Berger, James Hertog and Dong-Jin Park (2002), Craig Carroll and Max McCombs (2003), Patricia Curtin (1999), and numerous others confirms that corporations and organizations act as agenda builders, as well as contribute to framing, priming, and agenda setting (Berger, 2001; Ragas, 2012).

Media agenda setting, framing, priming, and agenda building are also influenced by *intermedia agenda setting* identified by Leon Danielian and Stephen Reese

(1989) and discussed by many others since. This refers to the way in which radio and television news tend to pick up stories from morning newspapers and how smaller media are influenced by the choice of topics and angles of larger influential media. Intermedia agenda setting takes on new dimensions in the age of social media, in which traditional media source leads and stories from blogs, microblogging sites such as Twitter, social networks, and video sharing sites, as well as vice versa. As well as having billions of individual users, social media are also used by organizations and corporations and Chapter 7 will examine how new channels of public communication can be used for framing, priming, agenda building, and agenda setting.

Agenda cutting

As noted in Chapter 3, one of the roles of PR is to sometimes keep information and even whole issues out of the media. J. Mallory Wober and Barrie Gunter (1988) refer to this practice as *agenda cutting* in their book *Television and Social Control* and it is further discussed by Wober (2001) in a conference paper on the phenomenon of agenda cutting and its importance. Wober and Gunter describe agenda cutting as the "process whereby problems or issues have attention directed away from them by receiving little or no media coverage" (1988, p. 128). In her analysis of agenda building, frame building, and agenda cutting, Rita Colistra (2012) identifies agenda cutting occurring in three ways: (1) by "placing an item low in the news agenda" (i.e., burying it), (2) by "removing it from the agenda once it is there, or by completely ignoring it", or (3) "never placing it on the agenda in the first place" (p. 100). Colistra notes that while placing ideas, information, and issues on the news agenda and giving them salience has been studied extensively for many years, keeping issues and information off the agenda "has largely been ignored in scholarly research" (2012, p. 100).

However, even in Colistra's analysis, the focus is mainly on internal media processes and influences that affect news selection and treatment such as "logistical constraints, journalists' own prejudices and internal…influences", although she does refer to "external influences" as well and cites a notorious example of PR burying news, which has been referred to by Wober (2001) and many others. On September 11, 2001, while the twin towers of the World Trade Center in New York were burning and thousands of lives were being lost, a PR practitioner for the British Transport Ministry, Jo Moore, issued an e-mail to her colleagues saying: "It's now a very good day to get out anything we want to bury. Councillors' expenses?" (Morris & Goldsworthy, 2008, p. 40). After the e-mail was leaked and created a media storm in the UK and US, Moore was forced to apologize and resigned in 2002 after further allegations that she again attempted to bury bad news by releasing it on the day of Princess Margaret's funeral. However, beyond these extreme examples, Wober and Gunter's point about how "problems and issues have attention directed away from them" is not explored in any detail in media studies literature. Research reported in Chapter 6 casts some further light on this largely hidden aspect of PR.

Agenda melding

Building on the work of McCombs and others, Donald Shaw and David Weaver (2014) have introduced the concept of agenda melding. This theory relates more to how audiences use different types of media, proposing that they meld agendas, issues, and attributes gleaned from various media in forming their views. However, this variation on the original agenda setting theory is useful in understanding how mass media and social media interrelate and feed off each other, as discussed in Chapter 7, and it could be applied to analyzing the interrelationship between journalism and PR.

Strategic Vs. Communicative Action

In addition to using Habermas's grand theory of the public sphere as an overall framework for analysis of journalism and PR (Habermas, 1989, 2006), another mid-range theoretical framework in which journalism and PR can be productively examined is Habermas's theory of communicative action. Building on his earlier reformulation of historical materialism (Habermas, 1979), in which he discusses how social learning processes make social evolution possible, Habermas (1984, 1987) identifies two broad models of communication in modern societies: *communicative* and *strategic*[2]. In Habermas's typology, communicative action is designed to achieve understanding in a group and to promote consensus and cooperation. It involves dialogue and co-orientation. What Habermas refers to as strategic action is designed solely or primarily to achieve one's own goals and primarily focuses on persuasion (see Habermas, 1984, pp. 84–101). In Habermas's terms, notwithstanding its many failings, journalism can be seen to mostly fit the criteria of communicative action, serving to create an informed public and consensus based on "reasoned debate" and 'the truth' (however problematic the latter concept is). Despite claims of co-orientation and symmetry in normative PR theory, PR is more appropriately categorized as strategic action. The field's own literature acknowledges this. For instance, in their third and seminal text on PR Excellence theory, identified as a dominant framework of PR worldwide by Magda Pieczka (2006), Jacquie L'Etang (2008), and others, Grunig et al. (2002) list the first of 17 characteristics of excellent PR as being "managed strategically" (p. 9). A focus on strategy and being strategic is further emphasized in Grunig et al.'s updated summary of Excellence theory in which they describe PR as a "strategic managerial function" and say:

> The senior public relations executive is involved with the *strategic management* processes of the organization, and communication programs are developed for *strategic* publics identified as a part of this *strategic management* process (J. Grunig, L. Grunig, & Dozier, 2006, p. 38) [italics added for emphasis].

No fewer than three uses of the term 'strategic' appear in this one sentence. While arguing that strategic communication need not be as manipulative as some suggest, Kirk Hallahan et al. (2007) acknowledge that "strategic communication has been used synonymously for public relations" in much of the literature (p. 9) and that a common definition of strategic organizational communication is "purposeful use of communication to fulfil its mission" (p. 3). In Europe, where the practices referred to as public relations or PR in Anglo-American terms are widely used (Bentele, 2004) but "rarely under that name" (van Ruler & Verčič, 2004, p. 1), the term 'strategic communication' is a common alternative title for the function and activities referred to in this book as PR (Aarts, 2009; Aarts & Van Woerkum, 2008). Furthermore, one of the leading journals in the field is titled *International Journal of Strategic Communication*.

Viewing journalism and PR using Habermas's concepts of communicative action and strategic action lends support to calls by a number of practitioners and scholars that the two fields are, and should be, quite separate and that integration is problematic for society. Using Habermas's theory of communicative action as an analytical lens, Lee Salter (2005) says: "There is a quite explicit danger of merging public relations and journalism that can only diminish the effectiveness of journalism in fulfilling its normative role" (p. 90). She adds that "it is with good reason that good journalists reject the use of public relations techniques in their own practices".

This does not make PR illegitimate, or justify labels such as spin, propaganda, flackery, and fakery, or prove that PR involves lies. It simply suggests that journalism and PR are different functions with different objectives and purposes and, therefore, their interrelationship and interdependence needs to be closely monitored and managed. Habermas's theory of communicative action, along with framing, priming, agenda building, agenda setting, and agenda cutting theories provide informative frameworks for analysis of the research findings reported in the next chapter.

So Now We Know *What* Happens, *Why* and *How* Does it Occur and Does it Matter?

In *Flat Earth News*, Nick Davies argues that the substantial influence of PR on media content is a matter of concern. He states, somewhat graphically:

> Like the civilian population of a war zone, the billions of people who rely on the mass media for information have suffered the worst injuries of all under a bombardment of falsehood, distortion and propaganda (2009, p. 186).

In short, Davies is saying, it matters. The attitudes of journalists suggest it matters. Research summarized in this chapter shows that journalists generally hold highly negative attitudes towards PR, often openly stating that PR involves hype, puffery, and spin at best and lies, deceit, manipulation, obfuscation, and propaganda in its worst manifestations. Even if media rhetoric about PR is exaggerated, and there are indications that it is, there is evidence of questionable and unethical practices in PR occurring on a far too regular basis and with far too little being done about it.

One would assume then that journalists resist PR or even refuse to use PR material. But research reported in this chapter shows that this is far from the case, with empirical evidence showing anywhere from half to 90 plus per cent of the content of our media containing substantial influence of PR, if not being directly placed PR information. This, we are told, is because of cutbacks in journalist staff levels and the double whammy of having to produce more content for an increasing range of online media with fewer staff and less time. However, while these matters are of concern, data show that the use of PR material preceded the current crisis in journalism—it is a well-established trend over more than 100 years.

So what is happening? The reality is that most if not all journalists work with PR every day and use some or a lot of PR information and assistance in their research and reporting. But, as a number of editors and journalists have acknowledged, they don't like to talk about it. As well as criticizing the activities of PR, Davies says the lack of transparency is a key issue. He reports that "most of the quotes which come through press officers have never been anywhere near the mouth of those who are supposed to have said them. Reporters know that. As long as the readers don't realize, nobody is worried" (2009, p. 174). He adds that "every PR adviser to whom I have spoken agrees that the best PR conceals its own hand" (p. 167). Meanwhile, Davies reports that "the same churnalists who complain constantly about dishonesty in…PR, themselves turn to the same PR sources, like babies in a high chair, waiting to be spoon-fed their stories" (2009, p. 197) and they seldom disclose their true sources.

The result, as I first reported back in 1993 in a Master's degree by research thesis, is:

> Many media consumers are unknowingly reading press releases every day in both the popular and quality press, obscured behind a veil of complicity between journalists and public relations practitioners. The programs broadcast by the electronic media are also heavily influenced by public relations in a range of ways (Macnamara, 1993, p. 105).

That matters. The lack of transparency matters in the view of many. Furthermore, the complicity matters because it disguises how, why, and on what terms journalists and PR practitioners interact.

And these things matter now more than ever because of what many are calling the 'crisis in journalism' at the same time as the continuing rapid escalation of social media use that is reshaping 'owned media' as well as 'earned media' and 'paid media' and introducing new techniques of media communication and promotion. It is more important than ever to examine the interactions and interdependencies of these key political actors.

As shown in this book so far, the discourse of denial, the discourse of victimhood, and the discourse of spin do not stand up to scrutiny and are revealed to be, as Foucault said of discourse, discursive practices that "form the objects of which they speak", but which often misrepresent reality in order to maintain power relations and the status quo (1972, p. 49). To attempt to unpack the contradictions, anomalies, and paradoxes, expose myths, shatter stereotypes, and understand how journalists and PR practitioners interact and maintain relationships, and what this means for the public interest, additional research was considered necessary and undertaken in 2008 (a pilot), in 2012 in an analysis for *Australian Journalism Review* (Macnamara, 2012b), and then in 2013 using in-depth qualitative interviews with an international sample of senior journalists and PR practitioners. Their views, concerns, explanations, recommendations, and prognoses for the future are reported in the next chapter.

Notes

1. Jim Parker worked as a journalist for 26 years with newspapers, wire services, commercial and public radio, television, and online media in the UK, Australia, New Zealand, and Asia, before going to work in corporate communication.
2. Habermas originally proposed four types of human action, which he called teleological action, normatively regulated action, dramaturgical action, and communicative action. However, he later introduced a simpler two-type typology of strategic action and communicative action (Habermas, 1984, 1987).

CHAPTER SIX

Journalism and PR Today—An International Qualitative Study

This chapter reports the findings of an international qualitative study of the inter-relationship between journalism and PR based on in-depth interviews with 32 senior journalists and PR practitioners in the US, UK, Australia, and in one developing country. Nine of the interviews were conducted during a pilot study in 2008, leading to a critical analysis of this data and extant literature in 2012, followed by 20 interviews specifically conducted during 2013 as part of researching this book. A further three interviews conducted as part of another study of media in developing countries were drawn on for the unique perspective that they provide.

Methodology

Sample

The pilot study used a purposive sample of information technology and telecommunications (IT) journalists (n = 4) and IT sector PR practitioners (n = 5) in Australia to explore relationships and interactions. This sector was selected for the pilot study as it is serviced by a large contingent of specialist media and writers, and IT companies are among leading spenders on PR (World PR Report, 2013). Then, to gain more broad-based and informed insights, the sampling frame for the 20 interviews conducted in 2013 was journalists and PR practitioners with 20 years or more experience in their fields across multiple sectors in the UK, US, and Australia. As it turned out, a number of interviewees had experience in both journalism and PR, a not unusual occurrence due to a long-standing trend of journalists moving into PR, and it is considered that this enhanced the sample's insights by affording multiple and comparative perspectives. Several interviewees had between 30 and 35 years of experience in journalism and/or PR and one had more than 40 years professional experience. Overall, the 32 interviewees had an average of 21.5 years of experience in journalism and/or PR, with IT journalists interviewed in the pilot study being younger than others in the sample, which is characteristic of the field. The main sample had an average of 26.9 years of experience in journalism and/or PR.

As well as ensuring a solid background of practical experience among interviewees, this sampling approach afforded a degree of reflectivity, as most interviewees were aged in their fifties, with several being in their sixties. Furthermore, the sampling frame prescribed that interviewees were drawn from general news and a range of industry and specialist sectors (i.e., 'rounds' or 'beats'). As well as IT and telecommunications, the sample included journalism and PR practitioners from business and finance, health, energy/petroleum and gas, food, agriculture, consumer products, transport, politics, and the non-profit sector.

The selection of journalists and PR practitioners to interview was undertaken using an initial stage of purposive sampling, followed by snowball sampling, with some limitations of a convenience sample. This limitation arose because a number of practitioners in both fields declined to be interviewed, either because of claimed lack of time, or restrictions imposed by their employer (e.g., senior government communication/PR executives), or because they did not want to be drawn out on the issues being examined. For instance, some journalists feel self-conscious about use of PR material and their relationship with PR practitioners and are reluctant to make admissions which they feel may impugn their professionalism and integrity. In general, PR practitioners were more willing to be interviewed than journalists—some were even happy to talk of their successes. However, the sampling frame applied meant that all interviewees were mature professionals with a range of experiences, and balance was sought between the sub-samples of journalists and PR practitioners—although this was not fully achieved (see 'Limitations'). Openness to speak frankly was assisted by selecting some recently retired journalists and PR practitioners, albeit this was restricted to retirement in the previous two years to ensure currency of information.

Purposive selection of interviewees began with identification of the senior PR/communication professional in or recently retired from a number of large multinational corporations, large government agencies, and international PR consultancies, as well as journalists in senior roles in major newspapers and broadcasting networks. Selected PR practitioners were also asked to nominate journalists with whom they had interacted to a substantial extent over a period of time. Similarly, journalists were asked to nominate PR practitioners with whom they had interacted to a substantial extent. Not all interviewees nominated others, but this snowball sampling element, while having some potential to introduce bias (e.g., referrals to friends), allowed claims to be compared and verified and the introductions offered gave the interviewer a greater level of access to practitioners. This is important in conducting in-depth qualitative research on potentially sensitive issues. Some journalists and PR practitioners are reluctant to speak with a stranger. Introductions paved the way for cooperation, trust, and frankness in the interviews.

Openness and frankness were further aided by offering anonymity to interviewees—both for their name and their organization's name. However, many were happy to speak on the record, including a number of very senior and experienced PR practitioners and journalists. Interviewees included, for example, the principal deputy assistant secretary of the Office of Public Affairs in the US Department of Homeland Security, Bob Jensen—although he made it clear that he was speaking in his personal capacity and not as a representative of any US government agency. Nevertheless, his 30-plus years of experience offered deep insights into domestic and international government communication and media relations. Prior to his senior role with DHS, he was deputy director of external affairs for the US Federal Emergency Management Agency (FEMA) in Washington, DC, where his experiences included setting up government communication field operations and handling media and public communication following the Haiti earthquake and the Deepwater Horizon oil spill in 2010 and during Hurricane Sandy in 2012. Other positions he has held include assistant press secretary for foreign affairs at the National Security Council based at the White House, executive officer and acting spokesman in Baghdad with the State Department, and director of communication operations for the US Department of Defense in Iraq and Afghanistan between 2006 and 2008. On the corporate and PR agency side, interviewees included the senior vice-president, corporate affairs of McDonald's (UK/Europe); the former head of PR for British Airways for a decade; the global head of corporate affairs for one of the largest American food and agriculture companies; and the CEOs of a number of the largest global PR agencies; as well as several specialist in-house communication heads and consultants working in fields such as finance, engineering, transport, and not-for-profit.

Experienced journalists interviewed included a former executive editor of Britain's top-rating morning TV program, a multi-award-winning BBC reporter, a former 'Fleet Street' editor, senior reporters from one of the major wire services and one of the leading newspapers in the US, a former editor in chief of one of Australia's leading daily newspapers, as well as a number of senior business, finance, technology, health, transport, and media writers and broadcasters in the US, UK, and Australia. Where interviewees requested anonymity, either in total or for parts of discussion, their comments are cited in this chapter as 'J1', 'J2', and so on, followed by a brief description where applicable, such as 'a senior reporter from a daily newspaper' or 'an IT trade journalist', and 'PR1', 'PR2', and so forth with a short descriptor such as 'head of communication for an NGO' when applicable.

Limitations

The sample contained a gender skew to men in both journalism and PR, with slightly less than one-third of participants being women. This can be explained to some extent by the purposive nature of the sample, which was designed to access the views and experiences of the most senior practitioners, such as editors and heads of PR and corporate communication. While journalism and PR are now characterized by gender balance in employment, or even a gender imbalance favouring women (Aldoory, 2007; Sha, 1996), practitioners in the most senior roles with 25–35 years of experience are more likely to be men, as they reflect employment patterns of the 1970s and 1980s.

The sample also included more PR practitioners than journalists and more years of PR experience than years of journalistic experience. The study set out to obtain a balanced mix of journalists' and PR practitioners' views, but the imbalance crept in during conduct of the research project because of a greater reluctance among journalists to be interviewed and comment freely on the topic. Nevertheless, in terms of years of experience, the sample was strongly representative of both fields, with participants having almost 300 years of journalism experience and slightly more than 400 years of PR experience in total. Thus, the interviews tapped a total of almost 700 years of experience in journalism and/or PR practice.

Data collection and analysis

All interviews, except one conducted in a noisy place, were either digitally recorded and transcribed, or obtained by e-interview in which the interviewee wrote comments and responses directly. Most interviews were conducted face-to-face and many involved multiple discussions, particularly interviews conducted via e-mail, which were supplemented with telephone, Skype, or Microsoft Lync conversations and/or multiple e-mail exchanges. Supplementary e-mail comments and responses to follow-up questions were copied and pasted into original interview transcripts to provide a full record for analysis.

Transcripts and text from interviews were analyzed using qualitative textual/content analysis techniques based on coding (Shoemaker & Reese, 1996). Manual coding of interview transcripts and notes was undertaken at two levels. As an initial *in vivo* or open stage (Glaser, 1978; Punch, 1998, pp. 210–211), content of interview transcripts was coded into 16 broad categories established *a priori*, as shown in Figure 6.1. A second level of *axial* coding, also referred to as *pattern* coding, was then undertaken to identify the specific views, perceptions, practices, concerns, proposals, and recommendations that emerged within these categories and reveal patterns and 'clusters' of views (Glaser & Strauss, 1967; Punch, 1998, p. 205). As well, particular attention was paid to using verbatim quotes from interviewees in relation to common themes and issues identified, to allow participants to 'speak in their own voice' for validity and authenticity.

No.	Category *(in vivo)*	Axial/pattern coding fields
1	Total years media experience	[n]
2	Years in journalism/PR	• Journalism [n=] • PR [n=]
3	Job/role	• Editor [y/n] • General news reporter [y/n] • Specialist round/beat [y/n, comment] • Freelancer [y/n] • Corporate PR [y/n] • Government PR [y/n] • NGO/non-profit PR [y/n] • PR consultancy [y/n] • Other [y/n, comment]
4	Sector	• General news [y/n] • Business/finance [y/n] • IT/telecommunications [y/n] • Transport/travel [y/n] • Engineering/construction [y/n] • Energy/petroleum [y/n] • Food/consumer/retail [y/n] • Government/politics [y/n] • Environment [y/n] • Other [y/n, comment]
5	Overall rating of journalists *(in ethics and professionalism)*[1]	[n=] on 1–10 scale

No.	Category *(in vivo)*	Axial/pattern coding fields
6	Overall rating of PR practitioners *(in ethics and professionalism)*	[n=] on 1–10 scale
7	Use of PR material	• Almost everything PR related [y/n] • A lot and often [y/n] • Some [y/n] • Not very much [y/n] • Do not use at all [y/n] • General comments [comment]
8	Reasons for PR use	• Loss of journalists jobs [y/n, comment] • Speed of deadlines/lack time [y/n, comment] • Cost (i.e., free content v production) [y/n, comment] • Convenience (free information available) [y/n, comment] • PR provides reliable quality content [y/n, comment] • No one knows, so why not [y/n, comment] • Laziness [y/n, comment] • Other [y/n, comment] • *(Multiple responses allowed)*
9	Spin	• Meaning of the term [comment] • Validity of the term [comment] • Personal use of the term [y/n, comment] • Other [y/n, comment]
10	Relationship in general *(view of the relationship between journalism & PR generally)*	• Avoidance [y/n, comment] • Antipathy and hostility [y/n, comment] • The enemy of media [y/n, comment] • Each has a different job to do [y/n, comment] • First point of contact, but not a source for content [y/n, comment] • Trusted sources for leads and content [y/n, comment] • Mutual respect [y/n, comment] • Symbiosis [y/n, comment] • Friends [y/n, comment] • Other [y/n, comment] • *(Multiple responses allowed)*

No.	Category *(in vivo)*	Axial/pattern coding fields
11	Personal relationship/s *(with journalists/PR practitioners you know)*	• Avoidance [y/n, comment] • Antipathy and hostility [y/n, comment] • The enemy of media [y/n, comment] • Each has a different job to do [y/n, comment] • A first point of contact, but not a source for content [y/n, comment] • Trusted source for leads and content [y/n, comment] • Mutual respect [y/n, comment] • Symbiosis [y/n, comment] • Friends [y/n, comment] • Other [y/n, comment] • *(Multiple responses allowed)*
12	Trust	• Level [comment] • How established [comment] • How maintained [comment] • What erodes trust [comment] • What builds trust [comment]
13	Ethics	• Standards in PR [comment] • Standards in journalism [comment] • Problems [comment] • Solutions [comment] • Role of codes of ethics [comment]
14	Transparency	• Disclosure of all sources (except for legal protection) [y/n, comment] • Disclosure of PR sources [y/n, comment] • Qualified disclosure [y/n, comment] Non-disclosure [y/n, comment]
15	Regulation	• Self-regulation [y/n, comment] • Some regulation by government [y/n, comment]
16	Education and training	• Education/training of journalists [comment] • Education/training of PR practitioners [comment] • Educating PR graduates about journalism [comment] • Educating journalists about PR [comment]

Figure 6.1. Coding scheme for analysis of interviews.

Research questions

The research questions that this study set out to explore were:

1. How do journalists and PR practitioners view each other and their respective roles?
2. How do journalists and PR practitioner negotiate the widely identified tensions between PR and journalism in their daily practice?
3. How can contradictions, such as journalists claiming that they do not use PR material while statistics incontrovertibly show that they do, be explained?
4. How do journalists simultaneously hold negative attitudes towards PR and yet deal with PR practitioners, often on a daily basis, and regularly use leads and information sourced from PR practitioners?
5. How do journalists and PR practitioners build and maintain working relationships, despite historical antipathies and tension between the fields of practice?
6. Do journalists and PR practitioners establish trust? If not, how do they overcome mistrust?
7. Do journalists and PR practitioners maintain integrity and ethics in dealing with each other? If so, how?
8. What do journalists and PR practitioners think of calls for greater transparency (e.g., the UK Media Standards Trust suggestion for declaration of sources of 'information subsidies' as well as calls for clear identification of all paid and subsidized content)?
9. What, if anything, should be done in journalism and PR education and training to address the issues raised in empirical studies and this research?
10. What other mechanisms, if any, should be put in place to ensure accuracy and independence of media content, while maintaining free media, free speech, and freedom of expression?

Pilot Study Findings

A pilot study undertaken by Amanda Millar (2008) as a postgraduate student under my supervision was informative as it probed relationships between IT journalists and specialist PR practitioners working in the IT sector through in-depth interviews with both journalists and PR practitioners. This research found a clear differentiation in journalists' minds between PR practitioners who they personally know and work with and PR in general. A common response in the pilot study was along the lines of 'I deal only with reputable PR people. I don't have anything to do with the charlatans of the trade'. This may seem to suggest that journalists are discriminating and avoid unreliable and manipulative PR practitioners. However, such responses need to be recognized in the context of the *third-person effect* identified by W. Phillips Davison (1983) and also discussed by Richard Perloff (2002). The third person effect is widely evident in media studies, such as investigations of the effects of advertising in which participants often state that advertising has significant effects on others but not on them. Among journalists who acknowledge using PR leads, contacts, and content, differentiation of their personal PR contacts as trustworthy mitigates the conflict and cognitive dissonance of their position and offers them some comfort, which may or may not be justified.

The third-person effect can also be seen in evidence among journalists in denial mode. When the substantial body of empirical evidence reported in Chapter 5 is pointed out to journalists who deny using PR material, their response is often along the lines of 'I don't use PR material, but I know other journalists do'. This strategy provides a narrative for explaining away the contradictions and paradox inherent in journalism–PR relations. In many cases, such claims are likely to be unjustified or simply untrue. In this sense, the third-person effect is similar to the "the doctrine of selective depravity", which Marvin Olasky says PR practitioners use to defend themselves and argue that it is a minority of "immoral outsiders who cause the trouble" (1989, p. 88).

However, it would be unfair to pass over this finding hastily and not consider that it might reveal something significant. While the pilot study involved only nine interviews, this finding echoes an early suggestion by Dennis Jeffers (1977) and other more recent findings (e.g., Ryan & Martinson, 1988; Shin & Cameron, 2003) that personal relationships are important in the interconnection between journalism and PR. Journalists tend to identify PR practitioners who they know personally and with whom they associate regularly as 'exceptions to the rule'. In several cases, journalists participating in the pilot study described PR practitioners who they know and deal with frequently in terms such as: "Oh, [name] is not really a PR person, she's more of an industry expert" (J1, Australian IT journalist, as cited in Macnamara, 2012b, p. 43).

In specialist fields such as IT, the research found that it is not uncommon for journalists to remove the label 'PR' from their thinking and vocabulary in their dealings with known PR practitioners and think of and describe them as "specialists", "experts", "sources", or "contacts". This is supported by industry data and surveys which show that many PR practitioners working in fields such as IT and finance have specialist expertise and are often more educated than journalists in the same field (Sallot, Steinfatt, & Salwen, 1998). The pilot study also demonstrated that there is a high degree of mutual dependency between journalists and PR practitioners in specialist fields. Journalists working in areas such as IT have a limited range of sources available for information on new products, corporate announcements, and technical information compared with general news reporters covering a broad range of topics.

Millar (2008) and Macnamara (2012b) reported that working relationships in specialist fields frequently exist over long periods, allowing time for trust and respect to be established. This is not universal, with some long-serving journalists continuing to hold generalized negative views of PR and PR practitioners. Anecdotes told in interviews reveal that these are based on specific "bad experiences" with PR, indicating that PR performance is patchy and inconsistent and that some journalists' concerns in relation to PR ethics and professionalism are valid. In fact, a general conclusion from the pilot study and the wider sample of interviews reported next is that it is rare to find a journalist who does not have a tale of woe about PR. This is a matter for the PR industry to take on board and will be further discussed in Chapter 8 in relation to future directions.

However, what the finding in relation to personal contacts suggests is that when journalists and PR professionals establish relationships, often working together over time, journalists incorporate these into their circle of contacts and 'trusted sources' and sometimes no longer see them as 'public relations' or 'PR'. Therefore, they are able to continue to hold generalized negative views of PR and seek to distance themselves from the practice, while simultaneously embracing their contacts and information provided by their trusted sources.

Influenced no doubt by the specialization that occurs in fields such as IT, perceptions of PR were found to be more positive than negative among IT journalists. All five of the journalists in this field interviewed see the function of PR as useful and important to them in achieving their day-to-day professional goals. One journalist stated emphatically: "I don't understand the antagonism towards the public relations industry that some journalists hold. My life would be a lot more difficult if it wasn't for PR people" (J2, Australian IT journalist, personal communication, May 7, 2008). Another described his interaction with PR practitioners as "just so constant, it's like breathing air" (J3, Australian IT journalist, personal communication, May 8, 2008).

In some cases, PR practitioners and journalists reported being friends. Three of the four PR practitioners interviewed in the pilot study said that they were friends with journalists and three of the five journalists interviewed considered themselves friends with a least one PR practitioner. Nevertheless, all interviewees—PR practitioners as well as journalists—expressed concern about the potential impact of personal relationships on their work. Comments included: "You need to be careful" and "I'm very wary" (Millar, 2008, p. 9). Such responses reflect international views, such as this comment by chief executive of *The Spectator,* Andrew Neil, on the launch of networking group Editorial Intelligence in the UK, which frequently brings journalists and PR practitioners together for networking. Neil was reported in *The Guardian* saying:

> I am very wary of journalists and PRs getting too close. The best journalism involves publishing things that powerful people don't want published. The danger is that it is a slippery slope and you become compromised and too close to the people you cover. If we as journalists are to do our jobs properly, we have to keep our distance (Plunkett, 2006, para. 4).

All IT journalists interviewed stated that they would not compromise their editorial or ethical standards to benefit a PR practitioner who is a friend. But most journalists interviewed agreed that there was "give and take" in their relationships with PR. One stated: "You give a bit of coverage on this" because "they give us access to that" (as cited in Millar, 2008, p. 10). Interestingly, PR practitioners interviewed also said they do not give preferential treatment to journalists who are friends. They said they do not necessarily give them better treatment, such as access to information, and that they do not expect favours from journalists who are friends.

A further interesting point that emerged in discussions with two IT journalists is that they referred to "operational checks and balances" that exist in media organizations—or ought to exist—to ensure favourable treatment is not offered and that standards are not compromised. One journalist said: "Even if they [journalists] try to give people preferential treatment, they still have to get past the editor and the editor still has to get it past the publisher" (J4, Australian IT journalist, personal communication, May 12, 2008). The qualification that these checks and balances ought to be in place is made because discussions with a former editor in chief reported later in this chapter suggest that this editorial management role has weakened or broken down in some cases and is a more serious concern than the numbers of journalists employed and the reporting activities of journalists.

It has to be emphasized that the PR practitioners interviewed in this pilot study were all experienced, seasoned professionals in the field. This is not a typical site of PR. 'Newbies' tend to not 'cut their teeth' in specialist fields such as IT or, if they do, it is usually under the mentorship of an experienced senior practitioner. As we will see later, this is not always the case in general PR practice, particularly in major PR agencies handling a range of accounts and in the marketing PR departments of consumer product companies. Even in the IT field, however, some journalists reported that an enduring problem with PR is lack of understanding of what they should be 'pitching' to journalists and what is of no interest or news value. All journalists interviewed perceived a negative side to PR, such as acting as organization gatekeepers—albeit not usually with the PR people who they dealt with regularly.

These preliminary findings were used to inform the design of the question guide for the main stage of this study and were further explored with the larger sample of journalists and PR practitioners interviewed internationally during the second half of 2013.

Journalists' and PR Practitioners' Perceptions of Each Other

International interviews confirmed findings of earlier studies that journalists have much more negative and prejudicial perceptions of PR practitioners than PR practitioners have of journalists (see DeLorme & Fedler, 2003; Jeffers, 1977; Kopenhaver, 1985; Kopenhaver, Martinson, & Ryan, 1984; Ryan & Martinson, 1988; Stegall & Sanders, 1986; White & Shaw, 2005). What may surprise journalists and journalism and media studies scholars is that PR practitioners rate journalists they deal with, on average, very highly in terms of ethics and professionalism (see Note 1 at the end of this chapter for the definition of professionalism used). Even more surprisingly, they rate their own field of practice, on average, much less ethical and professional than journalism. This seems to suggest a frankness and honesty among senior PR practitioners in recognizing a need to improve standards and practices in PR. It also suggests that at least some criticisms of PR are justified.

While this research was qualitative rather than quantitative, and therefore not generalizable, all participants were asked to give an average rating to both journalists and PR practitioners who they had dealt with on a 0–10 scale on which 10 was 'extremely ethical and professional' and zero was 'extremely unethical and unprofessional'. In these two questions, PR practitioners rated journalists who they had dealt with 7–9 out of 10, while they rated practitioners in their own field 5–7. Conversely, journalists rated themselves 8–9 and PR practitioners who they dealt with in the 4–6 range. To be fair, many interviewees split practitioners into categories. A common response from both sides was that a few practitioners in journalism and PR were 9 or higher out of 10 in terms of ethics and professionalism, while a lamentable 'rump' was 2–3 on a 10 scale. However, overall, journalists were less willing to admit poor standards of ethics and professionalism than PR practitioners were.

Journalism's secret supporters

A further somewhat surprising finding was that senior PR practitioners almost universally expressed concern for journalists and the future of independent journalism. Far from celebrating the depleted ranks of media gatekeepers and an ostensibly easier path to publication and broadcast of PR material, a number of senior PR practitioners in the US and UK, in particular, spoke sincerely about the importance of journalism to society. Some expressed grave concerns that a further collapse of independent media would see governments and disreputable companies operate without adequate checks and balances and without facing the 'court of public opinion'. Journalists might be surprised to learn that some of their strongest supporters and advocates are among the senior ranks of the PR industry. For example, the senior vice president, corporate affairs for the UK and Northern Europe for McDonald's Restaurants, Nick Hindle, said: "I'm a great admirer of journalism and journalists and we benefit from a free press in the United Kingdom and it's a real strength. It's…one of the strong parts of the foundation of our society" (personal communication, June 19, 2013). Further, he added:

> I think that journalists are being put under extraordinary pressure these days. They have had resources systematically taken away from them. There's been a long term decline in resources and at the same time that there has been a significant rise in resources going into public relations. I think that that makes them defensive and I completely understand that because they quite rightly believe that an independent press is important to a well-functioning society and they wear that badge with pride. I am genuinely concerned from a society perspective that, as it becomes harder and harder for independent or non-state media to be profitable and invest in their future, we will get this sort of increasing serving up of the news through search engines. That and more highly selective consumption of the news by consumers will actually have a detrimental effect on our understanding of the world. I think that that is quite frightening actually (Nick Hindle, personal communication, June 19, 2013).

The CEO for Europe, Asia, and the Middle East (EAME) of Ogilvy PR, Stuart Smith, spoke unprompted as a media consumer and concerned citizen rather than simply as a 'PR man' saying:

> I respect journalists that have deep integrity…as a consumer that's what I want. I'm hoping that journalists are looking at multiple sources which include the PR person, and what I read is a fair judgement from someone who has researched the issue and written a story about it.… I think if journalism and PR get too cosy, to some extent that doesn't serve the news-reading public (personal communication, June 26, 2013).

In addition to altruistic motives, PR practitioners interviewed also pointed out that they have a vested interest in the preservation of independent media, which is often unrecognized by critics of PR. Several noted that having information about their organization positively reported in respected independent media is more credible and more impactful than publicity in partisan media or saying it themselves through 'owned' media such as brochures, newsletters, or Web sites. While research studies have challenged some assumptions about the value of *third party endorsement*, particularly the assumed believability and impact of editorial publicity versus advertising (Hallahan, 1999b; Michaelson & Stacks, 2007), and the credibility of some major media has declined as noted in Chapter 2, balanced as well as positive reporting in independent media remain very important to governments, corporations, and other types of organizations. Biased and partisan media usually have less impact and value.

Journalism's hubris and elitist culture

That this respect and recognition are not reciprocated in most cases seems to be a mixture of justifiable suspicion of PR and media hubris and elitism. Journalists regard themselves as superior to PR practitioners in most respects, including in terms of ethics, social conscience, media knowledge, writing skills, and even in personal morals, a characteristic noted in research by Dennis Jeffers (1977) and Lillian Kopenhaver, who describes journalists as "self-righteous" (1984, p. 18). One senior journalist who did not want to be named stated proudly: "Journalists are truth seekers, that's what we are" (J5, UK newspaper journalist, personal communication, June 18, 2013). The same journalist also referred to PR practitioners as "sleazy", echoing not infrequent media sniping at PR (e.g., Simpson, 2002).

A number of former journalists who 'crossed over' to work in PR reflected soberly on the shift and acknowledged that their former prejudices were unfounded. For example, well-known UK journalist Martin Frizell, who became executive director of media at GolinHarris PR in London in 2011 after a decade as editor of the top-rating morning TV program GMTV in London and previously working for Reuters, Sky News, and ITV after starting his journalism career with newspapers in his home city of Glasgow, was frank. In discussing journalists' attitudes towards PR, he said: "There's snobbishness, there's an absolute snobbishness". He recounted going to "journalism college in Edinburgh", which had a PR course as well, and reflected that "there was this thing which came from our tutors…that clearly we were better than public relations people. They were failed journalists, they just didn't have that inquisitive, challenging, ethical, moral part of their backbone" (Martin Frizell, personal communication, June 24, 2013).

Andy Winstanley, a multi-award-winning transport and environment journalist with the BBC before 'crossing over' to PR in 2007, reported a similar introduction to PR during his journalism studies, saying:

> I can tell you that I did get a negative impression of PR. In fact, one lecturer said that most members of the course would probably end up as PRs as they wouldn't make it

as journalists. To him, PR was a second rate profession and this is the perception that many journalists start out with (personal communication, September 2, 2013).

In the US, the CEO of PR firm Ketchum's change communication and research business, and a former journalist with *Times Mirror* magazines, David Rockland, said "journalists see themselves on a pedestal as purveyors of all truths with no bias". He acknowledged that "PR practitioners are by definition biased" (personal communication, October 18, 2013). This modernist conceptualization of truth was discussed in Chapter 2 and the uneasy truth about truth in journalism is further discussed in the next section.

Furthermore, Andy Winstanley, who won four Royal Television Society Journalist of the Year awards and was named Reporter of the Year in the London Transport Awards of 2006 while working for the BBC, said that journalists do not understand and grossly underestimate the work of PR. Many journalists believe that their skills automatically translate to PR and make them excellent PR practitioners. However, after almost six years working in a senior PR role with engineering firm Atkins, Winstanley reflected:

> As a journalist you only get an impression of what PR people do and cannot fully understand the full breadth and depth of skills they must have in order to do their job well. I did already have a fairly good view of the complexity of PR, as a number of peers had transitioned into communication roles from journalism, but actually doing the job still came as an eye-opener. The main thing you don't see as a reporter is the scale of the stakeholder environment (personal communication, September 3, 2013)[2].

Brand editor of *PRWeek*, Ruth Wyatt, a journalist of 22 years with previous experience as feature editor of *Sunday Business* in the UK and writing for *Media Week*, as well as five years working as an in-house communication director and running her own small PR consultancy, commented:

> There seems to be a belief certainly among journalists that it's really easy to transfer your skills into PR. That's not necessarily true. PR is a different skill set.... I found that transferring over to PR I had a tremendous amount to learn (personal communication, June 26, 2013).

McDonald's SVP of corporate affairs for the UK and Northern Europe, Nick Hindle, added: "Good journalists have to work on their own. Good PR people have to be team players" (personal communication, June 19, 2013). While supporting journalists and speaking highly of most he has worked with, Hindle has experienced what Martin Frizell calls the "snobbishness" of journalists, saying "there are always journalists who talk to people in PR like they are a piece of dirt on the bottom of their shoe". He sees this as resulting from "a feeling of superiority" in some cases, but he also attributed journalists' attitudes to frustration and the pressure of deadlines (personal communication, June 19, 2013).

David Hickie, who spent 18 years at Fairfax Media in Australia including serving as editor in chief of *The Sydney Morning Herald* in a media career spanning 35 years in total, identified a further factor affecting journalism, particularly television news reporting. He said "the trap for me is the narcissism involved in the media. It offers high profile, look at me importance to people". He was frankly confessional stating: "When I first worked [in journalism]…I'm 23 years old and I'm just out of law school, all I want to do is see my by-line in the paper each week". Hickie says working in the media is "very seductive", particularly for young people, adding "if you suddenly can do very well quite quickly, you find yourself on a fast track to celebrity". He says narcissism and self-profile building influences interviews, particularly in broadcast media, and not in a good way, as it causes reporters to be focussed more on how they look and sound than on the story (personal communication, October 24, 2013).

Martin Frizell, who has worked as a journalist for 20 years and whose father was a journalist, believes the "whole thing of journalism versus PR…is cultural". He said "a lot of it is handed down almost in the DNA of journalists" (personal communication, June 24, 2013). This has implications for journalism education, as will be discussed in a later section in this chapter and in Chapter 8.

Modernist journalism

While not specifically identified by journalists or PR practitioners interviewed, there are also a number of broader underlying causes and factors that contribute to attitudes towards PR and use of PR material. These are apparent as sub-texts in the discussions, which reveal myths and metanarratives that frame journalists' thinking and behaviour. For example, interviewed journalists regularly talked about "the truth" and their role as "seekers of the truth"—a role that many feel they alone can perform. As part of this, many journalists wear cynicism like a badge of honour, referring to all official sources as "spinners" or even "lying bastards", which is used to justify a range of approaches and practices from aggressive 'attack dog' interviewing styles to negative reporting as the norm. This modernist singular understanding of truth drives journalists in a self-confident quest believing that because of their alleged independence, skill, and imagined innate perspicacity they can discover 'the truth', and that others such as PR practitioners are incapable of truth telling and deal in untruths. Interestingly, despite this underlying belief, journalists gravitate to official sources—and to PR practitioners—as this study and others have shown (e.g., Bennett & Serrin, 2011; McChesney, 2003, 2013; Perloff, 1998; Sigal, 1973, 1986).

Journalists interviewed also spoke regularly about there being "two sides to a story" (e.g., Hickie, personal communication, October 24, 2013). Postmodern thinking sensibly suggests that there are usually many perspectives, sometimes myriad. The binary modernist myth of 'two sides to a story' sees many journalists and even senior editors, when provided with information, seek an opposing or alternative view with the assumption that this provides balance to a story. Of course, it doesn't. High modernism is alive and well in the senior ranks of journalism.

PR's Achille's Heel

There is one aspect of PR, in particular, that contributes to the negative perceptions and experiences of journalists. Gordon Welsh, group corporate communications manager of Dana Petroleum based in Aberdeen, Scotland, who has spent 14 years in PR after nine years working as a journalist, including with daily newspapers, said "the problem is not PR per se, but in the large number of inexperienced practitioners who have come into PR" (personal communication, August 16, 2013). The rapid growth of PR in many countries has meant that, for every few senior experienced PR practitioners who are trusted by journalists, there are dozens, possibly hundreds, of young, enthusiastic, often overly excitable and dangerously inexperienced practitioners who pester journalists with irrelevant information and annoying requests. The international president of GolinHarris based in London, Matt Neale, is blunt about his own industry, saying:

> Can you imagine that, a dozen times a day, someone's who's 21, who's saying 'did you get my press release?' or 'I've got this …'? I've no idea who I'm targeting. I don't really understand the paper. I don't understand the service. I call on deadline. I think the problem is that many agencies in this vast industry in this country now have front line staff that…they're speaking to experienced journalists who have done one of the hardest degrees out there to get on, incredibly bright. You have these junior people who are untrained, just bothering them constantly (Matt Neale, personal communication, June 24, 2013).

Australian Stephen Woodhill, who has worked as head of communication with major media, telecommunications, and food companies and who was doing research for a PhD at the time of this study, is similarly concerned, saying "junior PR people who misunderstand the relationship or the time constraints on the journalist are a really big issue for our industry" (personal communication, October 30, 2013).

The producer of *Health Report* on Australia's ABC, Dr Norman Swan, who graduated in medicine from the University of Aberdeen in Scotland and is a multi-award-winning broadcaster and producer of several TV series in Australia and for Channel 4 in the UK, echoes this criticism. He said: "Many PRs are unsophisticated. They send out press releases and think they will be used. And then there are the follow-up phone calls. Often these are made by very junior staff" (personal communication, December 3, 2013).

Also, junior staff members in PR agencies and departments are often assigned to 'pitching' stories—the practice of phoning or e-mailing journalists, editors, and program producers to try to persuade them to write or broadcast a story. Brand editor of *PRWeek* in the UK, Ruth Wyatt, said "it's the people at the end of the food chain who are tasked with doing the initial sell in or follow up phone calls to journalists" (personal communication, June 26, 2013). Several PR veterans agreed that this approach is both ineffective and brings the whole PR industry into disrepute.

My former postgraduate student, Amanda Millar, who was director, trade marketing and corporate affairs for Yahoo!7 in Australia at the time of this study, refers to the young inexperienced practitioners who make up a significant part of the PR industry as the "Felicity Publicity" types (personal communication, October 10, 2013), because they are often young women, following a feminization of PR that has occurred in most countries over the past decade (Aldoory, 2007; Sha, 1996)[3]. Ruth Wyatt, brand editor of the trade journal *PRWeek*, spoke critically of "the fluffy bunny end of the market" saying "that's where you get the 22-year old junior trainee deputy acting assistant account executives ringing up—there are a million of them" (personal communication, June 26, 2013). Other PR practitioners similarly referred to "the pink and fluffies" because of a tendency of some young practitioners to be 'girly girls' who see PR as a glamorous job arranging social events and working with celebrities and media personalities (PR1, Australian corporate PR manager, personal communication, July 26, 2013). A Web search of the terms 'public relations' and 'pink' in 2013 brought up a staggering 65 million results (e.g., see a gushy profile in *EveryGirl* on the 25-year-old founder of Skirt PR in Chicago written by Melanie Stone, 2012).

Colin Browne, who was head of PR for British Telecom (BT) for seven years and director of corporate relations for the BBC for five years, agrees that the image and reputation of PR is negatively impacted by journalists' experiences in "dealing with junior PR people, particularly in the smaller consultancies" (personal communication, June 26, 2013). It should be stated, for fairness and balance, that his criticism, and those of many journalists including Ruth Wyatt, relate to inexperienced young men in PR, as well as women.

This finding is supported by industry literature and reports. For instance, writing in *Forbes*, Peter Himler (2013) elaborated on an address he gave to undergraduate students in the School of Journalism and Mass Communication at the University of North Carolina, Chapel Hill, saying one of the reasons for "acrimony between the two professions" is that "media relations is pushed to junior staffers at many big agencies—and in-house communications departments—with relatively little supervision or mentoring" (para. 7).

PR practitioners who are former journalists see both sides of the tensioned debate. For example, Peter Jones, who worked as a journalist before a 30-year PR career including 18 years with British Airways and its predecessors—10 years as head of PR for BA—and 12 years as communication director for Bupa, believes PR should "never try to sell something that is not saleable or that journalists cannot use". Speaking as a former journalist, he said young, inexperienced PR practitioners get caught in this trap.

> That's where a lot of this bad stuff comes from. You get a crap press release for some product or event that isn't really news, that's overwritten to the extent that it makes you giddy. You've got a first paragraph full of superlatives which of course are all sub-jective…then the PR phones you up on edition time to ask are you going to use it? These are old numbers now, but it used to be that the average news editor saw 200 press releases a day. I'm sure it's far more these days. A lot of them are just wasted trees (personal communication, June 20, 2013).

Dr Norman Swan noted that "those who have been around a long time know what to bring me. Usually that is research based information." Unfortunately for the PR industry, those who know what they are doing appear to be outnumbered substantially by those who do not. Swan stated bluntly: "I rarely come across a PR person who knows what they are talking about" (personal communication, December 3, 2013).

Other journalists are kinder, or simply more fortunate. Several of those interviewed pointed to the importance of PR contacts in emergency services and in government, and most IT journalists acknowledged that IT PR professionals mostly had a good understanding of the technologies and products they promoted. Financial and business journalists also differentiated the senior corporate relations and corporate affairs practitioners in large companies from PR generally, identifying these as specialists and often as high-level "sources" or at least "contacts". Some of these fields of PR are further discussed later in this chapter.

How and Why Journalists Use PR—The Pragmatic Perspective

Journalists and producers of radio and TV programs use leads and content supplied by PR practitioners, often to a substantial extent, for two reasons. The first is that they have no choice. This inevitability needs to be accepted and made transparent, but it should not be used to support simplistic arguments or assumptions about journalistic victimhood or the evils of PR. This lack of choice is the result of both structural change within journalism and structural change in industry and government to which journalism has to adapt. The structural issues in journalism are well known and have already been discussed in this book in Chapter 2. The declining number of journalists employed in many media, combined with requirements to write for online as well as print or broadcast editions, has led to time and resource scarcity in many news media. As noted previously, senior PR practitioners express concern rather than take delight in the challenges faced by journalists. Former journalist and head of PR for British Airways and Bupa, Peter Jones, said "it's a challenging world where your two main criteria are to be fast and to be accurate" (personal communication, June 20, 2013). Speed and accuracy do not easily go together—and their co-existence becomes even more unlikely when both journalist staff numbers and time are reducing.

However, as argued in Chapter 2, this is not the full story. Apportioning blame for reliance on PR to economic conditions, technological change, and rationalist management decisions by media proprietors ignores other important realities of contemporary societies and the media ecosystems that operate in them. Today PR practitioners are gateways to most government offices from the White House and Whitehall to the local mayor and to most corporations, institutions, associations, and even charities and activist groups, for media and public information. In many organizations, receptionists are required to ask for identification of all callers and direct media to the PR department or consultancy. Web site requests from media for information are routinely directed to PR staff. Journalists have no choice but to go through PR practitioners in an increasing number of instances.

On the face of it, this 'organization gatekeeping' may appear restrictive and uncooperative, and many journalists perceive it that way. However, experienced PR practitioners interviewed in this study collectively pointed out a number of factors which can actually be helpful to media and the public including:

1. PR practitioners understand media deadlines, whereas other departments in organizations are unlikely to respond within the required time;
2. PR practitioners in most organizations have access to the CEO and other senior managers and can "queue jump" media inquiries and requests for interviews into busy executives' diaries;
3. Sometimes PR practitioners will advocate on behalf of a journalist and help them gain an interview or comment. Almost a third of the senior PR practitioners interviewed spontaneously mentioned that they had "lobbied", "persuaded", or "hounded" a senior executive to grant an interview to a journalist that they otherwise would not have given. Mike Fernandez,

corporate affairs vice president of Cargill, said "that's a unique role that I think the public relations professional plays. They really have to see their job as a go-between between management and the reporter" (personal communication, October 21, 2013);

4. PR practitioners often have to 'translate' complex technical information into descriptions that are comprehensible for non-technical journalists and audiences;

5. PR practitioners can often provide valuable background briefing. Several senior PR practitioners interviewed said that on a number of occasions they had spent time "training" young, inexperienced reporters assigned to a round with which they were unfamiliar. For example, CEO of Ogilvy PR for Europe, Asia, and the Middle East, Stuart Smith, stated: "I think PR people are good at training some of the junior reporters who come on to certain beats, especially those who enter specialists areas such as technology" (personal communication, June 26, 2013). Anthony Tregoning from Australian PR firm Financial & Corporate Relations said "you're often helping younger journalists understand issues" (personal communication, October 21, 2013);

6. PR practitioners interviewed also reported giving trusted journalists special assistance, such as "going off the record so they could understand an issue" and "pointing them to someone who could talk when we couldn't" (PR2, US government public affairs director, personal communication, September 14, 2013). Peter Jones gave an example of a reporter who had missed a major story. "He needed a new angle or update to recover—he couldn't write what was already reported. So I gave him something extra. He walked away happy. I think we developed a mutual respect" (personal communication, June 20, 2013);

7. PR practitioners do also brief organization spokespersons to allow them to prepare for an interview or draft a statement, but this can result in more informed and thought-through comment and, thus, a better story. Besides, it is only fair that organization spokespersons prepare, given that journalists usually do research before contacting organizations. Mike Fernandez noted that "many corporate executives aren't well schooled in communication" (personal communication, October 21, 2013).

Many organizations have learned that leaving media inquiries to staff unfamiliar with media practices, giving statements or interviews without preparation, and distributing complex technical information such as scientific, medical, technological, financial, and research reports in their original form without summarization and interpretation result in lost opportunities in the least and often media criticism and misleading and inaccurate reporting. Governments, corporations, institutions, and most non-government bodies recognize that public communication is important and, accordingly, have established a specialist function to coordinate this role in the same way as they have done for finance, HR, marketing, customer service, and other areas. In short, PR—whether it is referred to as media relations, public information, corporate relations, or some other term—is part of the superstructure of contemporary societies (in both a general and Marxist sense). Media sociology informs us that media are situated and operate in a society, not separately outside it, and journalists need to navigate PR as an inevitable and unavoidable part of the societies in which they work. Furthermore, like all structures, PR can be enabling as well as disabling. Criticism should focus on particulars rather than ideologically and culturally motivated generalizations.

Scottish TV (STV) editor Shaun Milne pointed to the example of emergency services as a sector in which journalists are compelled to rely on organizations for vital information, much of which is compiled and released through PR professionals working under titles such as media relations, public information, public affairs, or simply communication. The 2013 Boston Marathon bombing provided an example of how the world's media rely on official statements—in this case the Boston Police Department working in cooperation with the FBI. Cheryl Fiandaca, bureau chief of public information for the Boston PD, and her staff played a key role in crafting, fact checking, gaining approval of, and releasing information via the department's Web site and on social media such as Twitter. That case study, highlighted at several conferences in 2013 and 2014, demonstrates that PR can play a central, important role in public communication. Gordon Welsh observed that, even beyond emergencies, "journalists feed off police information" (personal communication, August 16, 2013).

The 30 years of experience of Bob Jensen, whose roles in US government communication were briefly summarized at the beginning of this chapter under 'Sample', bear testimony to the central and essential role of PR practitioners in coordinating the flow of information from government departments and agencies. Reflecting on his time working at the White House, he said that on almost every major policy issue or international development "many journalists would call five seconds after something happened asking for a White House comment" (personal communication, September 14, 2013). Based on his experience at the White House during his role with FEMA and as assistant press secretary for foreign affairs with the National Security Council in 2010–2011, he made the point that there was no other accepted way in for journalists other than through the professional PR channels.

Jensen also spent two years in Baghdad, one year with the US State Department at the US Embassy (2004–2005), and one year coordinating trips for journalists to Iraq as well as working with the Baghdad bureaus to disseminate information (2006–2007), which included coordinating almost 1,500 satellite and phone interviews. Some of the journalists and broadcast teams reporting from Iraq were 'embedded' and some made short visits ('parachute' journalism). But in every case, journalists had to work through the official PR channels to get access to diplomatic and military officials and locations. Jensen rejects the notion that this constituted media manipulation. He acknowledges a long-standing belief among media that US federal government spokespersons are 'spin doctors' dating back to the daily briefings during the Vietnam War, which became known as "the five o'clock follies" because of their increasingly incredible optimistic reports. However, he said even though operations in Iraq and Afghanistan involved "media management", it was for the benefit of the media as well as the military and the US government, adding:

> We were responsible for their safety and welfare, as well as getting them to places where they could collect information and report. You can't have international journalists just wandering around a war zone—although there were some who did and several were killed or had very close calls (Bob Jensen, personal communication, September 14, 2013).

It should be no surprise that much information distributed to media and the public is channelled through professional communication staff in an age of specialization, particularly in cases such as emergencies, wars, on national security issues and other official government matters, as well as corporate reporting of financial results and announcements. Dealing with PR is a day-to-day reality for most journalists reporting on national affairs and specialist beats and rounds such as business and finance, technology, police and crime, health, science, and so on.

What is less understandable and less acceptable in the view of many is the widespread use of PR information unchecked and the lack of honesty and transparency about the processes involved. While criticizing PR and labelling it with a range of derogatory terms as listed in Figure 1.1, some journalists and program producers are regularly 'lined up at the trough' in terms of information hand-outs, exclusive interviews in return for favours, free products to trial and review, free photography and video footage, and other "information subsidies". Ketchum CEO for Europe, David Gallagher, is one of several PR practitioners who identify the consumer products sector as one in which PR material is regularly and voluminously used. He said:

> In the consumer sector I see lots of journalists, whether they're in general or specialist media, taking material and slapping it down, with very little change. It wasn't

something that they came asking for, so it's not like they were already on the trail or something and just asked if we could supply them some photos or information. They were approached with an idea for a story, given material for a story, given access to people who would talk about the story, and changed or added very little to it (personal communication, June 24, 2013).

Even more broadly, former GMTV and ITV reporter Martin Frizell said:

I think journalists like to put out the impression that they're getting scoops out of their own endeavours, their own originality. But a lot of the time they're not. A lot of the time they're getting things that are coming to them. PR will often target them exclusively (personal communication, June 24, 2013).

This particularly occurs in light entertainment and infotainment, such as morning TV shows, which David Hickie says engage in "quasi journalism". He explained:

They've got a never-ending demand for content and PR agencies representing the egg board or a promotion board for bananas or the apple and pear board or something come up with a creative gimmicky story…morning TV laps it up or one of the umpteen radio shows have a bit of fun with it…there's a big difference between what I'd call journalism as opposed to light entertainment (personal communication, October 24, 2013).

Many journalists feel a sense of silent shame at what has become of their once-grand institution and what has become of them. Journalism is one of the few fields in which a twenty-something with little more than an undergraduate degree and a sound recorder or notebook can rub shoulders with the mayor, CEOs of major corporations, Congress members, even the president or prime minister. They get to attend major events free of charge and are ushered to reserved seating. Even the mighty frequently quiver and cower in their presence. But all that is being steadily eroded. Now some blogger or citizen journalist breaks the news. They are too busy filing updates to the online edition to get out of their office to do research, so they repurpose PR releases, wire service stories, and free video clips to fill pages and programs. Their professional pride does not permit some to admit to such an emaciated existence. Some journalists blatantly lie about using PR material. It is what Robert McChesney calls their "dirty secret" (2013, p. 90). In such cases, greater transparency should not be an option; it should be insisted on by editors, producers, and media regulators.

However, former editor in chief David Hickie said that part of the problem is that the ranks of senior experienced editors and sub-editors have been routed in media cutbacks and those remaining are under pressure. He said that, beyond individual journalists, "check and balances have to be applied up the line. Bosses in the media need to say we've got this enthusiastic young journalist who's running around doing all this stuff, but is the source good enough? Media management has to take responsibility and provides checks and balances". He fears this is not happening in many media organizations (personal communication, October 24, 2013).

Former BBC reporter Andy Winstanley offered some explanation of why many journalists appear to lie about using PR information—the discourse of denial discussed in this analysis. Winstanley noted that "journalists mainly classify PR material as that given in press releases, events and conferences". He added that "many would not classify information gained in briefings and from those they view as 'contacts' as PR material" (personal communication, September 2, 2013). In other words, journalists apply a narrow definition of PR, restricted mainly to traditional PR outputs, and do not recognize many other sophisticated communication strategies as PR. For instance, most of the information on government and corporate Web sites is PR-generated or PR-related, as is much of their social media communication. Similarly, research studies and reports, seemingly spontaneously offered exclusive interviews, and visits by international VIPs, who journalists flock to meet and quote, are often largely and sometimes even wholly PR activities, conceptualized and coordinated by PR practitioners. Winstanley's observation is a significant insight which partly explains the paradoxes and contradictions in journalism–PR relations and indicates that the discourse of denial is not intentional lying or deceit—it is largely cultural interpretation of what is PR and who is PR versus a 'contact' or 'source'.

In other cases, journalists are caught in the middle between media management on one hand and PR and marketing on the other. While many journalists strive to maintain high standards of integrity and independence, their own advertising departments, business development managers, and new digital media divisions are soliciting 'partnerships' with organizations that guarantee positive exposure and promotional opportunities in return for a fee. Bob Jensen sees a "blurring of lines between journalism and infotainment", saying somewhat cynically and regretfully: "In the US, some journalists are being paid by companies and organizations to write stories and program anchors and guests are paid to talk about products" (personal communication, September 14, 2013). Often this is not their choice; it is the result of deals struck between media sales managers staring at a red balance sheet and advertisers looking for ways to get their message across in an era of declining impact of traditional advertising (de Pelsmacker & Neijens, 2012) and consumer resistance to advertising evidenced in the use of TiVo and ad blockers on the Internet. (See 'PR 2.0 and 3.0' and 'Embedded' marketing communication and promotion' in Chapter 7 for more details on new formats creating convergence of journalism and PR.)

Relationships—The Glue that Holds Journalism and PR Together

An unambiguous overall finding of this study was that, along with pragmatism, relationships are central and fundamental in journalism–PR interaction and provide the glue that holds them together in collaborative co-existence, or comes unstuck shattering the relatively fragile and tensioned bond. Almost every journalist and PR practitioner interviewed spoke of relationships. When interrogated on how these relationships are established and maintained and what underpinned them, several key themes emerged. Both journalists and PR practitioners referred to the importance of *reliability*, *honesty*, and *fairness* as essential elements that led to *trust*. While all interviewees referred to relationships as key to working together productively, there are mixed views on whether the relationships are primarily transactional (i.e., constantly under review based on each individual interaction) or enduring relationships based on accumulated experiences. Most journalists and PR practitioners agreed that relationships become established over time and that "track record" provides the framework for ongoing dealings. Corporate vice president, corporate affairs for US food giant Cargill, Mike Fernandez, who worked for National Public Radio (NPR) before going into PR, said:

> I think that for the first couple of times you have an interaction with a journalist, it's a bit like, show me. Both sides act cautiously. But I've been involved in very complicated stories that have had national consequences here in the United States where I would pick up the phone and talk to a reporter who I might have interacted with 12 years ago. He knows me, I know him. We've got history together and so he already has a sense that he can trust me (personal communication, October 21, 2013).

Track record also works the other way. *PRWeek* brand editor in the UK, Ruth Wyatt, said:

> If you experience somebody offering you something that subsequently turns out not to be exclusive or is old, or is a bit of a stitch up, or you feel overly manipulated by PR, then that impacts on all future dealings with that person (personal communication, June 26, 2013).

Veteran Australian PR practitioner Stephen Woodhill affirmed: "It's all relationships. There are times of course when it has to be transactional. You might be dealing with someone for the first time…but even then you try to engage so you're establishing a relationship." He added: "Trust can only be built by being available, honest and reliable. Be prepared to discuss the good with the bad." On the other hand, he said "an awful lot of PR people try to 'game' journalists. If you 'game' a journalist, you don't deserve to have a relationship" (personal communication, October 30, 2013).

CEO (EAME) of Ogilvy PR, Stuart Smith, confirmed the pilot study finding that closer relationships and interactions occur in specialist fields such as IT. He said "there is a different relationship between PR people in the 'tech' sector and the journalist because basically they're all geeks. So they actually connect at a very different level" (personal communication, June 26, 2013). (Stuart Smith, incidentally, has a PhD in environmental chemistry from Oxford—indicative of the expertise that exists in the PR sector in a number of cases.) Gordon Welsh from Dana Petroleum said "it's also much the same in industry sectors such as oil and gas" (personal communication, August 16, 2013).

However, the existence of cooperative, trusting, and even cordial relationships and friendships between journalists and PR practitioners does not mean, in most cases, preferential treatment and favouritism, deals, or compromise of principles. Rather, the research indicates that journalists and PR practitioners generally manage to separate personal feelings and relationships from their work and attempt to adhere to professional codes and standards even within close relationships that sometimes exist. Journalists interviewed stressed that, while relationships with PR practitioners make it easier to know who to contact and to get information, they give no guarantees of favourable media treatment or coverage. Equally and significantly, PR practitioners are unanimous in the view that relationships with journalists do not give them any expectation or guarantees of special consideration.

Scottish Television (STV) editor Shaun Milne, who previously was a newspaper journalist with publications including *The Daily Record*, *The Edinburgh Evening News*, and *The Glasgow Evening Times* in Scotland, as well as with *The Sunday Telegraph*, *The Daily Mirror*, and *The Sunday Mail* with 20 years' experience in journalism in total, said that "tensions should be expected" between journalists and PR practitioners. "If there were none, if there was some kind of content utopia, then neither side would be doing their jobs" (personal communication, September 23, 2013).

An important limitation pointed out is that "journalists by their nature often want more than a PR person can give…and PR people often want more than a journalist can give…so it's never going to be a completely satisfying relationship" (Nick Hindle, personal communication, June 19, 2013). Hindle expanded on this with a light-hearted but significant qualification to the trust that can develop between journalists and PR practitioners saying:

> It's a bit like the trust that forms between a lion tamer and a lion or an elephant and his handler. There is a trust and a relationship and they work together harmoniously, but at any stage an elephant is always an elephant and a lion is always a lion (personal communication, June 19, 2013).

From his experience working with the US government and internationally, Bob Jensen said he found the relationship between journalists and PR practitioners less adversarial in the US than in the UK. He described the relationship between journalists and PR practitioners as "a dance". He said there are steps and ground rules to follow, but there is dynamic interaction to negotiate. Jensen said it is departmental policy and his own view that all journalists should be treated fairly and given assistance. But he explained:

> Part of the dance is through agreed upon ground rules and a steady stream of timely, accurate and useful information being distributed to all media through well-established processes.... Journalists understand that there needs to be some give and take and those who get that will be given more access and assistance...journalists who use statements out of context or break ground rules or refuse to correct errors in fact usually get the minimum assistance. They get the standard statements and strictly worded responses (personal communication, September 14, 2013).

This research strongly confirmed the finding of other studies that relationships are an important factor in understanding the considerable interdependencies between journalism and PR, despite generalized public criticisms and hostility (e.g., Aronoff, 1975; Curtin, 1999; Jeffers, 1977; Shaw & White, 2004). Also, it confirmed studies showing that journalists view practitioners with whom they have regular contact as status equals (Shaw & White, 2004, p. 494), even though they maintain a sometimes justified and often ideologically based dislike and even disdain for PR. But this research also revealed some other interesting insights into these relationships.

The Flawed Theory of Symbiosis

Andrew Gowers, who left the role of editor of *The Financial Times* in the UK to become head of corporate communications for Lehman Bros bank, invokes a *Harry Potter* metaphor in writing: "I simply don't buy the idea that it's a Manichean struggle between knights in shining armour and the Voldemorts of PR". He believes journalists and PR practitioners should be able to co-operate on a "two-way street", although he does see his role in PR as quite different to journalism ("PR: It's not the dark side any more", 2006).

All senior journalists and PR practitioners interviewed acknowledged that the fields need to work together and most acknowledged that each helps the other to an extent. But their accounts of how working relationships operate do not support claims of symbiosis between journalism and PR in the sense that symbiosis is most often interpreted. Given choices of describing the role of PR practitioners and the relationship between journalists and PR practitioners that included 'first point of contact only', 'sources', 'symbiosis', a 'trade secret of PR', 'journalism's dirty little secret', 'problematic', 'the enemy', or 'other', most journalists and PR practitioners agreed that each has a job to do and that, even though their roles interrelate, their jobs are different. One option in the question guide was 'PR practitioners do their job for organizations and journalists do theirs for the public' and a number of journalists and PR practitioners specifically commented that this was a necessary and important distinction. Although scientists identify various levels and forms of symbiosis, most forms involve one species permanently or persistently living *on* or *in* another, ideally for mutual benefit (mutualism)—although commensalism (in which one party benefits) and parasitism are forms of symbiosis. In most analyses of journalism, PR is an external influence and, as discussed in Chapter 3, PR uses a wide range of other channels and sites. Likewise, while using PR sources and information, journalism should involve independent analysis and not depend on PR. These factors, and the ever-present tensions and frequent conflagrations that occur between the entities, indicate that the journalism–PR relationship is certainly not *obligate symbiosis* in which one or both entities entirely depend on each other for survival and enjoy mutualism or at least commensalism. It is at best *facultative symbiosis* in which entities live together and interact, but can exist independently of one another—although this research indicates that, in practice, this form of symbiosis does not exist either between journalism and PR in contemporary societies. Symbiosis seems to both overstate and simplistically understate the interrelationship between journalism and PR. So we need to look further into this complex interrelationship.

The Construction and Deconstruction of Trusted Sources

Many studies have shown that, in order to be news sources, individuals and organizations need to be seen by journalists as legitimate (e.g., Anderson, 1993; Berkowitz, 1992). Legitimacy is established in a number of ways, such as through qualifications, expertise, authority (e.g., official title or office), and trustworthiness which, as discussed previously, is established through reliability, honesty, and fairness. However, in probing relationships deeper, particularly interactions with regular sources, two further criteria emerge as important and even central to selection of sources and the construction of trusted sources.

A number of practitioners noted that, to a large extent, in contemporary media environments in which journalists are short-handed and in a hurry, sources are selected and used largely on the basis of access (i.e., availability). For example, former Fairfax editor in chief David Hickie said "things have changed a lot in the 35 years I've been in the business". He said that in the 1970s and even into the 1980s, corporations and even big accountancy, law, and business consultancy firms "were not geared to provide an expert to talk or comment on things that a journalist was interested in. Now, if you are a journalist…the companies are all set to provide an expert and give a comment at a moment's notice" (personal communication, October 24, 2013). Several PR practitioners interviewed also commented that one of their key functions is having spokespersons ready and willing to speak to the media at short notice—including outside of working hours. This confirms experiences reported in Chapter 4.

Producer of *Health Report* for the ABC (Australian Broadcasting Corporation) Dr Norman Swan identified another bias that affects sources selected for comment by media. He said "media seek so-called experts as sources. But often the person interviewed is the person who can talk—the person with the best media skills" (personal communication, December 3, 2013). Media, particularly television and radio, actively seek what they refer to as good *talent*, which they identify in practical terms as interviewees and guest commentators with a high level of media presentation skills (e.g., public speaking ability, well-modulated voice, personality, confidence, etc.).

While most journalism and media studies texts suggest that PR practitioners are 'organization gatekeepers' (often expressed pejoratively), or 'first point of contact' (i.e., 'gateway'), but that they are not legitimate sources, these additional criteria of availability and media skills propel PR practitioners towards the forefront of media source selection—either as conduits to access organization spokespersons and sometimes as sources themselves. Despite anti-spin rhetoric and public protestations against PR, a number of journalists nominated PR as "points for fact checking" as well as "contacts" (e.g., Shaun Milne, STV, personal communication, September 23, 2013).

Australian Anthony Tregoning, who has spent more than 40 years in publishing and PR, including heading a respected financial PR agency for several decades, made the provocative statement that "PR information can be more accurate than journalists' stories" (personal communication, October 21, 2013). While some journalists will take umbrage at and even be outraged by such a claim, Tregoning makes an important point that is widely overlooked. Financial institutions, such as banks and superannuation funds, and public companies are highly regulated, and media releases and public statements relating to earnings, mergers and acquisitions, joint ventures, and many other aspects of their operations are usually rigorously reviewed by corporate lawyers, they have to be signed off by the CEO and sometimes even the board of directors, and in some circumstances have to be submitted for approval by regulators such as stock exchanges or securities, investment, or superannuation watchdogs. Amanda Millar, head of trade marketing and corporate affairs at Yahoo!7 in Australia, supported Tregoning's claim, saying "corporate communication is highly regulated in the case of public companies" and the focus of PR is on "distributing factual information" (personal communication, October 10, 2013). A similar situation applies with medical and pharmaceutical institutions and companies. Before any announcement or claim can be made about products or services, strenuous approval procedures must be followed. PR practitioners report, often with a high degree of frustration, the difficulties of drafting, redrafting, and guiding statements through these approval procedures, while at the same time trying to retain comprehensibility for the public. Journalists are not bound by such strict legal requirements and PR practitioners in sectors such as science lament how media, in their haste and efforts to simplify information, regularly report inaccurately.

While some dismiss claims of accuracy in PR information, former editor in chief of *The Sydney Morning Herald* and 35-year veteran journalist David Hickie gave weight to the argument. In noting that there is always more than one side to a story, he said that "making contact with the public relations or the public affairs representative of an organization is valuable to your accuracy and to the story generally". He also stated that PR practitioners can "be very valuable because a journalist may not be exactly up to date with what is the latest law on this or that, or what's the latest developments in an area. The [PR] practitioner in a specific area will be. He or she is an expert or can direct you to an expert in the organization". He added on a philosophical note: "Big corporations are not always the enemy, although you might think that when you're just out of university" (personal communication, October 24, 2013).

Acculturation of PR as Trusted Sources

A number of interviewees gave at least qualified support to the pilot study finding that journalists acculturate PR practitioners into their coterie of contacts and trusted sources and, once admitted to this status, no longer view them as PR practitioners or associate them with PR. For example, former BBC journalist Andy Winstanley said that "the best PRs are actually not seen as PRs but as good contacts" (personal communication, October 8, 2013). From his experience as head of a leading US research company specializing in media, communication, and PR, David Rockland went further, saying journalists often contact him, as well as his clients, as "an expert source" (personal communication, October 18, 2013). Bob Jensen at the

US Department of Homeland Security reported a similar experience from his 30 years in government PR. He said he believed he was seen as both a government official and an expert source on a range of matters related to security, emergencies, and foreign affairs. Several US, UK, and Australian journalists acknowledged that those whom they refer to as "contacts", "specialists", "experts", and "trusted sources" include some whose job titles and roles are corporate relations, external relations, public affairs, and other positions that could be described as PR.

A *theory of acculturation* of PR as trusted sources and contacts, first proposed as a result of the pilot study discussed earlier in this chapter and reported in Macnamara (2012b), is supported by this research and at least partially explains why journalists often deny using PR material. Because of this process of acculturation, they simply do not see some people who have PR roles as PR. Andy Winstanley's observation that many journalists perceive PR narrowly as "news releases, events and conferences" and do not see many other tasks and activities undertaken by PR practitioners such as arranging interviews, providing background and facts, and answering questions as PR (personal communication, September 2, 2013), combined with the never-ending demand for information and content which requires accessible reliable sources, contributes to this phenomenon. Journalists need to "feed the hungry beast 24/7", as Bob Jensen put it (personal communication, September 14, 2013). To do so, they rely on sources and, in an age when most organizations have PR professionals fronting and coordinating their media and public communication, as well as often speaking for the organization, it is inevitable that some, if not many, PR practitioners become acculturated and absorbed into this special group that journalists trust and on whom they and the public rely. If journalists have established the veracity and trustworthiness of such sources through a professional working relationship over some time, this acculturation of PR as trusted sources is unproblematic and even beneficial. This further illustrates the fallacy of generalizing about PR. But it also turns critical attention back to the substantial part of the PR industry that does not meet these criteria.

Ethics—Can Journalists or PRs Pass the Test?

No journalists and only one PR practitioner interviewed had undergone formal training or education in ethics, other than an occasional lecture at university. All apply a subjective interpretation of ethics linked to personal morals and intuitive understandings. Concepts such as teleological and deontological ethical frameworks are unfamiliar to them and, while this might be expected among practitioners, the potential complexity of ethics and different perspectives that can be applied leading to different actions need to be better understood among both PR practitioners and journalists if high ethical standards are to be achieved. David Rockland from Ketchum in the US was the only interviewee who spoke strongly and specifically about ethics, saying: "There should be ethics training in every major PR agency with a test that you must pass or be fired" (personal communication, October 18, 2013). The CEO of Ketchum Europe, David Gallagher, said the agency required all staff to do ethical training every two years (personal communication, June 24, 2013).

Transparency—Maybe!

Robert McChesney describes the high proportion of media content that is sourced from PR as "the dirty secret of journalism" (2013, p. 90) and many scholars call for greater transparency in media sources. In 2010, as part of its Transparency Initiative, the UK Media Standards Trust called for journalists and publishers to disclose the original sources of all information, as well as the name of the author or authors, any affiliations or interests involved (such as sponsored travel and PR releases or other materials used), and the details of journalistic codes applied. A report for the Commission of Inquiry into the Future of Civil Society in the UK and Ireland by scholars from the Goldsmiths Leverhulme Media Research Centre similarly recommended:

> News organisations should be required to be accountable for their own coverage, be seen to embrace transparency in their news gathering activities and, wherever possible declare the source of their information to encourage original, investigative reporting and limit cannibalization and over-reliance on news agencies (Witschge, Fenton, & Freedman, 2010, p. 8).

The report further stated in its discussion: "We should move immediately to a system of transparency in the accurate labelling of the origins of all news reports" (p. 33).

However, most journalists rebuff such suggestions, claiming that any move to require full disclosure of sources would be "counter-productive" and an infringement of their right to protect their sources. They point out that most sources are disclosed in the text of articles, such as quotations from a named spokesperson. A flaw in this argument is the difference between primary and secondary sources. Journalists often do not differentiate between the two. For instance, information or a statement used in media content may be attributed to a person, such as the CEO of an organization, which appears to be transparent. However, the journalist may have extracted the quote and name from a media news release and never have spoken with the spokesperson. Several of the in-house PR practitioners interviewed reported that they had authority to speak for the CEO of their organization and issue statements in her or his name. Even though this practice is based on close consultation between PR practitioners and their CEOs and prior approval, it means that quotes in the media are not always what they appear to be. Worse, some media releases cite third-party research reports and data, which are often used by journalists without checking with the primary source. Information is often presented in media in a way that appears to be direct reporting by a journalist, when in fact it is secondary information that the journalist has not verified. In other cases, facts and figures are supplied by PR practitioners, such as industry statistics and financial data, and used either without attribution (which suggests they are the result of the journalist's own research) or disguised with quasi attribution such as 'industry sources'.

Ketchum CEO for Europe, David Gallagher, said a mild form of disclaimer such as 'this article was prepared in cooperation with [organization name]' could be beneficial, but he questioned whether media would go along with the idea and concluded: "I have a hard time seeing that work in practice" (personal communication, June 24, 2013). Martin Frizell, employed by GolinHarris PR in London since 2011 but with almost 25 years in journalism before that, said "I don't see how that would work" (personal communication, June 24, 2013). Some journalists and PR practitioners suggested that audiences did not want and would be "bored" by full disclosure of sources of information (PR5, UK PR consultant, personal communication, June 19, 2013).

ABC *Health Report* producer and award-winning health reporter Dr Norman Swan said he supports transparency in journalism, but he differentiated between journalists receiving information for consideration and commercial arrangements relating to media content. He said: "If journalists have received a lead from a PR person or been introduced to some specialist to interview, there's nothing wrong with that. Nothing needs to be declared. But journalists should disclose any funding arrangements involved in a story" (personal communication, December 3, 2013). He believes that sponsorships of media programs and content are particularly concerning.

Judging by the comments of journalists and PR practitioners interviewed in this study, despite a general concern for transparency, there does not seem to be much likelihood that greater transparency of sources of published and broadcast information will be introduced by media practitioners. New developments in media content discussed in the next chapter make this minimalist approach to transparency, which in some cases could be called lip service, concerning and an issue for further research.

Regulation

No journalists supported any form of regulation of practices beyond existing media laws and regulations applying in various countries. It could be said that journalists are resistant to regulation generally—even existing levels—and, given the importance of free media, that is probably a reasonable position to take. They fear encroachment by government on their freedoms and rights, which they see as essential to undertake their role as the Fourth Estate and 'watchdogs', and recent cases such as US government action against WikiLeaks founder Julian Assange, and other activist reporters and whistle blowers have exacerbated these fears.

PR practitioners have mixed views about regulation. All PR practitioners interviewed acknowledged unsavoury practices in their field, but they pointed to difficulties in enforcement of standards. Gordon Welsh of Dana Petroleum noted that "there are low barriers to entry to PR", which he said is part of the problem (personal communication, August 16, 2013). Practitioners also noted the voluntary nature of codes of ethics and codes of practice which the industry has adopted and their lack of teeth, not because of lack of industry conviction, but because of lack of any protective legislation. As noted in Chapter 4, most PR institutes and associations can expel members, but any public action against them, such as publishing details of offending behaviour ('naming and shaming'), can result in the organization and its officials being sued for defamation and/or damages. A number of practitioners in the UK and elsewhere point to the Chartered Institute of Public Relations (CIPR) in Britain as an example of legislative protection (a Royal Charter) which allows the organization to take action beyond a 'slap on the wrist' against practitioners who breach its standards. However, PR practitioners in the US and Australia believe that such powers are unlikely to be granted by governments which typically restrict such regulatory and legislative frameworks to what they regard as high risk fields such as medicine, law, and accountancy.

Education and Training

Almost all interviewees agreed with former BBC transport and environment reporter Andy Winstanley who said "I think there is a great deal of misunderstanding between the two professions" (personal communication, September 2, 2013). This appears to be pronounced among young journalists. Several of those interviewed stated that experienced journalists and corporate communication professionals "understand the game" and "know how to work together", while several PR practitioners expressed concern about inexperienced journalists who they said were arrogant, sometimes confrontational, and often naïve. Very few of the journalists interviewed had read a book about PR (other than critical texts such as Nick Davies' *Flat Earth News*), much less studied PR in a university subject or even a short course. As reported earlier in this chapter, a number of former journalists who 'crossed over' to work in PR acknowledged that they found themselves with a lot to learn (e.g., Ruth Wyatt, personal communication, June 26, 2013).

This echoes comments by senior media practitioners elsewhere. Canadian Broadcasting Corporation radio producer Ira Basen, who conducted training programs for CBC Radio journalists for a number of years, reported that he found "most journalists were largely ignorant of what public relations was and how it worked and were content to dismiss PR people as spin doctors and paid liars" and discuss PR in terms of "myths and clichés" (Gombita, 2012, para. 10). Academic research also has indicated prejudice based at least partly on ignorance. For instance, Lillian Kopenhaver (1984) observed in a study of journalists talking to PR students about ethics that "journalists have a narrow and self-righteous view of their work and know little about public relations" (p. 18).

PR practitioners unanimously stated that they had been taught about journalism and media practices, with many having done subjects or whole courses in journalism. Journalists interviewed agreed that PR practitioners need to have a sound understanding of "what journalists want", "how the media work", "deadlines, etcetera". Most university PR courses include lectures or whole subjects or units on media relations and media writing and, not surprisingly, PR practitioners interviewed enthusiastically supported journalism education in PR courses and PR education in journalism courses.

But journalists interviewed have mixed and vexed views on whether trainee journalists should receive some education in PR and some are strongly opposed to such suggestions. When pursued, those opposing education in PR for journalists either feel it is unnecessary because journalism graduates can learn about PR on the job (illustrating a lingering preference for on-the-job training rather than university education), or imply that somehow journalism students would be sullied or corrupted through lectures, briefings, or discussions of PR. Peter Jones, a journalist before spending 30 years handling PR for major global corporations including British Airways and Bupa, acknowledged that PR education for journalists could be seen as "a bit like inviting the fox into a hen house", but he supported the idea (personal communication, June 20, 2013).

However, there was some qualified support for education of journalism students about PR among some journalists and particularly among those who have crossed over to work in PR. Andy Winstanley stated that "trust comes from personal relationships and an understanding of each other's agenda" (personal communication, September 2, 2013). Dr Norman Swan from the ABC in Australia was one who said he "definitely supports students studying journalism receiving information about how PR works and what it does", although he added the proviso, with emphasis, that "it has to be ethical PR that is taught" (personal communication, December 3, 2013). His countryman, former Fairfax editor David Hickie, also supports the idea of journalism students learning about PR. He said:

> Journalism and seeking the truth will benefit from understanding...the subtleties and nuances involved in the public relations and public affairs industry and how some of that works. You will actually benefit if you hear that from the start and don't just find it out by experience five years into journalism (personal communication, October 24, 2013).

Martin Frizell, who despite working in PR since 2011, is a veteran journalist, said: "If you have a PR and journalism course running side by side, they [students] should be made to spend the first six months in the one classroom getting the basics of the world around them" (personal communication, June 24, 2013).

PR practitioners are strongly supportive of journalism students receiving an informed basic understanding of PR. Nick Hindle of McDonald's said: "I think the rules of engagement are rarely made clear on both sides. The rules of engagement are too often left unsaid" (personal communication, June 19, 2013). The CEO of Ketchum Europe, David Gallagher, himself a former journalist, commented:

> I think that has to be a good thing. I can't see any downside to every journalism graduate being subjected to some material about here's how best practice PR works, this is what you should look for and this is what you should be aware, and maybe what you should be cautious of. I don't see anything negative coming out of that (personal communication, June 24, 2013).

A number of other senior PR practitioners are equally supportive including Bob Jensen of the US Department of Homeland Security who commented that "it would make great sense for courses of study in journalism, communication and public relations to all include introductory courses about the other". He added: "I don't think there is any place for building negative impressions or beliefs in a university course about another line of work. I feel that is unprofessional and very unproductive" (personal communication, September 14, 2013).

There are also challenges for PR education within its own field of practice. A number of CEOs of leading PR consultancies said they prefer to hire graduates from liberal arts degrees, politics, economics, and other fields, including specialists such as doctors for health communication, rather than graduates of PR degrees. For example, GolinHarris international president, Matt Neale, expressed a view held by a number of employers in PR when he said: "I actually don't value the training that communication students get at university because it's just so theoretical as opposed to practice" (personal communication, June 24, 2013). Australian financial PR consultancy owner Anthony Tregoning specifically cited a "lack of writing skills" among PR graduates (personal communication, October 21, 2013), a complaint that is frequently made by employers in the PR industry who seek graduates with practical skills more than critical analytical capabilities and social and civic sensibilities (Macnamara, 2012c).

The Role and Impact of Social Media—Practitioners' Perspectives

Perhaps not surprisingly, no journalists interviewed believe that social media will replace independent professional media or serve as a viable Fifth Estate (Cooper, 2006; Dutton, 2007). Nor do PR practitioners, interestingly. All interviewees had given the matter considerable thought—social media came up regularly in all discussions—and all agreed with scholarly research findings that suggest media types will converge and hybridize to a significant extent (Jenkins, 2006; Macnamara, 2014), but also that most or all major forms will continue to co-exist at least for some time to come.

US PR researcher David Rockland said "great journalists will always be important" (personal communication, October 18, 2013). Andy Winstanley explained that "the growth of citizen generated content means there is an even greater need for good journalism now", given the volume of information produced and distributed on the Internet, much of which is unchecked, based on one perspective, and sometimes inaccurate (personal communication, September 3, 2013). The view of a number of scholars, including this author's analysis of the future of journalism in Chapter 2 of this book and in *The 21st Century Media (R)evolution: Emergent Communication Practices* (Macnamara, 2010, 2014), support this view.

PR practitioners do recognize and welcome the added channels for communication opened up through social media. Long-time journalist turned PR practitioner Martin Frizell said: "With being able to go direct to people, you are broadcasting yourself. A lot of what we do here [GolinHarris, London] is broadcasting straight to people...we're plugging into people directly now, bypassing the traditional routes" (personal communication, June 24, 2013). Similarly, SVP of corporate affairs for McDonald's in the UK and Northern Europe, Nick Hindle, commented that "PR can now talk directly to audiences rather than going via [traditional] media, so it's holding more and more cards" (personal communication,

June 19, 2013). In terms of the value that this brings, Australian PR consultant Anthony Tregoning explained:

> One of the weaknesses of going to your stakeholders through media is that you're relying on journalists' interpretation of what you say. If you go direct to people, you say what you want to say…. So to a certain extent, it's going to make communication much more effective (personal communication, October 21, 2013).

Mike Fernandez from Cargill similarly sees social media as a welcome development, commenting that "the technology today allows you to go direct in a way that you couldn't before". However, he and several other PR practitioners interviewed recognize social media as a "leveller" and a 'double edge sword'. Fernandez noted that, as well as providing a direct channel for organization–public communication, the ubiquitous nature of social media created transparency in terms of organizational behaviour, commenting that Cargill chairman and CEO, Greg Page, was "fond of saying, 'in a world where nothing can be hidden, you better not have anything to hide'" (personal communication, October 21, 2013). Interestingly, despite its theorization in media studies and PR texts and case studies reported in relation to mass media, no interviewee in this study feels that *agenda cutting*—keeping information out of media—is realistic in the age of social media. Bob Jensen from the US Department of Homeland Security said: "Today's digital and social media technology have changed how we do business. We are keenly aware that we can't hide the truth" (personal communication, September 14, 2013).

The Other Invisible Side of PR

While much of the activity and influence of PR in framing, priming, building, and setting the agenda of media coverage and public debate is surreptitious and largely invisible to the public, as pointed out by a number of authors, there is another even more invisible element of PR unseen and unrecognized even by journalists. As noted in Chapter 3 under 'PR as Counsellor' and in the sub-section titled 'Much PR Is Nothing to Do with Mass Media', a key role of senior PR practitioners is providing advice to management. This can include advice on opportunities for publicity and reputation building, such as advocating strategic sponsorship opportunities or proposing promotional events. However, the counsellor role of PR also often includes advising management on what not to do, what to stop doing, and what to fix or change. Senior ethical PR practitioners aware of poor environmental performance in parts of an organization's operations often urge management to address the issues before they become public and cause reputation damage.

Informed by research, senior PR practitioners are involved in warning management about rising concerns or dissatisfaction among stakeholders, shifting public attitudes and expectations, and anticipated negative reactions to proposals and plans. While PR practitioners are advisers and cannot direct management, many advocate and argue strongly for policies and actions that are socially responsible. This may not balance the interests of the organization and its stakeholders to the extent of symmetry and total co-orientation, but it is an underestimated part of the role of senior PR practitioners.

Colin Browne, the former head of PR for major UK companies including British Telecom (BT) and the BBC, estimates that during his career he spent 50 per cent of his time on internal counselling of management (personal communication, June 26, 2013). Corporate affairs head of Cargill, Mike Fernandez, agrees with this ratio, saying "for me it's at least 50–50, although sometimes it goes a little more external". He added: "We're representing the company to the outside. At the same time, we're representing the outside to the company" (personal communication, October 29, 2013). CEO of Ketchum Europe, David Gallagher, puts the percentage of internal counselling much higher at up to 80 per cent (personal communication, June 24, 2013). He estimates that only 20 per cent of his time and that of his senior consultants is devoted to disseminating information. Amanda Millar, my former postgraduate student who coordinated the pilot study and worked as director of trade marketing and corporate affairs for Yahoo!7 in Australia at the time of this research, estimates her time spent counselling management as high as 90 per cent. She reported that this included briefing senior executives and also "coaching" them. However, she was at pains to explain that coaching is not about making them scripted and rehearsed. She said that coaching "is more about getting management to explain things in a way that members of the public can understand" (personal communication, October 10, 2013). Such findings indicate that journalists see only a part of PR and sometimes a small part, although it must be said that the management counselling role is restricted to more senior PR practitioners.

Nevertheless, this invisible side of PR warrants more attention. It remains a contentious issue even in PR theory. As discussed in Chapter 3, Excellence theory calls for the senior PR practitioner to be a member of the senior management team—what some refer to as 'the dominant coalition' (Berger, 2005; Dozier, 1992). But others argue that, as a member of the "inner circle" (Thompson, 1967) or inner sanctum, the PR practitioner becomes inculcated into the culture and management style of the organization and, over time, becomes unable to see or represent the views of external stakeholders. Some argue that PR consultants are in a better position to advise management. However, PR consultancies are often more precarious than senior staff members in terms of their employment contract so arguing against management plans and proposal can be fraught. A further model is for PR advisors to be positioned outside organizations in the way legal counsel and auditors are positioned. However, this will require far greater professionalization, ethics training, and specialist education than currently exists in the PR industry in most countries.

Structure of the PR Industry

While this book discusses the structure of news media and journalism in Chapter 2 in terms of economic and technological influences that are changing practices, this study did not examine the structure of the PR industry in any detail. However, in addition to drawing attention to the advisory role of PR and where it might best be positioned to influence organization management, another interesting finding that emerged spontaneously from discussions is that a number of companies and government agencies are employing journalists for new roles in content production. After a trend of hiring journalists to do PR work that began with the birth of modern PR in the early 20th century and peaked in the 1970s and 1980s, before declining as an increasing number of specialized university PR courses became available, there are indications that organizations looking for expert content producers to support their growing investment in 'owned' media such as Web sites and social media sites are turning back to journalists.

Mike Fernandez reported that he has done this at Cargill and he is aware of a number of companies in the US that have recently hired journalists to produce content for them. He said: "In terms of hiring former journalists to work as part of our team, I think that that's only going to continue, particularly in a world of social media" (personal communication, October 21, 2013). In Australia, PR consultant Anthony Tregoning reported that a corporate client had similarly hired a journalist internally to produce content and, coincidentally, one of Australia's leading telecommunications companies reported at a seminar during the period of this research that it was recruiting journalists as content producers for its social media.

This is good news for journalists seeking employment—and potentially bad news for PR practitioners. While insufficient data are available to identify the extent or basis of this phenomenon, several interviewees noted that PR has become a broad role in organizations. Also, several commented that PR writing is often highly promotional and that organizations wishing to attract audiences to their owned media sites need content that is well-written, often produced quickly, and which is interesting and easy to understand for a wide audience—skills and processes in which journalists specialize.

Another trend emphasized by several participants in the study, including Mike Fernandez from Cargill, is that "because of PR getting a bad name, because of spin, most of our departments aren't called public relations any longer" (personal communication, October 21, 2013). This is a long-established trend in Europe (van Ruler & Verčič, 2004) and, as noted in Chapter 1, there is already a wide range of terms and titles used in the US, UK, Australia, and other countries. Unless it becomes rehabilitated, the connotations of 'PR' are likely to further influence the shape and branding of the industry over the next decade or two.

Professional PR Associations

While this study did not specifically examine the role and efficacy of professional associations and institutes, several interviewees commented on professional bodies in the context of education and training, standards, and ethics. Most were negative or mildly supportive at best of professional associations in their respective countries. Several senior PR practitioners, including CEOs of some of the largest PR agencies, were critical of organizations such as the Chartered Institute of Public Relations (CIPR) and the PR Consultants Association (PRCA) in the UK, and the Public Relations Institute of Australia (PRIA). Senior corporate relations and public affairs practitioners, in particular, feel that professional industry associations offer something to young practitioners but little to senior professionals. One high level corporate PR practitioner commented: "I don't think that the professional organizations that, in theory, represent PR people do us a great deal of service" (PR3, UK PR consultant, personal communication, October 30, 2013).

An interesting situation exists in the UK where the National Union of Journalists (NUJ) has established a Public Relations and Communications Council (PRCC) to represent PR practitioners and encourages PR members. Phil Morcom, who has spent almost 20 years in journalism including editing a trade magazine before becoming a media and social policy consultant working with non-profit organizations and being co-chair of the NUJ PRCC, admitted that "there is debate about whether that's a good thing or a bad thing". However, he commented:

> But it's certainly a reality. I think that there is a mix of people in the NUJ who are more pragmatic and realistic than others. Some take a strict ideological stand that there should be lots of demarcation and argue that we should continue to fight for that. Others take a view that, actually, that's not going to represent the world as it is (personal communication, June 26, 2013).

Figure 6.2. UK National Union of Journalists (NUJ) member recruitment brochure.

In the US, the Public Relations Society of America (PRSA) is well recognized and seen as doing "an OK job" (PR4, US PR consultant, personal communication, October 22, 2013), while industry research bodies such as the Institute for Public Relations (IPR) were known by only one of the practitioners interviewed. It should be emphasized that, as qualitative research with a relatively small sample, these findings cannot be generalized as an indication of the effectiveness or reputation of these bodies. However, the concerns expressed at senior level should be noted.

Developmental Media Relations

Two in-depth interviews were conducted by the author with journalists in the Solomon Islands in 2006, as well as with a senior PR practitioner working with AusAID[4], the major aid organization involved in relief operations in the island country at the time. While these were conducted some time ago as part of a separate research project to the main body of interviews reported here, these interviews afford insights into a particular area of journalism and PR that is little talked about other than in specialist studies of developmental communication. One journalist interviewed worked for the national newspaper, *The Solomon Star*, and the other was a reporter for the national radio network, Solomon Islands Broadcasting Corporation (SIBC). The PR practitioner interviewed was the director of public affairs of a national aid organization involved in the Regional Assistance Mission to the Solomon Islands (RAMSI). This mission was implemented to restore peace and stability in the Solomon Islands after a period of conflict and ethnic tensions that occurred between 1998 and 2006. These culminated in large-scale rioting and civil unrest in 2006 during which Australian, New Zealand, and Fijian police and troops were dispatched to restore order. The interviews took place in the national capital Honiara shortly after this period of heightened conflict.

The Solomon Islands is a western Pacific archipelago of more than 900 islands with a population of just over half a million, 80 per cent of whom live in rural areas and many of whom were still struggling to access health services, water, sanitation, and education in the early 21st century. The small nation is ranked 143 out of 187 countries in the United Nations Human Development Index (United Nations, 2013). Almost a quarter of the country's population lives below the basic needs poverty line.

These interviews were eye-openers in terms of understanding the role of media in developing countries as well as seeing a side of PR that many do not see or recognize. The journalists interviewed faced acute political pressures, with the incumbent government identified as corrupt. Aid received was often not reaching citizens and, in many cases, the citizens of the impoverished and unstable country were not aware that aid was even available. This was where media played a key role—radio in particular. While most villagers did not have TV and many were illiterate, radio reaches more than 95 per cent of the population. So, radio became a vital channel for providing timely information direct to citizens about aid that was available, such as medical services, clean water, and water purification equipment, and emergency food supplies. The national newspaper also was important for explaining developments such as the role of international police and troops and political change that was occurring to the nation's administrators, professionals, and businesses.

What also became apparent was that PR practitioners working with aid organizations, police, and other authorities played an indispensable role. Local journalists were too few and lacking resources to provide broadcasts on all relevant issues in the multiple languages and dialects spoken in the Solomon Islands. They also lacked technical knowledge on matters such as water purification and medical services and treatments. Professional communication staff of the aid organization on the ground in the Solomon Islands and in their international headquarters provided a steady stream of transcripts and recorded program segments that could be published and broadcast. These had no promotional content—the only mention of the aid organization was as a member of RAMSI (the Regional Assistance Mission to the Solomon Islands). Here was a form of true 'public relations' that I had not witnessed before and which is often ignored. Development (or developmental) journalism is recognized as an important element of emerging nations and democracies. But developmental PR plays a role too. More than in any other instance in my career, I saw journalists and PR practitioners working together.

Digging deeper, I also discovered that several of the leading journalists in the Solomon Islands received their initial training in journalism compliments of scholarships provided through the aid organization, promoted as part of its public affairs/communication function. Australia, of course, is not the only country that provides aid. USAID provides assistance to 35 or more countries around the world in various forms, including not only physical aid but also initiatives to strengthen journalists' skills, build economic self-sustainability of media outlets, and provide legal protection for free independent media (Moss & Koenig, 2013, para. 3). For example, USAID has been active in fostering freer, more professional media in Afghanistan since 2002. In Myanmar (formerly Burma), USAID has worked over a decade with more than 1,000 Burmese journalists. Journalists trained in the program's early years have gone on to become leaders of the local media industry. In Eastern Europe, the USAID-funded Regional Investigative Journalism Network helps connect practicing investigative journalists across borders who seek to uncover corruption, organized crime, and others engaged in the criminal services industry. The Building a Digital Gateway to Better Lives program in eight Middle East and North Africa countries has given more than 300 local journalists hands-on experience with digital tools to design and implement multimedia projects that report on public service issues affecting citizens (Moss & Koenig, 2013).

While most of the credit for these inspiring efforts must go to the aid workers and the brave journalists involved, I learned in the Solomon Islands that public information such as vital health communication also depends on support from PR practitioners working in aid organizations, the military, police, and various NGOs. That's a side of PR you will never see written about in the daily press.

A Taxonomy of PR Roles

What becomes apparent in analysis of extensive data from PR practitioners and journalists is that there is no one type of PR. PR comes in many shapes and forms and some categorization is necessary in order to identify characteristics. Figure 6.3 presents a taxonomy of PR, identifying five main types drawn from this analysis.

It is possible to categorize PR into many more types, but these five represent dominant types of PR practice observed by both journalists and PR practitioners. Figure 6.3 is not a column chart, so the proportions of the types are not to scale. The proportions are simply designed to give some indication of the approximate relativity between the types. The arrows indicate the primary direction of information flow and transactions and the dotted area indicates the approximate former proportion for types that have declined in use.

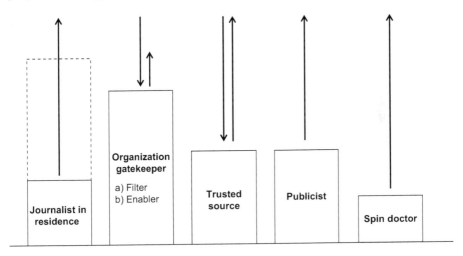

Figure 6.3. A taxonomy of public relations roles and their relationship with media.

1. The *journalist in residence* form of PR practice emerged and became common in the mid-20th century, comprised of public information officers, media relations officers, press secretaries, and the like who came from the ranks of journalism and saw their role predominantly as identifying news and information of public interest in an organization and working to release that information to the public via the media. In this sense, their work aligns with the 'press agentry' or publicity model of PR described by Grunig and Hunt (1984), but they are not sensationalists or promoters in the style of early 20th-century press agents. This type of PR practitioner applies a journalistic 'news sense', writes in a largely journalistic form, and the primary focus and objective is the outbound release of information from the organization through media news releases and arranging interviews with spokespersons. This category most accurately aligns with the "honest information broker" claim of PR noted by John Hohenberg (1973). After being a common approach, this form of PR declined in the late 20th century, as the role of PR broadened and became more strategic.

2. The *organization gatekeeper* serves as the central point of contact for much organization–media interaction. Unlike the journalist in residence whose focus (and often their loyalty) was towards the public and journalistic colleagues, the organization gatekeeper serves the organization and is usually part of middle management. Traditionally their role has been largely passive—that is, they respond to media inquiries, arrange interviews with spokespersons when requested, and produce approved communication such as annual reports to meet legal requirements and expectations of stakeholders. They guard and protect the organization and filter information that is released—and thus they can act as a block or barrier to media in some cases. However, this practitioner also serves as an enabler of public communication by facilitating interviews, events, and other activities in response to requests. This type of practitioner tries to be a 'boundary spanner', reflecting the organization outwards and also reflecting stakeholders' views inside the organization and provides some counsel to management, but the organization's interests always remain paramount.

3. The *trusted source*, as identified in this study, is a mostly overlooked category of PR practitioners who work closely with journalists on a regular basis and who are trusted—both internally within their organization and by journalists. They issue information on behalf of their organization through formal channels such as news releases and official statements and write speeches for their CEOs, but they also spend a lot of their time counselling and advising their organization's senior management, even guiding strategy to reflect stakeholders' interests and social responsibility, and they frequently background journalists to help them understand issues, brief journalists 'off the record', and sometimes can be quoted in their own name as they are often members of the senior executive team. They rarely or never lie and they are frank—for example, when they cannot reveal information or need to protect their organization's reputation, they honestly interact with senior journalists and tell them that they cannot tell them. The trusted source is highly interactive, working in a two-way flow of information with media and publics and endeavours to understand and recognize stakeholders' and societal, as well as organizational, interests.

4. The *publicist*, formally identified in Grunig and Hunt's (1984) landmark 'four models of PR', lives on today in a glitzier, gushier, and even more garrulous form than in the past and is the second most criticized and vilified type of PR practitioner. This category includes what Amanda Millar calls the "Felicity Publicity" types (personal communication, October 10, 2013) and what UK *PRWeek* editor Ruth Wyatt calls the "fluffy bunny

end of the market" (personal communication, June 26, 2013). International president of GolinHarris PR in London Matt Neale noted that "there's a definite distinction to be drawn between publicists and public relations practitioners". He said "publicists basically do lie and they're looking after celebrities" (personal communication, June 24, 2013). Neale, along with his executive director of media Martin Frizell, were among those who split PR into categories and, while giving a seven or eight out of 10 to corporate and business PR practitioners, rated publicists "two or three", with Neale commenting of them: "They have very little integrity, very little honesty. I almost see them as parasites". Publicists are promoters of events, products, celebrities, and themselves. Their currency is novelty, glamour, and often hype, gimmicks, and stunts, and their focus is solely on an outbound flow of information and media contact to generate publicity, rather than organization-public relations.

5. The *spin doctor* has spread to and become associated with the broad field of PR. But a number of interviewees, when asked for examples, pointed particularly to political media advisers and press secretaries working on election campaigns and with members of Congress, senators, and ministers in parliaments—and sometimes even to politicians themselves. For example, in discussing spin associated with Britain entering the second Iraq war, GolinHarris's Matt Neale reflected: "I don't think it was just the PRs, it was the politicians, the intelligence services…and journalists themselves in some cases". Gordon Welsh, group corporate communication manager for Dana Petroleum, said that "politics has given PR and spin a bad name" (personal communication, August 16, 2013). In Australia, 40-year veteran financial PR consultant Anthony Tregoning stated that "too many people came out of government and the political sector into PR", which he argued had brought the techniques of spin into the broader public sphere. He sees spin as the "rump of PR" and not an approach to be incorporated into or conflated with specialist PR such as financial and corporate relations or general PR practice (personal communication, October 21, 2013). Mike Fernandez, corporate vice president of corporate affairs for US food and agriculture giant Cargill, agreed saying: "I think it really started, unfortunately, in politics", although he added that the concept of spin is now "pretty generic" (personal communication, October 28, 2013). Senior career official with the US government Bob Jensen also noted that political parties regularly accuse the party in power of spin, with or without justification, and this is picked up by media, adding to the impression that PR is spin. While spin is used in the business world, by industry lobbyists, and

even by activist organizations which put their own spin on issues, interviewees suggested that spin is predominantly an artefact of politics and political communication. While journalists do not seem to see a difference, the conflation of PR generally with political rhetoric, partisanship, and hyperbole needs unpacking. Spin should be seen as one specific type of public communication, not as a synonym for PR.

It should be noted that this taxonomy of PR types is constructed in the context of journalist–PR relations (i.e., media relations). It does not include the multiple other functions and roles that PR has today, such as employee communication, community relations, and public affairs (i.e., dealing with government including writing submissions and lobbying). Nor does it include the work of PR in utilizing new direct channels of public communication such as social media, which are explored in the next chapter. The purpose of this taxonomy is to identify and explain the different approaches of PR towards what are referred to as mass media, traditional media, or mainstream media. Chapter 3 and Chapter 7 provide more complete analyses of PR and its myriad functions and activities beyond media relations.

Overall, this research found both senior journalists and senior PR practitioners refreshingly frank and reflective, although interestingly it was PR practitioners who were most prepared to be self-critical and call for higher standards. The PR industry and its relationship with journalism is perhaps best summed up by former journalist and experienced business and industry corporate communication executive Gordon Welsh who believes the PR industry exhibits the classic *Pareto Principle*. He said that, in some cases, the relationship is a case of "a love that dare not speak its name". But he added: "That probably applies to only 20 per cent. The other 80 per cent is puff and is not always entirely truthful" (personal communication, August 16, 2013). This, combined with research findings of the extent of the influence of PR reported in Chapter 5, indicates that educators, the PR industry, and journalists have work to do.

Notes

1. 'Professionalism' in this rating was defined as exhibiting high standards of performance and competence in all aspects of their work.
2. Where an interviewee is cited on more than one date, it is because the interview was conducted in several parts, such as a face-to-face interview followed by e-mail, telephone, or Skype discussions.

3. PR industry studies in a number of countries, such as those by Linda Aldoory (2007) and Bey-Ling Sha (1996), report that women now outnumber men in public relations.

4. AusAID has been the national agency responsible for administering Australia's international aid for several decades. In late 2013, the Australian federal government introduced a Bill to absorb AusAID into the Department of Foreign Affairs.

CHAPTER SEVEN

New Media Practices and the Blurring of Boundaries

As noted in the foreword, Brian Smith (2008) says that user-generated content and social media should be the focus of analysis in media content and influence today because "journalism and public relations are converging around new developments in social media" and traditional views of the relationship between journalism and PR are out-dated (p. 926). While this assertion ignores the continuing importance of traditional media in many societies, an analysis of journalism and PR today would not be complete without giving specific attention to new media practices. Again, PR is largely ignored in studies of what some call 'new media' (e.g., Lievrouw & Livingstone, 2002, 2005; Siapera, 2012) and others refer to as digital media (Bennett, 2008; Boler, 2008), or social media (Qualman, 2009; Solis & Breakenbridge, 2009). For instance, the only mention of PR in John Pavlik's *Media in the Digital Age* refers to video news releases (VNRs) which, in fact, are a traditional PR practice mostly targeted at television (2008, p. 262).

Discussion of new/digital/social media is comprised of a mixture of transformist views, cyberoptimism, techno-utopianism, and what Steve Woolgar (2002) calls *cyberbole*, on one hand, and cyberpessimism, techno-cynicism, and scepticism, on the other. In a recent analysis, Kevin DeLuca, Sean Lawson, and Ye Sun say "discussion of social media is too often simplified into a debate between techno-utopians and techno-cynics" (2012, p. 485). Robin Mansell (2012) and Robert McChesney (2013) describe the two 'camps' as the "celebrants" and the "sceptics". Most researchers now conclude that the reality is somewhere in between polarized views and *The 21st Century Media (R)evolution: Emergent Communication Practices* (Macnamara, 2010, 2014) endeavours to synthesize various competing narratives into an integrated balanced view, as recommended by Natalie Fenton (2007) and James Potter (2009) in his book *Arguing for a General Framework for Mass Media Scholarship*. Vincent Mosco's warning of "the digital sublime" (2004) cautions us about euphoria over new technologies and, at a practical level, Gartner Research (2008) warns its clients about the *hype cycle* which it says applies to all new technologies.

Nevertheless, there is substantial evidence that the mediascape has changed and continues to change and that a seismic shift has occurred in the tectonic plates of society in the early 21st century, particularly since around 2004. In *Convergence Culture: Where Old and New Media Collide*, Henry Jenkins states: "Media industries are undergoing another paradigm shift" (2006, p. 5). While focussing on negative impacts in *Digital Disconnect: How Capitalism Is Turning the Internet against Democracy*, Robert McChesney acknowledges the 'digital revolution' and its primary site, the Internet, as "the most extraordinary and important development of the past half century" (2013, p. xi). Traditional media industries are largely in the mess they are in because the management of most were Luddites when it came to recognizing what many now call 'the fourth media revolution' after the inventions of writing, the printing press, and broadcasting (Balnaves, Donald, & Shoesmith, 2009). For instance, in his 2005 speech to the American Society of Newspaper Editors in New York, Rupert Murdoch admitted that he and his empire had underestimated the importance of the Internet (Murdoch, 2005).

The Pew Research Center Project for Excellence in Journalism has warned for some time that these changes have major implications for journalism (e.g., Pew Research Center, 2004). Author of *The Vanishing Newspaper: Saving Journalism in the Information Age*, Philip Meyer, says the Internet is "as disruptive to today's newspapers as Gutenberg's invention of movable type was to the town criers, the journalists of the 15th century" (2008, para. 10). John Pavlik describes the rise of social media such as blogs as a "sea change" with "far reaching implications for the nature and function of journalism in modern society" (2008, p. 77).

Social Media—Let's All Be Friends!

While they are called 'new media' in many texts (e.g., Flew, 2008, 2014; Lievrouw & Livingstone, 2002; Lister, Dovey, Giddings, Grant, & Kelly, 2009; Siapera, 2012), the growing range of online communication applications that comprise what is referred to as Web 2.0—such as blogs, microblogging, social networks, and video and photo sharing—are referred to here as social media, noting that many are no longer new and also because the term 'social' more specifically denotes their key characteristics. Andreas Kaplan and Michael Haenlein provide a widely used definition of social media as "a group of internet-based applications that build on the ideological and technological foundations of Web 2.0 and that allow the creation and exchange of user generated content" (2010, p. 61). This provides a useful and informative description, as it points to the often overlooked but key fact that social media are characterized by a particular ideology, not only technology.

Megan Boler notes that the founder of the World Wide Web, Tim Berners-Lee, said the Web was designed for "shared creativity" and was never intended to be about delivering content to passive audiences (2008, p. 39). The term 'Web 2.0' was coined by Tim O'Reilly (2005)[1] as the theme of a conference in 2004 to refocus attention on Web-based services that feature openness for participation, collaboration, and interactivity. In a much-quoted essay titled 'What is Web 2.0?' O'Reilly says a central principle of Web 2.0 is harnessing "collective intelligence", a concept discussed extensively by sociologist Pierre Lévy (1997). O'Reilly summarizes: "You can visualize Web 2.0 as a set of principles and practices" (2005, para. 7).

The principles and practices of Web 2.0 have been further explicated by other Web 2.0 pioneers such as Peter Merholz who refers to Web 2.0 as a philosophy. In his blog *Peterme.com* under a salutary heading 'Web 2.0—it's not about the technology', Merholz states: "Web 2.0 is primarily interesting from a philosophical standpoint. It's about relinquishing control, it's about openness, trust and authenticity" (2005, para. 5). Richard MacManus, publisher of *ReadWriteWeb*, which is one of the world's top 20 blogs specializing in analysis of Web products and trends, presents a number of definitions of Web 2.0 including describing it as "an attitude not a technology" and specifically as "the underlying philosophy of relinquishing control" (2005, paras. 2, 3, and 5).

In scholarly analyses, Henry Jenkins similarly emphasizes that the convergence of communication and content on the latest iteration of the Web is about culture more than technology and, in particular, "participatory culture" (2006, p. 243). In *New Media & Society*, Teresa Harrison and Brea Barthel state that "Web 2.0 is founded on a radical reconceptualization of the user, from consumer of online products and information…to producer of online products and information that they share with others" (2009, p. 160), a point also made in Kaplan and Haenlein's definition of social media which points to "user-generated content" and "exchange" of information as key characteristics (2010, p. 61). This citizen who is both media producer and consumer has been popularly labelled the *prosumer* (Toffler, 1970, 1980) and the *produser* (Bruns, 2008).

Interactivity is also emphasized by Eric Bucy (2004) and Rob Cover (2004) as a defining element of Web communication, particularly Web 2.0—albeit interactivity is interpreted in multiple ways and needs clarification to fully appreciate the underlying logic of Web 2.0–based social media. Nico Carpentier identifies important distinctions between person-to-machine and person-to-person interactivity (2007, p. 221). Drawing on the work of Bohdan Szuprowicz (1995), Sally McMillan describes three levels of interactivity as *user-to-system* interactivity, *user-to-documents* interactivity, and *user-to-user* interactivity (2002, pp. 166–172). User-to-system interactivity, such as clicking a mouse and accessing menus (what Carpentier calls person-to-machine interaction), while significant in Human Computer Interface (HCI) terms, is a basic and largely perfunctory interaction in terms of human communication. It is user-to-user interactivity and open user-to-documents access to edit and create content rather than simply consume content that is most significant in Web 2.0 and social media applications.

The open, interactive characteristics of social media and contemporary communication practices are also informed by human communication theories derived from psychology, phenomenology, sociology, and sociocultural traditions, such as those of Hans Georg Gadamer (1989), Mikhail Bakhtin (1990), Martin Buber (1958, 2002), James Carey (2009), and understandings of the importance of participation in organizational communication (e.g., Macey & Schneider, 2008) and political communication (Carpentier, 2011). Gadamer's phenomenological admonition that one needs to be *open* to the views of others, willing to listen, and accepting, at least to some extent, of others' contributions in order for communication to be achieved and the experience of the 'other' to be interpreted positively, is salutary. Bakhtin's *dialogism* (Bakhtin, 1990; Holquist, 1981) and Buber's description of 'monologue', 'monologue disguised as dialogue', and 'dialogue' point emphatically to the oft-forgotten fundamental elements of communication—two-way interaction in the form of dialogue and conversation and the potential for collaboration. As discussed in Chapter 2, James Carey (2009) argues that media have a role to play in facilitating the conversations of a society and culture, not simply 'informing' people through top-down information transmission. Democratic political theory and organizational psychology similarly emphasize participation as a necessary ingredient of engagement (Carpentier, 2011; Macey & Schneider, 2008). Without engagement through conversation, dialogue, and collaboration, the "people formerly known as the audience" (Rosen, 2006) disengage and leave, as millions have done in relation to mass media.

Active Users on Social Media Sites 2013	
Facebook	1 billion
YouTube	800 million
QZone (China)	599 million
Twitter	500 million
Sina Weibo (China)	400 million
LinkedIn	187 million
Renren (China)	172 million
Google+	100 million
Instagram	100 million
Tumblr	96 million
Reddit	47 million
Wikipedia	38 million
Foursquare	25 million plus
Pinterest	25 million plus
MySpace	25 million

Figure 7.1. Leading social networks by number of active users (Macnamara, 2014).

Social media have enjoyed unprecedented growth over the past decade (See Figure 7.1), leading to a range of predictions in relation to the future of media and journalism, as well as the future of public communication broadly including the practices of PR and advertising. Some of these predictions and emergent trends warrant examination as part of this analysis, as they are increasingly changing the relationship between journalism and PR.

Citizen Journalism—The Fifth Estate or the End of Journalism?

In an example of transformist views of social media, cyberoptimism, and techno-utopianism, Stephen Cooper (2006) and William Dutton (2007) claim that the Internet, and social media in particular, will form a *Fifth Estate* to supplement or even replace the Fourth Estate comprised of mass media. They believe the watchdog role previously played by mass media will increasingly be taken over by watchful independent citizens connected online through networks, sharing information and with the ability to mobilize opinion and action. Partly they see this occurring because of a failure of mass media to live up to the promise of the Fourth Estate, which is described as "reporting, scrutinizing and commenting from a critical distance" (Gurevitch, Coleman, & Blumler, 2011, p. 51). Dutton (2007) argues that television networks in particular have moved from an outside critical observer position to become political insiders involved in the creation of political agendas and messages.

Many journalists, media commentators, and some media academics are sceptical about and even disparaging of social media and reject this thesis. Along with his criticisms of citizen journalists and amateur producers of media content in *The Cult of the Amateur* (Keen, 2007a), Andrew Keen launched an attack on what he called the "Web of deceit" in a newspaper article, saying:

> The Web 2.0 revolution is depleting the ranks of our cultural gatekeepers, as professional critics, journalists, editors, musicians, moviemakers and other purveyors of expert information are being replaced ('disintermediated') by amateur bloggers, hack reviewers, homespun moviemakers and attic recording artists (2007b, p. 27).

Keen describes citizen journalists as a "pyjama army" engaged in presenting opinion as fact, rumour as reportage, and innuendo as information. Web 2.0, according to Keen, is "the great seduction" and he claims that a "chilling reality in this brave new digital epoch is the blurring, obfuscation and even disappearance of truth" (2007b, p. 27). Similarly, writing in *Forbes* magazine, Daniel Lyons calls bloggers "an online lynch mob spouting liberty but spewing lies, libel, and invective" (2005, para. 1). In an article in *The Guardian*, Oliver Kamm (2007) describes political blogs as "error-strewn, insular and parasitic" and claims that they "tend not to enhance, but poison healthy debate". He adds: "They are, by definition, a self-selecting group of the politically motivated who have time on their hands…they are purely parasitic on the stories and opinions that traditional media provide" (paras. 4–5). Kamm concludes: "In its paucity of coverage and predictability of conclusions, the blogosphere provides a parody of democratic deliberation" (para. 7). One of the highest level media attacks on blogs was launched by the then CEO of News Limited[2] in Australia, John Hartigan, in an address to the National Press Club in 2009. Hartigan (2009) generalized blog content as "something of such limited intellectual value as to be barely discernible from massive ignorance" (para. 102). Blogs have also been described as "media for narcissists" (McDonald, 2005, p. 15) and as "egocasting" (Rosen, 2004/2005).

Some academics have joined in the criticism and expressions of deep concern. Echoing Andrew Keen, European media academic Geert Lovink (2007) describes bloggers and other citizen commentators as "pyjama journalists" in whose writing he says truth dissolves into pluralities of viewpoints and banalities.

In a comparative study of citizen media and traditional media coverage of local government affairs, Frederick Fico, Stephen Lacy, and colleagues (2013) found that citizen media sites such as blogs were more likely to contain opinion than news. Brian McNair (2003, 2006) says that emergent forms of citizen media such as blogs represent a change from the "control paradigm" of news and information to "cultural chaos" and, although he welcomes some aspects of this shift, he warns that it is creating a crisis of journalism.

However, many of these criticisms of blogs and other forms of social media are based on an assumption that they seek to emulate and/or replace journalism. As well as considerable diversity in social networks, which range from personal photo albums (e.g., Flickr, Pinterest, and Instagram) to Myspace[3], now a specialist music-sharing site, the media type referred to as blogs covers a wide range of styles, approaches, and levels of expertise and professionalism (Deuze, Bruns, & Neuberger, 2007, p. 4). A taxonomy of blogs was produced by Carolyn Miller and Dawn Shepherd (2004), which shows that "journalism is but one of many orientations for blogging" (Dahlgren, 2009, p. 178). More recently, Margaret Simons (2013) argued that the term 'blog' is "now manifestly inadequate" (para. 1) to allow sensible discussion and, drawing on historical communication and media formats, she proposes a taxonomy of blogs identifying nine types which she terms (1) pamphleteering blogs, (2) digest blogs, (3) advocacy blogs, (4) popular mechanics blogs, (5) exhibition blogs, (6) gatewatcher blogs, (7) diary blogs, (8) advertisements, and (9) news blogs. This provides a useful clarification that only some blogs purport to provide news and information. Others exist as a medium to exercise their authors' right to free speech for political advocacy and campaigning in the style of the 18th-century pamphleteers. Some wish to exercise their citizenship or consumer rights, or to engage in marketing in a market economy, while others are published for largely personal reasons with few or no pretensions to quality journalism or literary fame. Those who use social media as personal diaries, networking, entertainment, and for personal identity construction pose little threat to journalism or to standards of public communication generally.

Kaplan and Haenlein (2010) more recently suggested a classification scheme for social media generally, proposing six categories comprised of (1) collaborative projects (e.g., Wikipedia); (2) blogs and microblogs; (3) content communities (such as video sharing on YouTube and photo sharing on Flickr); (4) social networking sites (e.g., Facebook); (5) virtual game worlds (e.g., World of Warcraft): and (6) virtual social worlds (e.g., Second Life). There are differences between blogs and microblogs and the term 'content communities' could also apply to collaborative projects such as wikis or social bookmarking. However, this categorization further shows that reporting, analyzing, and commenting on news is only one use of social media. Sweeping generalizations about social media in the context of journalism are misguided and reveal journalism's ambivalent relationship with social media— seeing them as an unavoidable trend and possibly offering opportunities, on one hand, but resentful and territorial on the other.

Even when the activities of so-called citizen journalists overlap with or purport to be journalism, it further needs to be recognized that many of the authors are experts in their field. Technorati (2011) reports that the vast majority of bloggers have a university degree and almost half have a postgraduate degree. Bloggers and social media commentators (e.g., on Twitter) include scientists, academics, health and medical professionals, researchers, lawyers, economists, accountants, tax advisers, computer programmers, designers, collectors, engineers, and so on. It is disingenuous to suggest that such people should not have access to public communication other than when their words are interpreted and represented— and often misrepresented—by a journalist. Technorati also reports that almost one third of bloggers have worked or still work for traditional media.

Revenge of the Bloggers and 'The People Formerly Known as the Audience'

Apart from early forums for online chat (e.g., Newsgroups) and early social networks such as SixDegrees established in 1997 but closed in 2001, the first wave of interactive social media to reach the shores of our mediaworld was blogging, an abbreviation derived from Web logs, a form of online journal writing[4]. By 2008, Technorati (2009) reported that it was tracking 133 million blogs. By the end of 2011, the Nielsen/McKinsey research company NM Incite was tracking 181 million blogs around the world (Nielsen/NM Incite, 2012). However, the total number of blogs is likely to be much higher, as the China Internet Network Information Center (CINIC) claimed that there were 182 million blogs in China in 2009 (CINIC, 2009, p. 30) and it is unlikely that tracking companies such as NM Incite and Technorati include Chinese blogs, most of which are in Chinese language. Some estimates of the total number of blogs globally are as high as 450 million (Macnamara, 2014, p. 45).

Despite criticisms of social media and bloggers in particular, it has to be noted that a blogger, Matt Drudge, broke the Monica Lewinsky–Bill Clinton scandal in *The Drudge Report* under the noses of the throng of political reporters from America's and the world's leading newspapers and broadcast networks based in Washington, DC. *Salam Pax*, 'The Baghdad Blogger', became essential reading for behind-the-scenes independent accounts of the war in Iraq when CNN and other traditional media were 'embedded' within the US military machine where their access to information was controlled and their news spoon-fed (Balnaves, Donald, & Shoesmith, 2009, pp. 231–232). When veteran CBS newscaster and *60 Minutes* reporter Dan Rather claimed to have documents that showed President George Bush had evaded the military draft and used his family's influence to join the National Guard and later white-washed his record, amateur fact-checkers organized online and turned up evidence that showed the documents were forgeries. Following a post in *FreeRepublic.com* on September 8, 2004, a flurry of blog posts and links ultimately led to the resignation of Rather (Eberhart, 2005; Rheingold, 2008, p. 103).

In 2005 *AmericaBlog.org* revealed that a male prostitute was working in the White House press room amidst the nation's most experienced political reporters (Wrench, McCroskey, & Richmond, 2008, p. 313). *The Huffington Post*, which started essentially as a blog, has won a number of awards since it was founded in 2005 by Arianna Huffington, culminating in a Pulitzer Prize in 2012 in the national reporting category for a 10-part series about wounded veterans, titled *Beyond the Battlefield*, written by David Wood ("2012 journalism Pulitzer winners", 2012)[5].

While blogs are usually long-form writing with no word limit, microblogging has emerged as a related short-form practice and has grown even faster than blogging. While Twitter is the best-known microblogging service in Western countries (famous/infamous for its 140 characters limit)[6], other popular microblogging sites include Tumblr, Sina Weibo in China, and Plurk, which was launched in Canada before moving to Taiwan in 2012. Also, social networks such as Facebook and Google+ have microblogging services, such as Facebook Wall posts. Microblogging software is also available for internal organizational use, such as Yammer, Jive, and SocialText.

When US Airways Flight 1549 was forced to crash-land in the Hudson River in January 2009, Janis Krums, a passenger on a ferry that rushed to help, took a photograph of the downed plane as the first passengers evacuated and sent it to Twitpic, from which it was distributed worldwide as one of the first photos of the event (Cellan-Jones, 2009).

The first report of Michael Jackson's death came from a social media celebrity news Web site, TMZ (2009), and was passed on to millions of people around the world via Twitter and other social media, as it went 'viral'. Full-time television journalists including specialist entertainment reporters and international correspondents based in Los Angeles stood interview-less and fact-less outside Jackson's Bel Air mansion or the UCLA Medical Center where he was pronounced dead, as the news was tweeted around the world.

News of the death of Osama Bin Laden in May 2011 was broken on Twitter when a neighbour tweeted about the noise next door when US security forces attacked Bin Laden's hiding place (Laird, 2012). Twenty-seven minutes before mainstream media broke the news of singer-actor Whitney Houston's death in 2012, the story was on Twitter, reported by a man who tweeted the news to his 14 followers (Murphy, 2012, para. 1). Social media in the hands of citizens have brought what John Thompson (2005) calls "a new visibility" to news reporting and public communication.

A sign of the increasing acceptance and mainstream role of these new forms of media is that Clarence House (@ClarenceHouse) announced the engagement of Prince William to Catherine (Kate) Middleton on November 16, 2010 on behalf of the British Royal Family via Twitter at the same time as issuing an official media release (Kelly, 2010).

Whether journalists like it or not, the production and distribution of news and information, as well as their consumption, has changed extensively and irrevocably. While some resist these changes and see problems, others are embracing them and finding new ways to source and tell stories. As reported in Chapter 2 in discussing new forms of digital journalism, two journalists, Paul Lewis from *The Guardian* and Ravi Somaiya from *The New York Times*, collaborated with citizens on Twitter to obtain eye-witness information, obtain photos, and check facts during the four days of the London riots in August 2011. Similarly when 63 bushfires were burning around Sydney in September 2013, a series of Twitter hashtags, including #sydneyfires, #nswfires, and #londonderry (one of the areas most affected), were used by emergency services, citizens, and news media to share and distribute information, mostly in real time (Wu, 2013, para. 1). These are examples of social media and citizens (amateur media producers) working in complementary rather than substitutional ways with traditional mass media. We will return to this theme of cooperation and collaboration between journalists and citizens/amateur content producers later in this chapter. For now, it is important to examine how PR practitioners are reacting to and using social media and how journalism–PR interaction is changing with Web 2.0.

PR 2.0 and 3.0

While many journalists have been resistant to and sceptical about social media, many PR practitioners and some scholars have welcomed them with a burst of rhetorical enthusiasm and even evangelism. Social media advocate Brian Solis wrote in the foreword to Deirdre Breakenridge's (2008) book *PR 2.0: New Media, New Tools, New Audiences*: "Welcome to what just may be the greatest evolution in the history of PR" (Solis, 2008, p. xvii). He claims that with the shift to social media "monologue has given way to dialogue" (p. xviii). In the title of another book, Solis and Breakenridge (2009) claim that Web 2.0 is "putting the public back in public relations".

As well as potentially enabling contemporary theories of PR discussed in Chapter 3 to be operationalized—such as the two-way symmetrical model (Grunig & Hunt, 1984), Excellence theory (L. Grunig, J. Grunig, & Dozier, 2002), and the dialogic PR model (Kent & Taylor, 2002)—PR practitioners have welcomed social media and the Internet as a near ubiquitous distribution network because these technologies and practices allow them to bypass traditional media gatekeepers and directly reach their 'target audiences'. In the latest edition of *Corporate Communication: A Guide to Theory and Practice*, Joep Cornelissen (2011) enthusiastically states that social media "create new ways of reaching and engaging with stakeholders". He elaborates saying that the development of new media "provides an organization with the opportunity to engage in conversations and to tell and elaborate its story or key message to stakeholders or the general public in an interactive way", which he claims is a "real advance" compared with traditional media relations (p. 154).

With the advent of social media, organizations of all types can publish blogs and microblog through services such as Twitter, set up social network sites such as Facebook pages, and distribute photos on sites such as Flickr, Pinterest, and Instagram (i.e., publish themselves) and post videos to sites such as YouTube or even create a YouTube channel (broadcast themselves). Information can be produced and distributed directly to the public, without the need to deal with pesky journalists and go through media checks and balances. This environment in which everyone can be a media producer is reflected in the title of Dan Gillmor's 2004 book *We the Media.*

Research shows that PR practitioners are still coming to grips with these new media technologies and practices, with the rhetoric of PR 2.0 well ahead of implementation (Macnamara, 2011, 2012a, 2014; Macnamara & Zerfass, 2012). But in these new spaces, it is clear that the long-standing tension between journalism and PR continues and will continue. While some see opportunities as noted, many journalists remain fearful of social media and the Internet undermining the media and their craft. While social media have played a positive role in one sense by undermining media monopolies and oligopolies in which control of most daily newspapers and magazines, broadcasting, books, and movies worldwide fell into the hands of five corporations by the end of 20th century, as Ben Bagdikian (2004) identified[7], there are mixed views about the so-called "democratization of media" (Siapera, 2012, p. 55) and some of the emerging practices in what Mark Poster (1995) calls the "second media age".

The following are some of the concerning practices and developments occurring in PR 2.0 and what some even refer to as PR 3.0. For instance, the leading

PR trade journal *PRWeek* published an article in 2007 claiming that "what is happening now is so fundamental, it can only be described as the next iteration of the industry—or PR 3.0, as we have designated it". The claim was labelled "premature" and "absurd" even by industry optimists such as Brian Solis (2007). Nevertheless, evolving techniques of PR continue to be discussed at conferences and online (e.g., see Dinino, 2012), and *PRWeek* was again hyping the concept of PR 3.0 in 2013 in an article by Richard Grove (2013).

Advertorial

As discussed in Chapter 3 and Chapter 4, a long-standing practice that conflates PR and journalism is *advertorial*. While this practice has existed in newspapers and magazines for the past century, in print media this form of paid content is often notionally identified as promotion by being placed in supplements (segregated sections in newspapers and magazines) or under a header such as 'special feature'—although even these token efforts at transparency were often missing. In television news magazine and lifestyle programs, it is almost impossible to distinguish genuine news and critical review from paid messages. The *Sunrise* program in my home city regularly tells me about new products and airline 'price wars' to benefit consumers, but a little research soon reveals that the product marketers and the named airline are major sponsors of the program. These messages are not presented as advertising, but surreptitiously presented in editorial format on TV programs, including by journalist presenters[8], as well as in newspapers and magazines.

In online media, the boundaries collapse further. Supplements do not exist and even the flimsy separators between independent reporting and paid content are increasingly disappearing. Furthermore, the volume of content required to fill online editions, provide regular updates, and give additional background reading and viewing on Web sites of broadcast programs, is allowing more and more information subsidies, including blatant promotional content, to find their way into major media.

PR 2.0 also includes a number of new practices that appropriate and colonize social media for promotional, marketing, and propaganda purposes, as discussed in the following. Communication and media consultant Trevor Cook (2008) warns that "the opportunity to bypass the 'media gateway' can just mean an open invitation to pump out unfiltered propaganda" (para. 22), and he claims that social media are "starting to emerge as yet another wasteland for product pushers and shameless self-promoters" (para. 5). Also, a number of variations and new evolutions of advertorial are discussed later in this chapter in examining what is termed 'embedded' marketing communication.

'Flogging'

From its annual survey of how businesses are using Web 2.0 technologies, McKinsey & Company reported in 2011 that 79 per cent of companies were using social media for customer interaction and 66 per cent were using various Web 2.0 tools for internal communication (McKinsey, 2011). A more recent McKinsey survey of 3,542 executives globally found that 83 per cent of companies use at least one social media technology (McKinsey, 2013). An annual survey on social media adoption by Fortune 500 companies conducted by the University of Massachusetts Dartmouth Center for Marketing Research each year since 2008 reports that, in 2012, 73 per cent of Fortune 500 companies had a Twitter account and had tweeted in the previous 30 days, 66 per cent had a Facebook community page, 62 per cent had a corporate YouTube account, and 28 per cent had a corporate blog (Barnes, Lescault, & Andonian, 2012).

Corporate blogging and microblogging are now common practices and most institutions, associations, NGOs, non-profit organizations, and even many government departments and agencies regularly communicate with a range of stakeholders via blogs and microblogging. It has to be said that some, or even much, of this communication comprises genuine attempts to inform customers, members, employees, and citizens on issues of relevance to them. However, a growing practice is the use of social media channels for promotion of products, services, policies, and initiatives which is referred to as *flogging*. For example, L'Oreal came in for considerable criticism when it created a blog allegedly written by an independent beauty expert called Claire, but which was actually written by L'Oreal's PR department. The company was soon 'outed' and 'flamed' on the Internet (Crampton, 2005, p. 10).

Concern about practices such as flogging needs to be tempered with the anecdotal evidence that netizens seem to have an uncanny ability to detect inauthentic information on the Internet. The above example and the 'outing' of Walmart for its *Walmarting Across America* blog, and many other examples of citizens quickly identifying fakes, phonies, and shameless promotion, cautions us against over-reaction and generalization. Gunther Eysenbach (2008) argues that, even though *intermediaries* (where *inter* means standing in between media producers and receivers, such as media 'gatekeepers') are absent in many social media, *apomediaries* take their place—'apomediary' being a term derived from 'media' and 'apo', meaning stand by or alongside. The interconnections and sharing of information on social networks provides an emergent form of fact checking by peers and independent experts, resulting in what Andrew Flanagin and Miriam Metzger (2008) call *emergent credibility*. Nevertheless, flogging and related promotional uses of social media are growing and challenge cyberoptimist and techo-utopian views of Web 2.0 as a truly democratic public sphere.

Paid posts

Another growing practice is paying allegedly independent amateur and professional bloggers to post favourable comments about products, brands, or policies. Many independent bloggers are open to such an arrangement as they seek to monetize their media sites. Some accept advertising but, with traditional forms of advertising relatively unpopular on blogs and other social media sites, paid posts are a way to generate revenue from their efforts.

Organizations are particularly keen to gain posts of positive articles and reviews in blogs that have established a reputation for expertise in their field. It must be said that not all independent bloggers accept paid posts. But many do. In its 'State of the Blogosphere' report, Technorati (2009) estimated that four in five blogs post product or brand reviews. A number of these are independent, but an increasing number of posts praising particular products such as holiday destinations, hotels, restaurants, films, mobile/cell phones, computers, cosmetics, and even social networks themselves are paid messages disguised as independent reporting and reviews. Paid posts are also becoming a feature of microblogging, along with bots (Web robots) that automatically generate messages (Paine & Fysh, 2012).

Paid posts and flogging are examples of where the boundaries separating news, commentary, advertising, and promotion have blurred, in some cases beyond recognition. This means that, at times, citizens are unable to tell independent information from paid posts and flogging and, with media governance lacking or non-existent, they have to rely on their own media literacy.

Social media marketing and social network marketing

Much PR is put into the service of marketing and new forms of media are being eagerly exploited for marketing communication. Social media marketing refers to online marketing communication where the medium and the content are both social, according to social media consultant and *Advertising Age* 'Top 150' blogger Laurel Papworth (2008). She gives the example of marketing using fully user-generated content including text, sound, and video, music remixing, video mash-ups, and users interacting spontaneously with hosts and each other in social media. Papworth differentiates social network marketing as the use of social media or networks as a channel of communication for distribution of content produced by organizations or agencies (personal communication, February 3, 2009). While the former is truly social and authentic, as it involves citizens in all stages of production and distribution, the latter form of marketing is exploitation of social media and networks for distribution of corporate, organization, and government messages.

'Media catching'

An increasingly common practice that is contributing to PR access to media is ironically a collective initiative of journalists, not PR practitioners. A study by Richard Waters, Natalie Tindall, and Timothy Morton (2010) identifies what they call "media catching", which involves a reversal of the traditional interplay between PR practitioners and journalists. For most of the past century, a traditional and frequent media relations activity of PR practitioners has been 'pitching' stories to journalists. This was done by phone and e-mail and involved PR practitioners trying to convince journalists to write a particular story, use their information in a story, or interview their employer or client. Many journalists describe PR 'pitching' as the bane of their life, as discussed in Chapter 6, and a number of Web sites have been set up to 'out' bad, annoying, and fake 'pitches', such as *BadPitchBlog* (http://badpitch.blogspot.com.au), which is also on Twitter at https://twitter.com/bad-pitch, and the PR spammers wiki (http://prspammers.pbworks.com).

However, interestingly, journalists increasingly invite PR practitioners to send them information, leads, and content through messages posted on social media such as Twitter and specialist Web sites such as HARO (Help a Reporter Out). Founded in 2008 by American entrepreneur Peter Shankman, HARO (http://www.helpareporter.com) is reported to be "one of the fastest growing publicity services in North America" (HARO, n.d.) and has also now expanded to the UK. *WIRED* magazine described HARO as "crowdsourcing" for news (Buskirk, 2009) because HARO fields upwards of 220 queries a day from 30,000 reporters and bloggers and directs them to more than 150,000 sources, many of which are PR practitioners representing employers and clients ("Help a reporter out", 2012). Since its inception, HARO has published more than 75,000 journalist queries, facilitated nearly 7.5 million media pitches, and marketed and promoted close to 1,500 brands to the media, businesses, and consumers, according to the HARO Web site (HARO, n.d.). The site was purchased by Vocus, Inc. in 2010.

Media catching contrasts the traditional 'push' approach of PR, which journalists claim to resent and resist, with journalists calling for and catching content when it is passed to them (i.e., pull). While journalists have long used this approach to seek comments from experts, it is increasingly a practice in which "thousands of [PR] practitioners are being contacted at one time by journalists and others seeking specific material for stories, blog postings and Web sites" (Waters, Tindall, & Morton, 2010, p. 243). Such open and expansive channels for PR information to reach media were not possible before Web 2.0, and social media and practices such as media catching suggest that the use of PR material by media is likely to grow rather than reduce in the future and become even more invisible.

Editorial Intelligence, a business set up by Julia Hobsbawm in the UK, is similar to HARO in the sense that its purpose is to bring journalists and PR practitioners together. Editorial Intelligence (http://www.editorialintelligence. com) offers "networking opportunities" and "information" about 1,000 "opinion formers" in Britain's national media and hosts events at which "spin-doctors get to mingle with newspaper columnists and editors" (Plunkett, 2006, para. 3). The initiative has been criticized as a "backscratchers' club" and a "disgusting idea and ropy-sounding venture with a faintly unpleasant odour" (para. 1). But it continues to operate and journalists attend functions and communicate with PR practitioners through the service.

Brand/corporate journalism

What is called 'brand journalism' or 'corporate journalism', briefly discussed in Chapter 2 under 'New Forms of Journalism', is another practice that is blurring the boundaries of 'Church' and 'State' that once clearly demarcated journalism and PR. The growth of owned media is creating demand for increasing amounts of content to be produced. Now there are not only newspapers and broadcast bulletins to be filled, but millions of government, institutional, corporate, and non-government organization (NGO) Web sites needing content. Furthermore, the shift from 'push' to 'pull' modes of media consumption and the use of search engines require organizations to create content that scores highly in search engine algorithms in order to attract audiences. To rank highly in Web searches, sites need a constant stream of regularly updated quality content that goes beyond traditional corporate and marketing communication. Organizations need to become storytellers and develop interesting stories around their brands and products in an era of 'pull' media consumed by short-attention-span, spoilt-for-choice Web users. The days of 'push' media and force-fed advertising are long gone.

To meet this demand for content, many organizations are turning to specialist content creators such as journalists to write about their brands, rather than PR practitioners who are required to have a range of skills and responsibilities including event planning and management, strategic management advice, project and campaign planning, research, budgeting, evaluation, and management reporting. So 'crossing over' to 'the dark side' is likely to become an ever-increasing trend, as many journalists find themselves redundant or facing what foreign correspondent and satirist Russell Baker (2002) calls "journalism's age of melancholy".

Even worse in terms of transparency and boundaries, some journalists are 'moonlighting' part-time as brand journalists for PR agencies and departments. For example, writing in *Columbia Journalism Review*, Christine Russell reports that "many science reporters are left scrambling to find work as freelance or public information writers" (2008, para. 7). In such cases, the blending of journalism and PR becomes inevitable and moves further towards convergence. Such practices mean that not only are journalists receiving and even requesting PR information but they also are increasingly producing and placing the PR copy that proliferates in contemporary media.

'Embedded' marketing communication and promotion

A new form of promotional media communication that is emerging and growing rapidly, which fits somewhere between advertising and PR, is referred to as *embedded marketing* and *embedded marketing communication*, along with a number of related terms. The pioneer and relatively well-known example of embedded marketing is product placement, which involves the "covert" placement of branded products, services, or messages in media programming as a contextual part of the content rather than as an interruption and segregated element (Kuhn, Hume, & Love, 2010). Famous examples of product placement include the use of Aston Martin cars in James Bond movies and, more recently, Alpha Romeo and Ford vehicles. The 1997 James Bond film *Tomorrow Never Dies* reportedly grossed US$100 million even before cinema release through product placement deals (McDonnell & Drennan, 2010, p. 25). Today, judges on the TV talent show *Idol* around the world routinely sit with Coca-Cola drink cups prominently displayed in front of them, and advertising and promotion are increasingly being integrated with all types of entertainment, infotainment, and even news.

Traditional explicit approaches to product placement continue, but they frequently draw criticism and resistance from media consumers and critics. For example, the 2009 movie *Couples Retreat* attracted criticism by reviewers when a five-minute scene was written specifically to satisfy a paid placement by ActiVision, the developer of the Guitar Hero 5 video game. The movie also received a number of other negative reviews for actor Vince Vaughan repeating the name Applebee's five times in a prominent scene (Kokemuller, 2013).

Along with criticisms of blatant product placement, a number of other factors are fuelling the evolution and growth of a range of new embedded techniques that are blurring the boundaries between editorial media content, advertising, and PR. These include:

- Declining impact of traditional advertising (de Pelsmacker & Neijens, 2012, p. 1);
- The availability of new technologies for avoiding, deleting, or blocking advertising, such as video on demand, TiVo, and 'ad strippers' (e.g., Adblock[9]); and

- A search to avoid *persuasion knowledge*—recognition by consumers of content as intentional persuasion, which reduces the effect of persuasion (Friestad & Wright, 1994). Conversely, media content that "looks natural and 'innocent' and which does not trigger persuasion knowledge" is found to have more impact (de Pelsmacker & Neijens, 2012, p. 1).

Hence, marketers are increasingly trying to hide the persuasive intent of their messages and campaigns in interviews with paid spokespersons and sponsored celebrities, talk and chat shows, content such as advergames (Cauberghe & de Pelsmacker, 2010), and even in the storylines of TV drama shows and sitcoms (Russell & Stern, 2006). Furthermore, research findings which show that content passed along and shared among friends and followers in social media and social networks has significantly more effect on recall, brand awareness, and purchase intent than "paid advertisements" (Wauters, 2010) is spurring the application of embedded marketing communication techniques to social media and social networks.

While product placement in media content, particularly in movies, has been widely studied (e.g., Gupta & Lord, 1998; Kokemuller, 2013), the growing plethora of new techniques designed to at least partially "hide the truth" (de Pelsmacker & Neijens, 2012, p. 1), or even fully conceal marketing and promotional messages in media content, have been little researched to date (Wouters & de Pelsmacker, 2011, p. 300). There is also a lack of clear definitions of these new techniques and a burgeoning range of terminology. A search of scholarly and professional literature show that these go by 25 or more different names, including *branded content* (Canter et al., 2013), *brand placement* (Thomas & Kholi, 2011; Wouters & de Pelsmacker, 2011), *native advertising* (Glick & Neckes, 2013; Wasserman, 2013), *embedded marketing* (Kokemuller, 2013), and even "stealth marketing" (Roy & Chattopadhyay 2010). See Figure 7.2 for a summary of these and other terms for embedded marketing communication techniques grouped by disciplinary focus.

Product focussed	Brand focussed	Advertising focussed	Entertainment focussed	Other and related
Product placement	Brand placement	Native advertising	Branded entertainment*	Paid content
Product plugs	Branded content	Natural advertising	Advertainment	Paid syndication
'In show plugs'	Branded entertainment*	Advertiser-funded programming	Edutainment	Paid integration

(continued on next page)

Product focussed	Brand focussed	Advertising focussed	Entertainment focussed	Other and related
'Showing the can'	Brand integration	Sponsored content	Celebrity endorsements	Paid co-creation
Product integration	Brand casting	Sponsored messages	Advergames	Advertorial
	Branded storytelling	Content integration		Editorial integration
				Embedded marketing communication

Figure 7.2. Terms used for paid advertising and promotional content or messages embedded in media programming. (*Listed under both brand focussed and entertainment focussed.)

While these formats and practices have received little scholarly attention at this stage, many media organizations and marketers are agog with what is being hailed as the possible "salvation" of the troubled advertising industry (Wasserman, 2013, para. 2)—although they could just as easily be called PR. So-called native or natural advertising is being accepted and even promoted by a number of leading newspapers and magazines including *Forbes, The Washington Post, and The Atlantic* in the form of sponsored articles, sections, and even whole publications (Vega, 2013). For example, see the Web site of Atlantic Media, which now also publishes a number of sponsored publications including *Idea Lab* for GE (Atlantic Media, 2014). Also, an article on the *Gigaom* blog[10] describing and lauding native advertising says "sponsored content on Buzzfeed, 'brand stories' on Facebook, promoted trends on Twitter—all of these are commonly cited examples of advertising gone native" (Glick & Neckes, 2013). Writing in *Mashable*, Todd Wasserman (2013) notes that while one view is that native advertising is "a bold new path for brands and publishers", another is that "it's the hoary advertorial dressed up in 21st-century clothes" (para. 1).

A relatively new industry body, the Branded Content Marketing Association (BCMA), has published guidelines on brand placement and branded content and claims that these forms of paid content are ethical (BCMA, 2012). The American Society of Magazine Editors (AMSE), which published guidelines in response to concern about print media advertorials in 1982, released updated guidelines for editors and publishers in September 2013 on native advertising as well as advertorial, sponsored content, and paid links (ASME, 2013).

However, *The New York Times* has published a number of articles questioning these techniques, reporting that "almost all of the publishers running branded content say they abide by the traditional church-and-state separation" of editorial and advertising. But, it added, "the sponsored content runs beside the editorial on many sites and is almost indistinguishable" (Vega, 2013, para. 15). Furthermore, not all new formats are easily categorized as product placement, advertising, editorial, or sponsorship, and media organizations and marketers facing severe economic pressures are likely to exploit loopholes and gaps in codes and regulations. As *Ad Week* noted in late 2013: "Marketers and publishers continue to fall all over themselves to create messaging that doesn't look like advertising and that doesn't annoy the reader" (Moses, 2013). The intention of advertisers and marketers to hide paid promotional messages in media content is evident in a comment by Stephanie Loosie, managing editor at Dell Computer, who told *Mashable*: "Native advertising is not like porn: If it's done well, people don't know it when they see it" (Wasserman 2013, para. 7).

To date it seems that many marketers are not doing embedded well. *The Atlantic*'s first foray into paid content, an article titled 'David Miscavige Leads Scientology to Milestone Year', published in January 2013, caused reader outrage that resulted in an apology from the vice-president and general manager of The Atlantic Digital, Kimberly Lau. Admitting "we screwed up", Lau said the article "read like warmed-over PR" (Wasserman, 2013, para. 5). In other words, *The Atlantic* was not saying that its approach was inappropriate; it was simply saying that it did not embed the paid content deeply enough or subtly enough so as to be invisible to readers.

In mid-2013 the New York head office of the world's largest PR consultancy firm, Edelman, released a report titled 'Sponsored Content: A Broader Relationship with the US News Media' in which it noted that, like other PR and marketing communication firms, Edelman is "teaming up with the advertising arm of publishers on sponsored content partnerships", which it noted are also referred to as "paid content" and "native advertising" (Edelman, 2013b, p. 2). Edelman acknowledged "major ethical hurdles" and committing itself to disclosure of paid media content, warning that "it is likely that the US government will get involved if it feels consumers are being deceived and that self-regulation is not working well" (p. 8).

Other national governments are being urged to monitor these developments carefully. On July 22, 2013, the Australian *Media Watch* program on the national public broadcaster ABC TV criticized "branded content", "content integration", and "editorial integration", citing examples in which News Corporation newspapers published editorial articles that were highly promotional of major advertisers, as well as TV segments on morning programs that were thinly disguised promotion for sponsors. Even greater concerns are being expressed about the largely unregulated mediascape of social media.

Scrutiny of these practices is an urgent imperative, as embedded marketing communication formats are growing fast and spreading through all forms of online and offline media, as media organizations search for new business models and consumer product, political and social marketers search for new formats to reach 'consumers'. Using the term 'brand placement' to refer to this growing marketing communication practice, Wouters and de Pelsmacker (2011) report research showing that paid brand placement spending grew more than 40 per cent from 2002 to 2007 when it was worth almost $3 billion a year. Media research firm PQ Media estimated spending on the broadening practices of paid content at $8.25 billion worldwide in 2012 and forecast it would double by 2016 (PQ Media, 2013).

In his review of whether or not the Internet has changed the propaganda model of media identified by Edward Herman and Noam Chomsky (1988), Sheldon Rampton (2007) concludes that the five filters that Herman and Chomsky identify in *Manufacturing Consent*—media ownership, advertising, reliance on selective sources, 'flak', and anti-communism—are partly related to a particular time and place (e.g., American fears during the Cold War) and "may not apply in the same ways to the internet". But he adds: "Techniques of moulding and directing public opinion are emerging along with new media" (para. 35). Major challenges for media-saturated, mediatized, and PR-ized societies are to allow new media business models to evolve, while at the same time avoiding convergence of journalism, PR, and promotion, which would be counter-productive and even catastrophic for democracies and civil societies.

Notes

1. First use of the term Web 2.0 dates back to a 1999 article in *Print* magazine by Darcy DiNucci (1999, p. 32). However, DiNucci used the term mainly in relation to design and aesthetics in her article targeted at Web designers. The more common broad use of Web 2.0 is attributed to Tim O'Reilly (2005).
2. News Limited is an Australian subsidiary of Rupert Murdoch's News Corporation.
3. Myspace is now owned by Specific Media LLC and pop music singer and actor Justin Timberlake and was relaunched in a new format in 2012.
4. The term 'Web log' or 'Weblog' was created in 1997 (Wortham, 2007) before being shortened to 'blog' in 1999 by pioneering blogger Peter Merholz (1999) in a post on his blog, *Peterme.com*.
5. *The Huffington Post* (www.huffingtonpost.com) was sold in 2011 to AOL for US$315 million.
6. It is sometimes assumed that microblogging is limited to 140 characters. But this limit is a feature of Twitter, adopted to allow 'tweets' to be sent as single files over the Short Message Service (SMS) to mobile/cell phones. Tumblr allows both long and short postings with no

word limit, Plurk allows 210 characters, and, even though Sina Weibo restricts posts to 140 characters, Chinese characters represent whole words and phrases rather than single letters as in English.

7. Ben Bagdikian's (2004) analysis found that, at the end of the 20th century, the output of daily newspapers, magazines, broadcasting, books, and movies worldwide was dominated by five corporations: Time Warner, Disney, News Corporation, Viacom, and Bertelsmann.

8. The lead presenter of the *Sunrise* TV program in Australia is David Koch, who started his career as a cadet journalist with *The Australian* newspaper before becoming a business and financial journalist with *BRW* (*Business Review Weekly*) magazine and then founding *Personal Investment* magazine in Australia, New Zealand, and the UK.

9. Adblock Plus is a free Web browser plug-in originally developed for Firefox but now also available for Internet Explorer, Chrome, Opera, and Android.

10. *Gigaom* is a leading technology, media, and business blog founded in 2006 by Om Malik.

CHAPTER EIGHT

Future Directions for Journalism, PR, and the Public Sphere

Extensive literature reviewed in this book and empirical data from international research reported in the previous chapters affirm that independent journalism remains relevant and important for societies, particularly democracies and those aspiring to democracy. Research also indicates that, despite the reported 'crisis in journalism', there is a future for journalism and a role for professional journalists— or multiple futures and roles to be more correct—some, or many of which, will be enacted outside of traditional media organizations and will include new forms of journalism.

But new forms and roles of journalism should not be allowed to further converge or become conflated with PR, which is in danger of occurring because of the 'crisis' in traditional journalism caused by collapsing media business models, continuing rapid growth of PR, the global phenomenon of social media in which everyone and every organization is potentially a publisher and a broadcaster, and proliferation of new media practices and formats such as 'corporate journalism' and 'embedded marketing', as discussed in this analysis. A convergence of journalism and PR is not in the interests of journalism, or PR, in the view of many practitioners interviewed, and certainly not society, and, therefore, the issues raised should receive serious attention by scholars and practitioners in journalism and PR as well as those in media studies, sociology, politics, and cultural studies.

The concerns raised do not, however, justify demonization of PR, which occurs widely as shown in Chapter 1 and Chapter 5. It has to be recognized that, in free speech societies, the activities that comprise PR, as discussed in Chapter 3, are legitimate and age-old practices. While it has been renamed many times and become professionalized and theorized with a specific body of disciplinary knowledge in the 20th century, PR has been around since the Egyptian and ancient Greek civilizations, and in ancient Chinese civilizations from what we can tell. PR was used in the colonization of America to attract Europe's oppressed as immigrants and in promoting the settlement of 'the West'. It was used to promote British industry and products during the Industrial Revolution, such as in the great exhibitions. It was used to entice immigration to Australia and attract workers to its vast development projects such as the Snowy River Irrigation Scheme. Only through persuasive information would people pack up their families and move to the other side of the world. PR has been and continues to be used by churches, charities, environmental groups, and other activist and civic reform groups to communicate their messages. To deny or marginalize PR is therefore practically and intellectually misguided. But this is what is happening to a significant extent, as noted in the foreword and discussed in Chapter 1 and this informs the first of several recommendations for the future drawn from this analysis.

Countering *PRegemony* through 'Discursive Reflection' and Debate

Because PR seeks to operate subtly and even invisibly, and because many journalists and editors do not wish to acknowledge it or talk about it, contemporary media and public communication systems are characterized by what could be called *PRegemony*, drawing on Antonio Gramsci's concept of hegemony. Rather than exert force, hegemony relies on voluntary consent and compliance achieved through coercion and seduction. PR operates on hegemonic principles, never having any power to exert force or compel. However, hegemony is insidious because, as James Lull explains, in most cases "hegemony...serves to preserve the economic, political, and cultural advantages of the already powerful" (2000, p. 54).

As Jean Charron (1989) concluded a quarter of a century ago: "The relationship between journalists and public relations practitioners is both complex and ambiguous. It is characterized by both cooperation and conflict" (p. 42). It is also characterized by both silence and public name calling—the latter often presenting a pretence of critical review. Rather than continue within these dichotomous frameworks, it is argued that a much needed and more constructive approach for countering hegemony and other forms of power and influence in relation to media is *discursive reflection*, which communication theorists Robert Craig and Heidi Muller describe as "discourse that reflects on assumptions that may be distorted by unexamined habits, ideological beliefs and power relations" (2007, p. 425).

Discursive reflection should not begin from a position of opposition to PR or support for PR and nor should its starting point be stereotypes, myths, or clichés. Instead, there needs to be a sustained commitment to informed discussion and debate among scholars and practitioners in journalism, media studies, public relations, politics, sociology, cultural studies, and other interested fields, as well as policy makers, regulators, and concerned citizens. Such discussion needs to ensure that the free speech rights of employers, investors, and even campaigning politicians are recognized and respected, while also ensuring the rights and interests of society are recognized and respected in equal measure.

The sociocultural movement in PR and the not-insubstantial number of critical PR scholars in Europe, the UK, US, Australia, New Zealand, South Africa, Asia, and elsewhere are a resource available to make a significant contribution to such debate, as well as proponents of the dominant paradigm (i.e., PR Excellence theory) concerned about ethics and social equity. Journalism and media scholars concerned about the future of journalism equally are an essential part of such discursive engagement.

However, even before getting to discuss specific measures that might be taken, reviewing and changing some of the practices and trends identified in this analysis will require much more open minds among journalists and PR practitioners. First, it will require rejection of the discourse of denial, which is shown by substantial evidence to be fallacious and either delusional or deliberately deceptive. Second, it requires rejection of the media discourse of victimhood. It may sound unwarranted and provocative to suggest that journalists need to exercise greater social responsibility, given that mottos and slogans such as 'watchdog of society' are deeply embedded in the culture of journalism. But the rhetoric of independent media reporting and the normative ideals of democratic models grounded in Western liberalism are commonly not matched by reality. This partly occurs through no fault of journalists, who struggle against ever tighter deadlines, information overload, and a reduced workforce caused by collapsing media business models. But historical data, interviews with senior practitioners on 'both sides of the fence' reported in Chapter 6, and autoethnographic reporting of experiences and reflections reported in Chapter 5, show that journalists are also often complicit and willing participants in cosy cartels of communication that are resulting in the convergence of journalism and PR. Some are creators of spin themselves, in opinionated commentary blended with reporting, column and blog rants, and self-aggrandizing talk to camera monologues on TV. In the very least, some are lazy or have simply given up or given in, dispirited and disillusioned. Blaming PR for the embattled state of journalism is reductionist and hugely hypocritical.

Equally, the rhetoric of PR often rings hollow, given the mostly unregulated environment in which it operates; the largely generic and unenforceable codes of ethics and practice adopted by only partially representative voluntary membership industry associations; the normative theories of two-way symmetrical relationships and dialogue that PR scholars admit are rarely operationalized; and all-too-frequent revelations of misuse of PR for unethical ends. The discourse of honest brokers of information perpetrated by PR practitioners and the discourses of dialogue, two-way communication, relationships, and symmetry advanced in dominant theories and models of PR are built on aspiration and noble sentiment more than empirical foundations. That is no disrespect to the senior practitioners interviewed. They themselves referred to the *Pareto Principle*. For every honest socially responsible PR professional balancing the public interest with organizational interests, there are five who either naïvely gush hype and hyperbole or intentionally manipulate the channels of public communication. Politicians and governments, which, more than any section of democratic societies, should be concerned for and responsive to citizens, are seen as primary perpetrators of spin and their PR and media advisers are key instruments in this process.

Despite efforts to rehabilitate the term 'strategic' in a new more socially responsible and mutually beneficial form (e.g., Falkheimer & Heide, 2011; Hallahan et al., 2007; King, 2010; Torp, 2011), PR mostly comprises organization-centric *strategic action* rather than *communicative action*, as contrasted in Habermas's theory of communicative action (Habermas, 1984, 1987). Notwithstanding the role of counselling management and claims of 'boundary spanning' identified in both PR theory and practice in this analysis, the focus of PR is primarily on protecting and advancing the interests of employer organizations.

The acknowledgements and concerns of senior PR practitioners themselves, as well as those of journalists, as reported in Chapter 6, indicate that despite its positive uses and contributions in society, PR corrupts the public sphere in many instances, as warned by Peter Dahlgren (2009, p. 49), and contributes to what Deacon and Golding (1994) and Ward (2007) call the *PR State*. It also contributes to *promotional culture* (Davis, 2006; Wernick, 1991), which is seen as excessive and deleterious in developed and many developing societies. While Aeron Davis notes that promotion has propelled the economies of liberal capitalist democracies such as the US and UK, he also points out that these countries are among the OECD market leaders in obesity, cardiovascular disease, inequality, per capita waste and environmental pollution, personal debt, and citizen disillusionment and disengagement in politics (Davis, 2006 p. 159).

It is also clear from the description of PR practices in Chapter 3 and Chapter 4 and the research reported in Chapter 6 that PR is intricately and extensively involved in *framing* and *priming* issues in public debate and in *agenda building*, *agenda setting*, and occasionally *agenda cutting*. While PR practitioners do not use these theoretical terms, these concepts are operationalized in common PR tactics such as identifying and distributing 'key messages' (i.e., the organization's messages), 'staying on message', creating 'buzz', 'embedding' journalists (such as in military units), 'keeping things out of the media' or 'flying under the radar', and in the whole range of activities encompassed within media relations such as arranging media visits and tours, providing briefings, issuing reports and 'White Papers', and so on. Sites for framing, priming, agenda building, and agenda setting are also expanding with the growth in organizational use of social media sites as *owned media* and direct public communication, as discussed in Chapter 7.

Having made these criticisms, it is important to proceed further towards *praxis* as advocated by Karl Marx (1845), one of the founders of critical theory, drawing on the work of Hegel. The following proposals and recommendations are put forward as issues to be addressed in discursive reflection and to inform future research, teaching, and practice.

Transparency—Disclosure and Attribution of PR Material

In an epilogue in the fourth edition of his classic text, *Media Today: An Introduction to Mass Communication*, Joseph Turow (2011) calls for individuals and groups "to convince mass media organizations to be more open about the corporate connections that go into creating their content". Under the heading 'The need for transparency', he advocates: "Demand that entertainment and news organizations routinely disclose when press releases or public relations organizations are involved in instigating or contributing to a story. Insist that media firms prominently divulge all product placements" (pp. 596–597).

However, as reported in Chapter 6, few journalists or PR practitioners support calls for disclosure of use of PR material and many reject the idea outright, calling it impractical, unnecessary, an infringement of journalists' rights to protect sources, and even unwanted and "boring" for the public (PR5, UK PR consultant, personal communication, June 19, 2013). Also, Jordi Xifra (2012) has reported that attempts to explicitly identify PR-supplied information appearing in media content in Europe have failed, having been seen as "interventionism and censorship of freedom of expression and citizens' right to information" (p. 43).

Notwithstanding past failures to achieve transparency, evolving formats and practices discussed in Chapter 7 indicate that, even though it will be difficult to define and implement, some greater level of transparency through disclosure and attribution of PR/advertising/promotional material used by media claiming to be independent is a key issue for consideration as part of media ethics. The words of one of the most highly qualified reporters interviewed during research for this book, Dr Norman Swan from the Australian Broadcasting Corporation (ABC), say it succinctly and well: "The best ethical weapon is sunlight" (personal communication, December 3, 2013). There is a body of research that can inform media ethics and responsibility, including that published in journals such as *Journal of Mass Media Ethics*, recent books such as *Ethics of Media* (Couldry, Madianou, & Pinchevski, 2013), and analyses of media governance (e.g., Ginosar, 2013).

Rules of Engagement

Along with a need for constructive open dialogue in place of PR industry rhetoric and prevailing media discourses of denial, victimhood and spin, and increased transparency, a key recommendation of this study is that journalism and PR need to agree on and make clear their rules of engagement. The conflicted positions of journalists and PR practitioners are not the problem in need of resolution, as some propose, through either limiting PR or further 'symbiosis' between the fields. To the contrary, the presence of tension and conflict signals integrity and health in the system. A lack of difference and conflict suggests that one or the other has succumbed, usurped by the other. Complex societies operate and benefit from a number of social, cultural, political, and legal systems that involve pluralist, oppositional, and even adversarial relationships—such as prosecutor–defence roles enacted in courts, the government–opposition structure of parliaments, and even public debating. The problem that becomes evident from in-depth qualitative analysis is that many journalists and PR practitioners struggle with unwritten, often unspoken, unclear rules of engagement, whereas a characteristic of the aforementioned interactions is that they take place within very clear, well-defined protocols and procedures.

Senior journalists and PR practitioners report that they understand mutually accepted rules of engagement, but they acknowledge having had to work them out by trial and error through years of experience and admit that many young practitioners do not have a professional or moral compass to guide them through the complex and tangled maze of journalism–PR relations. Young reporters arrive confused at the threshold of their journalism careers, filled with ideology and idealism, but faced with the inevitability of dealing with PR. When they do interact with PR, most are forced to do so with barely a word of worthwhile advice from their journalism teachers and textbooks and often little by way of guidelines from their editors and colleagues. They are like maturing teenagers whose only advice on sex has been the unrealistic and impractical admonition 'don't'. As one former editor in chief observed in Chapter 6, there is also a lack of governance at senior editorial management level in many time-strapped newsrooms and media organizations today. Few editors check sources or demand corroborating sources, and few if any use technologies such as plagiarism software or Web sites such as SpinWatch (2014) or PRWatch (2014) to track the use of PR material. On the other side, young PR practitioners are eager to please employers and clients with high and often unrealistic expectations, sometimes naïve, and few have ethics education or training as reported in Chapter 6 and further discussed later in this chapter. While professional organizations in these fields broadly define and promote standards, more specific rules of engagement for journalism–PR interaction can be established through several of the following additional recommendations.

Codes of Practice and Self-regulation vs. Regulation

Codes of practice and ethics in both journalism and PR are typically broad and silent on many specifics such as disclosure and attribution in relation to PR material, what level of rewriting and checking is required to constitute independent reporting, and many of the other problematic issues raised in this analysis. For example, as noted in Chapter 7, no codes have substantially or effectively addressed new formats such as 'embedded' marketing communication and 'brand' and 'corporate' journalism. Social media are the "Wild West" in terms of rules and codes, according to some studies (Fitch, 2009).

European PR scholar Jordi Xifra notes that "the absence of legislation regulating the practice of public relations is an international phenomenon" (2012, p. 42). Apart from a few noteworthy examples, such as the Chartered Institute of Public Relations (CIPR) in the UK, which was awarded Chartered status by the Privy Council of the United Kingdom in 2005 giving it a range of powers to govern its members and legal protection while it carries out this role, the governments of most countries seem content to leave PR as a self-regulated industry. Recent controversies demonstrate a need for more specific and updated guidelines. For example, after a number of companies and PR agencies were 'outed' and publicly criticized for editing and/or rewriting Wikipedia entries, the CIPR issued specific guidelines on writing and editing articles for Wikipedia (CIPR, 2012) and the

Institute for Public Relations (IPR) in the US has drawn practitioners' attention to Wikipedia's conflict of interest policy (DiStaso, 2013; Wikipedia, 2013). Greater responsibility in other forms of media use would be a positive step for the PR industry.

Journalism, with justification, strenuously defends its right to be relatively free of regulation, other than laws on privacy, defamation, and media regulations in relation to ownership, foreign versus local content, and technology issues such as spectrum control in broadcasting. However, more specific codes of practice and guidelines would help practitioners—and improved self-regulation and governance would differentiate independent media from partisan sources of information and help redress falling public trust.

Educating Journalists

Given that a large proportion of journalists entering the field during the past few decades do so from undergraduate journalism courses, it can be concluded that, in addition to inherited ideology acquired in the workplace, journalists' attitudes towards PR largely originate in undergraduate journalism courses, and research confirms this hypothesis. In a 2005 analysis, Candace White and Thomasena Shaw (2005) conclude that journalists are "socialized to hold negative attitudes toward public relations, and that socialization begins in the academy". A US study by Donald Wright (2005) of a large sample of PR educators (n = 342) supports this finding. Wright found substantial evidence that professional prejudice and discrimination exists towards PR and PR education in universities. Almost 57 per cent of PR educators state that they had a dean, director, or department chair who was prejudiced against PR, and report that many university administrators use generalizations and stereotypes when discussing PR. Wright found this prejudice against PR more pronounced among journalism faculty than among other groups of educators.

Noting that the relationship between journalism and PR is plagued by misunderstanding and misconceptions, as a number of studies have shown (e.g., Jeffers, 1977), Sandra Stegall and Keith Saunders (1986) are among the first to propose that "one place to begin might be the education process of journalists" (p. 347). They suggest: "Perhaps journalists should be required to take a class in basic public relations, taught by someone who has experience in both professions" (p. 393).

However, most studies making such recommendations have been framed from a PR perspective and orientated towards making life easier and more productive for PR practitioners, rather than adopting a critical perspective based on the best interests of society. For instance, Stegall and Saunders continue: "It would seem that journalists could co-orient with PR practitioners better if they understood the history, principles and practices of the PR profession" (1986, p. 393). Journalists do not wish to "co-orient" with PR practitioners in most cases—and this analysis argues that it is unproductive for society if they do. A more realistic study by Holger Sievert in Germany concludes that "dialogue between the two camps certainly cannot hurt", but he argues that journalism and PR are not "two sides of a single coin" (2007, p. 191). His analysis reports that, even though the basic techniques of PR work, and media writing and media relations in particular, "correspond to journalists' professional competence and some aspects of communication competence", journalism has to be seen as "an autonomous social system that fulfils a unique function in society", while PR "is part of other social systems like business...politics, or culture" (Sievert, 2007, pp. 191–192). Sievert recommends separate specialist courses for journalists and PR practitioners for the sake of PR as much as journalism, noting that media relations and publicity is only one part of PR, as discussed in Chapter 3. However, he recognizes intersections and interrelationships and supports dialogue and exchange of information.

It is in relation to these intersections and interrelationships with PR that education and training of journalists is recommended in this analysis. As Trish Evans (2010) observes in *British Journalism Review*: "Today's young journalist...will deal with public relations operators many times in the normal course of a day—for her entire career—whether she likes it or not" (p. 32). As this analysis has shown, PR is ubiquitous in most contemporary societies and its influence is considerable. And it is growing, with budgets increasing by 10 per cent a year in mature markets and by more than 20 per cent a year in fast-growing economies, as reported in Chapter 3. Its practices are becoming ever more sophisticated and diverse. Sending young journalists out to work with little or no understanding of PR is counter-productive for journalism, as it leads to both abrasive interactions and "the dirty secret of journalism" (McChesney, 2013, p. 90), as journalists discover the inevitability of working with PR, but are not critically or technically equipped to do so, and are culturally, professionally, and ideologically disposed to deny doing so.

What is proposed here is not lectures or classes for journalism students that promote PR, or encourage them to use PR, or even to like PR. What is recommended, and what seems an obvious need, is a series of classes or seminars that give journalism students a general understanding of what PR is and what it entails, explains the functions and dysfunctions of PR, and examines and explains the specific practices, techniques, and formats that they are likely to encounter, and the ethical and professional ways of dealing with PR practitioners and material. Such education and training would equip graduate journalists with knowledge of how to negotiate this aspect of the contemporary mediascape in ways that respect the right of organizations to represent their views and opinions publicly and which allow them to interface with PR in an informed, open, and critical way. PR should be neither derided nor deified with the imprimatur of independent journalism.

Such an approach is strongly supported by almost all senior PR practitioners interviewed in the study reported in Chapter 6 and, interestingly, by most senior journalists and editors interviewed such as David Hickie and Martin Frizell. In talking about how the 'rules of engagement' between journalism and PR were often unclear and unspoken, Nick Hindle, senior vice president, corporate affairs for the UK and Northern Europe for McDonald's Restaurants, stated: "I would say that the rules of engagement should be talked about openly...that's a really sensible idea and it will be...very advantageous to journalists to hear from PR people at different stages in their career and their training" (personal communication, June 19, 2013).

There is also support for education of journalists about PR in industry discussion. As Alex Murray, former editor of *The Sunday Telegraph* in the UK, says: "PR people are sources just like anyone else and to discriminate against them simply for being PR people would be illogical" (as cited in McCrystal, 2008, p. 50). Young Australian journalist Matthew Knott, who completed a journalism degree in 2011, wrote in a report on media titled 'The Power Index: The World of Spinners and Advisers': "Dealing with the PR industry should be a crucial element of modern-day journalism education—both in universities and professional training programs". Reflecting on his training, he noted:

> In my otherwise excellent journalism degree...I learnt a lot about defamation law but little about how to interact with spinners and media advisers. How do you use a press release effectively? How do you get in touch with decision makers, not just spokespeople? What are the tricks of the trade used by those in the PR game? These are the type of questions up-and-coming journalists need help answering (Knott, 2012b, p. 54).

Part of the resistance to university classes or courses in PR for journalism students may be the lingering aversion to academic perspectives that exists within journalism in a number of countries including the UK (Frith & Meech, 2007; Keeble, 1998; Snoddy, 1992). However, even in the US where "most...journalists have gone to university journalism schools" (Sievert, 2007, p. 153), journalism scholars have often been engaged in 'academic wars' with PR academics, and co-location within mass communication schools has been contentious (see Wright, 2005, and the next section). Susan Bovet (1992) argues that 'J schools' have not parted company with public relations only because PR courses have become "cash cows" due to growth in PR enrolments and employment. Studies such as those cited strongly suggest that journalism practitioners and academics need to broaden their views beyond stereotypical understandings of public relations and ideologically framed prejudices and engage in informed critical debate.

Also, the decline of mass media and reduced jobs for journalists in traditional media industries have implications for journalism education. Donica Mensing notes that "the central theme of journalism education has been that of a professionally orientated program focussed on educating students for jobs in the media industries" (2010, p. 513). With structural change in traditional media and public communication, including the developments outlined in Chapter 7, educators need to consider broadening this approach. Rather than only producing journalists to work as reporters for newspapers, magazines, or radio and TV programs, journalism education needs to recognize that many graduates will work as freelancers, bloggers, activists, in advocacy or alternative journalism, and as content producers for corporate and organization 'owned media'. Some traditionalists will howl in indignation at such suggestions, but there is a marketplace for professional writers in a wide range of fields and the Columbia Journalism School report 'Educating Journalists' notes that "journalism can honourably be practiced in different settings" (Folkerts, Hamilton, & Lehmann, 2013, p. 64). A broader approach need not involve abandoning the values of traditional journalism—to the contrary, it could help bring these values to the broadening field of media and public communication.

Educating PR Practitioners

Given the expanding roles and influence of PR, as identified in this analysis, there is a compelling argument that PR education also needs to change. In an Oxford University report titled 'What's Happening to Our News?' Andrew Currah concludes:

> The long-term challenge is not simply how to make journalism more transparent about its many sources, which necessarily include PR feeds, but also how to convince non-media organizations such as PR firms that they too have a social responsibility to be honest in their reporting of the world (2009, p. 65).

A study of the PR field by US academic Shannon Bowen reports what she calls a "troubling finding" that 70 per cent of PR practitioners have little or no training in ethics, with 30 per cent saying they have had "no academic ethics study of any kind" and another 40 per cent saying they have had "a few lectures or readings on ethics" (Bowen, 2007, para. 24). In a following analysis, Bowen (2008) reports "a pronounced state of neglect among public relations professionals in a plethora of areas related to ethical understanding…and the ability to enact the role of ethics counsel" (pp. 271–272). Furthermore, she reports that many PR practitioners are unwilling to "embrace situations in terms of ethics" (p. 272). Michael Ryan and David Martinson (1983) argue that "the proper location of an ethical conscience in an organization is within the top echelon of the public relations function", but Bowen concludes that PR practitioners are singularly ill-equipped for such a role.

Despite widespread and sustained criticism of PR, as identified in Chapter 1 and Chapter 3, when asked, "Do you have a vision for the future of public affairs and public relations?" in a feature interview published in *Communication Director*[1] in 2012, the co-founder of one of the world's leading PR firms, Harold Burson, did not mention improving standards, practices, or ethics, or even improving the reputation of PR. Burson, who was described recently by *PRWeek* in the US as "the century's most influential PR figure" (Klose, 2012, p. 47), spoke of playing a greater part in decision making, how it was getting harder to "get your message out" with the proliferation of information, and criticized other disciplines includ-ing management consulting firms and human resources consultants for "trying to muscle in" on communication (Klose, p. 47).

Burson's response reflects a tension between academic and professional goals that creates a 'split personality' in PR education (see Kruckeberg, 1998). While Burson's reference to seeking a greater role in management decision making could potentially mean making management decisions more stakeholder friendly, his reference to "get your message out" and his concern that other management ser-vices "are trying to muscle in" reflect a functionalist perspective of PR[2]. Dominant functionalist PR thinking based largely on systems theory focusses on what is most effective and useful (functional) for the organization (getting its messages out) as well as the industry itself (protecting its turf).

Furthermore, despite useful studies by the Commission on Public Relations Education (2006, 2012), PR education is fractured and lacking standardization because of ongoing debate over the disciplinary 'home' of PR—that is, whether it is part of journalism, mass communication, speech communication, commu-nication, media studies, or one of 25 other schools and departments identified as offering PR education by Rowena Briones and Elizabeth Toth (2013), ranging as far afield as professional studies, culture, business, and executive education. Bri-ones and Toth (2013) note that PR continues to be studied and examined largely through the lens of journalism and mass communication in the US, as reported in a number of previous studies (e.g., Aldoory & Toth, 2000; Baines & Kennedy, 2010; Kruckeberg, 1998; Toran, 1977), as well as through functionalist manage-ment perspectives. While some scholars call for increased social and cultural focus in PR, others argue for even closer links between PR and business (e.g., Duhé, 2013). Resolving these disciplinary dilemmas and moving beyond normative theories to positive theories and applications of PR with a social conscience are key challenges for PR scholars, industry bodies, and practitioners.

Educating Educators

These changes to the education of journalists and PR practitioners will also require change among educators. A much more open perspective among journalism educators has already been suggested and, at the risk of offending colleagues teaching journalism, this must be emphasized. The cloistered, separatist, and somewhat elitist approach of some journalism academics and 'J schools' in relation to other media-related disciplinary fields such as advertising, public relations, and even social media to a significant extent leaves them cut off from reality in many respects, and it denies these fields the valuable insights of journalism scholarship. Journalism does not exist outside society in a bubble of objective reflectivity; it exists in society with all the messy interactions and interdependencies that this entails.

While celebrating and respecting the substantial body of knowledge that has developed in public relations over the past 100 years, and particularly since the 1980s, PR educators need to be more open to diversity and cautious towards paradigms and grand theories. These can too easily close down research and thinking and marginalize criticism. Diversity is advocated in three respects.

- First, PR scholarship should further reach out to neighbouring disciplines in the arts, social sciences, and humanities, including anthropology and emerging fields such as cultural anthropology, as well as sociology, psychology, political science, public diplomacy, history, cultural studies, literature, and philosophy. Furthermore, Americacentrism and Eurocentrism need to be challenged. Metatheoretical and methodological concepts such as *Asiacentricity* (Miike, 2010) and *Afrocentricity* (Asante, 2007; Karenga, 2002) can be used, not as replacements but to de-Westernize and broaden theory and research. The North American crusade for PR to be part of management and business has closed disciplinary doors and seen many of these frameworks ignored.
- Second, engagement in arts and humanities perspectives requires much greater deployment of *qualitative* research methods. The preponderance of quantitative research in PR influenced by behaviourism, positivism, and empiricism, particularly in North America, needs to complemented with humanist understandings gained through methods such as depth interviews,

longitudinal qualitative studies, ethnography, participatory action research, discourse and narrative analysis, and ethnomethodology. The search for a 'science of public relations' is largely paradoxical, as human communication and relationships can at best be only partially understood through such analysis.

- Third, PR and its various related fields of practice need to decide their intellectual home. That does not necessarily mean choosing a single home—to the contrary, diversity, specialization, and integrity may benefit from having several homes. For example, *corporate communication*, by virtue of its very name, could realistically and logically see its home in business. Similarly, *communication management* appears to concern itself with the processes of managing communication activities and *communication controlling* (Zerfass, 2010), suggesting an alignment with management studies. But *public relations* scholarship needs to resolve its ambiguity and its flawed attempt to be all things to all people. If the first word of PR is 'public', then the interests of publics should loom large. Accordingly, public relations should not be aligned with, let alone part of, the 'dominant coalition' in organization management, as scholars continue to argue (e.g., Kanihan, Hansen, Blair, Shore, & Myers, 2013). A more neutral or externalized position and disposition seems necessary, such as those adopted by external legal counsel, auditors, and ombuds. If those professional roles seem too lofty for PR, then the model of the diplomat is within easy reach for inspiration, with diplomatic services delivered at a range of levels from junior civil servants to ambassadors and the practices of public diplomacy offering insights for PR (L'Etang, 2008; Snow, 2009).

Rethinking Media and the Public Sphere

Writing in *Media Ethics*, Kimberley Blessing and Joseph Marren (2013) ask the following provocative question and provide their response.

> What happens to a culture that promotes spinners to the rank of 'doctor' and BS-ers[3] to artists? We end up being more easily confused about distinctions between true and false, right and wrong, reality and appearance (para. 6).

That is a good question, as it goes beyond more narrow questions about the future of journalism and the future of PR. The bigger issue that we all should be concerned about is what happens to our culture, our society, and our public sphere as a result of the developments and trends that have been discussed. This book has almost certainly not fully answered this question. But hopefully it has shed some light on issues, contradictions, and paradoxes, exploded some of the myths, exposed stereotypes, and put forward some suggestions that will have educational and practical benefits in journalism and public relations and spur sociologists, political scientists, and media studies and cultural studies researchers to pay more attention to PR and related practices.

Summary of Conclusions and Recommendations

- Journalism, PR, and media studies academics and leading practitioners should be engaged in forums for informed critical debate on the issues discussed in this book. Different perspectives should be expected and respected, but dialogue and collaboration are desirable and necessary to agree on 'rules of engagement' (e.g., a codes of practice for journalist–PR interaction, protocols, and guidelines) in place of vague, unwritten, and often unspoken *modus operandi* and rhetoric based on inherited ideology, stereotypes, and media mythology. Rules of engagement need to address the vexed issue of transparency and provide some level of governance at senior editorial management level (e.g., through source checking, use of PR tracking, or plagiarism software, etc.).
- All undergraduate and postgraduate journalism students should receive an informed practical and critical description and analysis of PR and its various elements and activities. This should not be 'PR for PR'. Rather, it should equip journalists to work with PR through having greater knowledge and practical understanding while retaining and even increasing their critical skills to differentiate, evaluate, interpret, and 'decode' various types and sources of information.
- As well as gaining knowledge and skills in writing and media practices, which could involve lectures or courses conducted by journalism scholars and/or practitioners, all PR undergraduate and postgraduate public relations students should receive theoretical and practical education in ethics and a stronger social perspective (see next point).
- PR research and teaching need to further review dominant functionalist models of PR, which make unrealistic claims that practitioners can act as both promoters of and social conscience within organizations through concepts such as 'boundary spanning' and that they can best perform this dual role while being a member of the 'dominant coalition' (i.e., the senior

management team or the government in power). Conceptual and theoretical contradictions at the heart of PR need to be resolved and greater attention given to alternative models such as public diplomacy.

- Scholars in political science and policy studies, sociology, cultural studies, and related disciplinary fields such as social and cultural anthropology, as well as historians, should recognize public relations as a significant influence in contemporary societies, including the role of PR in the public sphere and as cultural intermediaries. Overcoming this blind spot will broaden these disciplines as well as public relations scholarship.

- The PR, advertising, marketing, and media industries need to work together to develop consistent responsible codes of practice in relation to emerging practices such as 'embedded' marketing communication in its various guises such as 'native advertising', 'integrated content', and new forms of 'advertorial' to address their potential negative effects on the public sphere through the blurring of boundaries between paid promotion and independent news, analysis, and commentary. Media regulators and policy makers should also pay close attention to these developments.

Notes

1. *Communication Director* is a trade journal published by the European Association of Communication Directors.

2. Even though functionalism emerged in early sociology with a broad macro-societal approach and some early functionalist PR theories, such as the work of Franz Ronneberger and Manfred Ruhl, had a "society-orientated" focus (L'Etang, 2008, p. 11), functionalism has been heavily criticized for naïvely arguing that the various parts of society operate and evolve as systems towards consensus and equilibrium (i.e., social order), ignoring conflict, inequalities, power, and human agency including self-interest. Contrary to early claims of structural functionalism, critics argue that parts of society do not always work collaboratively and *communicatively* to form a cohesive and stable whole. Rather, some operate (function) *strategically* to serve their own ends (Habermas, 1987). Hence there is considerable criticism of functionalism in contemporary practices such as PR.

3. This term references philosopher Harry Frankfurt's (2005) book *On Bullshit*, the abbreviation BS, and the colloquial expression of 'bullshit artists'.

References

2012 journalism Pulitzer winners. (2012, April 16). *The New York Times*. Retrieved from http://www.nytimes.com/2012/04/17/business/media/2012-Journalism-Pulitzer-Winners.html

Aarts, N. (2009). *Een gesprek zonder einde* [A never end conversation]. Amsterdam: Vosspuspers.

Aarts, N., & Van Woerkum, C. (2008). *Strategische communicatie* [Strategic communication]. Assen, The Netherlands: Van Gorcum.

Abbott, E., & Brassfield, L. (1989). Comparing decisions on releases by TV and newspaper gatekeepers. *Journalism Quarterly, 66*(4), 853–856.

Adorno, T. (1991). *The culture industry: Selected essays on mass culture*. London, UK: Albert Britnell and Routledge.

Adorno, T., & Horkheimer, M. (1972). *Dialectic of entertainment*. New York, NY: Herder and Herder. (Original work published 1947)

AFSC (American Friends Service Committee) & Rustin, B. (1955). *Speak truth to power: A Quaker search for an alternative to violence*. USA: Author. Retrieved from https://afsc.org/document/speak-truth-power

Aldoory, L. (2007). Reconceiving gender for an 'excellent' future in public relations scholarship. In E. Toth (Ed.), *The future of excellence in public relations and communication management* (pp. 399–411). Mahwah, NJ: Lawrence Erlbaum.

Aldoory, L., & Toth, E. (2000). An exploratory look at graduate public relations education. *Public Relations Review, 26*(1), 115–125.

Altheide, D., & Snow, R. (1991). *Media worlds in the post-journalism era*. New York, NY: Aldine de Gruyter.

Anderson, A. (1993). Source-media relations: The production of the environmental agenda. In A. Hansen (Ed.), *The mass media and environmental issues* (pp. 51–68). Leicester, UK: Leicester University Press.

Anderson, A. (1997). *Media, culture and the environment.* London, UK and Bristol, PA: UCL Press.

Anderson, C. (2006). *The long tail.* New York: Hyperion.

Anderson, C., Bell, E., & Shirky, C. (2012). Post-industrial journalism: Adapting to the present. Tow Center for Digital Journalism, Columbia Journalism School, Columbia University, New York, NY. Retrieved from http://towcenter.org/research/post-industrial-journalism/

Andrews, L. (2006). Spin: From tactic to tabloid. *Journal of Public Affairs, 6*(1), 31–45.

Aronoff, C. (1975). Credibility of public relations for journalists. *Public Relations Review, 1*(1), 45–56.

Asante, M. (2007). *An Afrocentric manifesto: Toward an African renaissance.* Cambridge, UK: Polity.

ASME (American Society of Magazine Editors). (2013). ASME guidelines for editors and publishers. Updated September 2013. Retrieved from http://www.magazine.org/asme/editorial-guidelines

Atkinson, J. (2005). Metaspin: Demonization of media manipulation. *Political Science, 57*(2), 1–27.

Atlantic Media. (2014). About Atlantic Media Strategies. Retrieved from http://www.atlantic-media.com/brands/atlantic-media-strategies/

Australian Mobile Telecommunications. (n.d.). Ten years of GSM in Australia. Retrieved from http://transition.accc.gov.au/content/item.phtml?itemId=796056&nodeId=22eafe1c4bc-caf8a96411d083794d3f3&fn=4%20AMTA,%20Ten%20years%20of%20GSM%20in%20Australia,%20www.amta.gov.au.pdf

Bagdikian, B. (2004). *The new media monopoly.* Boston, MA: Beacon.

Baines, D., & Kennedy, C. (2010). An education for independence: Should entrepreneurial skills be an essential part of the journalist's toolbox? *Journalism Practice, 4*(1), 97–113.

Baker, R. (2002, July 18). What else is news? [Review of the book *Into the buzzsaw: Leading journalists expose the myth of a free press.*] *The New York Review of Books.* Retrieved from http://www.nybooks.com/articles/archives/2002/jul/18/what-else-is-news

Bakhtin, M. (1990). Art and answerability. In M. Holquist (Ed.), *Art and answerability: Early essays by M. M. Bakhtin* (V. Liapunov, Trans., pp. 1–3). Austin, TX: University of Texas Press. (Original work published 1919)

Balnaves, M., Donald, S., & Shoesmith, B. (2009). *Media theories and approaches: A global perspective.* Basingstoke, UK: Palgrave Macmillan.

Baran, S., & Davis, D. (2009). *Mass communication theory: Foundations, ferment and future* (5th ed.). Boston, MA: Wadsworth Cengage Learning.

Barnes, N., Lescault, A., & Andonian, J. (2012). Social media surge by the 2012 Fortune 500: Increase[d] used of blogs, Facebook, Twitter and more. Retrieved from http://www.umassd.edu/cmr/socialmedia/2012fortune500/

Basen, I. (2012, November 30). Ira Basen: The fight to regulate Britain's 'outrageous' press. *CBCNews,* World: Analysis. Retrieved from http://www.cbc.ca/news/world/ira-basen-the-fight-to-regulate-britain-s-outrageous-press-1.1183313

Bates, D., & Arno, A. (2009, February). How the press uses and values public relations and other media resources. Report of a national study of editors and journalists. Cision and George Washington University School of Political Management Strategic Public Relations Program. Retrieved from http://www.gwu.edu/~media/research_report.pdf

Bateson, G. (1955). A theory of play and fantasy. *Psychiatric Research Reports, 2*, 39–51.

Bauer, M., & Bucchi, M. (Eds.). (2007). *Journalism, science and society: Science communication between news and public relations.* New York, NY and Abingdon, Oxon, UK: Routledge.

BCMA (Branded Content Marketing Association). (2012). Guide to advertising funded programming. Retrieved from http://www.thebcma.info/best-practices/guide-to

Bean, C. (2012). Are we keeping the bastards honest? Perceptions of corruption, integrity, and influence on politics. In C. Pietsch & H. Aarons, *Australia: Identity, fear and governance in the 21st century* (Chapter 7). Canberra, ACT: ANU E-press. Retrieved from http://epress.anu.edu.au/apps/bookworm/view/Australia%3A+Identity,+Fear+and+Governance+in+the+21st+Century/10171/ch07.html

Becker, J. (2004). Lessons from Russia: A neo-authoritarian media system. *European Journal of Communication, 19*(2), 139–163.

Beckett, C., & Mansell, R. (2008). Crossing boundaries: New media and networked journalism. *Communication, Culture & Critique, 1*(1), 92–104.

Beecher, E. (2008). Look to the future: The future of journalism. *Walkley Magazine, 50*, April–May, Media Entertainment and Arts Alliance, Sydney, pp. 14–15.

Bell, P., & van Leeuwen, T. (1994). *The media interview: Confession, content, conversation.* Sydney, NSW: University of New South Wales Press.

Bennett, J. (Ed.). (2008). *Civic life online: Learning how digital media can engage youth.* Cambridge, MA: MIT Press.

Bennett, W. (1990). Toward a theory of press–state relations. *Journal of Communication, 40*, 103–125.

Bennett, W., & Serrin, W. (2011). The watchdog role of the press. In D. Graber (Ed.), *Media power in politics* (pp. 395–405). Washington, DC: CQ. (Original work published in 2005)

Bent, S. (1927). *Ballyhoo: The voice of the press.* New York: Boni & Liveright.

Bentele, G. (2004). New perspectives of public relations in Europe. In B. van Ruler & D. Verčič (Eds.), *Public relations and communication management in Europe* (pp. 485–496). Berlin and New York, NY: Mouton de Gruyter.

Bentele, G., Liebert, T., & Seeling, S. (1997). Von der determination zur intereffikation. Ein integriertes modell zum verhältnis von public relations und journalismus. In G. Bentele & M. Haller (Eds.), *Aktuelle entstehung von öffentlichkeit. Akteure, strukturen, veränderungen* (pp. 225–250). Germany: Konstanz.

Bentele, G., & Nothhaft, H. (2008). The intereffication model: Theoretical discussions and empirical research. In A. Zerfass, B. Van Ruler, & K. Sriramesh (Eds.), *Public relations research: European and international perspectives and innovations* (pp. 33–48). Wiesbaden, Germany: VS Verlag fur Sozialwissenschaften (Springer Science + Business Media).

Berger, B. (2001). Private issues and public policy: Locating the corporate agenda in agenda-setting theory. *Journal of Public Relations Research, 13*, 91–126.

Berger, B. (2005). Power over, power with, and power to relations: Critical reflections on public relations, the dominant coalition, and activism. *Journal of Public Relations Research, 17*(1), 5–28.

Berger, B. (2007). Public relations and organisational power. In E. Toth (Ed.), *The future of excellence in public relations and communication management: Challenges for the next generation* (pp. 221–234). Mahwah, NJ: Lawrence Erlbaum.

Berger, B., Hertog, J., & Park, D. (2002). The political role and influence of business organizations. In W. Gudykunst (Ed.), *Communication Yearbook, 26* (pp. 196–200). Mahwah, NJ: Lawrence Erlbaum.

Berkowitz, D. (1992). Who sets the media agenda? The ability of policy makers to determine news decisions. In J. Kennamer (Ed.), *Public opinion, the press and public policy* (pp. 81–102). Westport, CT: Praeger.

Berkowitz, D., & Adams, D. (1990). Information subsidy and agenda-building in local television news. *Journalism Quarterly, 67,* 723–731.

Bernays, E. (1923). *Crystallising public opinion.* New York, NY: Boni & Liveright.

Bernays, E. (1928). *Propaganda.* New York, NY: Liveright.

Bernays, E. (1952). *Public relations.* Norman, OK: University of Oklahoma Press.

Bernays, E. (1955). *The engineering of consent* (1st ed.). Norman, OK: University of Oklahoma Press.

Bimber, B., Flanagin, A., & Stohl, C. (2012). *Collective action in organizations: Interaction and engagement in an era of technological change.* New York, NY: Cambridge University Press.

Bird, G., & Merwin, F. (Eds.). (1955). *The press and society: A book of readings.* New York, NY: Prentice-Hall. (Original work published 1951) Retrieved from http://archive.org/stream/pressandsociety030075mbp/pressandsociety030075mbp_djvu.txt

Bixler, P. (1930). The reporter's last stand. *The North American Review, 229,* January, 113–116.

Black, S., & Sharpe, M. (1983). *Practical public relations.* Englewood Cliffs, NJ: Prentice-Hall.

Blessing, K., & Marren, J. (2013). Is the PR-ization of media…BS? *Media Ethics, 24*(2). Retrieved from http://www.mediaethicsmagazine.com/index.php/browse-back-issues/145-spring-2013/3998865-is-the-pr-ization-of-media-bullshit

Bleyer, W. (1973). *Main currents in the history of American journalism.* New York, NY: Da Capo Press. (Original work published 1927)

Blood, W. (1989). Public agendas and media agendas: Some news that may matter. *Media Information Australia, 52,* May, 7–15.

Bloomberg. (2014). Company overview of Upstream Australia Pty Ltd. *Businessweek.* Retrieved from http://investing.businessweek.com/research/stocks/private/snapshot.asp?privcapId=32693960

Blumer, H. (1948). Public opinion and public opinion polls. *American Sociological Review, 13,* 542–554.

Blumler, J. (1990). Elections, the media and the modern publicity process. In M. Ferguson (Ed.), *Public communication: The new imperative* (pp. 101–113). London, UK: Sage.

Bock, M. (2009). Who's minding the gate: Pool feeds, video subsidies, and political images. *International Journal of Press/Politics, 14*(2), 257–278.

Boczkowski, P. (2005). *Digitizing the news.* Cambridge, MA: MIT Press.

Boler, M. (Ed.). (2008). *Digital media and democracy: Tactics in hard times.* Cambridge, MA: MIT Press.

Boorstin, D. (1961). *The image: What happened to the American dream.* London, UK: Weidenfeld & Nicolson.

Bourdieu, P. (1984). *Distinction: A social critique of the judgement of taste* (R. Nice, Trans.). Cambridge, MA: Harvard University Press; London, UK: Routledge. (Original work published 1979)

Bovet, S. (1992). Educators need to communicate better on and off campus. *Public Relations Journal, 48,* 14–17.

Bowden, M. (2009, October). The story behind the story. *The Atlantic.* Retrieved from http://www.theatlantic.com/magazine/archive/2009/10/the-story-behind-the-story/307667/

Bowen, F. (2012, September 4). Spot the difference: Public relations and journalism. *London Progressive Journal.* Retrieved from http://londonprogressivejournal.com/article/view/1246

Bowen, S. (2007, October). Ethics and public relations. Gainesville, FL: Institute for Public Relations. Retrieved from http://www.instituteforpr.org/essential_knowledge/detail/ethics_and_public_relations/

Bowen, S. (2008). A state of neglect: Public relations as 'corporate conscience' or ethics counsel. *Journal of Public Relations Research, 20,* 271–296.

Breakenridge, D. (2008). *PR 2.0: New media, new tools, new audiences.* Upper Saddle River, NJ: FT, Pearson Education.

Briones, R., & Toth, E. (2013). The state of PR graduate curriculum as we know it: A longitudinal analysis. *Journalism and Mass Communication Educator, 68*(2), 119–133.

Broom, G. (1977). Co-orientational measurement in public issues. *Public Relations Review, 3,* 110–119.

Broom, G. (1982). A comparison of sex roles in public relations. *Public Relations Review, 8*(3), 17–22.

Broom, G. (2009). *Cutlip & Center's effective public relations* (10th ed.). Upper Saddle River, NJ: Pearson Education.

Broom, G., & Dozier, D. (1990). *Using research in public relations: Applications to program management.* Englewood Cliffs, NJ: Prentice-Hall.

Brown, J., Bybee, C., Wearden, S., & Straughan, D. (1987). Invisible power: News sources and the limits of diversity. *Journalism Quarterly, 4*(1), 45–54.

Brown, J., & Duguid, A. (2000). *The social life of information.* Boston, MA: Harvard Business School Press.

Bruns, A. (2005). *Gatewatching: Collaborative online news production.* New York, NY: Peter Lang.

Bruns, A. (2008). *Blogs, Wikipedia, Second Life and beyond: From production to produsage.* New York, NY: Peter Lang.

Bryant, J., & Miron, D. (2004). Theory and research in mass communication. *Journal of Communication, 54*(4), 662–704.

Buber, M. (1958). *I and thou* (W. Kaufmann, Trans.). New York, NY: Charles-Scribner.

Buber, M. (2002). Dialogue (R. Smith, Trans.). In *Between man and man* (pp. 1–45). London, UK: Routledge. (Original work published 1947)

Bucy, E. (2004). Interactivity in society: Locating an elusive concept. *Information Society, 20*(5), 373–383.

Burke, K. (1969). *A rhetoric of motives.* Berkeley, CA: University of California Press.

Burns, L. (2002). *Understanding journalism.* London, UK and Thousand Oaks, CA: Sage.

Burrowes, C. (2011). Property, power and press freedom: Emergence of the fourth estate, 1640–1789. *Journalism & Communication Monographs, 13*, 1–66.

Burt, T. (2012). *Dark art: The changing face of public relations.* London, UK: Elliott & Thompson.

Burton, B. (2007). *Inside spin: The dark underbelly of the PR industry.* Crows Nest, NSW: Allen & Unwin.

Buskirk, E. (2009, September 14). 'Help a reporter out' crowdsources news sources. *WIRED.* Retrieved from http://www.wired.com/business/2009/09/help-a-reporter-out-hits-paydirt-crowdsourcing-news-sources/

Butterick, K. (2011). *Introducing public relations: Theory and practice.* London, UK: Sage.

Cadzow, J. (2001, May 26). The hidden persuaders. *Sydney Morning Herald, GoodWeekend* magazine, pp. 20–24.

Cameron, G., Sallot, L., & Curtin, P. (1997). Public relations and the production of news: A critical review and theoretical framework. In B. Burleson (Ed.), *Communication yearbook, 20* (pp. 111–155). Thousand Oaks, CA: Sage.

Canadian Journalism Project. (2009, September). Conference report: The future of journalism, Cardiff, Wales. Retrieved from http://jsource.ning.com/profiles/blogs/conference-report-the-future

Canter, A., Kirby, J., McFarlane, G., & Welland, M. (2013). *Best of branded content.* London, UK: Digital Media Communications. Retrieved from http://www.thebcma.info/products-services

Carey, J. (1992). The press and the public discourse. *Kettering Review,* Winter, 9–22.

Carey, J. (2009). *Communication as culture.* New York, NY: Routledge. (Original work published 1989)

Carlyle, T. (1840). The hero as man of letters, Johnson, Rousseau, Burns. Lecture V, May 19. Retrieved from http://www.victorianweb.org/authors/carlyle/heroes/hero5.html

Carlyle, T. (1993). The hero as man of letters, Johnson, Rousseau, Burns. In T. Carlyle, *Heroes, hero worship and the heroic* (pp. 349–350). Berkeley, CA: University of California Press. (Original work published 1840)

Carpentier, N. (2007). Participation, access and interaction: Changing perspectives. In V. Nightingale & T. Dwyer (Eds.), *New media worlds: Challenges for convergence* (pp. 214–230). South Melbourne, Vic: Oxford University Press.

Carpentier, N. (2011). *Media and participation: A site of ideological democratic struggle.* Chicago, IL: Intellect.

Carragee, K., & Roefs, W. (2004). The neglect of power in recent framing research. *Journal of Communication, 54*(2), 214–233.

Carroll, C., & McCombs, M. (2003). Agenda-setting effects of business news on the public's images and opinions about major corporations. *Corporate Reputation Review, 6*, 36–46.

Case, J. (2007, November). Recovering the radical: Biocybernetic subversion in guerrilla video primer. Paper presented at the 93rd National Communication Association Annual

Convention, Chicago, IL. Retrieved from http://citation.allacademic.com/meta/p_mla_apa_research_citation/1/9/5/5/8/p195585_index.html

Castells, M. (1996). *The rise of the network society*. Oxford, UK: Blackwell.

Castells, M. (2000). *The rise of the network society* (2nd ed.). Oxford, UK: Blackwell.

Castells, M. (2009). *Communication power*. Oxford, UK and New York, NY: Oxford University Press.

Cauberghe, V., & de Pelsmacker, P. (2010). Advergames: The impact of brand prominence and game repetition on brand responses. *Journal of Advertising, 39*(1), 5–18.

Cawson, A. (1986). *Corporatism and political theory*. New York, NY: Basil Blackwell.

Cellan-Jones, R. (2009, January 16). Twitter and a classic picture. *BBC News*. Retrieved from http://www.bbc.co.uk/blogs/technology/2009/01/twitter_and_a_classic_picture.html

Charron, J. (1989). Relations between journalists and public relations practitioners: Cooperation, conflict and negotiation. *Canadian Journal of Communications, 14*(2), 41–54.

Chase, H. (1982). Issue management conference: A special report. *Corporate Public Issues and Their Management, 7*, 1–2.

Cho, S. (2006). The power of public relations in media relations: A national survey of health PR practitioners. *Journalism & Mass Communication Quarterly, 83*(3), 563–580.

Chomsky, N. (2002) *Media control*. New York, NY: Seven Stories.

Christians, C., Glasser, T., McQuail, D., Nordenstreng, K., & White, R. (2009). *Normative theories of the media: Journalism in democratic societies*. Urbana, IL: University of Illinois Press.

CINIC [China Internet Network Information Center]. (2009). 24th statistical report on internet development in China. Retrieved from http://www.cnnic.cn/html/Dir/2009/07/28/5644.htm

CIPR (Chartered Institute for Public Relations). (2012). Wikipedia best practice guidance for public relations professionals. London, UK: Author. Retrieved from http://www.cipr.co.uk/sites/default/files/CIPR_Wikipedia_Best_Practice_Guidance.pdf

Claussen, D. (2012). If even journalism professors don't know what journalism is, then all really is lost. *Journalism & Mass Communication Educator, 67*, 327–331.

Cobb, R., & Elder, C. (1972). *Participation in American politics: The dynamics of agenda building*. Boston, MA: Allyn & Bacon.

Cohen, A. (2009, May 7). The flak over flacks. *CBS News*, Sunday Morning. Retrieved from http://www.cbsnews.com/stories/2008/06/01/sunday/main4142947.shtml

Cohen, B. (1963). *The press and foreign policy*. Princeton, NJ: Princeton University Press.

Colistra, R. (2012). Shaping and cutting the media agenda: Television reporters' perceptions of agenda- and frame-building and agenda-cutting influences. *Journalism & Communication Monographs, 14*(2), 85–146.

Commission on Public Relations Education. (2006). The professional bond: Public relations education for the 21st century. New York, NY: Author. Retrieved from http://www.commpred.org/_uploads/report2-full.pdf

Commission on Public Relations Education. (2012). Standards for a Master's degree in public relations: Educating for complexity. New York, NY: Author. Retrieved from http://www.commpred.org/educatingforcomplexity

Commission on the Freedom of the Press. (1947). *A free and responsible press: A general report on mass communication*. Chicago, IL: University of Chicago Press.

Common Courage Press. (2001). Toxic sludge: Lies, damn lies and the public relations industry. Retrieved from http://www.commoncouragepress.com/index.cfm?action=book&bookid=060

Conley, D. (2010, December 17). Is WikiLeaks journalism? *The Australian*, Media. Retrieved from http://www.theaustralian.com.au/media/is-wikileaks-journalism/story-e6frg996-1225972790493

Cook, T. (2008, July 25). The revolution may not be blogged. *The Drum*, ABC (Australian Broadcasting Corporation). Retrieved from http://www.abc.net.au/unleashed/32158.html

Cooper, S. (2006). *Watching the watchdog: Bloggers as the fifth estate.* Spokane, WA: Marquette.

Cornelissen, J. (2011). *Corporate communication: A guide to theory and practice* (3rd ed.). London and Thousand Oaks, CA: Sage.

Corner, J. (2007). Media, power and political culture. In E. Devereux (Ed.), *Media studies: Key issues and debates* (pp. 211–230). London, UK: Sage.

Corporate Watch. (2002). Hill & Knowlton: A corporate profile. The Gulf War. Retrieved from http://www.corporatewatch.org.uk/?lid=380#war

Cosic, M. (2008, August 23). Without fear or favour. *The Weekend Australian*, Inquirer. Retrieved from http://www.theaustralian.com.au/business/media/without-fear-or-favour/story-e6frg996-1111117275507

Cottle, S. (Ed.). (2003). *News, public relations and power.* London, UK: Sage.

Couldry, N. (2004). Theorizing media as practice. *Social Semiotics, 14*(2), 115–132.

Couldry, N. (2010). *Why voice matters.* London, UK and Thousand Oaks, CA: Sage.

Couldry, N. (2012). *Media, society, world.* Cambridge, UK: Polity.

Couldry, N., Madianou, M., & Pinchevski, A. (Eds.). (2013). *Ethics of media.* Basingstoke, Hampshire, UK: Palgrave Macmillan.

Cover, R. (2004). New media theory: Electronic games, democracy and reconfiguring the author–audience relationship. *Social Semiotics, 13*(2), 173–191.

Craig, R., & Muller, H. (Eds.). (2007). *Theorizing communication: Readings across traditions.* Thousand Oaks, CA: Sage.

Crampton, T. (2005, August 22). Blogosphere increasingly international. *International Herald Tribune*, Business, Media and Communications, p. 10.

Creswell, J. (2009). *Research design: Qualitative, quantitative and mixed methods approaches* (3rd ed.). Thousand Oaks, CA: Sage.

Croteau, D., Hoynes, W., & Milan, S. (2012). *Media/society: Industries, images, and audiences.* Thousand Oaks, CA: Sage.

Cunningham, S., & Turnbull, S. (Eds.). (2014). *The media and communications in Australia* (4th ed.). Crows Nest, NSW: Allen & Unwin.

Cunningham, S., & Turner, G. (Eds.). (2010). *The media and communications in Australia* (3rd ed.). Crows Nest, NSW: Allen & Unwin.

Currah, A. (2009). What's happening to our news. Oxford, UK: Reuters Institute for the Study of Journalism, Oxford University. Retrieved from https://reutersinstitute.politics.ox.ac.uk/about/news/item/article/whats-happening-to-our-news.html

Curran, J. (2002). *Media and power*. London, UK: Routledge.

Curran, J. (2010). Future of journalism. *Journalism Studies, 11*(4), 464–476.

Curran, J. (2011). *Media and democracy*. Abingdon, Oxon, UK: Routledge.

Curran, J., Fenton, N., & Freedman, D. (2012). *Misunderstanding the internet*. New York, NY: Routledge.

Curran, J., & Morley, D. (Eds.). (2006). *Media and cultural theory*. Abingdon, Oxon, UK: Routledge.

Curtin, P. (1999). Re-evaluation public relations information subsidies: Market-driven journalism and agenda-building theory and practice. *Journal of Public Relations Research, 11*(1), 53–90.

Curtin, P., & Gaither, T. (2007). *International public relations: Negotiating culture, identity and power*. Thousand Oaks, CA: Sage.

Cutlip, S., Center, A., & Broom, G. (2006). *Effective public relations* (9th ed.). Upper Saddle River, NJ: Pearson Education.

Dahlgren, P. (2009). *Media and political engagement: Citizens, communication and democracy*. Cambridge, UK: Cambridge University Press.

Dahlgren, P. (2013). Online journalism and civic cosmopolitanism: Professional vs. participatory ideals. *Journalism Studies, 14*(2), 156–171.

Danielian, L., & Reese, S. (1989). A closer look at intermedia influences on agenda setting: The cocaine issue of 1986. In P. Shoemaker (Ed.), *Communication campaigns about drugs: Government, media and the public* (pp. 47–66). Hillside, NJ: Lawrence Erlbaum.

Davey, E. (2013, March 13). London NHS spends 13 million on public relations. *BBC News*, London. Retrieved from http://www.bbc.co.uk/news/uk-england-london-21762939

Davies, N. (2008). PR versus journalism. Debate organised by the Media Standards Trust and the University of Westminster, London, UK, April 9. Retrieved from http://www.youtube.com/watch?v=93615UWeXac

Davies, N. (2009). *Flat earth news*. London, UK: Random House.

Davis, A. (2000). Public relations, news production and changing patterns of source access in the British national media. *Media Culture Society, 22*, 39–59.

Davis, A. (2002). *Public relations democracy: Politics, public relations and the mass media in Britain*. Manchester, UK: Manchester University Press.

Davis, A. (2006). Placing promotional culture. In J. Curran & D. Morley (Eds.), *Media and cultural theory* (pp. 149–163). Abingdon, Oxon, UK: Routledge.

Davison, W. (Phillips). (1983). The third person effect in communication. *Public Opinion Quarterly, 47*, 1–15.

Day, M. (2013, May 27). Bitter pill for spin doctors. *The Australian*. Retrieved from http://www.theaustralian.com.au/archive/media/bitter-pill-for-spin-doctors/story-e6frg9tf-1226650913146#mm-premium

Deacon, D., & Golding, P. (1994). *Taxation and representation: The media, political communication and the poll tax*. London, UK: John Libbey.

Deans, J. (2011, June 3). Julian Assange wins Martha Gellhorn journalism prize. *The Guardian*. Retrieved from http://www.theguardian.com/media/2011/jun/02/julian-assange-martha-gelhorn-prize

de Bussy, N. (2009). Reputation management: A driving force for action. In J. Chia & G. Synnott (Eds.), *An introduction to public relations: From theory to practice* (pp. 222–247). South Melbourne, Vic: Oxford University Press.

Deception on Capitol Hill. (1992, January 15). *The New York Times.* Retrieved from http://www.nytimes.com/1992/01/15/opinion/deception-on-capitol-hill.html

Defren, T. (2008, April 18). Social media template, version 1.5. *PR-Squared* blog. Retrieved from http://www.pr-squared.com/index.php/2008/04/social_media_release_template

Delli Carpini, M., & Keeter, S. (1996). *What Americans know about politics and why it matters.* New Haven, CT: Yale University Press.

DeLorme, D., & Fedler, F. (2003). Journalists' hostility toward public relations: An historical analysis. *Public Relations Review, 29*, 99–124.

Deluca, K., Lawson, S., & Sun, Y. (2012). Occupy Wall Street on the public screens of social media: The many framings of the birth of a protest movement. *Communication, Culture & Critique, 5*(4), 483–509.

De Mente, B. (2012). *China: Understanding and dealing with the Chinese way of doing business!* Nanjing, China: Cultural Insight/Phoenix.

Demetrious, K. (2013a). Kristen Demetrious discusses public relations, activism and social change. Routledge 'Communication'. Retrieved from http://www.routledge.com/communication/articles/kristin_demetrious_discusses_public_relations_activism_and_social_change

Demetrious, K. (2013b). *Public relations, activism and social change.* New York, NY and Abingdon, Oxon, UK: Routledge.

de Pelsmacker, P., & Neijens, P. (2012). New advertising formats: How persuasion knowledge affects consumer response. *Journal of Marketing Communications, 18*(1), 1–4.

Deuze, M. (2005, July 4). Towards professional participatory storytelling in journalism and advertising. *First Monday, 10*(7). Retrieved from http://firstmonday.org/htbin/cgiwrap/bin/ojs/index.php/fm/rt/printerFriendly/1257/1177

Deuze, M. (2007). *Media work.* Malden, MA and Cambridge, UK: Polity.

Deuze, M., Bruns, A., & Neuberger, C. (2007). Preparing for an age of participatory news. *Journalism Practice, 1*(3), 322–338.

Devereux, E. (2007a). *Understanding the media* (2nd ed.). London, UK: Sage.

Devereux, E. (Ed.). (2007b). *Media studies: Key issues and debates.* London, UK: Sage.

Dewey, J. (1927). *The public and its problems.* Chicago, IL: Swallow; New York, NY: Henry Holt and Holt, Rinehart & Winston.

Dickinson, R., Matthews, J., & Saltzis, K. (2013). Studying journalists in changing times: Understanding news work as social situated practice. *The International Communication Gazette, 75*(1), 3–18.

Dinino, K. (2012). PR 3.0: The new frontier. KCD PR presentation. Retrieved from http://www.slideshare.net/kcdpr/pr-30-the-new-frontier

DiNucci, D. (1999). Fragmented future. *Print, 53*(4). Retrieved from http://darcyd.com/fragmented_future.pdf

DiStaso, M. (2013). Rules for Wikipedia editing for public relations. Research Conversations. Gainesville, FL: Institute for Public Relations. Retrieved from http://www.instituteforpr.org/2013/12/rules-wikipedia-editing-public-relations

Doherty, M. (2013, May 16). First the Sultan, now Bill Gates comes to town. *The Canberra Times*. Retrieved from http://www.canberratimes.com.au/act-news/first-the-sultan-now-bill-gates-comes-to-town-20130516–2jo7j.html

Donsbach, W. (Ed.). (2008). *The international encyclopedia of communication, Vol. 10*. Malden, MA and Oxford, UK: Blackwell.

Dormfield, A. (1983). *Behind the front page*. Chicago, IL: Academy.

Dougoud, C. (2009, October 28). Hit the road Jack: Getting coverage by not paying transportation fees. East-West Public Relations, Beijing. Retrieved from http://www.eastwestpr.com/2009/10/hit-the-road-jack-getting-coverage-by-not-paying-transportation-fees

Dozier, D. (1992). The organizational roles of communications and public relations practitioners. In J. Grunig (Ed.), *Excellence in public relations and communication management* (pp. 327–356). Hillsdale, NJ: Lawrence Erlbaum.

Dozier, D., & Broom, G. (2006). The centrality of practitioner roles to public relations theory. In C. Botan & V. Hazelton (Eds.), *Public relations theory II* (pp. 137–170). Mahwah, NJ: Lawrence Erlbaum.

Dozier, D., Grunig, L., & Grunig, J. (1995). *Manager's guide to excellence in public relations and communication management*. Mahwah, NJ: Lawrence Erlbaum.

DTI/IPR [Department of Trade & Industry/Institute for Public Relations]. (2003, November). Unlocking the potential of public relations: Developing good practice. Report. Retrieved from www.ipr.org.uk

Duhé, S. (2013). Teaching business as a second language. *Research Conversations*. Gainesville, FL: Institute for Public Relations. Retrieved from http://www.instituteforpr.org/2013/12/teaching-business-second-language

Dunlop, T. (2013a, July 10). Fact-checking sites are a symptom, not a cure. *The Kings Tribune*. Retrieved from http://www.kingstribune.com/index.php/weekly-email/item/1841-fact-checking-sites-are-a-symptom-not-a-cure

Dunlop, T. (2013b). *The new front page: New media and the rise of the audience*. Melbourne, Vic: Scribe, Penguin.

Dunwoody, S. (1978). Science journalists: A study of factors affecting the selection of news at a scientific meeting. PhD dissertation, Indiana University, Bloomington.

Durrer, V., & Miles, S. (2009). New perspectives on the role of cultural intermediaries in social inclusion in the UK. *Consumption Markets & Culture, 12*(3), 225–241.

Dutton, W. (2007). *Through the network of networks: The fifth estate*. Oxford, UK: Oxford Internet Institute.

Dvorkin, L. (2012). *The Forbes model for journalism in the digital age*. San Francisco, CA: Hyperink.

Dyer, G. (2012a, February 10). Latest circulation figures: Read all about it…or not. *Crikey*. Retrieved from http://www.crikey.com.au/2012/02/10/latest-circulation-figures-read-all-about-it-or-not

Dyer, G. (2012b, May 11). Newspaper circulation carnage: Biggest March fall on record. *Crikey*. Retrieved from http://www.crikey.com.au/2012/05/11/newspaper-circulation-carnage-biggest-march-fall-on-record

Eberhart, D. (2005, January 31). How the blogs torpedoed Dan Rather. *NewsMax.com*. Retrieved from http://archive.newsmax.com/archives/articles/2005/1/28/172943.shtml

Edelman. (2013a). Edelman Trust Barometer; Executive Summary. New York, NY: Author. Retrieved from http://www.edelman.com/insights/intellectual-property/trust-2013/about-trust

Edelman. (2013b). Sponsored content: A broader relationship with the US news media. New York, NY: Author. Retrieved from http://www.edelman.com/insights/intellectual-property/sponsored-content-report

Edwards, L. (2012). Defining the 'object' of public relations research: A new starting point. *Public Relations Inquiry, 1*, 7–30.

Edwards, L., & Hodges, C. (Eds.). (2011). *Public relations, society and culture: Theoretical and empirical explorations.* Abingdon, Oxon, UK: Routledge.

Edy, J., & Meirick, P. (2011). Wanted, dead or alive: Media frames, frame adoption, and support for the war in Afghanistan. In D. Graber (Ed.), *Media power in politics* (6th ed., pp. 141–151). Washington, DC: CQ.

Eliasoph, N. (2004). Can we theorise the press without theorising the public? *Political Communication, 21*(3), 297–303.

Ellerbach, J. (2004). The advertorial as information pollution. *Journal of Information Ethics, 13*(1), 61–75.

Elliott, S. (1992, May 14). A dispute in the public relations industry. *The New York Times*, Business Day. Retrieved from http://www.nytimes.com/1992/05/14/business/the-media-business-advertising-a-dispute-in-the-public-relations-industry.html

Eltham, B. (2009, April 27). The rotten elite. *New Matilda*. Retrieved from http://newmatilda.com/2009/04/27/rotten-elite

Entman, R. (1993). Framing: Toward a clarification of a fractured paradigm. *Journal of Communication, 43*, 5–58.

Ericson, R., Baranek, P., & Chan, J. (1989). *Negotiating control: A study of news sources.* Toronto, Canada: University of Toronto Press.

Eriksson, G., & Östman, J. (2013). Co-operative or adversarial: Journalists' enactment of the watchdog function in political news production. *International Journal of Press/Politics, 18*(3), 304–324.

Erjavec, K. (2005). Hybrid public relations news discourse. *European Journal of Communication, 20*(2), 155–179.

Esser, F. (2008). 'Spin doctor'. In W. Donsbach, (Ed.), *The international encyclopedia of communication* (pp. 4783–4787). Malden, MA: Blackwell.

Esser, F., Reinemann, C., & Fan, D. (2001). Spin doctors in the United States, Great Britain and Germany. *International Journal of Press/Politics, 6*(1), 16–45.

European Commission. (2013). Product placement, audio-visual and media policies. Retrieved from http://ec.europa.eu/avpolicy/reg/tvwf/advertising/product/index_en.htm

Evans, T. (2010). We are all in PR now. *British Journalism Review, 21*(2), 31–36.

Ewen, S. (1996). *PR! A social history of spin.* New York, NY: Basic.

Eysenbach, G. (2008). Credibility of health information and digital media: New perspectives and implications for youth. In M. Metzger & A. Flanagin (Eds.), *Digital media, youth and credibility* (pp. 123–154). Cambridge, MA: MIT Press.

Falconi, T. (2006). How big is public relations (and why does it matter)? The economic impact of our profession. Gainesville, FL: Institute for Public Relations. Retrieved from http://www.instituteforpr.org/research_single/how_big_is_public_relations

Falkheimer, J., & Heide, M. (2011, May). Participatory strategic communication: From one- and two-way communication to participatory communication through social media. Paper presented at the International Communication Association 2011 pre-conference, Strategic Communication: A Concept at the Center of Applied Communications, Boston, MA.

Fallows, J. (1996). *Breaking the news: How the media undermine democracy*. New York, NY: Pantheon.

Featherstone, M. (1991). *Consumer culture and postmodernism*. London, UK: Sage.

Fenton, N. (2007). Bridging the mythical divide: Political economy and cultural studies approaches to the analysis of media. In E. Devereux (Ed.), *Media studies: Key issues and debates* (pp. 7–31). London, UK: Sage.

Fico, F., Lacy, S., Wildman, S., Baldwin, T., Bergan, D., & Zube, P. (2013). Citizen journalism sites as information substitutes and complements for United States newspaper coverage of local governments. *Digital Journalism, 1*(10), 152–168.

Finlay, L., & Gough, B. (2003). *Reflexivity: A practical guide for researchers in health and social sciences*. Oxford, UK: Blackwell.

Fitch, K. (2009). Making friends in the Wild West: Singaporean public relations practitioners' perceptions of working in social media. *Prism, 6*(2). Retrieved from http://praxis.massey.ac.nz/global_pr.html

Flaherty, R. (2013, November 18). The future of PR. Keynote address to the Public Relations Institute of Australia National Conference, Adelaide, South Australia.

Flanagin, A., & Metzger, M. (2008). Digital media and youth: Unparalleled opportunity and unprecedented responsibility. In M. Metzger & A. Flanagin (Eds.), *Digital media, youth and credibility* (pp. 5–27). Cambridge, MA: MIT Press.

Flew, T. (2008). *New media: An introduction* (3rd ed.). South Melbourne, Vic: Oxford University Press.

Flew, T. (2014). *New media* (4th ed.). South Melbourne, Vic: Oxford University Press.

Flew, T., Spurgeon, C., Daniel, A., & Swift, A. (2012). The promise of computational journalism. *Journalism Practice, 6*(2), 157–171.

Flor, A. (1992). Development communication: The fifth theory of the press. In C. Maslog (Ed.), *Communication values and society* (chapter 5). Quezon City: Philippine Association of Communication Educators. Retrieved from http://www.academia.edu/178798/The_Fifth_Theory_of_the_Press

Foley, M. (2004). Lies, lies, and damned PR. *Index on Censorship, 33*(2), 76–77.

Folkerts, J., Hamilton, J., & Lehmann, N. (2013, October). Educating journalists: A new plea for the university tradition. New York, NY: Columbia Journalism School, Columbia University.

Foremski, T. (2006, February 27). Die! Press release! Die! Die! Die! *Silicon Valley Watcher* blog. Retrieved from http://www.siliconvalleywatcher.com/mt/archives/2006/02/die_press_relea.php

Foucault, M. (1972). *The archaeology of knowledge*. New York, NY: Harper & Row.

Fox News. (2009, February 5). Pentagon spending billions on PR to sway world opinion. Retrieved from http://www.foxnews.com/politics/2009/02/05/pentagon-spending-bil-lions-pr-sway-world-opinion/

Frankfurt, H. (2005). *On bullshit.* Princeton, NJ: Princeton University Press.

Frankfurt, H. (2006). *On truth.* New York, NY: Knopf.

Franklin, B. (1994). *Packaging politics: Political communication in Britain's media democracy.* London, UK: Edward Arnold.

Franklin, B. (1997). *Newzak and news media.* London, UK: Edward Arnold.

Franklin, B. (2006). *Local journalism and local media: Making the local new.* London, UK: Routledge.

Fraser, N. (1990). Rethinking the public sphere. *Social Text, 25/26,* 56–80.

Fraser, N. (1992). Rethinking the public sphere: A contribution to the critique of actually existing democracy. In C. Calhoun (Ed.), *Habermas and the public sphere* (pp. 109–142). Cambridge, MA: MIT Press.

Freeman, R. (1984). *Strategic management: A stakeholder approach.* London, UK: Pitman.

Friestad, M., & Wright, P. (1994). The persuasion knowledge model: How people cope with persuasion attempts. *Journal of Consumer Research, 21*(1), 1–31.

Frith, S., & Meech, P. (2007). Becoming a journalist: Journalism education and journalism culture. *Journalism, 8*(2), 137–164.

Gadamer, H. (1989). *Truth and method* (2nd ed.; J. Weinsheimer & D. Marshall, Trans.). New York, NY: Crossroad.

Gamson, W., & Modigliani, A. (1989). Media discourse and public opinion on nuclear power: A constructionist approach. *American Journal of Sociology, 95*(1), 1–37.

Gandy, O. (1982). *Beyond agenda setting: Information subsidies and public policy.* Norwood, NJ: Ablex.

Gans, H. (1979). *Deciding what's news: A study of CBS evening news, NBC nightly news, Newsweek and Time.* New York, NY: Vintage.

Gantz, J., & Reinsel, D. (2010, May). The digital universe decade: Are you ready? Framingham MA: IDC. Retrieved from http://australia.emc.com/collateral/analyst-reports/idc-digital-universe-are-you-ready.pdf

Gartner Research. (2008). Hype cycles: Interpreting technology hype. Stanford, CA: Author. Retrieved from http://www.gartner.com/it/products/research/methodologies/research_hype.jsp

Geertz, C. (1973). Thick description: Toward an interpretive theory of culture. In *The interpretation of cultures: Selected essays* (pp. 3–30). New York, NY: Basic.

Gentile, B. (2013). Backpack journalism project. Washington, DC: American University School of Communication. Retrieved from http://www.american.edu/soc/backpack

Gieber, W., & Johnson, W. (1961). The City Hall 'beat': A study of reporter and source roles. *Journalism Quarterly, 38,* 289–297.

Gilder, G. (1994). *Life after television.* New York, NY: W.W. Norton.

Gillmor, D. (2004). *We the media: Grassroots journalism by the people, for the people.* North Sebastopol, CA: O'Reilly.

Ginosar, A. (2013). Media governance: A conceptual framework or merely a buzz word? *Communication Theory, 23*(4), 356–374.

Gitelman, L. (2008). *Always already new: Media history, and the data of culture.* Cambridge, MA: MIT Press.

Gitlin, T. (1978). Media sociology: The dominant paradigm. *Theory & Society, 6*(2), 205–253.

Gitlin, T. (1980). *The whole world is watching.* Berkeley, CA: University of California Press.

Gitlin, T. (1998). Public spheres or public sphericles? In T. Liebes & J. Curran (Eds.), *Media, ritual and identity* (pp. 170–173). New York, NY: Routledge.

Gitlin, T. (2001). *Media unlimited.* New York, NY: Metropolitan.

Gitlin, T. (2009, May 25). Journalism's many crises. *Open Democracy.* Retrieved from http://www.opendemocracy.net/article/a-surfeit-of-crises-circulation-revenue-attention-authority-and-deference

Glaser, B. (1978). *Theoretical sensitivity.* Mill Valley, CA: Sociology.

Glaser, B., & Strauss, A. (1967). *The discovery of grounded theory: Strategies for qualitative research.* Chicago, IL: Adline.

Glick, J., & Neckes, J. (2013, September 22). Native advertising 101: Understanding the native continuum. *Gigaom,* 'Roadmap'. Retrieved from http://paidcontent.org/2013/09/22/native-advertising-101-understanding-the-native-continuum

Global Alliance for Public Relations and Communication Management. (2010). The global protocol on ethics in public relations. London, UK: Author. Retrieved from http://www.globalalliancepr.org/project.php?id=5

Goc, N. (2012). WikiLeaks and journalism in the 21st century. In S. Greenland, J. Bainbridge, C. Galloway, & R. Gill (Eds.), *Strategic communication: Cases in marketing, public relations, advertising and media* (pp. 61–69). Frenchs Forest, NSW: Pearson.

Goffman, E. (1974). *Frame Analysis.* Cambridge, MA: Harvard University Press.

Gogoi, P. (2006, October 9). Wal-Mart's Jim and Laura: The real story. *BusinessWeek.* Retrieved from http://www.businessweek.com/stories/2006–10–09/wal-marts-jim-and-laura-the-real-storybusinessweek-business-news-stock-market-and-financial-advice

Goldman, E. (1948). *Two-way street: The emergence of the public relations counsel.* Boston, MA: Bellman.

Goldstein, T. (2007). *Journalism and truth: Strange bedfellows.* Evanston, IL: Northwestern University Press.

Gombita, J. (2012, July 31). The intersection of public relations and journalism in the digital age. *PR Conversations.* Retrieved from http://www.prconversations.com/index.php/2012/07/the-intersection-of-public-relations-and-journalism-in-the-digital-age/

Goode, L. (2005). *Jürgen Habermas: Democracy and the public sphere.* London, UK: Pluto.

Graber, D. (Ed.). (2011). *Media power in politics* (6th ed.). Washington, DC: CQ.

Gray, J. (2010). Entertainment and media/cultural/communication/etc studies. *Continuum: Journal of Media & Cultural Studies, 24*(6), 811–817.

Gray, J., Bounegru, L., & Chambers, L. (2012). *The data journalism handbook.* Sebastopol, CA: O'Reilly.

Green, J. (1940, September). Crazy like a fox. *American Magazine, 130,* p. 57.

Green, N. (2010, April 12). Police PR spending hits £30 million a year. *Spinwatch.* Retrieved from http://www.spinwatch.org/index.php/issues/pr-industry/item/477-police-pr-spend-ing-hits-£30-million-per-year

Greenslade, R. (2012, December 12). Fall in advertising revenue mirrored by fall in print circu-lations. *The Guardian,* Greenslade blog. Retrieved from http://www.guardian.co.uk/media/greenslade/2012/dec/13/abcs-advertising

Griffin, E. (2009). *A first look at communication theory* (7th ed.). New York, NY: McGraw-Hill.

Grossberg, L., Wartella, E., Whitney, D., & Wise, J. (2006). *Media making: Mass media in a popular culture* (2nd ed.). Thousand Oaks, CA: Sage.

Grove, R. (2013. June 10). Is PR 3.0 a Trojan horse? *PRWeek.* Retrieved from http://www.prweekus.com/is-pr-30-a-trojan-horse/article/297021

Grunig, J. (Ed.). (1992). *Excellence in public relations and communication management.* Hillsdale, NJ: Lawrence Erlbaum.

Grunig, J., Grunig, L., & Dozier, D. (2006). The excellence theory. In C. Botan & V. Hazelton (Eds.), *Public relations theory II* (pp. 21–62). Mahwah, NJ: Lawrence Erlbaum.

Grunig, J., & Hunt, T. (1984). *Managing public relations.* Orlando, FL: Holt, Rinehart & Winston.

Grunig, J., & White, J. (1992). The effect of worldviews on public relations theory and practice. In J. Grunig (Ed.), *Excellence in public relations and communication management* (pp. 31–64). Hillsdale, NJ: Lawrence Erlbaum.

Grunig, L., Grunig J., & Dozier D. (2002). *Excellent organisations and effective organisa-tions: A study of communication management in three countries.* Mahwah, NJ: Lawrence Erlbaum.

Gupta, P. (2013, June 29). The five biggest PR disasters of the past year. *Salon.* Retrieved from http://www.salon.com/2013/06/28/the_5_biggest_pr_disasters_of_the_past_year

Gupta, P., & Lord, K. (1998). Product placement in movies: The effect of prominence and mode on audience recall. *Journal of Current Issues in Advertising, 20*(1), 47–59.

Gurevitch, M., Coleman, S., & Blumler, J. (2011). Political communication: Old and new media relationships. In D. Graber (Ed.), *Media power in politics* (pp. 45–56). Washington, DC: CQ.

Guth, D., & Marsh, C. (2007). *Public relations: A values-driven approach* (3rd ed.). Boston, MA: Pearson Education.

Habermann, P., Kopenhaver, L., & Martinson, D. (1988). Sequence faculty divided on PR value, status and news orientation. *Journalism Quarterly, 65,* 490–496.

Habermas, J. (1979). *Communication and the evolution of society.* London, UK: Heinemann.

Habermas, J. (1984). *Theory of communicative action, Vol. 1: Reason and the rationalization of society* (T. McCarthy, Trans.). Boston, MA: Beacon. (Original work published 1981 in German)

Habermas, J. (1987). *The theory of communicative action, Vol. 2: Lifeworld and system: A critique of functionalist reason* (T. McCarthy, Trans.). Boston, MA: Beacon. (Original work published 1981 in German)

Habermas, J. (1989). *The structural transformation of the public sphere* (T. Burger, Trans.). Cambridge, UK: Polity. (Original work published 1962 in German)

Habermas, J. (1991). *The structural transformation of the public sphere* (T. Burger, Trans.). Cambridge, MA: MIT Press. (Original work published 1962 in German)

Habermas, J. (2006). Political communication in media society: Does democracy still enjoy an epistemic dimension? The impact of normative theory on empirical research. *Communication Theory, 16*(4), 411–426.

Hagan, L. (2007). For reputation's sake: Managing crisis communication. In E. Toth (Ed.), *The future of excellence in public relations and communication management: Challenges for the next generation* (pp. 413–440). Mahwah, NJ: Lawrence Erlbaum.

Hallahan, K. (1999a). Seven models of framing: Implications for public relations. *Journal of Public Relations Research, 11*(3), 205–242.

Hallahan, K. (1999b). No, Virginia, it's not true what they say about publicity's 'implied third-party endorsement' effect. *Public Relations Review, 25*(3), 331–350.

Hallahan, K. (2010). Being public: Publicity as public relations. In R. Heath (Ed.), *Handbook of public relations* (2nd ed., pp. 523–545). Thousand Oaks, CA: Sage.

Hallahan, K., Holtzhausen, D., van Ruler, B., Verčič, D., & Sriramesh, K. (2007). Defining strategic communication. *International Journal of Strategic Communication, 1*(1), 3–35.

Hallin, D. (1992). The passing of the 'high modernism' of American journalism. *Journal of Communication, 42*(3), 14–25.

Hallin, D. (1994). *We keep America on top of the world: Television journalism and the public sphere.* London, UK: Routledge.

Hallin, D., & Mancini, P. (2004). *Comparing media systems.* Cambridge, UK: Cambridge University Press.

Hanson, V. (2008, November 7). Post-journalism. *National Review Online,* The Corner. Retrieved from http://www.nationalreview.com/corner/173630/post-journalism/victor-davis-hanson

Harcup, T. (2009). *Journalism: Principles and practices* (2nd ed.). London, UK: Sage.

HARO [Help a Reporter Out]. (n.d.). About HARO. Retrieved from http://www.helpareporter.com/about-haro

Harrison, T., & Barthel, B. (2009). Wielding new media in Web 2.0: Exploring the history of engagement with the collaborative construction of media products. *New Media & Society, 11*(1 & 2), 155–178.

Hartigan, J. (2009, July 1). Australia's right to know: Freedom of speech campaign. Speech to the National Press Club, Canberra, Australia. Retrieved from http://www.crikey.com.au/2009/07/01/hartigan-the-blogosphere-is-all-eyeballs-and-no-insight

Hartley, J. (1999). What is journalism? The view from under a stubbie cap. *Media International Australia Incorporating Culture and Policy, 90*, 15–31.

Hartman, I. (2011). What WikiLeaks reveals about critical media. *Berkeley Political Review,* March. http://bpr.berkeley.edu/2011/03/what-wikileaks-reveals-about-critical-media

Hatherell, W., & Bartlett, J. (2005, July). Positioning public relations as an academic discipline in Australia. *Asia Pacific Public Relations Journal, 6*(2). Retrieved from http://www.deakin.edu.au/arts-ed/apprj/vol6no2.php

Heath, R. (2001). *Handbook of public relations.* Thousand Oaks, CA: Sage.

Heath, R. (Ed.). (2005). *Encyclopaedia of public relations, Vol. 1.* London, UK and Thousand Oaks, CA: Sage.

Heath R. (Ed.). (2010). *The Sage handbook of public relations* (2nd ed.). Thousand Oaks, CA: Sage.

Heath, R., Toth, E., & Waymer, D. (Eds.). (2009). *Rhetorical and critical approaches to public relations II.* New York, NY: Routledge.

Held, D. (1989). *Political theory and the modern state.* Stanford, CA: Stanford University Press.

Held, D. (2006). *Models of democracy.* Cambridge, UK: Polity.

Help a Reporter Out (HARO) launched UK categories. (2012, July 6). *PR Web,* Vocus. Retrieved from http://uk.prweb.com/releases/Help-A-Reporter-Out-UK/HAOR-UK/prweb9668102.htm

Herman, E., & Chomsky, N. (1988). *Manufacturing consent: The political economy of the mass media.* New York, NY: Pantheon.

Hesmondhalgh, D. (2007). *The cultural industries* (2nd ed.) London, UK and Thousand Oaks, CA: Sage.

Hess, K., & Waller, L. (2008). An exploratory study of relationships between local government media officers and journalists in regional Australia. *Asia Pacific Public Relations Journal, 9,* 151–160.

Hiebert, R. (1966). *Courtier to the crowd: The story of Ivy Lee.* Ames, IA: Iowa State University Press.

Himelboim, I., & McCreery, S. (2012). New technology, old practices: Examining news websites from a professional perspective. *Convergence, 18*(4), 427–444.

Himler, P. (2013, March 14). The journalist and the PR pro: A broken marriage? *Forbes,* Media & Entertainment. Retrieved from http://www.forbes.com/sites/peterhimler/2013/03/14/the-journalist-the-pr-pro-a-broken-marriage

Hirst, M., & Harrison, J. (2007). *Communication and new media: From broadcast to narrowcast.* South Melbourne, Vic: Oxford University Press.

Hodges, C. (2006). PRP culture: A framework for exploring public relations practitioners as cultural intermediaries. *Journal of Communication Management, 10*(1), 80–93.

Hohenberg, J. (1973). The professional journalist (3rd ed.). New York, NY: Holt, Rinehart & Winston.

Hohenberg, J. (1983). The professional journalist (5th ed.). New York, NY: Holt, Rinehart & Winston.

Holquist, M. (Ed.). (1981). *The dialogic imagination: Four essays by M. M. Bakhtin* (C. Emerson & M. Holquist, Trans.). Austin, TX: University of Texas Press. (Original work published 1975)

Holtz, S., & Demopoulos, T. (2006). *Blogging for business.* Chicago, IL: Kaplan.

Hon, L., & Grunig, J. (1999). Guidelines for measuring relationships in public relations. Gainesville, FL: Institute for Public Relations. Retrieved from http://www.instituteforpr.org/research_single/guidelines_measuring_relationships

Howell, G. (2009a). Issues and crisis management: James Hardie Industries. In M. Sheehan & R. Xavier (Eds.), *Public relations campaigns* (pp. 189–205). South Melbourne, Vic: Oxford University Press.

Howell, G. (2009b). An issues-crisis perspective. In J. Chia & G. Synnott (Eds.), *An introduction to public relations: From theory to practice* (pp. 270–298). South Melbourne, Vic: Oxford University Press.

Hunt, T., & Grunig, J. (1994). *Public relations techniques*. Fort Worth, TX: Harcourt Brace.

IABC (International Association of Business Communicators). (2014, February 21). Spin your words into gold. News. Sydney, NSW: Author.

ICCO (International Communications Consultancy Organization). (2011, May). ICCO world report: A return to growth. London, UK: Author. Retrieved from http://www.iccopr.com/fckeditor/editor/filemanager/connectors/aspx/fckeditor/userfiles/file/ICCOWR2011_Return2Growth_final.pdf

Ingram, D. (2012). *The news manual: A professional resource for journalists and the media*. Retrieved from http://www.thenewsmanual.net/index.htm

IPRA (International Public Relations Association). (2001). E-group, 10 March. Retrieved from ipra@yahoogroups.com

IPRA (International Public Relations Association). (2014). Campaign for media transparency. Retrieved from http://www.ipra.org/secciones.php?sec=2&subsec=4

It's the links, stupid. (2006, April 20). *The Economist*. Retrieved from http://www.economist.com/surveys/displaystory.cfm?story_id=6794172

Iyengar, S. (1991). *Is anyone responsible? How television frames political issues*. Chicago, IL: University of Chicago Press.

Iyengar, S., & Kinder, D. (1987). *News that matters*. Chicago, IL: University of Chicago Press.

Iyengar, S., Peters, M., & Kinder, D. (1982). Experimental demonstrations of the 'not-so-minimal' consequences of television news programs. *American Political Science Review, 76*, 848–858.

Jarvis, J. (2008, April–May). Towards 2020 vision. *Walkley Magazine, 50*, Walkley Foundation, Media, Entertainment and Arts Alliance, Sydney, pp. 19–20.

Jeffers, D. (1977). Performance expectations as a measure of relative status of news and PR people. *Journalism Quarterly, 54*, 299–307.

Jenkins, H. (2006). *Convergence culture: Where old and new media collide*. New York, NY: New York University Press.

Jensen, K. (Ed.). (2012). *A handbook of media and communication research*. Abingdon, Oxon, UK: Routledge.

Jie, L. (2004, December 22). Association to boost healthy growth of PR sector. *China Daily*. Retrieved from http://www.chinadaily.com.cn/english/doc/2004–12/22/content_402264.htm

Johnston, J., Zawawi, C., & Brand, J. (2009). Public relations: An overview. In *Public relations: Theory and practice* (3rd ed., pp. 3–25). Sydney, NSW: Allen & Unwin.

Jones, A. (2011). Losing the news: The future of the news that feeds democracy. In D. Graber (Ed.), *Media power in politics* (pp. 57–65). Washington, DC: CQ.

Jones, J., & Salter, L. (2012). *Digital journalism*. London, UK: Sage.

Journalist reveals bribery practice in Indonesian media. (2011, November 11). *Bernama*. Retrieved from http://www.mole.my/content/journalist-reveals-bribery-practice-indonesian-media

Jowett, G., & O'Donnell, V. (1986). *Propaganda and persuasion*. London, UK: Sage.

Jowett, G., & O'Donnell, V. (2006). *Propaganda and persuasion* (4th ed.). Thousand Oaks, CA: Sage.

Kamm, O. (2007, April 9). A parody of democracy. *The Guardian*. Retrieved from http://www.guardian.co.uk/commentisfree/2007/apr/09/comment.politics2

Kanihan, S., Hansen, K., Blair, S., Shore, M., & Myers, J. (2013). Communication managers in the dominant coalition: Power attributes and communication practices. *Journal of Communication Management, 17*(2), 140–156.

Kaplan, R., & Haenlein, M. (2010). Users of the world, unite! The challenges and opportunities of social media. *Business Horizons, 53*(1), 59–68.

Karenga, M. (2002). *Introduction to black studies* (3rd ed.). Los Angeles, CA: University of Sankore Press.

Keane, J. (2009). *The life and death of democracy*. London, UK: Simon & Schuster.

Keeble, R. (1998). *The newspapers handbook* (2nd ed.). London, UK: Routledge.

Keeble, R., Tulloch, J., & Zollman, F. (Eds.). (2010). *Peace journalism, war and conflict resolution*. New York, NY: Peter Lang.

Keen, A. (2007a). *The cult of the amateur: How today's internet is killing our culture*. New York, NY: Doubleday.

Keen, A. (2007b, August 4). Disentangle it now, this web of deceit. Extract from *The cult of the amateur*. *The Weekend Australian*, Inquirer, p. 27.

Kelly, G. (1995). *Managing the interview* (2nd ed.). Mt Waverley, Vic: Kelly Communications.

Kelly, L. (2010, November 16). Prince William's engagement news comes courtesy of Twitter. *The Washington Post*, Celebritology 2.0. Retrieved from http://voices.washingtonpost.com/celebritology/2010/11/prince_williams_big_news_comes.html

Kent, M., & Taylor, M. (2002). Toward a dialogic theory of public relations. *Public Relations Review, 28*, 21–37.

Kersten, A. (1994). The ethics and ideology of public relations: A critical examination of American theory and practice. In W. Armbrecht & U. Zabel (Eds.), *Normative aspekte der public relations* (pp. 109–130). Opladen, Germany: Westdeutscher Verlag.

Kim, B., Pasadeos, Y., & Barban, A. (2001). On the deceptive effectiveness of labeled and unlabeled advertorial formats. *Mass Communication and Society, 4*(3), 265–281.

King, C. (2010). Emergent communication strategies. *International Journal of Strategic Communication, 4*(1), 19–38.

Kinnick, K. (2005). Puffery. In R. Heath (Ed.), *The encyclopedia of public relations, Vol. 2*. Thousand Oaks, CA: Sage.

Kitzinger, J. (2007). Framing and frame analysis. In E. Devereux (Ed.), *Media studies: Key issues and debates* (pp. 134–161). London, UK and Thousand Oaks, CA: Sage.

Klose, M. (2012). The big interview: Harold Burson. *Communication Director, 4*, 44–47.

Knott, M. (2012a, February 6). The Power Index: The world of spinners and advisers. *Crikey, The Power Index.* Retrieved from http://www.crikey.com.au/2012/02/06/the-power-index-the-world-of-spinners-and-advisers/?wpmp_switcher=mobile

Knott, M. (2012b.) Journalists can pull out of the spin cycle. In Walkley Foundation, *Kicking at the cornerstone of democracy: The state of press freedom in Australia.* Redfern, NSW: Media, Entertainment & Arts Alliance.

Kohut, A., Doherty, C., Dimock, M., & Keeter, S. (2012, September). Trends in news consumption 1991–2012: In changing news landscape, even television is vulnerable. Washington, DC: Pew Internet Research Center for People and the Press. Retrieved from http://www.people-press.org/2012/09/27/in-changing-news-landscape-even-television-is-vulnerable

Kokemuller, N. (2013). Concept of embedded marketing and product placement. *Chron.com (The Houston Chronicle),* Small Business. Retrieved from http://smallbusiness.chron.com/concept-embedded-marketing-product-placement-20278.html

Kopenhaver, L. (1984). Local journalists teach PR students about news ethics. *Journalism Educator, 39*(3), 17–19.

Kopenhaver, L. (1985). Aligning values of practitioners and journalists. *Public Relations Review, 11,* 34–42.

Kopenhaver, L., Martinson, D., & and Ryan, M. (1984). How public relations practitioners and editors in Florida view each other. *Journalism Quarterly, 61*(4), 860–888.

Kornblut, A. (2005, January 29). Third journalist was paid to promote Bush policies. *The New York Times,* Washington DC. Retrieved from http://www.nytimes.com/2005/01/29/politics/29column.html?_r=2&

Kovach, B., & Rosenstiel, T. (2001). *The elements of journalism: What newspeople should know and the public should expect.* New York, NY: Three Rivers.

Kovach, B., & Rosenstiel, T. (2007). *The elements of journalism: What newspeople should know and the public should expect* (Rev. ed.). New York, NY: Three Rivers.

Krosnick, J., & Kinder, D. (1990). Altering support for the president through priming. The Iran-contra affair. *American Political Science Review, 84,* 497–512.

Krotz, J. (2009). Six tips for taking control of media interviews. Microsoft Small Business Center. Retrieved from http://www.microsoft.com/smallbusiness/resources/management/leadership-training/6-tips-for-taking-control-in-media-interviews.aspx#tipsfortaking-controlinmediainterviews

Kruckeberg, D. (1998). The future of PR education: Some recommendations. *Public Relations Review, 24*(2), 235–248.

Kuhn, K., Hume, M., & Love, A. (2010). Examining the covert nature of product placement: Implications for public policy. *Journal of Promotion Management, 16*(1), 59–70.

Kunelius, R. (2001). Conversation: A metaphor and a method for better journalism? *Journalism Studies, 2*(1), 31–54.

Kunhardt, P., Jr., Kunhardt, P., III, & Kunhardt, P. (1995). *P. T. Barnum: America's greatest showman.* New York, NY: Alfred A. Knopf.

Kurtz, H. (1998). *Spin cycle: How the White House and the media manipulate the news.* New York, NY: Touchstone.

Lacy, S., Fico, F., & Simon, T. (1989). Relationship among economic, newsroom and content variables: A path model. *Journal of Media Economics, 2*(2), 51–66.

Laird, S. (2012, April 18). How social media is taking over the news industry. *Mashable.* Retrieved from http://mashable.com/2012/04/18/social-media-and-the-news

Lamble, S. (2011). *News as it happens: An introduction to journalism.* South Melbourne, Vic: Oxford University Press.

Lamme, M. (2012). Partners and pioneers in public relations. *Communication Director, 4,* 36–39.

Lamme, M., & Miller, K. (2010). Removing the spin: Towards a new theory of public relations history. *Journalism and Communication Monographs, 11*(4), 281–362.

Lancaster, P. (1992). *Gentlemen of the press: The life and times of an early reporter, Julian Ralph of the Sun.* New York, NY: Syracuse University Press.

Lang, A. (2013). Discipline in crisis? The shifting paradigm of mass communication research. *Communication Theory, 23*(1), 10–24.

Lang, G., & Lang, K. (1981). Watergate: An exploration of the agenda-building process. In *Mass Communication Review Yearbook, 2* (pp. 447–469). Beverly Hills, CA: Sage.

Lang, G., & Lang, K. (1983). *The battle for public opinion: The president, the press and the polls during Watergate.* New York, NY: Columbia University Press.

Lasswell, H. (1927). *Propaganda techniques in the world war.* New York, NY: Knopf.

Lasswell, H. (1948). The structure and function of communication in society. In L. Bryson (Ed.), *The communication of ideas* (pp. 37–51). New York, NY: Harper.

Ledingham, J. (2006). Relationship management: A general theory of public relations. In C. Botan & V. Hazelton (Eds.), *Public relations theory II* (pp. 465–483). Mahwah, NJ: Lawrence Erlbaum.

Ledingham, J., & Bruning, S. (Eds.). (2000). *Public relations as relationship management: A relational approach to the study and practice of public relations.* Mahwah, NJ: Lawrence Erlbaum.

Leeds Metropolitan University. (2008). Towards a global curriculum: A summary of literature concerning public relations education, professionalism and globalisation. Report for the Global Alliance of Public Relations and Communication Management, February. Leeds, UK: Author.

Leitch, S., & Walker G. (Eds.). (1997). Public relations on the edge. *Australian Journal of Communication, 24*(2), vii–ix.

Len-Ríos, M., Hinnant, A., Park, S., Cameron, G., Frisby, C., & Lee, Y. (2009). Health news agenda building: Journalists' perceptions of the role of public relations. *Journalism & Mass Communication Quarterly, 86*(2), 315–331.

L'Etang, J. (1995). Clio among the patriarchs: Historical and social scientific approaches to public relations: A methodological critique. Paper presented to the Second International Public Relations Symposium, Bled, Slovenia.

L'Etang, J. (2008). *Public relations: Concepts, practice and critique.* London, UK and Thousand Oaks, CA: Sage.

L'Etang, J. (2009). Radical PR: Catalyst for change or an aporia? *International Journal of Communication Ethics, 6*(2), 13–18.

L'Etang, J., McKie, D., Snow, N., & Xifra, J. (2014). *The Routledge handbook of critical public relations*. London, UK: Routledge.

L'Etang, J., & Pieczka, M. (1996). *Critical perspectives in public relations*. London, UK: International Thomson Business.

L'Etang, J., & Pieczka, M. (2006). *Public relations—critical debates and contemporary practice*. Mahwah, NJ: Lawrence Erlbaum.

Levy, M. (1981). Disdaining the news. *Journal of Communication, 32*(3), 24–31.

Lévy, P. (1997). *Collective intelligence: Mankind's emerging world of cyberspace*. Cambridge, MA: Perseus.

Lewin, K. (1947). Frontiers in group dynamics II: Channels of group life, social planning and action research. *Human Relations, 1*(2), 143–153.

Lewis, J. (2001). *The end of cinema as we know it: American film in the nineties*. New York, NY: New York University Press.

Lewis, J., Williams, A., Franklin, B., Thomas, J., & Mosdell, N. (2008). The quality and independence of British journalism: Tracking the changes of 20 years. Research report. Cardiff School of Journalism, Media and Cultural Studies, Cardiff University, Wales. Retrieved from http://www.cardiff.ac.uk/jomec/research/researchgroups/journalismstudies/fundedprojects/qualitypress.html

Lewis, P. (1992, April 14). Personal computers: Microsoft smooths some bumps. *The New York Times*, Technology. Retrieved from http://www.nytimes.com/1992/04/14/science/personal-computers-microsoft-smooths-some-bumps.html

Lievrouw, L., & Livingstone, S. (Eds.). (2002). *The handbook of new media*. London, UK: Sage.

Lievrouw, L., & Livingstone, S. (Eds.). (2005). *The handbook of new media* (2nd ed.). London, UK: Sage.

Lincoln, Y. (1997). Self, subject, audience, text: Living at the edge, writing in the margins. In W. Tierney & Y. Lincoln (Eds.), *Representation and the text: Reframing the narrative voice* (pp. 37–54). Albany, NY: State University of New York Press.

Lippmann, W. (1922). *Public opinion*. New York, NY: Free.

Lister, M., Dovey, J., Giddings, S., Grant, I., & Kelly, K. (2009). *New media: A critical introduction* (2nd ed.). Abingdon, Oxfordshire, UK and New York, NY: Routledge.

Littlewood, T. (2002). *The true picture in the PR age: A casebook for journalists*. Chicago, IL: Burnham.

Lomax, A. (2006, March 23). Advertising, disrupted. *The Motley Fool*. Retrieved from http://www.fool.com/investing/general/2006/03/23/advertising-disrupted.aspx

Louw, E. (2005). *The media and political process*. London, UK: Sage.

Louw, E. (2010). *The media and political process* (2nd ed.). London and Thousand Oaks, CA: Sage.

Lovink, G. (2007, February 1). Blogging, the nihilist impulse. *Eurozine, Lettre internationale 73*. Retrieved from http://www.eurozine.com/articles/2007-01-02-lovink-en.html

LSE (London South East). (2007, February 15). Upstream Marketing buy Macro Consulting in all-share deal. Finance and Stock Market News. Retrieved from http://www.lse.co.uk/FinanceNews.asp?ArticleCode=yg3gh0rgfvt9ljp&ArticleHeadline=Upstream_Marketing_buys_Macro_Consulting_in_allshare_deal

Lull, J. (2000). *Media, communication, culture: A global approach*. Cambridge, UK: Polity.

Lyons, D. (2005, November 14). Attack of the blogs. *Forbes*. Retrieved from http://www.forbes.com/forbes/2005/1114/128.html

Macey, W., & Schneider, B. (2008). The meaning of employee engagement. *Industrial and Organizational Psychology, 1*(1), 3–30.

Machin, D., & Van Leeuwen, T. (2007). *Global media discourse: A critical introduction*. Abingdon, Oxon, UK, and New York, NY: Routledge.

MacIntyre, D. (2003, July 5). Alastair Campbell: The spin doctor who became the story. *Independent.co.uk*. Retrieved from http://www.independent.co.uk/news/people/profiles/alastair-campbell-the-spin-doctor-who-became--the-story-585828.html

MacManus, R. (2005, September 7). What is Web 2.0? *ZDNet*. Retrieved from http://blogs.zdnet.com/web2explorer/?p=5

Macnamara, J. (1983). *Public relations handbook for clubs and associations*. Canberra, ACT: Promac.

Macnamara, J. (1985). *Public relations handbook for clubs and associations*. Melbourne, Vic: Margaret Gee Information Group. (Original work published 1983)

Macnamara, J. (1992). *The Asia Pacific public relations handbook*. Sydney, NSW: Archipelago.

Macnamara, J. (1993). *Public relations and the media*. Unpublished Master of Arts by research thesis, Deakin University, Geelong, Vic, Australia.

Macnamara, J. (1996a). *Public relations handbook for managers and executives*. Melbourne, Vic: Information Australia.

Macnamara, J. (1996b). *How to handle the media*. Sydney, NSW: Prentice Hall.

Macnamara, J. (2000). *Jim Macnamara's public relations handbook*. Melbourne, Vic: Information Australia.

Macnamara, J. (2005). *Jim Macnamara's public relations handbook* (5th ed.). Sydney, NSW: Archipelago.

Macnamara, J. (2009). Public relations in the interactive age: New practices, not just new media. *Asia Pacific Public Relations Journal, 10*, 1–16.

Macnamara, J. (2010). *The 21st century media (r)evolution: Emergent communication practices*. New York, NY: Peter Lang.

Macnamara, J. (2011). Social media governance: A major gap, risk and opportunity in PR and reputation management. *Asia Pacific Public Relations Journal, 12*, 41–60.

Macnamara, J. (2012a). *Public relations theories, practices, critiques*. Sydney, NSW: Pearson.

Macnamara, J. (2012b). Journalism and public relations: Unpacking myths and stereotypes. *Australian Journalism Review, 34*(1), 33–50.

Macnamara, J. (2012c). The global shadow of functionalism and Excellence theory: An analysis of Australasian PR. *Public Relations Inquiry, 1*(3), 367–402.

Macnamara, J. (2014). *The 21st century media (r)evolution: Emergent communication practices* (2nd ed.). New York, NY: Peter Lang.

Macnamara, J., & Crawford, R. (2013). Australia Day: A study of PR as cultural intermediaries. *Continuum: Journal of Media and Cultural Studies, 27*(2), 294–310.

Macnamara, J., Mirandilla, K., & Wang, S. (2013, August). Measurement and evaluation of embedded anti-tobacco embedded social marketing. Report for the Cancer Institute NSW by the Australian Centre for Public Communication, University of Technology Sydney.

Macnamara, J., & Zerfass, A. (2012). Social media communication in organizations: The challenges of balancing openness, strategy and management. *International Journal of Strategic Communication, 6*(4), 287–308.

Macquarie University. (2013). Master of future journalism. Sydney, NSW: Author. Retrieved from http://courses.mq.edu.au/postgraduate/master/master-of-future-journalism

Madden, T. (1997). *Spin man: The topsy-turvy world of public relations...a tell-all tale.* Boca Raton, FL: TransMedia.

Maltese, J. (1994). *Spin control: The White House Office of Communications and the management of presidential news* (2nd ed.). Chapel Hill, NC: University of North Carolina Press.

Manning, P. (2001). *News and news sources: A critical introduction.* London, UK: Sage.

Manning, P. (2013, April 8). Fairfax journo hits out: Fear and favour in *AFR* takeover. *Crikey.* Retrieved from http://www.crikey.com.au/2013/04/08/fairfax-journo-hits-out-fear-and-favour-in-afr-takeover

Mansell, R. (2012). *Imagining the internet: Communication, innovation, and governance.* Oxford, UK: Oxford University Press.

Marchand, R. (1998). *Creating the corporate soul: The rise of public relations and corporate imagery in American big business.* Berkeley and Los Angeles, CA: University of California Press.

Marchionni, D. (2013). Journalism-as-a-conversation: A concept explication. *Communication Theory, 23*(2), 131–147.

Maréchal, G. (2010). Autoethnography. In A. Mills, G. Durepos, & E. Wiebe (Eds.), *Encyclopedia of case study research, Vol. 2.* (pp. 43–45). Thousand Oaks, CA: Sage.

Markson, M. (2009, October 20). Max Markson on PR puppetry. *mUmBRELLA*, Mumbo Report. Retrieved from http://mumbrella.com.au/mumbo-report-max-markson-on-pr-puppetry-dmgs-dean-buchanan-on-ratings-stress-triple-ms-paul-murray-on-anti-ad-dickheads-why-we-hate-telstras-brad-and-emma-10574

Marsh, A. (2012, September 2). Journalist shares 7 common PR sins to avoid. *Ragan's PR Daily.* Retrieved from http://www.ragan.com/Main/Articles/A_reporters_inbox_Show_a_little_respect__42715.aspx

Marx, K. (1845). Theses on Feuerbach. In *Marx/Engels Selected Works, Vol. 1, Part 11* (Trans. W. Lough, pp. 13–15). Moscow, Russia: Progress. Retrieved from http://www.marxists.org/archive/marx/works/1845/theses/theses.htm

Matchett, S. (2010, July 14). The profession that dare not speak its name. *The Australian*, Higher Education, p. 26. Retrieved from http://www.theaustralian.com.au/higher-education/the-profession-that-dare-not-speak-its-name/story-e6frgcjx-1225891321598

Mayer, H. (1968). *The press in Australia.* Sydney, NSW: Lansdowne. (Original work published 1964)

McChesney, R. (2003). The problem of journalism: A political economic contribution to an explanation of the crisis in contemporary journalism. *Journalism Studies, 4*(3), 299–329.

McChesney, R. (2013). *Digital disconnect: How capitalism is turning the internet against democracy.* New York, NY: Free.

McChesney, R., & Nichols, J. (2010). *The death and life of American journalism: The media revolution that will begin the world again.* Philadelphia, PA: Nation.

McChesney, R., & Scott, B. (Eds.). (2003). *The brass check: A study of American journalism.* Urbana and Chicago: University of Illinois Press.

McCombs, M. (2004). *Setting the agenda: The mass media and public opinion.* Cambridge, UK: Polity.

McCombs, M. (Ed.). (2014). *Setting the agenda: The mass media and public opinion* (2nd ed.). Cambridge, UK: Polity.

McCombs, M., & Bell, T. (1996). The agenda-setting role of mass communication. In M. Salwen & D. Stacks (Eds.), *An integrated approach to communication theory and research* (pp. 93–110). Mahwah, NJ: Lawrence Erlbaum.

McCombs, M., & Evatt, D. (1995). Los temas y los aspectos: Explorando una nueva dimension de la agenda setting. *Communicacion y Sociedad, 8*(1), 7–32.

McCombs, M., & Ghanem, S. (2001). The convergence of agenda setting and framing. In S. Reese, O. Gandy, & A. Grant (Eds.), *Framing in the new media landscape* (pp. 67–91). Mahwah, NJ: Lawrence Erlbaum.

McCombs, M., & Reynolds, D. (2002). News influence on our pictures of the world. In J. Bryant & D. Zillman (Eds.), *Media effects: Advances in theory and research* (2nd ed., pp. 1–18). Mahwah, NJ: Lawrence Erlbaum.

McCombs, M., & Shaw, D. (1972). The agenda-setting function of mass media. *Public Opinion Quarterly, 36*, 176–187.

McCombs, M., & Yu, J. (2005). Shaping feelings. *Media Tenor, 151*, 18–20.

McCrystal, D. (2008). It's more fun on the 'dark side'. *British Journalism Review, 19*(2), 47–51.

McCrystal, D. (2012). Is PR's future so dark? [Review of the book *Dark art: The changing face of public relations*]. *British Journalism Review, 23*, 75–76.

McDonald, R. (2005). Introduction. In J. Mills (Ed.), *Barons to bloggers: Confronting media power.* Melbourne, Vic: Miegunyah.

McDonnell, J., & Drennan, J. (2010). Virtual product placement as a new approach to measure effectiveness of placements. *Journal of Promotion Management, 16*(1 & 2), 25–38.

McKinsey. (2011, November). Business and Web 2.0. *McKinsey Quarterly*, Interactive reporting feature. Retrieved from https://www.mckinseyquarterly.com/Business_and_Web_20_An_interactive_feature_2431

McKinsey. (2013). Evolution of the networked enterprise. McKinsey & Company. Retrieved from https://www.mckinseyquarterly.com/Evolution_of_the_networked_enterprise_McKinsey_Global_Survey_results_3073

McKnight, D., & O'Donnell, P. (2008, September 3). The winter of journalism's content. *The Australian.* Retrieved from http://www.theaustralian.news.com.au/story/0,25197,24283745-13480,00.html

McMillan, S. (2002). Exploring models of interactivity from multiple research traditions: Users, documents and systems. In L. Lievrouw & S. Livingstone (Eds.), *Handbook of new media* (pp. 163–182). London, UK: Sage.

McNair, B. (2003). From control to chaos: Toward a new sociology of journals. *Media, Culture and Society, 24*(6), 547–555.

McNair, B. (2006). *Cultural chaos: Journalism, news and power in a globalized world.* New York, NY: Routledge.

McQuail, D. (1994). *Mass communication theory: An introduction.* London, UK: Sage.

McQuail, D. (2005). *McQuail's mass communication theory* (5th ed.). London, UK and Thousand Oaks, CA: Sage.

McQuail, D. (2010). *McQuail's mass communication theory* (6th ed.). London, UK and Thousand Oaks, CA: Sage.

Media Training Worldwide. (2009). Media training. Retrieved from http://www.mediatraining-worldwide.com/media-train.html

MediaWise. (2003, July 9). Back to basics or why are these bastards lying to us? Retrieved from http://www.mediawise.org.uk/back-to-basics-or-why-are-these-bastards-lying-to-us/

Mencher, M. (2010). *Melvin Mencher's news reporting and writing.* New York, NY: McGraw-Hill.

Mensing, D. (2010). Rethinking (again) the future of journalism education. *Journalism Studies, 22,* 511–523.

Merholz, P. (1999). For what it's worth. *Peterme.com.* Retrieved from http://web.archive.org/web/19991013021124/http://peterme.com/index.html

Merholz, P. (2005). It's not about the technology. Retrieved from http://www.peterme.com/archives/000560.html

Merkel, B., Russ-Mohl, S., & Zavaritt, G. (Eds.). (2007). *A complicated, antagonistic and symbiotic affair: Journalism, public relations and their struggle for public attention.* Lugano, Switzerland: Giampiero Casagrande.

Merriam-Webster Online Dictionary. (2013). Bunco. Retrieved from http://www.merriam-webster.com/dictionary/bunco

Meyer, P. (2002). *Precision journalism: A reporter's introduction to social science methods* (4th ed.). Lanhan, MD: Rowman & Littlefield.

Meyer, P. (2004). *The vanishing newspaper: Saving journalism in the information age.* Columbia, OH: University of Missouri Press.

Meyer, P. (2008, October/November). The elite newspaper of the future. *American Journalism Review.* Retrieved http://www.ajr.org/Article.asp?id=4605

Michaelson, D., & Stacks, D. (2007). Exploring the comparative communications effectiveness of advertising and media placement. Gainesville, FL: Institute for Public Relations. Retrieved from http://www.instituteforpr.org/topics/advertising-media-placement-effectiveness

Miike, Y. (2010). An anatomy of Eurocentrism in communication scholarship: The role of Asiacentricity in de-Westernizing theory and research. *China Media Research, 6*(1), 1–11.

Miles, M., & Huberman, M. (1994). *Qualitative data analysis.* Thousand Oaks, CA: Sage.

Millar, A. (2008, June). Attitudes to information subsidies and source relationships among Australian technology media and PR practitioners. Unpublished MA research paper, University of Technology, Sydney.

Miller, C., & Shepherd, D. (2004). Blogging as social action: A genre analysis. In L. Gurak, S. Antonijevic, L. Johnson, C. Ratli, & J. Reymann (Eds.), *Into the blogosphere: Rhetoric, community and the culture of weblogs* (n.p.). Minneapolis, MN: University of Minnesota. Retrieved from http://blog.lib.umn.edu/blogosphere/blogging_as_social_action.html

Miller, D. (1994). *Don't mention the war: Northern Ireland, propaganda and the media.* London, UK: Pluto.

Miller, D., & Dinan, W. (2008). *A century of spin: How public relations became the cutting edge of corporate power.* London, UK: Pluto.

Miller, G. (1989). Persuasion and public relations: Two 'Ps in a pod'. In C. Botan & V. Hazelton (Eds.), *Public relations theory* (pp. 45–66). Hillsdale, NJ: Lawrence Erlbaum.

Moloney, K. (2000). *Rethinking public relations: The spin and the substance*. Abingdon, Oxon, UK: Routledge.

Moloney, K. (2006). *Rethinking public relations: PR propaganda and democracy* (2nd ed.). New York, NY: Routledge.

Moloney, K., McQueen, D., Surowiec, P., & Yaxley, H. (2012). Dissent and protest public relations. Bournemouth, UK: Public Relations Research Group, the Media School, Bournemouth University. Retrieved from http://www.prconversations.com/wp-content/uploads/2013/09/Dissent-and-public-relations-Bournemouth-University.pdf

Morales, L. (2012, July 10). Americans' confidence in television news drops to new low. Gallup Politics. Retrieved from http://www.gallup.com/poll/155585/americans-confidence-television-news-drops-new-low.aspx

Morris, T., & Goldsworthy, S. (2008). *A persuasive industry? Spin, public relations and the shaping of the modern media*. Basingstoke, Hampshire, UK: Palgrave MacMillan.

Morris, T., & Goldsworthy, S. (2012). *PR today: The authoritative guide to public relations*. Basingstoke, Hampshire, UK: Palgrave Macmillan.

Mosco, V. (2004). *The digital sublime: Myth, power and cyberspace*. Cambridge, MA: MIT Press.

Mosco, V. (2009). *The political economy of communication* (2nd ed.). London, UK: Sage.

Moses, L. (2013, October 20). The roadblocks of native advertising: Clients and agencies need to get out of the way. *Ad Week*. Retrieved from http://www.adweek.com/news/advertising-branding/roadblocks-native-advertising-153261

Moss, J., & Koenig, M. (2013, May 3). Free press: The cornerstone of democracy. USAID. Retrieved from http://blog.usaid.gov/2013/05/free-press-the-cornerstone-of-democracy/

Murdoch, R. (2005, April 13). Speech to the American Society of Newspaper Editors, New York, NY. Retrieved from http://www.newscorp.com/news/news_247.html

Murphy, P. (1991). Limits of symmetry. In J. Grunig & L. Grunig (Eds.), *Public relations research annual, Vol. 3* (pp. 115–131). Hillsdale, NJ: Lawrence Erlbaum.

Murphy, S. (2012, February 12). Twitter breaks news of Whitney Houston's death 27 minutes before press. *Mashable*. Retrieved from http://mashable.com/2012/02/12/whitney-houston-twitter

Museum of Public Relations. (2013). 1929: Torches of freedom. Retrieved from http://www.prmuseum.com/bernays/bernays_1929.html

National Health and Medical Research Council. (2013). Asbestos related diseases. Retrieved from http://www.nhmrc.gov.au/your-health/asbestos-related-diseases

Negus, K. (1992). *Producing pop: Culture and conflict in the popular music industry*. London, UK: Arnold.

Negus, K. (1999). *Music genres and corporate cultures*. London, UK: Routledge.

Negus, K. (2002). The work of cultural intermediaries and the enduring distance between production and consumption. *Cultural Studies, 16*(4), 501–515.

Nerone, J. (Ed.). (1995). *Last rights: Revisiting Four Theories of the Press*. Urbana, IL: University of Illinois Press.

Neuendorf, K. (2002). *The content analysis guidebook*. Thousand Oaks, CA: Sage.

Neuman, W. [Russell]. (2006). *Social research methods: Qualitative and quantitative approaches* (6th ed.). Boston, MA: Pearson.

Neuman, W., Just, M., & Crigler, A. (1992). *Common knowledge: News and the construction of political meaning*. Chicago, IL: University of Chicago Press.

Newbold, C., Boyd-Barrett, O., & Van den Bulck, H. (2002). *The media book*. London, UK: Arnold-Hodder Headline.

Newcomb, T. (1953). An approach to the study of communicative acts. *Psychological Review, 60*, 393–404.

New South Wales Government. (2004). Report of the Special Commission of Inquiry in the Medical Research and Compensation Foundation, Part B. Retrieved from http://www.dpc.nsw.gov.au/about/publications/publications_categories_list

Newspaper Association of America. (2012a, September 4). Newspaper circulation volume. Retrieved from http://www.naa.org/Trends-and-Numbers/Circulation/Newspaper-Circulation-Volume.aspx

Newspaper Association of America. (2012b, September 4). Advertising expenditures: Annual (all categories). Retrieved from http://www.naa.org/Trends-and-Numbers/Advertising-Expenditures/Annual-All-Categories.aspx

Newspaper revenue forecast to drop 4% in 2013. (2013, January 7). *Marketing*. Retrieved from http://www.marketingmag.com.au/news/newspaper-revenues-forecast-to-drop-4-in-2013-32825

Nielsen/NM Incite. (2012, March 8). Buzz in the blogosphere: Millions more bloggers and blog readers. *Nielsenwire*. Retrieved from http://blog.nielsen.com/nielsenwire/online_mobile/buzz-in-the-blogosphere-millions-more-bloggers-and-blog-readers

Nip, J. (2006). Exploring the second phase of public journalism. *Journalism Studies, 7*(2), 212–236).

Nip, J. (2008). The last days of civic journalism: The case of the Savannah Morning News. *Journalism Practice, 2*(2), 179–196.

Nip, J. (2010). Routinization of charisma: The institutionalization of public journalism online. In J. Rosenberry & B. St. John III (Eds.), *Public journalism 2.0: The promise and reality of a citizen-engaged press* (pp. 135–148). New York, NY: Routledge.

Nixon, S., & du Gay, P. (2002). Who needs cultural intermediaries? *Cultural Studies, 16*(4), 495–500.

Oakham, K., & Kirby, B. (2006). Feeding the chooks in the country: A study of successful public relations media strategies in regional Victoria. *Asia Pacific Public Relations Journal, 7*, 95–108.

O'Donnell, P., McKnight, D., & Este, J. (2012). *Journalism at the speed of bytes: Australian newspapers in the 21st century*. Sydney, NSW: Walkley Foundation.

Olasky, M. (1989). The aborted debate within public relations: An approach through Kuhn's paradigm. *Journal of Public Relations Research, 1*(1–4), 87–95.

O'Reilly, T. (2005, September 30). What is web 2.0: Design patterns and business models for the next generation of software. *O'Reilly* blog. Retrieved from http://oreilly.com/pub/a/web2/archive/what-is-web-20.html?page=1

Oriella. (2013). The new normal for news: Have global media changed forever? Oriella PR Network global digital journalism study 2013. Retrieved from http://www.oriellaprnetwork.com/research

O'Shaugnessy, M., & Stadler, J. (2008). *Media and society* (4th ed.). South Melbourne, Vic: Oxford University Press.

O'Sullivan, J., & Heinonen, A. (2008). New media, old values: Journalism role perceptions in a changing world. *Journalism Practice, 3*(3), 357–371.

Over half your news is spin. (2010, March 15). *Crikey.* Report of Australian Centre for Independent Journalism. Retrieved from http://www.crikey.com.au/2010/03/15/over-half-your-news-is-spin

Packard, V. (1957). *The hidden persuaders.* Philadelphia, PA: David McKay. (Reissued 1960 by Penguin, New York, NY and Harmondsworth, Middlesex, UK)

Paine, K., & Fysh, H. (2012). Dissecting 'buzz'—it's not what you think it is. A detailed analysis of social media 'buzz' around controversial topics. Retrieved from http://kdpaine.blogs.com/files/kdpp2012buzzanalysis.pdf

Paper Cuts. (2012). Web site. Retrieved from http://newspaperlayoffs.com/home/

Papworth, L. (2008). How new media has changed the role of PR and communications—and what you need to know to survive. Speech to Public Relations Institute of Australia seminar, Sydney, NSW, May.

Parker, J. (2011, May 15). The dark side inside. *The Failed Estate*, blog post. Retrieved from http://thefailedestate.blogspot.com.au/2011/05/dark-side.html

Parkinson, M. (2001). The PRSA code of professional standards and member code of ethics: Why they are neither professional nor ethical. *Public Relations Quarterly, 46*(3), 27–31.

Pavlik, J. (2001). *Journalism and new media.* New York, NY: Columbia University Press.

Pavlik, J. (2008). *Media in the digital age.* New York, NY: Columbia University Press.

Pavlik, J. (2013). A vision for transformative leadership: Rethinking journalism and mass communication education for the twenty-first century. *Journalism & Mass Communication Quarterly, 68*(3), 211–221.

Peacock, M. (2011). *Killer company: James Hardie exposed.* Melbourne, Vic: HarperCollins.

Perloff, R. (1998). *Political communication: Politics, press and public in America.* Mahwah, NJ: Lawrence Erlbaum.

Perloff, R. (2002). The third-person effect. In J. Bryant & D. Zillman (Eds.), *Media effects: Advances in theory and research* (2nd ed., pp. 480–506). Mahwah, NJ: Lawrence Erlbaum.

Perloff, R. (2013). Progress, paradigms, and a discipline engaged: A response to Lang and reflections on media effects research. *Communication Theory, 23*(4), 317–333.

Peters, B. (2009). And lead us not into thinking the new is new: A bibliographic case for new media history. *New Media & Society, 11*(1 & 2), 13–30.

Peters, T., & Waterman, R., Jr. (1982). *In search of excellence: Lessons from America's best-run companies.* New York, NY: Harper & Row.

Pew Research Center. (2004). The state of the news media. Washington, DC: Pew Research Center Project for Excellence in Journalism. Retrieved from http://stateofthemedia.org/2004

Pew Research Center. (2009). How news happens: A study of the news ecosystem of one American city. Washington, DC: Author. Retrieved from http://www.journalism.org/analysis_report/how_news_happens

Pew Research Center. (2010). The state of the news media. Online—summary essay. Washington, DC: Pew Research Center Project for Excellence in Journalism. Retrieved from http://stateofthemedia.org/2010/online-summary-essay/

Pew Research Center. (2012). The state of the news media 2012. Washington, DC: Pew Research Center Project for Excellence in Journalism. Retrieved from http://stateofthemedia.org/2012

Pew Research Center. (2013). The state of the news media 2013. Washington, DC: Pew Research Center Project for Excellence in Journalism. Retrieved from http://stateofthemedia.org/2013

Pieczka, M. (1996). Paradigms, systems theory and public relations. In J. L'Etang & M. Pieczka (Eds.), *Critical perspectives in public relations* (pp. 124–156). London, UK: International Thomson Business.

Pieczka, M. (2006). Paradigms, systems theory and public relations. In J. L'Etang & M. Pieczka (Eds.), *Public relations: Critical debates and contemporary practice* (pp. 331–358). Mahwah, NJ: Lawrence Erlbaum.

Pilger, J. (2010). Foreword. In R. Keeble, J. Tulloch, & F. Zollman (Eds.), *Peace journalism, war and conflict resolution* (pp. ix–xi). New York, NY: Peter Lang.

Plunkett, J. (2006, April 10). Press and PR partnership—networking or not working? *The Guardian*, p. 3. Retrieved from http://www.theguardian.com/media/2006/apr/10/monday-mediasection4

Pollay, R. (1990). Propaganda, puffing and the public interest. *Public Relations Review, 16*(3), 39–53.

Poster, M. (1995). *The second media age*. Cambridge, UK: Polity.

Potter, W. (James). (2009). *Arguing for a general framework for mass media scholarship*. Thousand Oaks, CA: Sage.

Potter, W. (2010). *An insurance company insider speaks out on how corporate PR is killing health care and deceiving Americans*. New York, NY: Bloomsbury.

PQ Media. (2013). PR media global product placement spending forecast 2012–2016. Retrieved from http://www.pqmedia.com/globalproductplacementforecast-2012.html

PRCA. (2012). 2011 PR Census. Public Relations Consultants Association, London, UK.

PRIA (Public Relations Institute of Australia). (2009, May 12). Managing media interviews. *PRIA Events E-Bulletin*, Sydney, NSW.

PriceWaterhouseCoopers. (2009). Moving into multiple business models: Outlook for newspaper publishing in the digital age. Report of online survey of 4,900 consumers in seven countries. Author. Retrieved from http://www.pwc.com/gx/en/entertainment-media/publications/outlook-newspaper-publishing-in-digital.jhtml

PR: It's not the dark side any more. (2006, May 29). *The Independent*. Retrieved from http://www.independent.co.uk/news/media/pr-its-not-the-dark-side-any-more-480156.html

Pross, A. (1986). *Group politics and public policy*. New York, NY: Oxford University Press.

PRSA (Public Relations Society of America). (2013). PRSA MBA initiative. Retrieved from http://www.prsa.org/Intelligence/BusinessCase/MBAInitiative/

PR Watch. (2005). How PR sold the war in the Persian Gulf. Excerpt from *Toxic Sludge is Good for You* (Stauber & Rampton, 1995). Retrieved from http://www.prwatch.org/books/tsigfy10.html

PR Watch. (2014). About us. Retrieved from http://www.prwatch.org/cmd

Punch, K. (1998). *Introduction to social research: Quantitative and qualitative approaches.* London, UK: Sage.

Purcell, K., Rainie, L., Mitchell, A., Rosenstiel, T., & Olmstead, K. (2010). Understanding the participatory new consumer: How internet and cell phone users have turned news into a social experience. Washington, DC: Pew Research Center Project for Excellence in Journalism. Retrieved from http://www.pewinternet.org/Reports/2010/Online-News.aspx

Qualman, E. (2009). *Socialnomics: How social media transforms the way we live and do business.* Hoboken, NJ: John Wiley & Sons.

Quinn, S. (2012). *MOJO: Mobile journalism in the Asian region.* Singapore: Konrad-Adenauer-Stiftung. Retrieved from http://www.kas.de/wf/doc/kas_29755-1522-2-30.pdf?130201092225

Radio ad revenue softer for 2012. (2013, January 8). *Campaign Brief.* Retrieved from http://www.campaignbrief.com/2013/01/radio-ad-revenue-softer-for-20.html

Ragas, M. (2012). Issue and stakeholder intercandidature agenda setting among corporate information subsidies. *Journalism & Mass Communication Quarterly, 89*(1), 91–111.

Ramli, J. (2008, April 16). TV and newspapers 'no longer credible'. *New Straits Times*, p. 13.

Rampton, S. (2007, May 22). Has the internet changed the propaganda model? *PR Watch.* Retrieved from http://www.prwatch.org/node/6068

Reich, Z. (2009). *Sourcing the news.* Cresskill, NJ: Hampton.

Reich, Z. (2013). The impact of technology on news reporting: A longitudinal perspective. *Journalism and Mass Communication Quarterly, 90*(3), 417–434.

Reuters. (2013, February 11). BCC journalists to strike over job cuts: Union. London, UK: Author. Retrieved from http://www.reuters.com/article/2013/02/11/us-britain-bbc-strike-idUSBRE91A0P020130211

Rheingold, H. (2008). Using participatory media and public voice to encourage civic engagement. In W. Bennett (Ed.), *Civic life online: Learning how digital media can engage youth* (pp. 97–118). Cambridge, MA: MIT Press.

Ritchie, P. (2010). *The spin doctor's guide to effective authentic communication.* Fremantle, WA: Vivid.

Robie, D. (2011). Conflict reporting in the South Pacific: Why peace journalism has a chance. *Journal of Pacific Studies, 31*(2), 221–240.

Robinson, S. (2011). Journalism as process: The organizational implications of participatory online news. *Journalism & Communication and Monographs, 13*, 137–210.

Rogers, E., & Dearing, J. (1988). Agenda-setting research: Where has it been, where is it going? *Communication Yearbook, 11*, 555–594.

Romano, A. (2010). Deliberative journalism: American public journalism versus other international models. In A. Romano (Ed.), *International journalism and democracy: Civic engagement models from around the world* (pp. 16–32). New York, NY and London, UK: Routledge.

Rosebraugh, C. (Producer & Director). (2012). *Greedy lying bastards.* [Documentary]. United States: One Earth Productions.

Rosen, C. (2004/2005). The age of egocasting. *The New Atlantis: Journal of Technology & Society, 7* (Fall 2004–Winter 2005), 51–72. Retrieved from http://www.thenewatlantis.com/archive/7/rosenprint.htm

Rosen, J. (1999). *What are journalists for?* New Haven, CT: Yale University Press.

Rosen, J. (2006, June 27). The people formerly known as the audience. *PressThink*, blog post. Retrieved from http://journalism.nyu.edu/pubzone/weblogs/pressthink/2006/06/27/ppl_frmr.html

Rosen, J. (2008, July 14). A most useful definition of citizen journalism. *PressThink*, blog post. Retrieved from http://archive.pressthink.org/2008/07/14/a_most_useful_d.html

Rosenberry, J., St John, B., III. (Eds.). (2010). *Public journalism 2.0: The promise and reality of a citizen-engaged press.* New York, NY: Routledge.

Roskos-Ewoldsen, D., Roskos-Ewoldsen, B., & Dillaman Carpentier, F. (2002). Media priming: A synthesis. In J. Bryant & D. Zillman (Eds.), *Media effects: Advances in theory and research* (2nd ed., pp. 97–120). Mahwah, NJ: Lawrence Erlbaum.

Ross, K. (2010). Danse macabre: Politicians, journalists and the complicated rumba of relationships. *International Journal of Press/Politics, 15*(3), 272–294.

Roy, A., & Chattopadhyay, S. (2010). Stealth marketing as a strategy. *Business Horizons, 53*(1), 69–79.

Roy Morgan Research. (2007, August). Large majority of Australians think the media are often biased. Finding 4194. Sydney, NSW: Author. Retrieved from http://www.roymorgan.com/news/polls/2007/4195

Rushton, K. (2012, October 24). Guardian moves towards compulsory job cuts. *The Telegraph*, para. 1. Retrieved from http://www.telegraph.co.uk/finance/newsbysector/mediatechnologyandtelecoms/media/9630985/Guardian-moves-towards-compulsory-job-cuts.html

Russell, C. (2008, November 14). Science reporting by press release. *Columbia Journalism Review*, The Observatory. Retrieved from http://www.cjr.org/the_observatory/science_reporting_by_press_rel.php

Russell, C., & Belch, M. (2005). A managerial investigation into the product placement industry. *Journal of Advertising Research, 45*(1), 73–92.

Russell, C., & Stern, B. (2006). Consumers, characters and products: A balance model of sitcom product placement effects. *Journal of Advertising, 35*(1), 7–21.

Ryan, M., & Martinson, D. (1983). The PR officer as corporate conscience. *Public Relations Quarterly, 28*(2), 20–23.

Ryan, M., & Martinson, D. (1984). Ethical values, the flow of journalistic information and public relations persons. *Journalism Quarterly, 61*(1), 27–34.

Ryan, M., & Martinson, D. (1988). Journalists and public relations practitioners: Why the antagonism? *Journalism Quarterly, 65*(1), 131–140.

Ryan, M., & Martinson, D. (1994). Public relations practitioners, journalists view lying similarly. *Journalism Quarterly, 71*(1), 199–211.

Ryan, M., & Tankard, J., Jr. (1977). *Basic news reporting.* Palo Alto, CA: Mayfield.

Sachsman, D. (1976). Public relations influence on coverage of the environment in San Francisco area. *Journalism Quarterly, 53*, 54–60.

Sallot, L. (2002). What the public thinks about public relations: An impression management experiment. *Journalism & Mass Communication Quarterly, 79*(1), 150–171.

Sallot, L., & Johnson, E. (2006). Investigating relationships between journalists and public relations practitioners: Work together to set, framed and build the public agenda, 1991–2004. *Public Relations Review, 32*, 151–159.

Sallot, L., Steinfatt, T., & Salwen, M. (1998). Journalists' and public relations practitioners' news values: Perceptions and cross-perceptions. *Journalism and Mass Communication Quarterly, 75*, 366–377.

Salter, L. (2005). The communicative structures of journalism and public relations. *Journalism, 6*(1), 90–106.

Scammell, M. (1995). *Designer politics: How elections are won.* London, UK: Macmillan.

Schelling, T. (1960). *The strategy of conflict.* Cambridge, MA: Harvard University Press.

Scheufele, D. (1999). Framing as a theory of media effects. *Journal of Communication, 49*(1), 103–122.

Scheufele, D., & Tewksbury, D. (2007). Framing, agenda setting, and priming: The evolution of three media effects models. *Journal of Communication, 57*(1), 9–20.

Schlesinger, P., Miller, D., & Dinan, W. (2001). *Open Scotland? Journalists, spin doctors and lobbyists.* Edinburgh, Scotland: Polygon.

Schmitter, P. (1974). Still the century of corporatism? *The Review of Politics, 36*, 85–131.

Schmitter, P. (1979). Still the century of corporatism? In P. Schmitter & G. Lehmbruch (Eds.), *Trends towards corporatist intermediation* (pp. 7–52). London, UK: Sage.

Schudson, M. (1998). *The good citizen: a history of American civic life.* New York, NY: Free.

Schudson, M. (1999). What public journalism knows about journalism but doesn't know about 'public'. In T. Glasser (Ed.), *The idea of public journalism* (pp. 118–133). New York, NY: Guilford.

Schultz, J. (1998). *Reviving the fourth estate.* Cambridge, UK: Cambridge University Press.

Schultz, T. (1999). Interactive options in online journalism: A content analysis of 100 US newspapers. *Journal of Computer-Mediated Communication, 5*(1), n.p. Retrieved from http://onlinelibrary.wiley.com/doi/10.1111/j.1083–6101.1999.tb00331.x/full

Seib, P., & Fitzpatrick, K. (1995). *Public relations ethics.* Orlando, FL: Harcourt Brace.

Seitel, F. (1998). *The practice of public relations* (7th ed.). Upper Saddle River, NJ: Prentice Hall.

Severin, W., & Tankard, J. (2001). *Communication theories: Origins, methods, and uses in the mass media.* New York, NY: Addison Wesley Longman.

Sexton, E. (2007, February 17). When 'spin' spun out of control. *The Sydney Morning Herald,* Weekend Business, p. 39.

Sha, B. (1996, May). Does feminisation of the field make public relations more ethical? Paper presented to the International Communication Association Annual Conference, Chicago, IL.

Shafer, J. (2010, August 30). Who said it first? Journalism is 'the first rough draft of history'. *Slate* blog. Retrieved from http://www.slate.com/articles/news_and_politics/press_box/2010/08/who_said_it_first.html

Shaw, D., & McCombs, M. (Eds.). (1977). *The emergence of American political issues: The agenda-setting function of the press.* St. Paul, MN: West.

Shaw, D., & Weaver, M. (2014). Media agenda setting and audience agenda melding. In M. McCombs (Ed.), *Setting the agenda: The mass media and public opinion* (2nd ed., pp. 145–150). Cambridge, UK: Polity.

Shaw, T., & White, C. (2004). Public relations and journalism educators' perceptions of media relations. *Public Relations Review, 30*, 493–502.

Sheth, J., & Sisodia, R. (2002). Competitive markets and the rule of three. *Ivey Business Journal*, September–October. Retrieved from http://www.iveybusinessjournal.com/topics/strategy/competitive-markets-and-the-rule-of-three

Shin, J., & Cameron, G. (2003). The potential of online media relations to address false consensus between source and reporter: A co-orientational analysis of PR professionals and journalists in Korea. *Journalism & Mass Communication Quarterly, 80*(3), 583–602.

Shin, J., & Cameron, G. (2005). Mixed views of public relations practitioners and journalists for strategic conflict management. *Journalism and Mass Communication Quarterly, 82*(2), 318–338.

Shoemaker, P. (1989). Public relations versus journalism: Comments on Turow. *American Behavioural Scientists, 33*(2), 213–215.

Shoemaker, P., & Reese, S. (1996). *Mediating the message: Theories of influence on mass media content.* White Plains, NY: Longman.

Siapera, E. (2012). *Understanding new media.* London, UK: Sage.

Siapera, E. (2013, February 15). From post-industrial to post-journalism. *The Guardian*, Media Network blog. Retrieved from http://www.theguardian.com/media-network/media-network-blog/2013/feb/14/post-industrial-journalism-changing-society

Siebert, F., Peterson, T., & Schramm, W. (1956). *Four theories of the press: The authoritarian, libertarian, social responsibility, and Soviet communist concepts of what the press should be and do.* Urbana, IL: University of Illinois Press.

Sievert, H. (2007). Why differentiation between PR and journalism is necessary. In B. Merkel, S. Russ-Mohl, & G. Zavaritt (Eds.), *A complicated, antagonistic and symbiotic affair: Journalism, public relations and their struggle for public attention* (pp. 185–195). Lugano, Switzerland: Giampiero Casagrande.

Sigal, L. (1973). *Reporters and officials.* Lexington, MA: D.C. Heath.

Sigal, L. (1986). Who? Sources make the news. In R. Manoff & M. Schudson (Eds.), *Reading the news* (pp. 9–37). New York, NY: Pantheon.

Signitzer, B., & Wamser, C. (2006). Public diplomacy: A specific governmental public relations function. In C. Botan & V. Hazelton (Eds.), *Public relations theory II* (pp. 435–464). Mahwah, NJ: Lawrence Erlbaum.

Simons, M. (2013). Towards a taxonomy of blogs. *Creative Economy.* Queensland University of Technology Creative Industries Faculty. Retrieved from http://apo.org.au/commentary/towards-taxonomy-blogs-0 (Original work published 2008)

Simpson, G. (1990). Not all of us are 'no' men: A PRO view. *British Journalism Review, 1*(4), 39–41.

Simpson, P. (2002, March 29). Analysis: Truth, the conference watchword. *PR Week.* Retrieved from http://www.prweek.com/uk/news/141025/analysis-truth-conference-watchwordprweeks-pr-themedia-conference-last-week-londons-dorchester-hotel-revealed-thatthe-industry-need-reputation-management-ever-beforesays-peter-simpson

Sinclair, J. (2014). The media and communications: Theoretical traditions. In S. Cunningham & S. Turnbull (Eds.), *The media and communications in Australia* (4th ed., pp. 15–29). Crows Nest, NSW: Allen & Unwin.

Sinclair, L. (2013, February 7). Radio revenue dips 3 per cent in January. *The Australian*, Media. Retrieved from http://www.theaustralian.com.au/media/radio-revenue-dips-3pc-in-january/story-e6frg996-1226572851486

Sissons, H. (2012). Journalism and public relations: A tale of two discourses. *Discourse & Communication, 6*(3), 273–294.

Sitrick, M. (1998). *Spin: How to turn the power of the press to your advantage.* Washington, DC: Regnery.

Smith, B. (2008). [Review of *A complicated, antagonistic, symbiotic affair: Journalism, public relations and their struggle for public attention*]. *Journalism & Mass Communication Quarterly, 85*, 925–927.

Smith, M. (2011, May 24). WikiSecrets' Julian Assange full interview footage. Video interview with Martin Smith, PBS *Frontline*. Retrieved from http://wikileaks.org/WikiSecrets-Julian-Assange-Full.html

Snoddy, R. (1992). *The good, the bad and the unacceptable.* London, UK: Faber & Faber.

Snow, N. (2009). Rethinking public diplomacy. In N. Snow & P. Taylor (Eds.), *Routledge handbook of public diplomacy* (pp. 3–11). New York, NY: Routledge.

Solis, B. (2007, April 24). *PRWeek* claims industry enters age of PR 3.0—they couldn't be more wrong. *@BrianSolis*. Retrieved from http://www.briansolis.com/2007/04/prweek-claims-industry-enters-age-of-pr

Solis, B. (2008). Foreword. In D. Breakenridge, *PR 2.0: New media, new tools, new audiences* (xvii–xx). Upper Saddle River, NJ: FT, Pearson Education.

Solis, B. (2009, May 18). Reviving the traditional press release. *@BrianSolis* blog. Retrieved from http://www.briansolis.com/2009/05/reviving-traditional-press-release/

Solis, B., & Breakenridge, D. (2009). *Putting the public back in public relations: How social media is reinventing the aging business or PR.* Upper Saddle River, NJ: FT, Pearson Education.

Somerland, E. (1950). *Mightier than the sword: A handbook on journalism, broadcasting, propaganda, public relations and advertising.* Sydney, NSW: Angus & Robertson.

Sorrell, M. (2008). Public relations: The story behind a remarkable renaissance. Speech to the Yale Club, New York, 5 November. Retrieved from http://www.instituteforpr.org/edu_info/pr_the_story_behind_a_remarkable_renaissance1

Spicer, C. (2000). Public relations in a democratic society: Value and values. *Journal of Public Relations Research, 12*(1), 115–130.

Spicer, C. (2007). Collaborative advocacy and the creation of trust: Toward an understanding of stakeholder claims and risks. In E. Toth (Ed.), *The future of excellence in public relations and communication management: Challenges for the next generation* (pp. 27–40). Mahwah, NJ: Lawrence Erlbaum.

Spin. (2002, November 4). Present at the creation. NPR (National Public Radio). Retrieved from http://www.npr.org/programs/morning/features/patc/spin

Spin doctors and manipulators exposed. (2000, November 12). *Crikey.* Retrieved from http://www.crikey.com.au/2000/11/12/spin-doctors-and-manipulators-exposed

Spinwatch. (2014). About us. Retrieved from http://www.spinwatch.org/index.php/about/about-spinwatch

Sproule, J. (1997). Propaganda and democracy: The American experience of media and mass persuasion. New York, NY: Cambridge University Press.

Sriramesh, K. (2004). *Public relations in Asia: An anthology.* Singapore: Thomson.

Stauber, J., & Rampton, S. (1995). *Toxic sludge is good for you: Lies, damn lies and the public relations industry.* Monroe, ME: Common Courage.

Stegall, S., & Sanders, K. (1986). Co-orientation of PR practitioners and news personnel in education news. *Journalism Quarterly, 63*(2), 341–347.

Stern, M. (2010, October 4). Among the young, radio is in decline. *MediaLife,* paras. 2–3. Retrieved from http://www.medialifemagazine.com/among-the-young-radio-is-in-decline

Sterne, G. (2008). Public relations among the functions of management: A New Zealand perspective. *Public Relations Journal, 2*(3), 2–16.

Stone, M. (2012). The ladies of Skirt PR. *The EveryGirl,* Career Profiles. Retrieved from http://theeverygirl.com/feature/the-ladies-of-skirt-pr

Strahan, L. (2011). Sources of arts journalism: Who's writing the arts pages? In B. Franklin & M. Carlson (Eds.), *Journalists, sources, and credibility: New perspectives* (pp. 127–137). Abingdon, Oxon, UK and New York, NY: Routledge.

Study shows why BN lost media war. (2008, April 2). *New Straits Times.* Retrieved from http://derstrasse.wordpress.com/2008/04/02/study-shows-why-bn-lost-media-war/

Sumpter, R., & Tankard, J. (1994). The spin doctor: An alternative model of public relations. *Public Relations Review, 20*(1), 19–27.

Szuprowicz, B. (1995). *Multimedia networking.* New York, NY: McGraw-Hill.

Tang, L. (2013). Consuming news in Chinese cyberspace: A case study. *Continuum: Journal of Media & Cultural Studies, 27*(5), 740–751.

Tanner, A. (2004). Agenda building, source selection, and health news at local TV stations: A nationwide survey of local television health reporters. *Science Communication, 25,* 350–363.

Tanner, L. (2011). *Sideshow: Dumbing down democracy.* Brunswick, Vic: Scribe.

Taylor, M. (2000). Toward a public relations approach to nation building. *Journal of Public Relations Research, 12*(2), 179–210.

Taylor, M., & Kent, M. (2006). Public relations theory and practice in nation building. In C. Botan & V. Hazelton (Eds.), *Public relations theory II* (pp. 341–359). Mahwah, NJ: Lawrence Erlbaum.

Technorati. (2009). State of the Blogosphere 2008. Retrieved from http://technorati.com/social-media/feature/state-of-the-blogosphere-2008/

Technorati. (2011). State of the blogosphere 2011. San Francisco, CA: Author. Retrieved from http://technorati.com/social-media/article/state-of-the-blogosphere-2011-introduction

Tedlock, B. (2008). The observation of participation and the emergence of public ethnography. In N. Denzin & Y. Lincoln (Eds.) *Strategies of qualitative inquiry* (3rd ed., pp. 151–171). Thousand Oaks, CA: Sage.

Tench, R., & Yeomans, L. (2009). *Exploring public relations* (2nd ed.). Harlow, UK: Prentice Hall-Pearson Education.

Tennison, N. (2008). *My spin in PR: A memoir.* Hampton, Vic: Media Relations.

Tewksbury, D., Jones, J., Peske, M., Raymond, A., & Vig, W. (2000). The interaction of news and advocate frames: Manipulating audience perceptions of a local public policy issue. *Journalism & Mass Communication Quarterly, 77*(4), 804–829.

Thomas, S., & Kholi, C. (2011). Can brand image move upwards after *Sideways?* A strategic approach to brand placements. *Business Horizons, 54,* 41–49.

Thompson, J. (1967). *Organizations in action.* New York, NY: McGraw-Hill.

Thompson, J. (2005). The new visibility. *Theory, Culture & Society, 22*(6), 31–51.

Tilley, E., & Hollings, J. (2008). Still struck in a 'love-hate relationship': Understanding journalists' enduring and impassioned duality toward public relations. In E. Tilley (Ed.), *Power and Place: ANZCA 2008: Refereed proceedings of the Australian and New Zealand Communication Association Conference 2008,* 9–11 July, Massey University, Wellington, New Zealand. Retrieved from http://www.anzca.net/conferences/past-conferences/35-anzca08.html

TIME. (1982, May 10). Flack attack: *The Post* spurns PR wolves. *TIME,* p. 101.

Times reporter who resigned leaves long trail of deception. (2003, May 11). *The New York Times.* Retrieved from http://www.nytimes.com/2003/05/11/national/11PAPE.html

TMZ. (2009, June 25). Michael Jackson—Cardiac arrest. Retrieved from http://www.tmz.com/2009/06/25/michael-jackson-rushed-to-the-hospital/

Toffler, A. (1970). *Future shock.* New York, NY: Random House.

Toffler, A. (1980). *The third wave.* New York, NY: William Morrow.

Toran, W. (1977). Does PR belong in journalism school? *Journalism Educator, 32,* 35–38.

Torp, S. (2011, May). The strategic turn: On the history and broadening of the strategy concept in communication. Paper presented at the International Communication Association 2011 pre-conference, Strategic Communication: A Concept at the Center of Applied Communications, Boston, MA.

Toth, E. (Ed.). (2007). *The future of excellence in public relations and communication management: Challenges for the next generation.* Mahwah, NJ: Lawrence Erlbaum.

Turk, J. (vanSlyke). (1986). Public relations' influence on the news. *Newspaper Research Journal, 7*(4), 25–26.

Turner, G. (2001). Ethics, entertainment, and the tabloid: The case of talkback radio in Australia. *Continuum: Journal of Media & Cultural Studies, 15*(3), 349–357.

Turner, G. (2010). Public relations. In S. Cunningham & G. Turner (Eds.), *The media and communications in Australia* (3rd ed., pp. 207–216). Crows Nest, NSW: Allen & Unwin.

Turow, J. (2011). *Media today: An introduction to mass communication* (4th ed.). New York, NY: Routledge.

TV revenues down across the board. (2012, February 3). *mUmBRELLA.* Retrieved from http://mumbrella.com.au/tv-revenues-down-73267

Tye, L. (1998). *The father of spin: Edward L. Bernays and the birth of public relations.* New York, NY: Crown.

Tye, L. (2002). *The father of spin: Edward L. Bernays and the birth of public relations*. New York, NY: Henry Holt & Company.

Unethical media practices revealed by IPRA report. (2002, June 13). *PR Newswire*. Retrieved from http://www.prnewswire.com/news-releases/unethical-media-practices-revealed-by-ipra-report-77891562.html

United Nations. (2013). International human development indicators: Solomon Islands. Retrieved from http://hdrstats.undp.org/en/countries/profiles/SLB.html

Valin, J. (2005). One profession—one voice—public relations around the world. Paper presented the Global Alliance for Public Relations and Communication Management All India Conference, New Delhi.

Van Der Haak, B., Parks, M., & Castells, M. (2012). The future of journalism: Networked journalism. *International Journal of Communication, 6*, Special Feature, 2923–2938.

Van Riel, C. (1995). *Principles of corporate communication*. London, UK: Prentice Hall.

Van Riel, C., & Fombrun, C. (2007). *Essentials of corporate communications*. New York, NY: Routledge.

van Ruler, B., & Verčič, D. (2004). Overview of public relations and communication management in Europe. In B. van Ruler & D. Verčič (Eds.), *Public relations and communication management in Europe* (pp. 1–11). New York, NY: Mouton de Gruyter.

van Ruler, B., & Verčič, D. (2005). Reflective communication management, future ways for public relations research. In P. Kalbfleisch (Ed.), *Communication yearbook 29* (pp. 238–273). Mahwah, NJ: Lawrence Erlbaum.

van Ruler, B., Verčič, D., Bütschi, G., & Flodin, B. (2001). Public relations in Europe: A kaleidoscopic picture. *Journal of Communication Management, 6*(2), 166–175.

Vega, T. (2013, April 7). Sponsors now pay for online articles, not just ads. *The New York Times*, Media & Advertising. Retrieved from http://www.nytimes.com/2013/04/08/business/media/sponsors-now-pay-for-online-articles-not-just-ads.html?pagewanted=all

Verel, P. (2010, February). Authors advocate government subsidies for journalism. Report of an address to students by Robert McChesney and John Nichols. New York, NY: Fordham University. Retrieved from http://www.fordham.edu/Campus_Resources/eNewsroom/topstories_1771.asp

Vis, F. (2013). Twitter as a reporting tool for breaking news. *Digital Journalism, 1*(1), 27–47.

Walker, S. (1999). *City editor*. Baltimore, MD: Johns Hopkins University Press.

Walkley Foundation. (2012). Kicking at the cornerstone of democracy: The state of press freedom in Australia. Redfern, NSW: Media, Entertainment & Arts Alliance. Retrieved from http://www.walkleys.com/files/media/PF2012_2.pdf

Walmart, Edelman flogged for blog. (2006, October 16). *WebProNews*. Retrieved from http://www.webpronews.com/insiderreports/2006/10/16/walmart-edelman-flogged-for-blog

Ward, I. (2003, July). An Australian PR state. Refereed paper presented to the Australian & New Zealand Communication Association ANZCA 2003 conference, Brisbane. Retrieved from http://www.bgsb.qut.edu.au/community/ANZCA03/Proceedings/papers/ward_full.pdf

Ward, I. (2007). Mapping the Australian PR state. In S. Young (Ed.), *Government communication in Australia* (pp. 3–18). Port Melbourne, Vic: Cambridge University Press.

Warner, M. (2002). *Publics and counterpublics.* Brooklyn, NY: Zone.

Wasserman, T. (2013, September 26). Why native advertising is the opposite of porn. *Mashable.* Retrieved from http://mashable.com/2013/09/25/native-advertising-porn

Waters, R., Tindall, N., & Morton, T. (2010). Media catching and the journalist—public relations practitioner relationships: How social media are changing the practice of media relations. *Journal of Public Relations Research, 22*(3), 241–264.

Wauters, R. (2010, April 20). Measuring the value of social media advertising. *Techcrunch.* Retrieved from http://techcrunch.com/2010/04/20/social-media-advertising

Weaver, D., & Elliot, S. (1985). Who sets the agenda for the media? A study of local agenda-building. *Journalism Quarterly, 62,* 87–94.

Welsh, D. (2013). *Propaganda: Power and persuasion.* London, UK: British Library.

Wernick, A. (1991). *Promotional culture: Advertising, ideology and symbolic expression.* London, UK and Thousand Oaks, CA: Sage.

White, C., & Shaw, T. (2005, August). Portrayal of public relations in mass communication textbooks. Paper presented at the Association for Education in Journalism and Mass Communication, San Antonio, Texas.

White, D. (1950). The gatekeeper: A case study in the selection of news. *Journalism Quarterly, 27,* 383–390. (Reprinted in L. Dexter & D. White [Eds.]. [1964]. *People, society and mass communications.* New York, NY: Free.)

Whitney, D., Fritzler, M., Jones, S., Mazzarella, S., & Rakow, L. (1989). Geographic and source biases in network television news. *Journal of Broadcasting & Electronic Media, 33*(2), 159–174.

Wikipedia. (2013). Wikipedia: Conflict of interest. Retrieved from http://en.wikipedia.org/wiki/Wikipedia:Conflict_of_interest

Wilcox, D., & Cameron, G. (2006). *Public relations: Strategies and tactics* (8th ed.). Boston, MA: Pearson Education/Allyn & Bacon.

Wilcox, D., & Cameron, G. (2010). *Public relations: Strategies and tactics* (9th ed.). Boston, MA: Allyn & Bacon.

Wilcox, D., & Cameron, G. (2011). *Public relations: Strategies and tactics* (10th ed.). Boston, MA: Allyn & Bacon.

Wilkinson, J., Grant, A., & Fisher, D. (2012). *Principles of convergent journalism.* New York, NY: Oxford University Press.

Williams, E. (1999, August). You don't owe PR anything. *The American Editor,* p. 19.

Wilson, D., & Supa, D. (2013). Examining modern media relations: An exploratory study of the effect of Twitter on the public relations–journalist relationship. *Public Relations Journal, 7*(3), 1–20.

Witschge, T. (2009, March 27). Street journalists versus 'ailing journalists'? *Open Democracy.* Retrieved from http://www.opendemocracy.net/article/street-journalists-as-an-answer-to-ailing-journalism

Witschge, T., Fenton, N., & Freedman, D. (2010). Protecting the news: Civil society and the media. London, UK: Goldsmiths Leverhulme Media Research Centre, University of

London. Retrieved from http://www.carnegieuktrust.org.uk/getattachment/1598111d-7cbc-471e-98b4-dc4225f38e99/Protecting-the-News--Civil-Society-and-the-Media.aspx

Wober, J. (2001, October). Agenda cutting: Some remarks on the phenomenon and its importance. Paper presented to the Media Tenor Agenda-Setting Conference, Bonn, Germany.

Wober, J., & Gunter, B. (1988). *Television and social control.* Aldershot, UK: Avebury.

Wood, R. (2001a, June 25). The dark side of communications. *Information Week*, IDG Communications, Sydney, NSW, n.p.

Wood, R. (2001b, July 9). Editor replies. *Information Week*, IDG Communications, Sydney, NSW, n.p.

Woolgar, S. (2002). Five rules of virtuality. In *Virtual society? Technology, cyberbole, reality* (pp. 1–22). Oxford, UK: Oxford University Press.

World PR Report. (2013). London, UK: The Holmes Group and International Communications Consultancy Organisation (ICCO). Retrieved from http://www.slideshare.net/ArunSudhaman/world-reportsmaller

Wortham, J. (2007, December 17). After 10 years of blogs: The future's brighter than ever. *WIRED*. Retrieved from http://www.wired.com/entertainment/theweb/news/2007/12/blog_anniversary

Wouters, M., & de Pelsmacker, P. (2011). Brand placement in scripted and non-scripted Belgian and US programs on Belgian television. *Journal of Marketing Communications, 17*(5), 299–318.

Wrench, J., McCroskey, J., & Richmond, V. (2008). *Human communication in everyday life: Explanations and applications.* Boston, MA: Pearson Education.

Wright, D. (2005). We have rights too: Examining the existence of professional prejudice and discrimination against public relations. *Public Relations Review, 31*(1), 101–109.

Wu, M. (2013, September 10). How Twitter helped journalists report on the #sydneyfires. *The Rise of Citizen Journalism*. Retrieved from http://theriseofcitizenjournalism.wordpress.com/2013/09/11/how-twitter-helped-journalists-report-on-the-sydneyfires-10092013

Xifra, J. (2012). On decrees, dispute and definitions. *Communication Director, 4*, 40–43.

Young, P. (2006). Astroturfing: Dark art of politics turned scourge of the blogosphere. *Blog Campaigning*. Retrieved from http://blogcampaigning.com/2006/10/astroturfing-dark-art-of-politics-turned-scourge-of-the-blogosphere/

Zawawi, C. (1994). Source of news: Who feeds the watchdogs? *Australian Journalism Review, 16*(1), 67–72.

Zawawi, C. (2001). Feeding the watchdogs: An analysis of relationships between Australian public relations practitioners and journalists. Incomplete doctoral thesis, Queensland University of Technology, Brisbane, Qld.

Zawawi, C. (2009). A history of public relations in Australia. In J. Johnston & C. Zawawi (Eds.), *Public relations: Theory and practice* (3rd ed., pp. 26–46). Crows Nest, NSW: Allen & Unwin.

Zerfass, A. (2008). Corporate communication revisited: Integrating business strategies and strategic communication. In A. Zerfass, B. van Ruler, & K. Sriramesh (Eds.), *Public relations research* (pp. 65–96). Wiesbaden: VS Verlag für Sozialwissenschaften.

Zerfass A. (2010). Assuring rationality and transparency in corporate communications. Theoretical foundations and empirical findings on communication controlling and communication performance management. In M. Dodd & K. Yamamura (Eds.), *Ethical issues for public relations practice in a multicultural world, 13th International Public Relations Research Conference* (pp. 947–966). Gainesville, FL: Institute for Public Relations.

Ziegler, H. (1988). *Pluralism, corporatism, and Confucianism: Political association and conflict resolution in the United States, Europe, and Taiwan*. Philadelphia, PA: Temple University Press.

Zolotow, M. (1949, December 10). The great bamboozler. *Saturday Evening Post*, p. 22.

Index

Also by the Author

The 21st Century Media (R)evolution: Emergent Communication Practices

Public Relations Theories, Practices, Critiques

Media and Male Identity: The Making and Remaking of Men

Jim Macnamara's Public Relations Handbook

The Asia Pacific Public Relations Handbook

Public Relations Handbook for Managers & Executives

Public Relations Handbook for Clubs & Associations

How to Handle the Media

The Modern Presenter's Handbook

About the Author

Jim Macnamara, PhD, FPRIA, FAMI, CPM, FAMEC*, brings a unique perspective to this analysis of the controversial relationship between journalism and public relations, having worked as a journalist, as a PR practitioner, and as a media researcher for many years, before becoming a media and communication academic.

He began his career writing for small country newspapers in Australia. These were "inauspicious and inconspicuous beginnings" according to the author. However, over the next decade he wrote as either a staff reporter or freelancer for *The Sydney Morning Herald*, *The Land*, *Country Life*, *People* magazine, *Walkabout*, *Overlander*, and *Australian Playboy*.

As happens with many journalists, the financial lure of public relations brought a career change and he then spent almost 20 years working in PR roles, including serving as deputy manager of international PR consultancy Hill & Knowlton in Sydney, before co-founding and heading a successful communication consultancy where he coordinated corporate and marketing communication for clients including Microsoft, Dell Computer, Vodafone, and Singapore Airlines.

In 1994, after completing a Master of Arts by research examining the influence of PR on the media, he established the Asia Pacific office of the leading international media research firm CARMA International (Computer Aided Research and Media Analysis) and worked as a media researcher for a decade before selling the company and taking up an academic post as Professor of Public Communication at the University of Technology, Sydney.

Jim holds a Bachelor of Arts majoring in journalism, media studies, and literary studies and a Master of Arts by research in media studies from Deakin University, Geelong; a Graduate Certificate in Writing from the University of Technology, Sydney; and a Doctor of Philosophy (PhD) in media research from the University of Western Sydney.

Note

* Fellow of the Public Relations Institute of Australia; Fellow of the Australian Marketing Institute of Australia; Certified Practicing Marketer; Fellow, International Association for Measurement and Evaluation of Communication.